Studies in Economic Transition

General Editors: **Jens Hölscher**, Reader in Economics, University of Brighton; and **Horst Tomann**, Professor of Economics, Free University Berlin

This new series has been established in response to a growing demand for a greater understanding of the transformation of economic systems. It brings together theoretical and empirical studies on economic transition and economic development. The post-communist transition from planned to market economies is one of the main areas of applied theory because in this field the most dramatic examples of change and economic dynamics can be found. The series aims to contribute to the understanding of specific major economic changes as well as to advance the theory of economic development. The implications of economic policy will be a major point of focus.

Titles include:

Irwin Collier, Herwig Roggemann, Oliver Scholz and Horst Tomann (*editors*)
WELFARE STATES IN TRANSITION
East and West

Hella Engerer
PRIVATIZATION AND ITS LIMITS IN CENTRAL AND EASTERN EUROPE
Property Rights in Transition

Michał Federowicz and Ruth V. Aguilera (*editors*)
CORPORATE GOVERNANCE IN A CHANGING ECONOMIC AND POLITICAL
ENVIRONMENT
Trajectories of Institutional Change

Hubert Gabrisch and Rüdiger Pohl (*editors*)
EU ENLARGEMENT AND ITS MACROECONOMIC EFFECTS IN
EASTERN EUROPE
Currencies, Prices, Investment and Competitiveness

Jens Hölscher (*editor*)
FINANCIAL TURBULENCE AND CAPITAL MARKETS IN TRANSITION
COUNTRIES

Jens Hölscher and Anja Hochberg (*editors*)
EAST GERMANY'S ECONOMIC DEVELOPMENT SINCE UNIFICATION
Domestic and Global Aspects

Mihaela Kelemen and Monika Kostera (*editors*)
CRITICAL MANAGEMENT RESEARCH IN EASTERN EUROPE
Managing the Transition

Emil J. Kirchner (*editor*)
DECENTRALIZATION AND TRANSITION IN THE VISEGRAD
Poland, Hungary, the Czech Republic and Slovakia

Julie Pellegrin
THE POLITICAL ECONOMY OF COMPETITIVENESS IN AN ENLARGED EUROPE

Stanislav Poloucek (*editor*)
REFORMING THE FINANCIAL SECTOR IN CENTRAL EUROPEAN COUNTRIES

Gregg S. Robins
BANKING IN TRANSITION
East Germany after Unification

Johaness Stephan
ECONOMIC TRANSITION IN HUNGARY AND EAST GERMANY
Gradualism and Shock Therapy in Catch-up Development

Hans van Zon
THE POLITICAL ECONOMY OF INDEPENDENT UKRAINE

Adalbert Winkler (*editor*)
FINANCIAL DEVELOPMENT IN EASTERN EUROPE
The First Ten Years

Studies in Economic Transition
Series Standing Order ISBN 0-333-73353-3
(*outside North America only*)

You can receive future titles in this series as they are published by placing a standing order. Please contact your bookseller or, in case of difficulty, write to us at the address below with your name and address, the title of the series and the ISBN quoted above.

Customer Services Department, Macmillan Distribution Ltd, Houndmills, Basingstoke, Hampshire RG21 6XS, England

Corporate Governance in a Changing Economic and Political Environment

Trajectories of Institutional Change

Edited by

Michał Federowicz
Senior Researcher
Polish Academy of Sciences
Poland

and

Ruth V. Aguilera
Assistant Professor
University of Illinois
USA

First published 2003 by
PALGRAVE MACMILLAN
Houndmills, Basingstoke, Hampshire RG21 6XS and
175 Fifth Avenue, New York, N. Y. 10010
Companies and representatives throughout the world

PALGRAVE MACMILLAN is the global academic imprint of the Palgrave Macmillan division of St. Martin's Press, LLC and of Palgrave Macmillan Ltd. Macmillan® is a registered trademark in the United States, United Kingdom and other countries. Palgrave is a registered trademark in the European Union and other countries.

ISBN 1–4039–2076–1

This book is printed on paper suitable for recycling and made from fully managed and sustained forest sources.

A catalogue record for this book is available from the British Library.

Library of Congress Cataloging-in-Publication Data

Corporate governance in a changing economic and political environment : trajectories of institutional change / edited by Michał Federowicz and Ruth Aguilera.
       p. cm. – (Studies in economic transition)
     Papers from a workshop organized by the WZB–IFiS PAN.
     Includes bibliographical references and index.
     ISBN 1–4039–2076–1
       1. Corporate governance–Europe, Western–Congresses.
2. Organizational change–Europe, Western–Congresses. 3. Corporate governance–Europe, Eastern–Congresses. 4. Organizational change–Europe, Eastern–Congresses. 5. Comparative management.
I. Federowicz, Michał. II. Aguilera, Ruth V. III. Series.

HD2741.C7752 2003
338.6′094–dc21   2003053619

10   9   8   7   6   5   4   3   2   1
12   11   10   09   08   07   06   05   04   03

Printed and bound in Great Britain by
Antony Rowe Ltd, Chippenham and Eastbourne

For Adam Ferran and Dariusz

Contents

List of Boxes, Figures and Tables   viii

Preface and Acknowledgements   x

Notes on the Contributors   xii

1   Introduction: Corporate Governance from a Comparative Perspective – Bridging East and West
Michał Federowicz   1

2   Are Italy and Spain Mediterranean Sisters? A Comparison of Corporate Governance Systems
Ruth V. Aguilera   23

3   Ukraine: the Newly Built State and Economic Institutions
Volodymyr Sidenko and Oksana Kuziakiv   71

4   Bulgaria: the Rise of Capitalism and Actors' Rationality
Douhomir Minev and Maria Jeliazkova   100

5   The Czech Republic: the Case of Delayed Transformation
Marek Havrda   121

6   Poland: Worker-driven Transformation to Capitalism?
Michał Federowicz   144

7   Ownership and Corporate Governance in the Hungarian Large Enterprise Sector
Éva Voszka   170

8   Revisiting the French Model: Coordination and Restructuring in French Industry (in the 1980s and 1990s)
Bob Hancké   195

9   The Specificity of Corporate Governance in Small States: Institutionalization and Questioning of Ownership Restrictions in Switzerland and Sweden
Thomas David and André Mach   220

10   European Integration and Corporate Governance in Central Europe: Trajectories of Institutional Change
Heather Grabbe   247

Bibliography   267

Index   291

List of Boxes, Figures and Tables

Boxes

10.1   The Copenhagen Conditions   256
10.2   Short-term economic reform priorities for 1998 (Accession
       Partnerships)   258

Figures

9.1   Proportion of Swiss quoted companies with a "single share"
      in their capital structure, 1989–2001   236
9.2   Mergers and acquisitions in Switzerland, 1977–99   237

Tables

2.1   Summary of historical institutional factors shaping
       economic organization in selected OECD countries   26
2.2   Direct investment inflows, selected OECD countries,
       1990–99   30
2.3   Direct investment outflows, selected OECD countries,
       1990–99   32
2.4   Country breakdown of global amount raised from
       privatization   34
2.5   Receipts from privatization   34
2.6   Main privatizations in Italy, 1993–2001   36
2.7   Spanish privatizations, 1985–99   37
2.8   Ownership of listed companies in selected countries in 1996 44
2.9   Significant shareholdings in Italian listed companies   45
2.10   Ownership concentration in individual firms in
       OECD countries   45
2.11   Ownership concentration of Italian listed companies
       as percentage of total market capitalization   46
2.12   Bank-lending to nonfinancial enterprises in Italy   49
2.13   Number of bank mergers in Italy, 1980–97   50
2.14   Italian banks by size and composition of loans   51
2.15   Number of listed domestic companies, 1989–2000   53
2.16   Market capitalization of listed domestic equity issues at
       year end in selected OECD countries   54
2.17   Corporate finance resources for 300 Italian small and
       medium firms in 1993   55

2.18   Debt/equity ratios of nonfinancial enterprises at book
       values, OECD countries   56
2.19   Bank debt as percentage of total debt in 1998   57
2.20   Financial assets of institutional investors   57
2.21   Significant shareholdings in listed Spanish companies   59
2.22   Ownership percentage among the first three shareholders   60
       for Spanish quoted firms
2.23   Likelihood of corporate control change among Spanish
       quoted firms, 1997   60
2.24   Corporate financial structure of Spanish manufacturing
       firms, 1983–92   63
3.1   Main instruments of payments and transactions   87
3.2   The main performance differences between privatized and
       successful newly established private companies in Ukraine   92
5.1   GDP growth in the Czech Republic   123
5.2   Ownership concentration in listed firms   128
7.1   Ownership structure of companies   172
7.2   Big and medium-size firms according to number of
       owners and majority ownership, 1995   173
7.3   The presence of different types of owners in "top 100", 1997   173
7.4   Number of owners and the presence of majority
       shareholders   173
7.5   Ownership types of "top 100" according to the owners
       and ownership concentration, 1997   174
8.1   Financial results of large firms, 1981–85   203
9.1   Ownership concentration in some developed countries,
       early 1990s   223
9.2   One-share-one-vote distortion in some developed
       countries, 1995   227
9.3   Nestlé's capital structure on November 15, 1988   228
9.4   Voting right differentials between classes of shares in
       Swedish listed companies, 1992   230
9.5   Outward and inward FDI stocks in some developed
       countries, 1985–2000   232
9.6   Evolution of market capitalization as a percentage
       of GDP, 1975–99   233
9.7   Distribution of stock market value according to ownership
       categories   240
9.8   The percentage of listed companies on the Stockholm stock
       exchange with dual class shares, selected years, 1968–98   241

Preface and Acknowledgements

> If social sciences are to meet the challenge of understanding East European transitions, with particular regard to the simultaneity of economic and political transitions, it is necessary to re-examine the methodological principles and models of explanation of the main approaches, or "paradigms", competing within the field of research.
>
> Michel Dobry (2000: vii)

This book bridges two different kinds of experience that grew up in the Western and Eastern parts of Europe, which were symbolically separated by the Berlin Wall. The period of almost a decade and a half that has followed the physical dismantling of the Wall has demonstrated how difficult the integration process has been, and how individual national responses to new challenges and opportunities have differed. At the same time, Western European countries also confronted a new wave of integration processes, as well as global challenges, and, in turn, responded in their individual ways. This book examines the evolution of economic institutions that affect corporate governance, but to do so in a comparative way it necessarily refers to political evolution as well. The lesson from this exercise is that key concepts and "models" are to be reconsidered in order to satisfy cross-country comparative studies.

This comparative exercise results from more than symbolic cooperation between East and West, namely between the Wissenschaftszentrum Berlin (WZB) and the Institute of Philosophy and Sociology (IFiS PAN) Warsaw. In this regard, the authors and editors of the volume address special thanks personally to Dr Georg Thurn who is *spiritus movens* of this cooperation and to both institutions. Michal Federowicz is also grateful to the Kościuszko Foundation for its generous funding of his individual study program in the United States, a good place to study Europe as Europe looks more integrated from there than from the inside. The idea of the volume was conceived in that period. Ruth Aguilera is grateful for the support received from the Center of Advance Study and CIBER at the University of Illinois in Urbana-Champaign. The authors of the Bulgarian, Czech Republic, Hungarian, Polish, and Ukrainian case studies acknowledge significant support from the Research Support Scheme in Prague that funded field research in these countries.

We are indebted for valuable insight to Bernard Chavance, Steven Casper, David Soskice, Sigurt Vitols, Hans van Zon, and other participants of the Workshop organized by the WZB and IFiS PAN that preceded the final stage of the project. The volume would not have taken its present shape without extensive editorial assistance of Greg Allen, Adina Dabu, Grażyna Drażyk, Niti Pandey, and Zeynep Yalabik.

M.F. R.A.

Notes on the Contributors

Ruth Aguilera is an Assistant Professor at the College of Business and the Institute of Labor and Industrial Relations at the University of Illinois at Urbana-Champaign. She got her Bachelor's and Master's degree in Economics from the College of Economics at the University of Barcelona. She also undertook a graduate program in Business Analysis at the Management School in Lancaster University, England, and completed her PhD in Sociology at Harvard University in December 1999, specializing in economic sociology and comparative methods. Professor Aguilera has spent considerable time conducting research in Europe at the Wissenschaftszentrum Berlin für Sozialforschung (WZB), Universitá Luigi Bocconi in Milan, and Juan March Institute in Madrid. Professor Aguilera's research interests lie in the intersection of international management and economic sociology. She is currently conducting research on comparative corporate governance, and cross-border mergers and acquisitions. Her main academic journal publications are: "The Cross-National Diversity of Corporate Governance: Dimensions and Determinants," *Academy of Management Review* (2003, with G. Jackson); "The Spread of Codes of Good Governance Worldwide: What's the Trigger?" *Organization Studies* (with A. Cuervo-Cazurra, forthcoming, 2004); and "Directorship Interlocks in Comparative Perspective: the Case of Spain" *European Sociological Review* (1999).

Thomas David is lecturer in Economic and Social History at the universities of Lausanne (Institute of Economic and Social History) and Neuchâtel (Department of Economics). His main fields of research include economic nationalism (in Eastern Europe), economic growth (in particular Switzerland since 1850) and corporate governance. He edited (with Jean Batou) two books: *Uneven Development in Europe. The Obstructed Growth of the Agricultural Countries*, 1918–1939 (1998); and a special issue of *Economie appliquée* entitled "La mondialisation: perspectives historiques" (No. 2, June 2002).

Michał Federowicz is senior researcher in the Institute of Philosophy and Sociology of the Polish Academy of Sciences, and lecturer at the Central European University. Among his works are: *Poland's Economic Order: Persistence and Transformation* (1994); "Works Councils in Poland: under Communism and Neo-liberalism", in *Works Councils: Consultation, Representation, and Co-operation in Industrial Relations* (1995, with A. Levitas); "Prywatyzacja jako nurt przemian instytucjonalnych" (Institutional Meaning of Privatisation), in *Elementy Nowego Ładu* (1997); "*Corporate Governance*: the Problem of the Concept in a Post-communist

Context, in *Sisyphus: Social Studies*, (Vol. XIII/XIV, 2000); "Anticipated Institutions: the Power of Path-finding Expectations, in *Democratic and Capitalist Transitions in Eastern Europe. Lessons for Social Sciences* (2000).

Heather Grabbe is Research Director at the Centre for European Reform, a cross-party, independent think tank on European affairs based in London. She is also a non-stipendiary JRF at Wolfson College, Oxford University. She has a BA (Hons) from Oxford University and a PhD from Birmingham University. She has worked extensively on EU enlargement at the Royal Institute of International Affairs, the European University Institute (Florence), the European Union Institute for Security Studies (Paris) and the Centre for International Relations (Warsaw). Her publications include *Germany and Britain: an Alliance of Necessity* (2002, with Wolfgang Münchau), *Profiting from EU Enlargement* (2001), and *Enlarging the EU Eastwards* (1998, with Kirsty Hughes).

Bob Hancké is lecturer in European Political Economy at the London School of Economics and Political Science. He holds a PhD in Political Economy from the Massachusetts Institute of Technology (MIT). Until 2000 he was a Senior Research Fellow at the Wissenschaftszentrum Berlin, where he contributed to the project that led to *Varieties of Capitalism*, edited by Peter Hall and David Soskice. Previous appointments include Fellowships at Harvard University (J.F. Kennedy School and Center for European Studies). He published *Large Firms and Institutional Change* (2002). His work has appeared in *European Political Economy Review, International Journal of Urban and Regional Research, Industry and Innovation, Politics and Society, Organization Studies, European Journal of Industrial Relations, British Journal of Industrial Relations, Small Business Economics, Travail et Emploi, and New Technology, Work* and *Employment*.

Marek Havrda is Managing Director of EUROPEUM Institute for European Policy, Prague, where he also leads the Socioeconomic Research Program. He spent the 2000/1 academic year as a Fulbright visiting researcher at the School of Advanced International Studies, Johns Hopkins University. He received an MA in Economics and an MA in International Studies from Charles University in 2000 and 1997 respectively. In 1998, he graduated with an MA from the Department of Sociology of the Central European University. He also studied business and government relations at Georgetown University. His research activities include transformation of post-communist economies and societies, corporate governance, and public finance.

Maria Jeliazkova has a PhD in Sociology, and is research associate in the Department of Sociology of Labor and Social Policy at the Institute of Sociology, Bulgarian Academy of Sciences. Her main fields of research are social policy and economic sociology. Selected publications include: "The

Low Level of Industrial Democracy: Consequences", in *Changing Faces of Democracy* (2000); "Poverty Level and Fragmentation of Bulgarian Society" (1996); "Mass Unemployment in Transition of Economy" (1995).

Oksana Kuziakiv is research associate of the Institute for Economic Research and Policy Consultation (IER), Kiev, Ukraine, and project coordinator of the Ukrainian Enterprise Survey. She specializes in surveys in business trends, business development, and the business climate in Ukraine. She has worked with numerous nongovernment institutions and foreign technical assistance projects such as the Soros International Economic Advisory Group, the International Centre for Policy Studies, and the Economic Education and Research Consortium. She graduated from the Kiev National Taras Shevshenko University (MA with honors in Sociology), and undertook postgraduate studies at the Institute of Sociology of NASU.

André Mach is lecturer in Comparative Political Economy at the Institute of Political and International Studies (University of Lausanne). His research interests include competition policy, industrial relations, corporate governance, and more generally the impact of globalization on national politics and policies. His major publications are: "Globalisation, néo-libéralisme et politiques publiques dans la Suisse des années 1990". Zurich: Seismo (1999) (ed.) and 'Switzerland: Adjustment Politics within Institutional Constraints' in F. Scharpf and V. Schmidt (eds) (2000). 'Welfare and Work in the Open Economy. Diverse Responses to Common Challenges'. Oxford: Oxford University Press: pp. 131–73 (with Giuliano Bonoli).

Douhomir Minev is senior research associate in Sociology and in Economics. He is also Head of the Sociology of Politics and Organizations Department at the Institute of Sociology, Bulgarian Academy of Sciences. His main fields of research are: economic sociology, sociology of organization, and sociology of social policy. Some publications: *The Bulgarian Economy: Reforms, Changes and Prospects* (1996); *The Transition: Elites and Strategies* (1996); *Reforms in the Social Sphere* (1996).

Volodymyr Sidenko holds the post of Director of Economic Programs at the Ukrainian Centre for Economic and Political Studies named after Olexander Razumkov. Author of 120 scientific publications, including: "The Shocks and Traps of Postcommunist Economic Transformations" in *Political Thought* (No. 4, 1997); "Economic Development and International Institutions: a View from Ukraine" in *European Conflicts and International Institutions: Cooperating with Ukraine* (1998); "The Conceptual Foundations of Ukraine's Strategy of Integration into European Union Structures', in *Economy and Forecasting* (No. 2, 2001, in Ukrainian); "The Impact of EU Enlargement on Ukraine in Trade and Economic Sphere" in *Foreign Trade* (Nos 3–4, 2001, in Ukrainian, with Ihor Burakovsky).

Éva Voszka is senior researcher of the independent think tank Financial Research Ltd, Budapest and Associate Professor at the University of Economics in Budapest. She got her PhD in economics from the Academy of Sciences of Hungary. Her research interests include economic transformation of Central-East European countries, especially privatization, competitive market structures and corporate governance. She has published seven books in Hungarian. Her recent publications include: "The Revival of Redistribution in Hungary", in *Economic Institutions, Markets and Competition* (1996), pp. 274–92, "Privatization as a 'Learning Process': the Case of Hungary", in *Successful Transitions* (Political Factors of Progress in Postsocialist Countries), (2001), pp. 139–52; "Privatization in Hungary 1988–1998", in *Transitional Societies in Comparison: East Central Europe vs. Taiwan* (2001), pp. 443–57.

1
Introduction: Corporate Governance from a Comparative Perspective – Bridging East and West

Michał Federowicz

1.1 The problem[1]

1.1.1 The scope of analysis and comparative perspective

The main challenge of cross-national analyses is to identify and conceptualize the most significant concepts so that they can be applied across borders. Corporate governance, the key notion of this book, has evolved over the last ten years from the single principal–agency problem to a much more complex structure of stakeholders' relations in the agency game (Aguilera and Jackson, 2003). This development is the result of comparative studies of advanced economies, which took the concept of the agency problem from the American-based debate over managerial incentives and set it in the institutional context of other countries, most notably Germany and Japan (Hoshi et al., 1991; Gerlach, 1992; Roe, 1993; Berglöf and Perotti, 1994; Soskice, 1994; Lehrer, 1996; Vitols et al., 1997; Casper, 1999; Aoki, 2000). The broader meaning of corporate governance, utilized by the authors in this book, contributes to an understanding of the profound differences between institutional settings of the three leading national economies in contemporary capitalism. The triad comparisons – US/UK, Germany, Japan – became the most persuasive evidence in debates over the deeply rooted divergence between advanced economies that persists in spite of strong converging pressures. It has also contributed to the Variety of Capitalism (VoC) approach (Dore et al., 1999; Hall and Soskice, 2001), which points, in political economy terms, to the "comparative institutional advantage" of each country. The lesson from the substantial body of literature in this field is that not only the three leading models but also other advanced economies operate in significantly different institutional settings at the national level, which was the result of long-term evolution, and carried out institutional adjustment in very individual ways (Albert, 1991; Berger and Dore, 1996; Zigler, 1997; Rhodes and Apeldoorn, 1998).

This book builds on the literature devoted to the varieties of capitalism. It takes the three most extensively researched models as a point of reference, but it goes beyond them and beyond the scope of advanced and stable economies. The book is the result of a number of country-based research projects on corporate governance, which implicitly had a common purpose of developing a definition of corporate governance that might contribute to understanding the dynamically changing institutional settings for business activity. As these projects overlapped in their research questions we could envision a common language and understanding of corporate governance issues across countries. The volume bridges Western and Eastern Europe. It covers the cases of ten countries on the European continent, from Spain to Ukraine, and focuses on understanding how institutional settings at the national level will affect micro-level decisions. The book concludes with a chapter discussing the impact of European integration on the national settings of corporate governance, which is more binding for candidate countries than for member states.

We selected ten European countries so that we can examine the dynamics of changing corporate governance in both the advanced economies that have well-established institutional settings but are still exposed to internal and external pressures for change, and economies in the process of transformation from planned economies to market economies with hardly any consolidated institutions. We do not suggest that there is a continuum between the countries nor any linear vision of development. Although the question of "stage of consolidation" or "degree of consistency among corporate governance institutions" may be addressed, we do not claim that one country necessarily follows the path of another. In this sense, we hope to avoid any simplified analogies between country cases. Instead, we discuss the very individual ways each country has of coping with internal and external uncertainties of a changing environment. If there are a variety of models among the advanced economies, then one may also observe a large diversity of trajectories towards sound governance in countries that are deeply transforming their institutional settings (Chavance and Magnin, 2000).

The broad comparative perspective in this book suggests that institutions do not travel well. That results from the "tightness of fit" (Berger, 1996) in the national models of capitalism in advanced economies. We can take for granted, after 12 years of post-communist transformation, that with few exceptions any attempts at direct institutional transplant are first rejected in the new locations and then need a long evolution before they start functioning (Campbell and Pedersen, 1996; Swaan, 1996; Silitski, 1999; Kuzio et al., 1999; Higley and Pakulski, 2000; Zeman, 2000; Lane, 2001). The diffusion of institutional solutions does not work in a simple and direct way, although it certainly does exist. The perception of other countries' solutions does not go unnoticed. In addition, international commitments and the impact of international organizations on such relations within or with the European Union, attitudes towards foreign investors and the level of their engagement, and other pressures from international markets will affect the outcomes of the corporate governance. All of these external factors contribute to the continuous reshaping of the domestic dynamics of institutional change. Our comparative perspective is not about cookie-cutter solutions or specific models that might often be barely identifiable in a given country. It is more about the mechanisms of institutional change that in turn will define corporate governance. The question is how the national economies carry out institutional adjustment. It assumes examining the incremental change in a given country to identify both domestic and external factors of that change, and specifically seeing what constellations of economic and political interests have determined its dynamics and direction. This kind of question may travel much easier.

1.1.2   The challenges of conceptualizing diversity

The theoretical task is to find a way of comparing Eastern and Western Europe that helps in understanding and unpacking the complexity of the process of establishing and continuously adjusting sound corporate governance. The book focuses mainly on the eastern part of the continent and aims to show its dramatic diversity and to point out that the mechanisms of privatization that initiated institutional change in the early 1990s were largely incomplete (Hellman, 1998). The comparison with Western countries helps uncover inconsistencies in the emerging systems in the Central-Eastern European (CEE) countries. But conversely, some problems of contemporary capitalist evolution are revealed in a "distorting mirror" of the East, pointing the way towards a more general investigation of the future of capitalist development. In this sense the East–West comparisons may contribute to a more general theory of institutional adjustment (Dobry, 2000). The joint work in the book attempts to combine the debate on corporate governance in contemporary (advanced) capitalism with the debate on privatization, economic adjustment, and institutional reforms in the post-communist environment. The East–West comparisons refer to a more general comparison between "capitalism after communism" in the East and "continuously evolving capitalism" in the West.

Institutional fine-tuning is of vital importance nowadays (Hall, 1995; Gourevitch, 1996). The major problem is to develop a response to the constantly new pressures coming mostly from new product markets. This is necessary not only at the firm level but also at the national level in terms of a significant reconfiguration and modification of previously institutionalized practices (Hancké and Casper, 1996; Vitols et al., 1997; Amable and Hancké, 2001). In this regard, the East–West comparison may lead to new observations concerning the mechanisms and prospects of such reconfigurations. The question is where and how this may be successful, under what conditions, and how it risks reproducing the old institutions (Zon, 2000) that have not been able to meet new challenges.

The overall thesis of the book is that each national system copes with challenges of corporate governance in its own way, because it tries to rely as much as possible on its existing institutional resources. This is how the domestic elite and other domestically critical actors, including social actors such as unions, think about their adaptability to changing circumstances. In this sense, even under strong converging pressure, what tends to be experienced is "long-term resilience of national systems" (Berger, 1996) or "incremental change" (Vitols, 1999) rather than adaptation to external patterns or a radical shift to a different logic of institutional arrangements. The issue of "national institutional resources" (Hancké, 2002) is common to East and West, and in both interests arises to protect them as much as possible at the expense of external adaptability. That is why, using Stark's term, "recombination" of existing institutional assets is typically more likely to happen than radical institutional change.

However (here is the core of our thesis), the more stable the economic situation of a country, the more successful will be the institutional change that only "recombines" institutional assets with some new elements. Similarly, the more problematic the economic position of a given country, the more damaging this natural desire and attempt to preserve existing constellations of domestic forces may be, and the more promising it may be to abandon them as quickly as possible. The chapters on Bulgaria and Ukraine elaborate on this dilemma. In other words, recombination of the existing resources is likely to succeed in countries that, while facing the necessity of change, enjoy a stable economic situation and relatively coherent institutional settings, such as France (analyzed in this volume by Hancké) or Germany (Vitols, 1999). In contrast, the countries characterized by a weak position and disintegrating institutional settings (often initially not acknowledged by domestic actors), sooner or later face a massive and fundamental transformation and find that they must be open to the external factors of change. Spain, the latecomer to the European democratic family, had to quickly open to foreign investment in comparison to Italy or France. But Hungary had to do so much more than Spain, replacing initial attempts to "recombine" existing assets (Stark, 1996) with the profound "reconstitution" of capitalist institutional arrangements that underpin sound corporate governance (Gray and Hendley, 1995; Pistor, 2000), and let foreign direct investment (FDI) fill in the new structure. Alternately, Ukraine remained vague toward rudimental institutions of contemporary capitalism and tried to promote preexisting constellations of domestic economic and political actors (D'Anieri et al., 1999; Zon, 2000).

While the advanced economies have been powerful enough to withstand external pressures and modify their institutions in their own way, there has been little room for such a strategy in the transforming economies of

Central and Eastern Europe. A detailed understanding of this contrast, we believe, helps explain the successes and failures in the process of deep institutional transformation in Central-Eastern Europe. Moreover, it may also aid in suggesting necessary future transformations among advanced economies. Countries that wish to support the most successful business strategies must continuously reconsider their practices of corporate governance. The East–West comparisons also provide an opportunity to examine how the same terms used across country contexts may differ. For instance, the terms "the state" and "state regulation" may carry diverse associations and actually may refer to different types of political and economic relations. And in a less obvious example, "cross-ownership" may have different connotations in, say, Germany and Ukraine or Russia. Understanding these country differences helps in examining more precisely the institutional gaps and inconsistencies in incomplete processes of change.

1.1.3   Existing and changing institutions

There is one more point to raise in the context of dynamic change. This is the issue of the "path-dependence" approach (Granovetter, 1985; Stark, 1992). In the book we build upon an individualized perspective of each country and this is very much in line with path-dependence. On the other hand, however, we see significant limitations to the approach as far as explanatory capacity is concerned (Moss, 1997; Greskovits, 2000; Bohle, 2000). In *post facto* explanations everything might be interpreted as path-dependent, but this offers little insight into the mechanisms of institutional change.

If we object to the path-dependence approach, it is not to deny it entirely. History matters and we essentially agree that the role of national politics and national history is absolutely fundamental in framing specific incorporation of capitalist institutions in a given country. This is in fact how the path-dependent national embeddedness of capitalist institutions is manifested (Granovetter, 1985; Chavance and Labrousse, 1998; Chavance and Magnin, 1999, 2000). But while this may perhaps work for advanced economies, as they are relatively stable, when applied to the East it may often be misleading, for it does not solve the problem of massive and fundamental institutional change. It does not tell us how each of the countries, to a certain and differentiated degree, was able to both build on and go beyond its past. It promotes a bias towards easy *post facto* explanations, instead of focusing on the dynamics of the change. Even for stable economies, if we dig deeply the approach is not satisfying. For instance, France was able to overcome the *dirigiste* state coordination, but path-dependence does not offer much in understanding how a series of institutional innovations, together with standardized macroeconomic policies, led to a shift in the leading role of the state in favor of "firm-led" corporate adjustment. Such a dynamic eventually resulted in the substantial modification of institutional settings of French corporate governance, as discussed by Hancké in this volume.

Path-dependence should be supplemented and modified by some other concepts. We propose two of them. First is the concept of the hierarchy of institutions, which means that some institutions to a large extent determine some others. Thus, to explain a massive change, it is important to consider the more influential institutions and look at how they balance the "old" and "new" driving forces, as well as their influence on institutional change. For instance, the interplay between political and economic institutions may turn out to be an "influential" part of the explanation, such as in the Soviet Union where political institutions heavily determined the economy. The degree of political change in a given country might influence the nature and outcome of economic change. As Hellman demonstrates, relying on data from a large sample of transforming countries: the more democratic the regime, the more robust the economic development (Hellman, 1998). This was not so obvious to many researchers at the beginning of the post-communist transformation. The nature of political institutions also affects the nature of the dominant business networks that encompass business activity, which in turn contributes to the game between reshaping and reproducing economic institutions. This aspect was often neglected by network analyses, and the concept of a hierarchy of institutions helps to fill this gap.

But one can still argue that the "core institutions" are indeed path-dependent, even though a part of their evolution certainly contradicts historical dependency. The puzzle is how to conceptualize what is beyond path-dependence. Typically, the answer is that change comes from outside. In such an approach, domestic forces would be treated as path-dependent and external forces as innovative. We believe that this is wrong. The agents of change are both inside and outside the domestic arena. More importantly, both of them modify their strategies according to their future-oriented expectations and calculations. These future-oriented calculations of actors participating in and contributing to change are often a neglected step in analyses of institutional development.

Thus, the second aspect, besides the hierarchical nature of institutional settings, is the strong strategic orientation of (some) economic and political actors, based on *anticipated* outcomes. When the existing institutional settings are continuously less satisfying, these actors acquire a stronger voice and greater audience, and provoke other actors to more future-oriented speculations about likely change. In turn, their redefined expectations create a new environment, which may reinforce the change. What is essential in these "path-finding" cycles (Federowicz, 2000) is that some actors go beyond the existing institutional settings, and often devote a great deal of effort to escape from them. In their calculations about the future, they try to anticipate the change and take advantage of being ahead in this process.

Doing so, they contribute to the shift of the core institutions, or to establishing new ones. Then, in a medium- and long-term perspective, before a new institutional setting is really established, they may be praised or punished for their path-finding activity, according to the hierarchy of other intervening institutions. These two concepts: hierarchy of institutions and "anticipated institutions" that are employed by some actors before institutions are fully established may help in understanding radical institutional change.

1.2 The notion of corporate governance

The key definition of corporate governance should be a good tool for cross-country investigations and be able to identify to detect factors of dynamic change. The major focus of this book is on the conditions, mechanisms, and constraints in the process of establishing sound corporate governance and then adjusting them to meet the most immediate needs. We believe this kind of approach provides a bridge between the emerging markets and advanced economies, both experiencing internal and external pressures for institutional change, but each country with its own scope, starting point, and current position. The process is gradual, as it requires a series of agreements on the firm, country, and sometimes international levels, and involves a multiplicity of actors as stakeholders. But by definition it also needs some shaking and prodding to promote that change, and sometimes quite strong, for the implicit nature of social and economic institutions tends toward stability and status quo rather than change and adjustment.

We conceptualize sound corporate governance as an abstract goal rather than a concrete model of continuous institutional adjustment, which partly builds on path-dependent institutional stability, but also partly works against it by disrupting the status quo in order to reduce new internal and external tensions. By sound corporate governance we mean a set of institutionalized (but not only formal) settings and practices that orient the key actors of decision-making towards the sustainable development of the firm. By contrast, "distorted corporate governance" may provoke key actors, sometimes even the owners, to act against the firm, as is displayed in this volume.

1.2.1 Beyond the single principal–agent problem and beyond stylized models: a political economy perspective

Assuming the principal–agent problem and dealing practically with one-country institutional arrangement, the notion of corporate governance did not need to explicitly refer to the American institutional environment. Settings such as liquid capital markets, high-level market capitalization, dispersed banking systems, a highly competitive environment in inter-firm relations, or flexible labor market (not to mention the state's lack of involvement in microeconomic decisions) were taken for granted when considering managerial strategies in the game with the owners and their impact on the firm (Shleifer and Vishny, 1986; Roe, 1994; Shleifer and Vishny, 1997). However, the literature of the late 1970s and early 1980s, referring to the agency problem, implicitly asked a broader question: how was it that the earlier autonomy of managers, which brought the flourishing results of the preceding decades, contributed to the eventual deterioration of many large American concerns? There was no answer within the narrow paradigm of corporate governance, with its main focus on managerial incentives.

At that time, European economies were still not integrated or expansive enough to provoke serious analyses of a corporate model that would be distinctive from and provide comparative advantage to the American solution. The expansion of the Japanese economy in the 1970s and 1980s, especially through successful confrontation with American firms in their own markets, prompted a new agenda of scientific investigation into institutional arrangements. Not all of the literature devoted to the Japanese economy referred to the corporate governance issue; in fact, the term was not used initially. Mainstream research attempted to reconstruct Japanese economic relations within and outside a single firm, which is essentially a broader definition of corporate governance. This has led to a detailed description of institutional underpinnings that were behind Japanese firms' strategies, strategic alliances, and managerial decision-making (Gerlach, 1987, 1992). Not surprisingly, the Japanese system turned out to be closer to the German system than to the American, but is still quite distinct from the German (Kester, 1992; Soskice, 1994; Streeck, 1996). Among the most significant differences is that Japanese banks play a much larger role than those in Germany, and they have the technological capacity to monitor the effectiveness of corporations. The relation between owners and managers is based on regular formalized as well as informal meetings on the one hand, and long-standing financial ties on the other. But unlike large German firms, Japanese firms tend to compete among themselves in their home markets, which is more an American type of relation. Still, like German firms, they try to cooperate on some strategic goals, such as R&D.

The impact of the vast research on the Japanese economy was to weaken the dominant American position in an "intellectual market for institutions," and make room for Europe-oriented research. Together with ongoing European integration, in the late 1980s and early 1990s the concepts of "European," "continental," and "Rhenish" corporate governance were formulated, in contrast to the Anglo-Saxon (or Anglo-American) system. However, the Rhenish model relied mostly on the German matrix (with some elements of the Japanese model that seemed at the time the most valuable), only rather loosely referring to other European countries. It was more a desire than the reality of continental

Europe. In fact, each country continued with its own approach to institutional adjustment, trying to combine its typical institutional resources with some new solutions that would be more open to globalizing pressures than to any idea of pan-European institutional settings. Too many spheres of institutional systems are involved in real corporate governance to expect easy harmonization.

An example is France, that although relying on the leading role of the national elite, was able to develop a significant financial market, yet maintains stable shareholder agreements and long-standing financial systems. With strong management both within and outside the company, the French system is quite different from both the German and the Anglo-American systems, and more importantly, does not have much in common with the French *dirigiste* past.

We can also see significant changes in Italy and Spain. Although one might expect that these two countries would share similar systems by virtue of belonging to a Southern European–Mediterranean culture, they are in fact significantly different, as Aguilera persuasively demonstrates in this volume. Italy, while engaging in intensive industrialization after World War II and getting the state and politics involved in economic development, kept the banking sector out of industry, due to its earlier negative experiences. In addition, it has significantly reduced state engagement, looking rather for cross-country alliances with some major firms. Spain, in its post-dictatorship acceleration, relied on a relatively strong and state-protected banking system, as an asset of the past, but was more open to FDI, which largely contributed to economic development as well as to the institutional shift.

These national cases show the reality of a given economy from the perspective of stylized models and show the continuous change of institutional settings of advanced economies. Germany, too, although it exemplifies the most self-reproducing institutional system, has been witnessing a growing number of exceptions to governance arrangements, especially in new industries, where firms are trying to escape from, or modify, traditional arrangements and practices (Vitols et al., 1997; Casper, 1999). Yet, the desire of a synthesis of "best practices" is always debatable (Berger, 1996; Kester, 1996).

The political economy of corporate governance analyzes the structures in which the governance game takes place. Corporate governance, or governance structure, is considered here a coherent part of the institutional system that underpins economic life. It is the part of the system that sets the rules of the game for managers and other stakeholders who affect strategic decision-making. In a stable economic system, these are rather complex but coherent arrangements. The incentive structure explicitly addressed to top managers, or their formal relations to the shareholders, are only a part of the story. Thus, transposing just one or a few elements of corporate governance to one country from another does not really mean that corporate governance will work there. Considering corporate governance in the much broader framework of political economy means seeing the institutional gaps and inconsistencies within the system and looking for the economic and political forces behind them.

Nevertheless, the broad meaning of corporate governance cannot be expanded without limit. It should be explicitly stated that the center of investigation is the firm, and the rules of the game focus around top management and top managerial decision-making, which will eventually shape firm strategy. The political economy of corporate governance reconstructs the structures inside the firm. But to do so, it builds on a vast knowledge of the institutional environment of the firm, exploring a broad economic, political, and social context. It challenges the interplay between new and old constraints and opportunities in the game. These are different in each country and subject to different dynamics of institutional change. This is why a broad understanding of corporate governance helps establish a comparative perspective. The main question is not just the reconstruction of a model or models. It is, rather, seeing how coherent corporate governance is likely to be reshaped, responding to changing circumstances as is typically the case in well-established and stable economies, or established and consolidated in the emerging capitalist economies. The firm here is not considered as the object of typical organizational studies, but as one of the key segments of the political economy of contemporary capitalism. Corporate governance bridges the micro and macro levels of investigation.

1.2.2 What is still missing?

The importance of corporate governance lies precisely in its centrality, linking microeconomic (firm-level) decisions with critical institutional arrangements that may interfere with strategic decision-making, and which in fact constitute the economic system in a given country. This is also how politics may affect corporate governance. Let us now reconstruct the major aspects of corporate governance.

First of all, in the principal–agent relation the owners are the finance providers, expecting a return from their investments. But ownership is not the only form of channeling resources to the firm; the whole banking system and more broadly the system of financial flows are involved in a struggle for sound corporate governance. To put it more generally, what is in question is the provision of resources to the firm, where ownership is only part of the story.

Second, the question of management comprises at least a double principal–agent relation, between owners and top managers, and between managers and workers, each of them strongly capable of influencing strategic decisions. In this regard, not only is the traditional field of industrial relations involved but also the increasingly relevant field of training and education (Aguilera and Jackson, 2003).

Third, some other areas of institutional regulation strongly affect top managerial decisions, such as antitrust policies and those that more broadly regulate entry and exit from the market, as well as contract law, self-regulation, and legal policies (Pistor, 2000). Also relevant are interfirm relations and institutionalized policies that affect the firm's sharing of some nonfinancial assets with other firms in, for example, R&D.

Finally, various settings should be regarded not as universal and generating catch-all solutions, but as concrete product market needs, which largely determine the type of principal–agent relations, based on different skills, flexibility, and autonomy, and the likely monitoring at all levels (Soskice, 1994). It is specific product market arrangements that create concrete comparative advantage in international competition. The most visible pressure on continuous rearrangements comes from the highest value-added product markets.

This synthesized revision of critical aspects of corporate governance shows its complexity and provides the tools to examine this complexity. At the same time, it allows for the great diversity within the contemporary capitalist family of advanced economies. However, it still does not include some important aspects that may be at play in establishing sound corporate governance as the result of deep systemic change.

To do so, our analyses are also sensitive to the specific situation of "capitalism after noncapitalism," that is, the highly intensive process of capital formation. In the (re)constitution of capitalism that took place in Central and Eastern Europe the rapid capital formation provoked both large uncertainty and high potential gains to the actors involved. In this new situation formal settings often played a secondary role. Each of the aspects listed above contributed to a reinterpretation of governance structures, with the first one concerning finance provision certainly being the most important. Not surprisingly, it touches on the initial problem of corporate governance.

We need here to "reverse" the traditional perspective. According to Shleifer and Vishny's well-known assertion, corporate governance is about "the ways in which suppliers of finance to corporations assure themselves of getting a return on their investments" (Shleifer and Vishny, 1997: 737). Let us turn this upside down. Corporate governance concerns the ways in which top managers try to ensure finance for their companies, and they do this by different mechanisms available in the formal and informal institutional environment, with all the necessary economic and political commitments. This is why in the context of intensive capital formation, including massive privatization, not only financial sectors but also the state institutions (with their flows of public money) are the important parts of the system with which corporate governance interlocks, regardless of formal ownership ties.

The narrow meaning of corporate governance, of course, does incorporate the numerous regulations that largely determine business relations. The broad understanding of corporate governance, however, has to make sense of these detailed regulations. It helps to investigate the institutional and macroeconomic context of microeconomic strategies and see how the actors involved in corporate governance are continuously testing the micro–macro relations. This uncovers the real alternatives behind managerial choices. In considering corporate governance we need a broad and detailed understanding of the (un)available choices and (non)existing constraints on managers, owners, bureaucrats, politicians, labor, and other likely stakeholders.

Essentially, corporate governance is about the range of opportunities and types of constraints that mostly top managers face in their strategies related to the firm. It is here where a sound or distorted governance is conceived. The institutionalized opportunities and constraints differ across countries, and they may differ across product markets, but this general perspective is valid for both emerging and advanced economies. It ensures a flexible research framework that is very sensitive to country-specific performance and yet maintains the major attributes of corporate governance. Instead of forcing one-way directives, it helps to see the multiple international pressures, without losing sight of domestically determined interests.

1.3   Political economy of how to get there: East–West comparisons

The essence of the problem of corporate governance is actually capitalist development and its evolutionary nature. It initially came from the split in the roles of the owner and of management, which took place in the early decades of the last century. As John Scott put it: "industrial capitalist societies have undergone a transition from *personal* to *impersonal* forms of ownership and control" (Scott, 1997: 15). That split was the source of capitalist vitality in the twentieth century. It made capital more flexible and open to new possibilities of technological and organizational innovation, and made available a broad field for managerial selection (no longer based on heritage, political loyalty, or tribal or mafia rule). Finally, it created a market for corporate control, if not through the stock market, then through mergers and strategic alliances.

This evolutionary transformation from *personal* to *impersonal* forms of ownership and control that took place within capitalist logic may be characterized by two poles. In its Anglo-American version (closer to a free market ideal but not equal to it), ownership became dispersed over time, but management was specialized and concentrated and subject to a highly competitive environment (Roe, 1994). In the German or Japanese versions of capitalist development (less oriented to a free market concept yet also subject to market-type competition), the ownership became institutionally interlocked within cross-ownership and in this way avoided dispersion, while management became less concentrated and had more obligations toward both finance providers and employees. The latter is more prevalent in the Japanese case although it is not as formalized there as in Germany (Soskice, 1994).

Now, to identify the most striking differences between East and West of Europe let us first underline that World War II and the cold war stopped the typical capitalist evolution in the central-eastern part of the continent. Both of the above-mentioned trajectories of institutional capitalist development (Anglo-Saxon and continental models) sharply contrast with the experience of socialist economies in the east of Europe. It is enough to notice that in the latter, the role of the owner disappeared in a nondefinable ideal of "social" (all society) ownership, and the role of management became dispersed in multilevel, hierarchical, and politically controlled bureaucracy. The vanishing sense of ownership and the growing complexity of structures (formal and informal) of decision-making characterized the evolution of governance under Communist Party regimes, with a dramatic increase in the significance of informal relations that eventually led to the ungovernability of the system. In the same period, and specifically since the 1970s, capitalist countries saw an intensive fine-tuning of all kinds of institutional arrangements related to governance and decision-making, such as capital flows and instruments, managerial incentives, the banking system, and the labor market.

The shift toward privatization in the post-communist countries in the early 1990s was not just an intellectual fashion or the result of pressure from international financial institutions. It targeted the weakest point of earlier microeconomic institutional settings. Privatization in the East has been the most significant part of institutional transformation. However, privatization has not dealt with all the institutional areas related to governance, even failing to question the likely governance structures after privatization in an environment that is still an institutional mix. This has inevitably led to the partial and noncoordinated course of reforms.

The inconsistency of the institutional system in the East is a critical difference in the East–West comparison. There were many reasons for this inconsistency during deep transformation, especially in the discrepancy between reformers' visions and real forces behind the change. Typically, the reformers both within and outside the involved countries opted for American-style development; to create as quickly as possible institutionally guaranteed competitive environments. At the same time, a part of the former *nomenclatura*, although not objecting to the American type of business relations, made steps toward cross-ownership to institutionally protect their long-term corporate control. As a result, the trajectories of institutional change were not coherent. On the one hand, the cross-ownership relations were not the same as in, say, Germany or France, mainly due to the weak financial sector. On the other hand, the financial markets did not resemble those in the US or the UK (Coffee, 1996, 1998) in terms of both their low market capitalization and poor transparency. The state, being still heavily involved through the nominal ownership of large portions of the economy and through huge financial flows, did not correspond to a Western understanding of state involvement. The more consistent policies were able to consolidate only after some serious macroeconomic tensions, like those in Hungary in 1995, or later and more seriously in the Czech Republic, in 1997. The price for the inconsistencies was always high, and sometimes extremely high, like the 1996/97 banking crash in Bulgaria.

It is now clearer than ever though that the most important goal of privatization is a healthy corporate governance structure. Among the CEE economies, the Hungarian experience displays the most efficient way of achieving this goal. Starting with an intentionally gradual, case-by-case approach, Hungarian leaders were the first to achieve positive results. In spite of early attempts by domestic groups to protect their interests in murky cross-ownership structures, the strategy of maximizing FDI in privatized firms eventually provided the most transparent corporate governance, as is systematically documented by Voszka in this volume.

But even if there is no such access to FDI, corporate governance remains the most significant outcome of privatization. It also puts the question of property rights transfer in a much broader context, because it inevitably addresses problems that are typically neglected in a single issue of transfer of titles. The point is that when facing deep institutional change, in order to build a healthy governance structure it is not sufficient to rely on one or another model of the relations between (new) owners and management, or management and workers, which are well-known from the advanced economies. As stated in the previous section, in addition to the formal principal–agent relations, it is crucial to know what kinds of choices, opportunities, and constraints the existing institutional system, together with its informal part, offers to all economic actors. The Hungarian success was not based solely on FDI, but rather on the most complete and coherent institutional settings in all other spheres such as bankruptcy law, contract law, banking law, and so on (Gray and Hendley, 1995; Pistor, 2000). From the political economy perspective of corporate governance the necessity and high level of FDI inflows became the best incentive for change in consecutive governments, regardless of the political option. It also allowed the building of relatively transparent institutions that could and did encourage further investments. In addition, in the Hungarian case, FDI inflows contributed to the consolidation of the political and economic elite, unlike in other countries where FDI divided the elites.

Another dimension to examine is the East and West difference and similarities in interconnection between corporate governance systems and the type of product markets, and vice versa. The success in particular product markets depends on initial corporate governance settings and their further development. Obviously, the departure point, in a time of growing interdependence of the globalizing world economy, may differ significantly. The impact of leading product markets in the global economy is clearly visible when comparing the outstanding performance of Japanese firms in the 1980s, before the era of telecommunications and other information technologies and their increasing difficulties in the decades that followed. This is also a challenge for Western European economies, which may need further changes in their corporate governance settings. Indeed, in countries such as Germany, Switzerland, Sweden, or France for that matter, it remains uncertain – and in recent times this uncertainty has significantly grown – whether they will follow the same course they have taken over the last 20 years. These European countries have become more flexible and competitive than they were before but have nonetheless retained an underlying form of capitalism that is distinctly different from the Anglo-Saxon system. It is not clear whether these sorts of internally changing but divergent paths will continue, or whether there will be a convergence toward a more Anglo-Saxon system. Leading technological developments of the last five to ten years put the weight toward the Anglo-Saxon experience, but this is surely not the last word. In our comparison of East and Western European corporate governance systems, we are interested in understanding the growing interdependence between firms, economies, and institutional systems. For this task, it is important to look at specific product markets, which tend to dominate economic development and evaluate what type of governance best promotes such development.

There exists a lot more uncertainty when it comes to the developing economies, including those of Central and Eastern Europe. The lesson from the product markets means that the question of corporate governance is not as abstract as some theories of capitalism would like us to believe. It is an open question regarding the transforming economies, which kind of market niches they are likely to explore, and how their efforts to consolidate the governance structures consort with their potential markets. For example, one of the determinants of recent Irish success, the most recent "newcomer," was its potential in terms of institutional resources. However, such a fortunate happy coincidence is an exception rather than the norm, and it is not the case in Central-Eastern Europe.

Markets produce their own specific hierarchy in the value chains, with some of them being more lucrative than others. In fact, this is the game in advanced economies when it comes to high-tech competition. It is also the reason for continuous modification in corporate governance and is a measure of its efficiency. In the case of the profoundly transforming economies, however, it is more complex. These countries do not actually freely pick up the desired elements of the existing models and practices.

Instead, besides their institutional legacy they face many constraints, lack capital and the capacity to enter international markets. They have to reconstruct their production regimes, and they also need to find a new place in product markets and (re)establish recognition in the international division of labor. Thus, they face deep reform of corporate governance in time of large uncertainty about potential niches in the markets, while national arrangements do matter as they largely determine adaptability of firms to global pressures of specific product markets.

The East–West comparison is also significant when considering the way international institutions influence the national and firm levels. This especially affects those countries and firms that badly need capital but are suffering from the inconsistency of institutional arrangements. Without doubt, core–periphery-type relations exist here. Early dependency literature taught that to a certain extent economic development in peripheral countries takes place as long as the core nation states accept it taking place. Although the accession of CEE countries is a different experience, it is not entirely clear how much equalization and dependency are behind the European harmonization. As Grabbe states in the closing chapter of this volume, the Copenhagen Conditions strongly suggest the necessary "capacity [of the candidate countries] to cope with competitive pressure and market forces within the Union." However, "the EU has so far focused on rote adoption of legislation, with little attention to the impact that the resulting micro-institutional structures have on efficiency." There is clearly no single European model of corporate governance and, as Grabbe argues, the EU seems to have more influence on market regulations in Central Europe than it has in Western Europe: "Europeanization may conflict with globalization where the EU is imposing rigid and potentially inappropriate policy frameworks." Although the perspective of accession generally encourages political and economic reform, the process of accession itself, in terms of European harmonization, is not necessarily equal to the economic transformation that would improve the firms' competitiveness. Still, much depends on domestic politics and the consistency of domestic institutional reforms, which clearly might improve the bargaining position of the candidates.

Finally, the East–West comparison highlights how the system of corporate governance interlocks with other key elements of capitalist systems, such as labor markets, education and training, or intercompany relations. The list of the other elements is very much country sensitive and has to refer to country-specific circumstances. For instance, as the French case shows, the arrangements of elite circulation may turn out to be crucial in reshaping corporate governance. In the case of the UK, it is the type of contracting arrangements that is important. And for countries transforming after communist periods, the emerging governance structure interlocks with the state, defined as a set of (exhausted) institutions. For example, the way the Ukrainian state was constructed after 1991 has hampered the reform of corporate governance and other economic institutions. In all countries, the nature of business networks with their political involvement affects intercompany relations. As stated before, in Central-Eastern Europe corporate governance is intertwined with a variety of arrangements that contribute to a rapid process of capital formation with preexisting non-financial capital exchanged for financial capital.

The level of consistency among various institutional segments of the political economic system encompasses the overall comparisons of the East and West. Surprisingly, however, the tensions between inconsistent institutional segments may provoke additional pressures for change. In this regard the nature of the political regime matters. Looking at the institutional dynamics of emerging systems, one can refer to a broader thesis of "low-level equilibrium," as formulated by Greskovits for countries transforming after the period of communist dominance (Greskovits, 1998). Low-level equilibrium addresses the relation between the political system and the economic system in these countries. It reflects the initial concerns about their capacity to consolidate democracy while at the same time facing deep economic reform, which could have led to massive social protests. The protests did not occur to the extent that would threaten the continuity of the reforms. As the low-level equilibrium thesis states, these countries managed to build formal democratic institutions and the foundations of market relations. However, these are rather poor democracies and deeply imperfect markets. The result is that a kind of equilibrium between those deficiencies makes the low level (low quality) of the system rather stable and durable.

The field of corporate governance, the subject of this book, suggests that the durability of low-level equilibrium would only be justified if the economic system were closed. The analysis points out the numerous partial disequilibria in the broadly approached issue of corporate governance. These disequilibria could of course be (and often have been) balanced by an "imperfect democracy" where the formally democratic mechanisms of political control do not really function. Yet growing economic pressures, coming from both international product markets and financial markets, make such a balance increasingly questionable. In addition, domestic social protests in this context may encourage further institutional change toward a more mature democratic system, because they precisely help to deconstruct such a perverse equilibrium. In other words, it is predicted that the more open the economic system, the more pressure there is to build upon a low-level balance among domestic institutions and improve their quality.

It is worthwhile to ask what contributes to the emergence of new institutions in Central and Eastern Europe. When the Soviet Union dissolved, the economies of the region found themselves typically between two poles, the

US and Western Europe. Not only the legacy of the past but also many other factors shaped the new corporate governance model, such as: a vision of the contradicting corporate traditions, the actual exercise of relations with individual countries, FDI inflows from various directions, and the countries' capacities for flexible policies resulting from domestic politics. Recently, the prospect of EU enlargement has come into the equation for candidate countries, although the outcome for the individual (pre and post) accession games is not entirely determined. This holds as well for the outcome of a larger game over globalization, which will affect all European countries, from Portugal to Ukraine.

There is not really a "market for institutions." Market forces do not directly decide the corporate governance settings in a particular country. The "best" arrangements (in a certain period, for certain product markets) do not necessarily go to where the highest demand is for them. The best models of corporate governance constantly change, and there is no strong selection mechanism at the institutional level. This is why the historically shaped domestic political scene plays a crucial role in the county's adaptability and contribution to permanent, capitalist, institutional change. Nevertheless, the long-term economic strength of a country, coming from its international market position, as well as its political position in the international power structure, strongly intervene in the process.

1.4   Conclusion

What can we learn from the East-West and cross-continent comparisons? The East–West comparison highlights the extraordinary transformation of the last decade as a long-standing outcome of specific historical development resulting from World War II. This general comparison points out major inconsistencies of partial reforms taking place in emerging markets in the former "post-war Eastern Europe." These are striking in comparison with the fine-tuning of institutional settings in the West. However, the country case studies presented in this volume show that the trajectory of institutional change is very much country-specific and the old East–West cleavages are becoming less and less relevant. Among the advanced economies, for instance, we do not observe any homogeneous continental model. Countries continue to search for their own way of institutional adjustment to the pressures of new markets. The stylized and contradicting models of governance structures are present in these efforts only as one of many points of reference. Similarly, the catching-up countries try to benchmark changes in the advanced economies, but the outcomes tend to be tailored to individual countries. In all cases, the dynamics of institutional change strongly depend on domestic politics even when the domestic scene interferes with international commitments, and it does so probably most visibly in the EU candidate countries.

Regardless of international commitments, the first and clear message of all country cases examined is that the role of national governments is of critical importance. Cross-country comparisons persuasively show that the state (government and other institutions) is the key actor in the game for sound economic performance. It is not surprising that, for example, privatization (de-statization) should be organized and controlled by the state, and in general, deregulation or a proper balance of regulations is also a matter of state activity. As in France, where the major move opposing *dirigisme* was provoked by concrete measures arranged by the state, seemingly post-communist transformations could be triggered only by the reformers' adequate use of state institutions. In the "hierarchy" of institutional settings, the proper functioning of the state comes prior to the proper functioning of business. The lesson is that the capability of state institutions is decisive in establishing and adjusting sound corporate governance. If the international or regional organizations want to address the issue of corporate governance, they have to be sensitive toward governability of the public sphere as well. Otherwise, they are not able to deal with a mixture of "public" and "private" (Wedel, 2003). Such a mixture exists everywhere, which is not to advocate that governments should not be encouraged toward increasing transparency of the links between the two spheres. There is no room here for ambivalence.

Second, the mixture of public and private spheres indicates that there is one more element to be considered when dealing with institutional change in the field of corporate governance. That is the framework of macroeconomic policy. The nature and consistency of macroeconomic policy affect all financial flows, and thus may significantly change the environment in which the influential actors shape their strategies, anticipate their likely gains and losses, and build their understanding of macro–micro relations. In this way, macroeconomic policy contributes to (re)shaping governance structures. It is probably the most influential factor in changing the nature of business networks in the continuum from rent-seeking (wealth distracting) to wealth creating. The context of macroeconomic policy helps in understanding the pace and quality of institutional change.

Finally, contrasting the countries with profound distortions of institutional settings and those most successful in permanent institutional adjustments/transformation helps to bring to light some phenomena amplified in the "distorting mirror." The normative aspect of capitalist transformation is explicitly taken up by Minev and Zheliazkov in the Bulgarian chapter of this book, but it certainly concerns other countries as well. The argument is that a capitalist order (like any other) is not possible without a clear social sense of the basic norms and values that underpin that order. The normative background that includes but goes beyond legal regulations has often been disregarded in the capitalist transformations of the last 30 years in the advanced economies, and has been neglected even more in the post-communist transformations. However, the normative sense directly affects governability of the system at the macro level and the efficiency of economic performance at the micro level. One of the issues raised in most of the chapters is the problem of the "real owner," that is the owner who cares about the property in the long run. Lack of real owners in privatization in the East resulted from various factors, like the large scale of the privatization, the lack of capital, and the lack of a middle class, but it was fostered by the ambience of the unconstrained (in the normative sense) conduct of the rule-makers. By contrast, if for instance the French state was able to bring about a significant shift in institutional settings, that was due to the French economic and bureaucratic elite's ability to keep the self-sanctioning mechanism working, in which shared and transparent values have remained a viable reference for individual participants in the game. This normative capability provided institutional resources for the French *noyau dur* solution. Nothing comparable happened on a national scale in the cases of post-communist interwoven ownership, which is why eventually FDI became a major factor in transforming corporate governance.

Without easy analogies, one may expect that concerns about the real owner, as well as more general concerns about the normative underpinnings of economic relations (one might say embedded in a social sense of fairness), are more universal than appears in the distorting mirror. The problem goes back to the source of capitalist dynamics. As mentioned before, not only real owners, but also the split between ownership and management lay behind capitalist development in the twentieth century. Each country has dealt with the problem of governability of the relations between managers, owners, and other stakeholders in its own way, building country-specific models within a few generations. But recently the dominant models have suffered turbulence. The once admired Japanese performance, attributed to the perfect design of *keiretsu*, can hardly meet the challenges triggered by new product markets, such as information processing. Until now, there has not been a clear sign that Japanese firms and banks are able to adjust the design of governance and overcome internal weaknesses. Together with the last boom in telecommunications and energy, American firms seemed best organized for the new product markets. That image vanished, however, when consecutive flagships turned out to be deeply defective and disappeared from view.

The universal problem is how to deal with the growing uncertainty of quickly changing social and economic realities. New product markets offered to firms, as well as to the financial sector, carry huge promises and risks. The Japanese *keiretsu* were too slow to react in time, but many other firms all over the world were too quick and too ambitious in taking new risks. In fact, the managers often took the risk, with little capacity on the owners' part to understand and control strategic decisions. The managers themselves had to rely on speculations that reflected more the dominant trends than economic calculations. As we now know from several cases, politicians at the highest levels were sometimes involved in the strategy building of large firms. The financial sector also contributed to shaping strategy, making use of the gaps in legal regulations and sometimes acting unlawfully. In the end, in spite of large corporate risks, individuals involved in the corporate game could also be observed taking less risk. Stories from the largest recent bankruptcies in the West resemble stories from post-communist privatization, which may have been on a smaller scale but were far more numerous. Essentially, Eastern "double bookkeeping" does not differ much from Western "creative/aggressive bookkeeping"; subordinated "supervisory boards" work similarly, not digging deeply into managerial decisions; and the politicians involved have similar motives. Finally, there are the managers who have to face uncertainty that is hardly calculable in purely economic terms, while being exposed to huge temptations offered by new and temporary opportunities, with little individual risk at the end. The problem is that the institutional systems lack the tools of adequate adjustment to the new situations that are continuously arising that expose a small number of participants in the game to quick and temporary gains while the others have limited means to impose accountability. The gaps in the institutional systems are more visible and damaging in the East, but the problem is much more general.

In the book, we undertake a broad West–East comparison of corporate governance national systems in five advanced economies and five catching-up economies. It helps us highlight and trace changes over time and the multiple paths to punctuated equilibrium. The cross-continental comparison underlines the individual nature of country-specific scenarios and outcomes of institutional change. It puts into question any stereotypic grouping of countries. Among the cases presented in the book are, for instance, three countries of Latin tradition – France, Italy, and Spain – but, as we can see, in terms of institutional development each of them is substantially different. Similarly, the countries of Central Europe – the Czech Republic, the Slovak Republic, Hungary, and Poland – show diverse trajectories of institutional change. Different pathways emerged in each of them in spite of their strong common roots in the prewar German legal tradition of the commercial law, which all of them reinstated during post-communist transformation, and yet modified in their individual ways. One may also uncover important differences in the institutional evolution of Balkan countries such as Bulgaria or Romania, or post-Soviet states such as Belarus, Russia, or Ukraine. These differences come from country-specific constellations of influential actors that affect the process of (re)making the institutions. In this sense domestic politics matter, and the lesson is that one cannot avoid the political dimension when looking for more sound and adequate corporate governance.

The sequence of the chapters intentionally avoids any grouping of the countries covered in this book. We start with an analysis of two Western countries, Italy and Spain, presented explicitly as two "outlier" models, to show the specific arrangements of each, as well as the way they have transformed over time. Then Ukraine, Bulgaria, the Czech Republic, Poland, and Hungary are presented. These countries are faced with deep institutional change, with differentiated pace and scope of the transformation process, and various approaches and constellations of actors behind them. In the end, we come back to a Western exemplification of a long-term transformation, that is: France, Switzerland, and Sweden, which were able to recombine national institutional resources when introducing some important new factors. Each chapter presentation builds on its own theoretical framework adjusted to specific national needs. The last chapter reassesses the evolution of corporate governance to explicitly put on the agenda the growing importance of the European Union dimension. This, at present, has a greater impact on candidate countries than member states.

Note

1. Special thanks go to Ruth Aguilera for her insights and engagement in editing this chapter. The author would also like to thank Steven Casper, Bernard Chavance, Bob Hancké, Uwe Mummert, Andrzej Rychard, Daved Soskice, Sig Vitols, Hans van Zon and other participants of the workshop at the WZB for their contribution to the discussions that enriched the theoretical perspective of the project. Thanks go as well to George Kolankiewicz and Tomasz Mickiwicz at the SSEES UCL for fruitful cooperation on this matter, and to the British Council and Polish Committee for Scientific Research for financial support for this cooperation.

2
Are Italy and Spain Mediterranean Sisters? A Comparison of Corporate Governance Systems

Ruth V. Aguilera

2.1 Introduction[1]

This chapter argues that corporate governance practices are influenced by institutional features of the economy in which they are embedded, and by the political and economic changes that take place in that economy. The purpose of this chapter is to describe and explain corporate governance models found in two rapidly changing countries, Italy and Spain, and contrast these countries' models with those in other OECD countries. I first describe existing corporate governance models. I then discuss Italy's and Spain's main triggers of change and analyze their respective corporate governance practices by reference to other industrialized countries. Finally, I compare corporate governance practices in these countries and assess where Italy and Spain lie on the spectrum of corporate governance models.

Italy and Spain are two latecomers to industrialization that experienced similar levels of economic development at the beginning of the twentieth century. However, by the late 1970s, there were major differences in these countries' economic organization. Whereas Italy was a developed industrial country and a full-fledged member of the European Community, Spain was a developing country that was beginning an economic and political transition period. Twenty years later, both countries exhibited considerable transformations, with Italy's gross national product ranked fifth among the Western economies in the early 1990s, and Spain's economy demonstrated remarkable development. For example, although Spain's population is about two-thirds of the Italian one and its economy is barely half the size of Italy's economy, in the 1990s the Spanish economy grew by an average of 2.5 percent while Italy reached only 1.6 percent (*The Economist*, July 7, 2001: 6). Furthermore, with the internationalization of these economies, there has been some convergence in their corporate governance models mostly due to European Union harmonization pressures – namely privatizations. Yet fundamental institutional differences in their economic organization still persist as a result of historical institutional legacies. In this chapter, I examine the differences and similarities among these two countries in the context of other industrialized countries (OECD).

2.2   Corporate governance models

Business corporations comprise different interest groups. These include shareholders, boards of directors, managers, and employees. Corporate governance refers to the relationships between those who own the firm and those who run it, with the key question being who ultimately controls the organization (Berle and Means, 1932; Roe, 1993; Charkham, 1994; Prowse, 1994; Fligstein and Freeland, 1995; Blair, 1995; Fukao, 1995). In trying to answer this quintessential question, the firm has been perceived in two sharply differentiated ways: as an *economic* unit and as a *social* unit.

Organizational economic approaches conceptualize the firm as an economic unit, and study its organization's internal dynamics. Organizational economics includes the following schools: managerial economics (Berle and Means, 1932; Baumol, 1959; Marris, 1964; Williamson 1964), agency theory (Jensen and Meckling, 1976; Fama, 1980; Fama and Jensen, 1983; Jensen, 1993), transaction cost analysis (Williamson, 1985), and property rights (Hart and Moore, 1990; Hart, 1995). They share the assumption that fundamental conflicts of interest exist between shareholders, directors, and managers. A principal drawback of such approaches is that they perceive the firm, in large part, as a black box and not as a nexus in a network or a unit in an organizational environment, and therefore fail to account for external influences on the shape of governance structures.

The social organizational perspective uses a broader lens than the economic account, placing the corporation into external contexts called "survival environments" (resource dependence), "institutional environments" (institutional school) or networks of relationships (Fligstein and Freeland, 1995; Smelser and Swedberg, 1994). In essence, firms are not treated as isolated social units, but instead as embedded in their environments (Granovetter, 1985). They may be constrained by scarcity of resources, by structures of economic and social ties, or by cultural and political structures. Sociological approaches to organizations are sensitive to variations in countries' legal and institutional arrangements. In this chapter, I view the corporation as a social unit influenced by its position in the economic structure and by the historical institutional features of the country within which it is embedded.

Different countries offer corporations varied institutional environments, and such variation is reflected in each country's corporate governance structure. There is an emerging literature discussing how varieties of capitalism are shaped by institutional factors (Hall and Soskice, 2001). These scholars have created a sharp division of national corporate governance models into a dichotomy of ideal-typical cases: the Anglo-Saxon model[2] and the Continental model[3] (Zysman, 1983; Berglöf, 1990; Albert 1993; Roe, 1993; Prowse, 1994; Steinherr and Huveneers, 1994; La Porta et al., 1998). Comparison of these two models of corporate structure suggests that pathways to industrialization, the role of the state in shaping economic policies, and a country's location in the international context will shape differences in corporate governance. These include, in particular, attributes of financial systems, legislation surrounding the structure of corporations, labor and product markets, and regulations affecting foreign capital penetration. These are institutional factors shaping corporate governance models, the influence and operation of which are presented in sections 2.4 and 2.5. Table 2.1 shows a comparison of some of these institutional factors in selected OECD countries.

The Anglo-Saxon model (exemplified by the British and United States country cases) presents an "entrepreneurial" pattern of industrialization. In this model, ownership which tends to be diffused, is held by individual shareholders, and more recently by institutional shareholders (Baums et al., 1994; Useem, 1996). Its market-based financial system exerts a strong influence on corporate structure. Markets play a leading role in managing capital (Steinherr and Huveneers, 1994: 272) through the provision of a wide range of financial instruments and highly developed capital markets (Berglöf, 1990: 244). The model is characterized by diffused ownership, high investor protection, and low employee protection. In addition, the Anglo-Saxon legal tradition draws a sharp line between commercial and investment banks, relies on severe antitrust regulations (for example the 1890 Sherman Act in the United States), and considers interlocking directorates among competing companies to be an illegal practice (the Clayton Act in 1914 in the United States). Further, United States corporate law (the Glass–Steagall Act in 1933) restricts ownership relations between bank and industrial enterprises (Roe, 1993), and thus prevents banks (commercial and investment) from becoming more influential in industry. As a consequence, American banks have been historically small and relatively weak given the size of the US economy.

The Continental model of corporate structure, by contrast, involves bank-controlled and bank-allied companies, and credit-based financial systems favoring low-risk, long-term financing. Banks, particularly the commercial banks, thus exert significant influence over corporate affairs through ownership and governance rights. In Germany, banking influence is accentuated by the organization of most large industrial firms as joint-stock companies (Kocka, 1980: 91). In addition, German banks may exercise direct and continuous power over industrial firms through the supervisory boards (*Aufsichtsrat*) characteristic of the dual board structure of

Table 2.1 Summary of historical institutional factors shaping economic organization in selected OECD countries

	US	Germany	Japan	Italy	Spain
1. *Timing of industrialization*					
First railroad track (a)	1825	1835	1872	1840	1850
Year in which agricultural employment fell below 20% (b)	1955	1955	1965	1970	1975
2. *Role of the state*					
Degree of state interventionism	Low	High	Intermediate	High	High
Financial system					
Role of banks	Weak	Strong	Medium	Weak	Strong
Role of stock market	High	Low	Low	Low	Low
3. *International influences*					
Inward direct foreign investment	Medium	Low	Low	Medium	High
Export orientation	Low	High	High	Medium	Medium
Membership in trade blocs	Late (NAFTA) (1989)	Early (1957)	None (1957)	Early (1986)	Late, EC
4. Main domestic entrepreneurs	Individuals and corporations	Banks Families	Sacho-kai State	Families State	Banks Families

Sources: (a) *International Historical Statistics: Europe 1750–1988*, pp. 655–63; (b) *The Fontana Economic History of Europe*, Vol. 5, edited by C. Cipolla (1976).

German corporations (Prowse, 1994). Universal banks are the predominant financial institutions in the Continental model. The coordination of financial activities is often orchestrated by the state, which supports bank lending or actively intervenes through regulation and control of credit allocation (Berglöf, 1990: 245). Direct state intervention in the economy can occur through either the provision of cheap credit to strategic industrial sectors or the establishment of state-owned enterprises. Long-term credit arrangements foster the relationship of banks with industry.

Another main feature of the Continental model is its comparatively underdeveloped capital market and low investor protection, mostly because banks are the chief financing lending institutions. Moreover, contrary to Anglo-Saxon corporate law, Continental model countries exhibit no enforced legal restrictions on the formation of intercompany economic agreements. Thus, in Germany "the 1897 verdict of the German Supreme Court (*Reichsgericht*) [upheld] cartel agreements as legally binding contracts under civil law, even in the cases involving a restraint of trade. And by the interwar period the 'regulated competition' of cartels had become a fully legitimate and accepted form of market organization" (Windölf and Beyer, 1996: 205–6). It was only after World War II that cartels were banned in Germany. Nonetheless, some coalitions of family shareholders (for example Thyssen, Krupp, Flick) and the "Big Three" universal banks were able to rapidly regain their dominant positions in the German economy. Thereafter, cartels came to be regarded favorably as an internal market strategy for international survival. In a nutshell, the main traits of the Continental model are concentrated ownership, low investor protection, a financial model based around banks, and high employment protection.

Finally, it is worth mentioning the Japanese model of corporate structure[4] which has been described as a special case. It is characterized by its main organizational form: the *keiretsu* which emerged as a prolongation of the *zaibatsu*, and as a defensive strategy against the fear of takeovers (Morikawa, 1992). *Keiretsus* are groups of Japanese firms tied together through reciprocal shareholdings, credit relations, trading relations, and interlocking directorships. They became an accepted form of economic organization by the mid-1950s. During the postwar occupation, Americans introduced legal measures modeled on the Glass–Steagall Act that were intended to separate commercial and investment banks. Most large Japanese financial corporations were exempted from these regulations, however, since they were considered strategically crucial for the economic recovery, especially given the underdeveloped stock market in Japan. The Japanese corporate system followed a path distinct from the Anglo-Saxon model, skewing industry financing toward banks and away from the securities market (Roe, 1993: 1955), and promoting a tight external labor market complemented with long-term employment relationships (Gilson and Roe, 1999).

In addition, as Johnson (1982) points out, Japan's "developmental state" became a central actor since the Japanese postwar "economic miracle," primarily through its different state financial institutions (Evans, 1995) and developmental agencies such as Japan's Ministry of International Trade and Industry (MITI). Hence, as in the Continental model, both Japanese banks and the state affected Japanese corporate structure. Contrary to the Continental model, however, the underdeveloped Japanese stock market provided opportunities for groups of investors to get involved as reciprocal shareholders (*Kabushiki mochiai*) (Lincoln et al., 1992). As a result, "[the] board of directors of the Japanese corporation looks remarkably similar to that of Anglo-Saxon corporation in structure" (Prowse, 1994: 42), in that large shareholders are not frequently represented on the board of directors, but rather prefer to influence the firm through informal networks (for example, the *keiretsu* presidents' council: *Shacho-kai*) (Lincoln et al., 1996).

Although there exists a vast research literature on corporate governance in Great Britain, Germany, the United States, and Japan, and a number of studies comparing these countries' models of corporate governance (Franks and Mayer, 1990; Roe, 1993; Charkham, 1994; Prowse, 1994; Bianco and Trento, 1995; Blair, 1995; Fukao, 1995; Shleifer and Vishny, 1997; O'Sullivan, 1996), research on Italian and Spanish corporate governance is scarce. In the following sections, I discuss the Italian and Spanish models of corporate governance, and place these cases within the typology of corporate models just discussed.

2.3   Triggers for change in economic organization

Differences in institutional environments will encourage particular kinds of economic organization over others through structuring the ways that collective actors are constituted, cooperate, and compete for resources and legitimacy (Whitley, 1999: 27). However, it would be naïve to state that the internationalization of markets has not brought industrialized countries together to some degree, if anything else because both communication and transfer of tangible and intangible assets across countries have become a lot easier as a result of globalization. In addition, certain aspects of economic and political institutions put pressures to adapt to the new era. Italy and Spain are at a crossroads in this debate, in the sense that they are shifting their governance models by undertaking major structural changes such as privatizations, deregulations, enacting new legislation, and ultimately furthering the growth of the stock market. Yet, they also need to craft the unique governance mechanisms to enhance their national competitiveness.

One of the possible ways that transformation toward the Anglo-Saxon model recently recoined *shareholder capitalism* may be occurring in Italy and Spain is through contagion. The values and mechanisms underlying shareholder capitalism were generally not created in Italy and Spain but rather were imported from the Anglo-Saxon world with English jargon; for instance *stock options* and *golden shares*. This contagion process began as Italy and Spain were exposed to Anglo-Saxon governance practices first with the entry of Anglo-Saxon multinational firms, and later with institutional investors as well as the perceived idea that companies could enhance their competitiveness by implementing such practices.

In this section, I will examine two economic and institutional factors in Italy and Spain that have exposed and introduced transformations in these countries' economic organization. These are (1) foreign direct investment, and (2) market liberalization resulting in a massive privatization process. A common trend in these macro-level pressures is that they are motivated by the state to strengthen national competitiveness or by suprastate forces such as the need to comply with European harmonization efforts.

2.3.1 Foreign direct investment

Foreign direct investment (FDI) in Italy and Spain was initially dominated by the entry of foreign multinational corporations. In the postwar era, the source of inexpensive labor, particularly suited to high-volume and medium/low-skill operations (such as car assembly) was multinationals' main motivation to settle in Southern Europe, and in the 1970s and 1980s an interest to access the European Union market triggered further foreign investment. The entry of multinational firms was particularly noteworthy in Spain as a consequence of the liberal economic policies implemented during the second period of the Franco regime (1957–77) when economic policy shifted from autarky industrialization to economic liberalization and removal of trade barriers. This trend continued up to the 1990s. Hence, the Spanish government provided significant incentives to attract foreign firms in contrast to Italian protectionism. This is exemplified by the fact that in 1995 the total FDI stock as a percentage of GDP represented 5.7 percent in Italy versus 17.6 percent in Spain (Guillén, 2000: 421).

Although FDI has increased over the years in both countries, the mode of FDI has changed. By the 1990s, foreign investment in Spain shifted from *direct foreign investment*, which does not include direct investment in listed shares but includes portfolio investment in nonlisted shares, to *portfolio foreign investment*, which includes direct investment in listed shares but does not include portfolio investment in nonlisted shares. Hence, while in 1995 direct foreign investment was roughly half of portfolio foreign investment (11,067 million euros), by the end of 2000, direct foreign investment was 39,742 million euros and portfolio foreign investment was 62,212 million euros (OECD, 2001: 24). This is explained by the entry of institutional investors and the internationalization of financial markets. Table 2.2 shows the direct investment inflows in an international comparative perspective for the 1990s. It shows that Spanish direct investment inflows have been above the OECD average and significantly higher than those in

Table 2.2 Direct investment inflows, selected OECD countries, 1990–99 (US$ million)

	1990	1991	1992	1993	1994	1995	1996	1997	1998	1999p
Australia[a]	6,513	4,042	5,036	3,007	3,951	13,202	5,171	7,510	6,502	4,441
Austria	647	359	940	982	1,314	636	4,429	2,656	4,902	2,952
Belgium–Luxembourg	7,966	9,292	11,326	10,751	8,313	10,558	14,061	12,093	22,724	15,868
Canada	7,562	2,870	4,717	4,748	8,431	10,780	9,407	11,470	16,499	24,268
Czech Republic	–	–	1,004	654	869	2,562	1,428	1,300	2,540	4,877
France	15,609	15,157	17,855	16,439	15,580	23,681	21,942	23,174	28,955	37,416
Germany	2,492	4,090	2,662	1,915	1,790	13,449	6,577	11,092	21,271	52,403
Hungary	311	1,462	1,479	2,350	1,144	4,453	2,275	2,173	2,036	1,944
Ireland[b]	258	1,168	1,244	850	420	621	1,888	1,676	3,904	5,422
Italy	**6,344**	**2,481**	**3,210**	**3,746**	**2,236**	**4,817**	**3,535**	**3,698**	**2,611**	**5,019**
Netherlands	12,165	6,552	7,824	8,561	7,586	11,611	15,055	14,499	41,977	33,341
Japan	1,806	1,286	2,755	210	888	41	228	3,224	3,193	12,378
Poland	88	359	678	1,715	1,875	3,659	4,498	4,908	6,365	6,471
Spain	**13,839**	**12,445**	**13,352**	**8,073**	**9,425**	**6,217**	**6,820**	**6,387**	**11,797**	**9,357**
Sweden	1,971	6,351	-41	3,843	6,346	14,455	5,076	10,968	19,569	59,102
Switzerland	5,485	2,644	411	-83	3,368	2,224	3,078	6,642	7,499	3,412
United Kingdom	32,889	16,027	16,214	15,468	10,497	22,738	26,084	33,245	64,388	82,176
United States	48,422	22,799	19,222	50,663	45,095	58,772	88,977	109,264	193,375	282,507
Total OECD	177,699	123,396	121,051	150,748	156,408	230,670	248,882	299,004	509,313	683,744

Notes: Data are converted using yearly average exchange rates; *p* = provisional;
As from 1995, data are based on the calendar year.
[a] Break in series.
[b] Results shown for Ireland are for net (inward and outward), direct investment capital flows. For 1999 and 1998, balance of payments data.
Data for years 1990–94 are from *Financial Market Trends*, No. 71, November 1998, p. 187 (Table 1). Data for years 1996–99 are from *Financial Market Trends*, No. 76, June 2000, p. 24 (Table 1).
Source: International Direct Investment Statistics Yearbook (for years 1990–94), 1998, OECD, OECD/FDI database (for years 1996–99) – based on national sources.

Italy which are consistently lower than in most European countries. A study based mostly on in-depth interviews with key informants in Italy suggests that low Italian foreign investment rates are due to "poor infrastructure, low labor productivity, and fear of organized crime in the South" (Vietor, 2001: 11). Table 2.3 presents the direct investment outflows. Contrary to inflows, outflows have been slightly higher in Italy up to 1996 when Spanish outflows overtook Italian ones mostly due to investments in Latin America. Unlike the case of inflows, the trend in outflows has remained more constant.

FDI continues to grow throughout the OECD countries, reaching $684 billion in inward investment and $768 billion in outward investment in 1999 (OECD, 2000). The primary contributor behind the increase in the 1990s FDI was mergers and acquisitions (M&As). According to the OECD *Financial Market Trends*, in 1999 Western Europe was the world's leading region for cross-border M&As (OECD, 2000: 23), reaching $1 trillion in 1999 and $800 billion in 2000 (*The Economist*, July 7, 2001: 75). Other vehicles behind FDI were deregulation and privatization. Deregulation processes in telecommunications, electricity, public utilities, and financial services industries were either initiated by the harmonization efforts of the European Union or by national governments as a mechanism to enhance competition. The sale of state-owned enterprises to international investors accounted for a large percentage of inward FDI.

2.3.2 Privatization process

Italy and Spain have historically shared strong state intervention through state-owned industrial holdings. The onset of the Italian financial crises in the early 1930s prompted heavy state intervention with the largest relocation of ownership in Italy, with the state at the core of Italian capitalism (Magnani and Trento, 2001). In this process, the Italian government rescued the troubled banks by buying out their industrial holdings and transferring them to a newly created institution, the IRI (Istituto per la Ricostruzione Industriale). IRI was created under the fascist regime in 1933 initially as a transient corporation to rescue troubled banks, although in 1937 it was transformed into a permanent institution. It quickly expanded and became during the postwar years a large industrial conglomerate and key industrializing institution (Castronovo, 1995). The second largest state holding company, ENI (Ente Nazionale Idrocarburi), was founded in 1953 originally to develop Italy's energy's industry. In the 1960s, Italian state-owned firms performed so comparatively well that they became the most dynamic sector of Italian business, and were seen as models to be emulated by other advanced industrial countries.

In Spain, state enterprises were largely developed under the Franco regime as a strategic institution for the import-substitution model of economic growth and also played a key role in the country's industrialization,

Table 2.3   Direct investment outflows, selected OECD countries, 1990–99 (US$ million)

	1990	1991	1992	1993	1994	1995	1996	1997	1998	1999p
Australia[a]	265	3,001	951	1,779	5,291	3,728	5,927	6,262	2,466	-3,192
Austria	1,663	1,288	1,871	1,467	1,201	1,043	1,935	1,948	2,948	2,703
Belgium–Luxembourg	6,130	6,493	10,389	4,693	1,205	11,786	8,065	7,273	28,453	24,937
Canada	5,222	5,813	3,586	5,868	9,090	11,165	12,879	22,054	26,575	17,362
Czech Republic	–	–	21	101	120	37	153	25	175	197
France	36,220	25,115	30,416	19,732	24,381	15,760	30,395	35,586	41,913	88,324
Germany	23,964	23,623	19,526	15,320	17,179	38,791	50,841	40,716	91,183	98,853
Hungary	–	–	–	11	49	43	-3	431	481	249
Ireland[b]	–	–	–	–	–	–	–	–	8,569	18,326
Italy	**7,612**	**7,326**	**5,948**	**7,221**	**5,109**	**5,732**	**6,465**	**10,619**	**12,078**	**3,038**
Japan	50,744	31,688	17,301	13,916	18,117	22,629	23,424	25,991	24,159	20,730
Netherlands	15,288	13,577	14,366	12,343	17,405	19,629	31,230	29,247	51,365	45,540
Poland	–	–	13	18	29	42	53	45	316	123
Spain	**3,442**	**4,424**	**2,171**	**2,648**	**3,900**	**3,608**	**5,590**	**12,547**	**18,935**	**35,421**
Sweden	14,743	7,053	409	1,357	6,698	11,221	4,664	12,648	24,376	18,951
Switzerland	6,709	6,212	6,050	8,765	10,798	12,214	16,150	17,747	16,631	17,910
United Kingdom	18,636	15,972	19,156	25,573	28,251	44,329	34,125	61,620	119,463	199,275
United States	30,982	32,696	42,647	78,164	73,252	92,074	92,694	109,955	132,829	152,152
Total OECD	231,018	191,430	178,589	202,230	237,418	307,366	340,977	414,079	636,480	767,814

Notes: Data are converted using yearly average exchange rates; *p* = provisional;
Break in series. As from 1995, data are based on the calendar year.
[a] Results shown for Ireland are for net (inward and outward), direct investment capital flows. For 1999 and 1998, balance of payments data.
Data for years 1990–94 are from *Financial Market Trends*, No. 71, November 1998, p. 188 (Table 1). Data for years 1996–99 are from *Financial Market Trends*, No. 76, June 2000, p. 24 (Table 1).
Source: International Direct Investment Statistics Yearbook (for years 1990–94), 1998, OECD, OECD/FDI database (for years 1996–99) – based on national sources.

mostly in the heavy industry sector and the military. State-owned firms were notably concentrated within the state industrial holding company INI (Instituto Nacional de Industria) created in 1941 following the Italian model (Martín Aceña and Comín, 1991). The state-owned systems of Italy and Spain are similar in that they did not emerge as a deliberate policy of nationalization but were the by-product of corporate salvage operations and import substitution models of economic development.

However, by the 1970s, state-owned firms began to experience operating losses, and developed a strong dependence on government funding. As Magnani and Trento point out, for the Italian state, but also applicable to the Spanish one, "as well as acting as an owner, the [Italian and Spanish] states have constantly made up for failures in the governance environment of private companies by providing them with a steady flow of resources and supplying subsidies to realize delayed restructuring" (2001: 17). In both countries, the state holdings bought out mismanaged companies, and particularly in the Italian case, because most banks were under the auspices of IRI, they transferred funds to entrepreneurs to overcome situations of financial distress, and guaranteed subsidized credit. In the 1980s, state-owned firms were riddled with managerial inefficiency and political corruption, and there were several attempts to restructure and privatize state holdings. As a consequence, state-owned firms have been subject to rationalization and restructuring with successive waves of privatization since the 1980s. IRI was liquidated following the European Commission mandate in mid-2000. In 1995, INI was dismantled into two strategic institutions whose economic goals were industrial restructuring, and in 1997 with the new Spanish conservative government, all industrial state-owned assets were transferred again under a single institutional umbrella, SEPI (Sociedad Estatal de Participaciones Industriales) for reorganization and further privatization (Gámir, 1999). Despite the common strong state intervention in both countries there are some differences in degree. Thus, in 1990, Italian state-owned firms still accounted for the highest percentage of public ownership as a percentage of the overall economy (20 percent) among the European countries closely followed by France (18 percent) (Macchiati, 1996: 27).

The major shift in state interventionism was the privatization process. Italy, France, and Spain experienced an extensive privatization process starting in 1992, as is shown in Tables 2.4 and 2.5. This privatization process became a central part of their national economic policies and was exceptionally accelerated in the years prior to the launching of the euro due to the governments' need to meet the fiscal objectives of the new monetary union (particularly decrease public debt), coupled with the European Union directives requiring liberalization of markets.

Privatization has been an important mechanism to bring small investors into the financial market, to expand the number of traded firms and to boost the overall capitalization of the domestic stock exchange. Individuals and

Table 2.4   Country breakdown of global amount raised from privatization (US$ million)

	1990	1992	1994	1996	1997	1998	1999p
Italy			**6,493**	**6,265**	**27,719**	**13,619**	**25,611**
France			5,479	5,099	8,189	12,951	9,509
Spain	**172**	**820**	**1,458**	**2,679**	**12,522**	**11,618**	**964**
Japan			13,773	6,379	4,009	6,641	14,856
Portugal	1,192	2,326	1,132	3,011	4,968	4,260	1,624
Greece			73	558	1,395	3,892	4,880
Austria	32	49	700	1,251	2,020	2,426	138
Poland	23	238	385	749	2,179	2,079	3,422
Finland			1,166	911	835	2,068	3,645
Belgium			549	1,222	1,562	2,277	–
Mexico	3,122	6,859	766	73	2,690	987	291
Czech Republic			1,077	994	442	469	781
Germany			240	13,228	1,125	364	6,734
Hungary	38	720	1,017	1,157	10966	353	88
Netherlands	716		3,766	1,239	831	335	1,481
Sweden		378	2,313	785	1,055	172	2,071
UK	12,906	604	1,341	7,610	4,544	–	–
Total OECD	24,822	16,617	47,284	69,347	95,955	85,886	100,765
of which EU 15	15,662	4,247	24,940	44,518	66,812	58,484	61,522
Other countries	5,078	19,845	18,111	27,911	57,827	45,153	44,000
Global total	29,900	36,462	65,395	97,258	153,782	131,039	144,765

Source: OECD (2000: 46).

Table 2.5   Receipts from privatization (as % of GDP)

	1993–95	1996–98
Portugal	1.4	3.9
Hungary	5.2	2.5
Spain	**0.5**	**1.6**
Greece	0.0	1.6
Italy	**0.5**	**1.4**
Poland	0.4	1.2
Czech Republic	1.7	1.2
Finland	0.6	1.0
Austria	0.3	1.0
France	0.6	0.6
Belgium	0.6	0.6
Mexico	0.3	0.3
Netherlands	0.8	0.2
Japan	0.2	0.1

Source: OECD (2000).

institutional investors become shareholders and the state slowly fades away. Moreover, privatizations tend to offer special issues for employees, who then also become minority owners. However, the hand of the state is not so invisible, since most of these privatizations are accompanied by *golden shares* where even in the case in which the state has a minority stake it might have a veto power over strategic decisions such as mergers or takeovers.

The first privatizations pre-1990s were undertaken with the method of sale to strategic buyers; in the 1990s public offerings became the main method of sale. Public offerings require sophisticated financial markets and a well-developed legal infrastructure for companies that are not already listed, and tend to be placed in the hands of institutional investors, some of them foreign. More recently, the initial public offering also includes incentives for minority shareholders to become involved. Consequently, for instance in Spain, the subscription of minority shareholders has almost doubled since the implementation of the "Spanish Privatization Plan" in 1996. The scenario is similar in Italy. In 1999, Enel (Italy's largest electricity company) undertook the world's largest IPO being oversubscribed five times by both retail and institutional investors (OECD, 2000). Enel's sale of the second tranche will take the government stake below 50 percent. In 1999, the breakdown of privatization offerings was 56 percent to the public in Italy, 5 percent to employees, and 39 percent to institutional investors and individuals abroad, which represents according to Consob (2000: 10) an increase in the proportion placed with institutional investors and a decrease in the proportion absorbed by the Italian public compared to offerings in the two previous years.

In Spain, the state coffers received 30 billion euros as a result of selling 40 state-owned enterprises: Endesa (electricity), Aceralia (steel), Iberia (flagship airline), and Telefonica (telecommunications) among others in the last four and a half years (between June 1996 and April 2001) (CCP, 2001). The Italian privatization is the largest ever realized in a European country. It generated a total gross proceeds of more than 85,000 million euros (Magnani and Trento, 2001: 24). Of the privatized companies since the start of the Italian privatization program in 1992, 13 have been included in the Mib30 index, accounting for 60 percent of the Mib30 (Italian blue chip index) and 48 percent of the total capitalization of the stock exchange (OECD, 2000: 47). The privatization process also resulted in the hostile takeover, a common economic action in shareholder capitalism, of a recently privatized Telecom Italia by Olivetti in February 1999. Tables 2.6 and 2.7 list the main privatizations in Italy and Spain respectively.

2.4 Corporate governance in Italy

Italian capitalism has been termed "political capitalism" (Amatori, 1997), "entrepreneurial capitalism," and "flexible capitalism" (Porter, 1990; Piore

Table 2.6   Main privatizations in Italy, 1993–2001

Year	Corporation (group)	Method of sale	Percentage sold
1993	Italgel (IRI)	Private agreement	62.12
	Cirio–Bertolli–DeRica (IRI)	Private agreement	62.12
	Credito Italiano (IRI)	Public offering	58.09
	SIV (RFIM)	Auction	100.00
1994	IMI – 1st tranche	Public offering	32.89
	COMIT (IRI)	Public offering	54.35
	Nuovo Pignone (ENI)	Auction	69.33
	INA – 1st tranche	Public offering	47.25
	Acciai Speciali Terni	Private agreement	100.00
	SME – 1st tranche	Private agreement	32.00
1995	Italtel (IRI)	Auction	40.00
	Ilva Laminati Piani (IRI)	Private agreement	100.00
	Enichem Augusta (ENI)	Auction	70.00
	IMI – 2nd tranche	Private agreement	19.03
	SME – 2nd tranche (IRI)	Accept takeover bid	14.91
	INA – 2nd tranche	Private agreement	18.37
	ENI – 2nd tranche	Public offering	15.00
	ISE (IRI)	Auction	73.96
1996	Dalmine (IRI)	Auction	84.08
	Italimpiati (IRI)	Auction	100.00
	Nuova Tirrena	Auction	91.14
	SME – 3rd tranche (IRI)	Accept takeover bid	15.21
	INA – 3rd tranche	Convertible bond issue	31.08
	MAC (IRI)	Auction	50.00
	IMI – 3rd tranche	Public offering	6.94
	Montefibre (ENI)	Public offering	65.00
	ENI – 2nd tranche	Public offering	15.82
1997	ENI – 3rd tranche	Public offering	17.60
	Aeroporti di Roma (IRI)	Public offering	45.00
	Telecom Italia	Core investors + public	39.54
	SEAT editoria	Core investors + public	61.27
	Banca di Roma (IRI)	Public offering + bond	36.50
1998	SAIPEM (ENI)	Public offering	18.75
	ENI – 4th tranche	Public offering	14.83
	BNL	Public offering	67.85
1999	ENEL	Public offering	35.00
	Autostrada (IRI)	Auction + public offering	57.00
2000	Autostrada (IRI)	Private agreement	30.00
	Finmeccanica (IRI)	Public offering	43.70
	Aeroporti di Roma (IRI)	Private agreement	51.20
	Banci di Napoli	Public offering	16.16
2001	ENI – 5th tranche	Accelerate book building	5.00

Sources: Magnani and Trento (2001: 30–1, Table 11); company accounts (various years); Ministry of Treasury, *Relazione sulle privatizzazion* (various years); financial press.

Table 2.7 Spanish privatizations, 1985–99

Year	Firm	Owner	Percentage sold	Buyer
1985	Textil Tarazona	INI	69.6	Cima Enursa
	Igenasa	INI (Enisa)	67.7[a]	ERT
	Igfisa	INI (Endiasa)	100.0	Pleamar
	Cesquisa	INI (Enisa)	45.4	Cepsa
	Secoinsa	INI	69.1	Fujitsu España/Telefónica
	SKF Española	INI	98.8	Aktiebogalet SKF
	Marsans	INI	100.0	Trapsatur
	Gossypium	DGPE/Itelhorce	100.0	Textil Guadiana
1986	Entursa	INI	100.0	CIGA
	Frigsa	INI (Endiasa)	100.0	Saprogal/ H. de Lujo Esp.
	Gypisa	INI (Endiasa)	100.0	Frig. Santana/Los Norteños
	La Luz	INI (Carcesa)	100.0	Prevert
	Insisa	INI (BWE)	60.0	Acctas. Privadas de Insisa
	Remetal	INI (Inespal)	66.6[b]	Remetal
	Issa	INI (Inespal)	100.0	Aluperfil
	Aluflet	INI (Aluminia)	40.0	Actas. Privadas de Aluflet
	Motores MBD	INI (Motores Barrera/ Sodiga)	60.0[c]	Klockner Humboldt Deutz AG
	Pamesa	INI (Ence)	100.0	Torras Hostench
	Fovisa	INI (Made)	100.0	Gekanor (GKN/Acenor)
	Indugasa	INI (Seat)	50.0	GKN
	Seat	INI	100.0[d]	Volkswagen
	Telesincro	INI (Inisel)	100.0[e]	Bull
	Gesa	–	30.0	IPO (Institutional)
1987	Dessa	INI (Bazán/Ast)	80.0	Forestal del Atlántico
	Evatsa	INI (Inespal/So)	100.0	Cebal
	Lifotan	INI (Inespal)	100.0	Baumgartner Ibérica
	Alumalsa	INI (Inespal)	44.0	Montuper
	Purlator	INI (CASA)	97.4	Knecht Filterwerk

Table 2.7 Spanish privatizations, 1985–99 *Continued*

Year	Firm	Owner	Percentage sold	Buyer
	Vict. Luzuriaga	INI	33.3	Eisenwerk Bruhl
	Diasa	INI (Endiasa)	50.0	Saudisa (Promodes)/BBV
	Miel Española	INI (Endiasa)	51.0	Sugemesa (Agrolimen)
	Miraflores	INI (Lac. Cast.)	–	Queserías Miraflores
	Acesa	INI (Bazán/Ast)	29.0	IPO (Institutional/Minority)
	Telfónica-87	INI (Inespal/So)	6.0	IPO (Institutional)
	Ence-87	INI (Inespal)	40.0[f]	IPO (Institutional)
1988	Endesa		20.4[g]	IPO (Institutional/Minority)
1989	Astican	INI	90.72	Italmar
	MTM	INI	100.0[h]	GEC Alsthom
	Ateinsa	INI	100.0[i]	GEC Alsthom
	Enfersa	INI	100.0[j]	Ercros
	Oesa	INI (Endiasa)	100.0	Ferruzzi
	Pesa	INI (Inisel)	97.4	Amper
	Ancoal	INI (Enisa)	75.2	Omnium Industrie
	Repsol	INH	26.0[k]	IPO (Institutional/Minority)
1990	Adaro Indonesia	INI (Enadimsa)	80.0	Indonesia Coal/Asmico, etc.
	Hytasa	DGPE	100.0	Textil Guadiana
	Imepiel	DGPE	100.0	DFG Grupo Cusi
	Dirsa	DGPE (Tabac.)	75.06	Diasa (Promodes/BBV)
	Seb. de la Fuente	DGPE	100.0	Cofidisa
	Salinas de Torrevieja	DGPE	38.5	U. Salinera de Esp. (Solvay)
	Coifer	DGPE (Tabac.)	50.0	Alimentos Naturales (BBV)
1991	Enasa	INI	100.0	Iveco
	G. Emp. Alvarez	INI	100.0[l]	Iveco
	TSD	INI (Enosa)	100.0	Telepublicaciones
	Fridarago	DGPE (Tab.)	100.0	Rústicas
	Coisa	DGPE (Tab.)	100.0	Rústicas

Table 2.7 Spanish privatizations, 1985–99 Continued

Year	Firm	Owner	Percentage sold	Buyer
1992	Jobac	Mercasa	100.0[m]	Eosmer Consm (Eroski)
	Icuatro	INI (Iniexport)	90.0	Grupo Alegre
1993	Automoción 2000	INI (Teneo)	100.0	Inversores Reo
	Fábrica S. Carlos	INI (Teneo)	100.0	G. Navacel/Total Chemical Trade
	Palco	INI (Inespal)	100.0 [n]	Alcan Deutschland
	Royal Brands SA	DGPE (Tabac.)	100.0	RJR Alimentación (50% Tabac.)
	Ineco	Renfe	66.0[o]	–
	Argentaria	INI (Teneo)	25.0[p]	IPO (Institutional/Minority)
1994	C. Trasatlántica	INI (Teneo)	100.0	Naviera de Odiel/Mar. Valenciana
	Arteespaña	INI (Teneo)	100.0	Medino, S.L.
	ASDL	INI (Ceselsa)	87.7	Quadrant Group
	Sodiga	INI	51.2	Xunta de Galicia
	Enagas	INH	91.0[q]	Gas Natural
	Caivsa	INH	100.0	Gas Natural
	RJR Alimentacio	DGPE (Tabac.)	10.7	RJR Nabisco
1995	Refinalsa	INI (Inespal)	50.0	Remetal
	Sidenor	AIE	50.0	Digeco-Roda
	Lesa	DGPE (Tabac.)	100.0	Leyma/Iparlat
	Telefónica		10.7[r]	IPO (Institutional/Minority)
1996	Almagrera	SEPI	99.98	Navan Resources
	Gas Natural	SEPI	3.81	IPO (Institutional)
	Sefanitro		52.65	
	Sodican		51.0	
1997	Aldeasa	SEPPa	80.0	IPO (Institutional/Minority)
	Aceralia	SEPI	52.8	IPO (Institutional/Minority)
	Iongraf	SEPI	100.0	MBO
	Sodical	SEPI	51.0	Shareholders + Caja R. del Duero
	Surgiclinic Plus	AIE	50.0	Hambros

Table 2.7 Spanish privatizations, 1985–99 Continued

Year	Firm	Owner	Percentage sold	Buyer
	Auxini	SEPI	60.0	OCP
	Retevisión	Mins. De Fomento	60.0	STET and Endesa
	CSI-Aceralia	AIE-SEPI	47.2	ARBED & Corp. J. M. Aristrain
	Elcano	SEPI	100.0	Grupo Marítimolbérico
	Tisa	SEPPa	23.78	Telefónica
	Ferroperfil	SEPI	100.0	MBO
	Inespal	SEPI	99.6	Alcoa
	Infoleasing	SEPI	100.0	Liscat (Caixa de Catalunya)
	Hijos de J. Barreras	SEPI	99.99	Grupo Barreras
	Sodicamán		51.0	
1998	Tabacalera	SEPPa	52.0	IPO (Institutional/Minority)
	Productos Tubulares	SEPI	100.0	Tubos Reunidos
	Inima	SEPI	100.0	Lain
	Comesa	SEPI	100.0	Several buyers
	Serausa	SEPPa	100.0	Areas, S.A.
	Grupo Potasas	SEPI	100.0	Dead Sea Works (DSW)
1999	Indra	SEPI	66.1	IPO (Institutional/Minority)
	Red Eléctrica de Esp	SEPI	31.5	IPO (Institutional/Minority)
	Icsa-Aya	SEPI	100.0	Mecanizaciones Aeronáuticas
	Enatcar	SEPI	100.0	Alianza Bus

Table 2.7 Spanish privatizations, 1985–99 *Continued*

Year	Firm	Owner	Percentage sold	Buyer
	Astander	SEPI	100.0	Italmar
	LM Compos Toledo	SEPI	50.0	LM Composites
	Iberia	SEPI	54.0	BA, AA, institutional domestic investors
	Initec	SEPI	100.0	Técnicas Reunidas & Westinghouse
	Casa (closed 2000)			

Notes: Companies are classified by date of first privatization.
[a] 51% in 1985; 14.2 in 1986; and 2.4 in 1989.
[b] 66.1 in 1986; 0.5 in 1990.
[c] 38.4 in 1986; 21.6 in 1989.
[d] 75 in 1986; 25 in 1990.
[e] 40 in 1986; 33.9 in 1988; 26.1 in 1994.
[f] 40 in 1987/8(?); 15 in 1995; 45 in 1996 and 1997.
[g] 20.4 in 1988; 8.6 in 1994; 25 in 1997; 46 in 1998.
[h] 85 in 1989; 15 in 1992.
[i] 85 in 1989; 15 in 1992.
[j] 80 in 1989; 20 in 1991.
[k] 26.4 in 1989; 4.2 in 1989; 2.9 in 1990; 2.1 and 9.8 in 1992; 14.1 in 1993; 19.5 in 1995; 11 in 1996; and 10 in 1997.
[l] 60 in 1991; 40 in 1993.
[m] 70 in 1991; 30 in 1995.
[n] 50 in 1993; 50 in 1994.
[o] 55 in 1993; 11 in 1994.
[p] 25 in April 93; 25 in November 1993; 25 in 1996; and 25 in 1998.
[q] 91 in 1994; 9 in 1997.
[r] 10.7 in 1995; 21 in 1996.
Sources: Gamir (1999: 100–3, 105, 118–21, 136–42); Fernández Ordóñez (2000: 160–1); Anuario El PAIS (2001: 428).

and Sabel, 1984). This is because the Italian economy includes a small number of large corporations that were already part of Italy's industrial capitalism at the outbreak of World War II,[5] together with a vast network of small- and medium-sized firms,[6] a highly interventionist state, and a fairly protectionist economy.

This section describes corporate governance patterns for Italian corporations, mostly large firms. I begin by describing the Italian corporate law and types of corporations, and the structure of corporate ownership and control. I then discuss the system of corporate finance, particularly the role of banks, the stock market, and institutional investors.

2.4.1   Corporate law and types of corporations[7]

The Italian Civil Code of 1942 is, with few exceptions, the principal source of Italian corporate law (Colombo and Portale, 1991; Galgano, 1997). Until very recently, the government had not created a suitable corporate legal framework within which modern business could develop and flourish in Italy, with little financial transparency and protection for minority shareholders. However, since the early 1990s, the harmonization of European corporate law, the internationalization of the economy, and the necessity to have a competitive business and financial system have led to reforms in the Italian corporate governance environment.[8]

Italian company law provides for three main forms of corporations: the Società per Azioni, SpA (stock company), the Società in Accomandita per Azioni, Sapa (stock company with personally liable directors), and the Società a Responsabilità Limitata, SrL (limited liability company) (Zattoni, 1994). The legislative company model is based on the SpA. Medium and large firms, as well as most publicly traded firms, are legally structured as SpA. The Sapa was intended as a device to facilitate the raising of capital by a personally liable entrepreneur, usually well-known to and trusted by the public. This is the characteristic corporate form for top holding companies of large business groups.[9] The limited liability corporate form (SrL) is adopted by small and medium-sized firms and is the predominant corporate form in the Italian economy. It becomes less common as a firm's size increases. According to Stranghellini (1995: 101), when companies grow, they adopt the form of SpA for corporate image reasons. SpA are considered more stable and "serious." The distribution of power in an SpA is legally allocated among three corporate bodies: shareholders, a board of directors, and a board of auditors.

As of 1993, of the 1000 largest Italian industrial companies, classified by annual turnover, 810 were SpA, and 116 SrL. The rest were cooperatives and consortia, foreign companies, or public entities. Of the top 100 companies, most are SpA; there are six SrL, and seven cooperatives. Most banks and insurance companies are required to adopt the legal form of SpA or *società cooperativa* (cooperative societies). Thus, in 1992, out of the

50 largest banks, classified by total assets, 39 were SpA, 10 were coopera-tives and one was a state-owned entity with a special regime (Monti dei Paschi di Siena). Finally, all of the 100 largest insurance companies (with the exception of a few mutual insurance companies), ranked by total pre-miums collected, were SpA (*Il Mondo Economico*, December 25, 1993).

2.4.2 Type of corporate ownership

Shareholders, mostly in the form of block holders, play an active role in Italian corporate governance, and have the final say in fundamental company matters such as capital structure, dividend policy, and firm strat-egy such as mergers. Shareholders govern a corporation via majority rule. Ownership entities involve the following: individuals, domestic enterprises (nonfinancial enterprises), financial holding companies, with no manufac-turing activity, foreign companies, and the state.

There is a distinction in ownership patterns between those companies that are listed in the stock market and those which are not. The latter, small to medium-sized companies, are usually controlled by a single individual (the founder) or by very homogeneous shareholders (a close group of share-holders, often members of the same family). They generally do not have state or foreign capital, nor do they receive institutional investments, because the family intends to retain control of the firm. Barca et al. (1994: 45–60) demonstrate that there is a strong negative relationship between number of employees and percentage of individual ownership for small and medium firms. From their survey of 286 Italian firms of 20–500 employees in 1993, they show that in those firms with less than 50 employees, 80 percent of the ownership belongs to individuals (1994: 51).

As for companies listed on the Italian stock market, aggregate statistics on direct ownership demonstrate the coexistence of different types of shareholders. Table 2.8 shows ownership percentages of listed companies in comparative perspective. It is to be noted that Italian financial cor-porations (including banks and domestic institutional investors) play a relatively small role compared to other selected OECD countries. Italian financial entities hold 14 percent of the shares in listed firms versus 21.2 percent in Spain, and 47 percent in the US and 68 percent in the UK. Even though 10.9 percent of bank ownership might seem high, it is impor-tant to note that these banks are mainly state-owned, as will be discussed in section 2.4.4. Foreign ownership is also rather low in Italy in compara-tive perspective, partly as a consequence of protectionist policies and the predominance of small and medium-size firms. By contrast, the domestic nonfinancial sector owns 82 percent of the capital of listed firms in Italy. The latter accounts for the large state-owned enterprise sector and family-run enterprises compared to other countries. According to Table 2.8, Italy has the highest percentage of state ownership of listed firms, at 28 percent, of the seven OECD countries selected.

Table 2.8   Ownership of listed companies in selected countries in 1996 (%)

	Italy	Spain	Germany	France	Japan	US	UK
Domestic institutional investors	3.0	7.2	20	20	27	40	58
Banks	10.9	14	10	10	15	7	10
Foreign institutional investors	4.3	27.6	9	25	11	5	9
State	28	11	4	3	1	0	1
Individuals (families)	32.2	23.6	23	15	20	49	21
Nonfinancial firms	21.6	6.9	42	19	26	–	1
Other[a]	–	9.7	–	–	–	–	–
Total	100	100	100	100	100	100	100

[a] Foreign noninstitutional.
Source: Eguidazu (1999: 250–1).

As a result of Italy's effort to create a more transparent stock market, some ownership data have recently been made public by the Regulatory Stock Commission, Consob. Table 2.9 shows a consistent yet updated pattern from Table 2.8. Two main trends are worth highlighting. First, there is a slight increase in the number of foreign investors and institutional investors, which is explained by the liberalization of financial markets and privatization public offerings. Second, there is a decreasing trend in the percentage of state owner- ship. The Consob Annual Report (2000) states that there has been a reduction in the share of market capitalization of companies controlled by the state from 28 percent in 1995 to 25.6 percent in 1998. State ownership of publicly traded firms is closely linked to the privatization efforts. While privatization efforts in Italy started in the early 1990s, the peak of this process was not until 1996, and it slowed considerably in the following years. Still the low visible turnover of ownership types can be explained by the financial obstacles to new entrants, stickiness of the model of family control, and collusion between top management teams of state-owned firms and politicians, which according to Magnani and Trento (2001: 20) cause adverse effects on long-term growth and on equity.

2.4.3   Corporate control

Until very recently it was difficult to know the ownership concentration of Italian and Spanish firms because of the lack of disclosure requirements. The European Commission's 1988 transparency directive required all member states to disclose large ownership stakes and voting rights (Becht and Röell, 1999). This directive in itself shakes the governance culture in both Italy and Spain.

Ownership concentration is assessed by examining the percentage of corporate control held by the largest owners. Table 2.10 demonstrates that

Table 2.9   Significant shareholdings in Italian listed companies[a]

	1997		1998		1999		2000	
	No.	%[b]	No.	%[b]	No.	%[b]	No.	%[b]
Foreign investors	166	5.0	176	5.9	193	6.2	233	6.5
Insurance	22	2.2	32	2.5	36	1.5	27	3.2
Banks	79	5.1	65	4.8	83	5.3	66	5.9
Foundations	42	3.1	31	5.1	43	4.5	49	5.0
Institutional investors	50	0.1	69	0.1	74	0.2	82	0.3
Companies	150	14.4	155	12.6	162	19.4	151	17.2
State	44	12.1	32	8.8	35	10.6	37	10.2
Individuals	266	4.8	233	3.8	253	4.5	254	4.9
Total	819	46.8	793	43.6	879	52.2	899	53.1

[a] Shareholding exceeding 2% of the voting capital.
[b] Percentage of the value of the shareholdings to market capitalization.
Source: Consob (1998, 1999, 2000).

Table 2.10   Ownership concentration in individual firms in OECD countries (% of largest owner's share of capital)

Largest owner's share	Italy* (1994)[a]	Spain (1990)[b]	France (1982)[c]	US (1986)[d]	Japan (1983)[e]	UK (1976)[f]	Germany (1985)[g]
> 50	60	49	55	9	5	2	66
30–50							23
25–30				29		9	
20–25					70		
15–20	40	49	42			5	12
10–15				10			
5–10				29	25	32	
< 5		2	2	23		52	

Sources:
[a] OECD (1994–95) Italy.
[b] Galve Gorriz and Salas Fumás (1993=213).
[c-g] Berglof (1990: 248).

corporate ownership is more concentrated in Italy than in any other major OECD country. For example, in 1994, 60 percent of the firms traded in the Italian stock market have a single majority owner, compared to only 9 percent in 1986 in the United States, and 5 percent in 1983 in Japan. The largest five shareholders held, on average, nearly 90 percent of outstanding shares of listed companies in Italy (OECD, 1994–95: 60). The Italian system of corporate governance was conceived with concentrated shareholders as a group, and this continues to be trend in the 1990s as shown in Table 2.11. In the 1990s, there was a small change in the corporate control of large

Table 2.11 Ownership concentration of Italian listed companies as percentage of total market capitalization[a]

	1996	1997	1998	1999	2000
First shareholder	50.4	38.7	33.8	44.2	44.0
First three shareholders	59.6	44.8	40.8	50.1	50.9
Market	38.9	52.9	56.5	47.6	46.6

[a] As a % of total capitalization of ordinary shares of all firms quoted in the Italian stock exchange.
Source: Consob (2001: 7).

Italian corporations due to the massive privatization and consequent owner-ship reorganization during 1997 and 1998 that led to a temporary trend of diffusion of ownership, and the successive process of control reorganization that led to an increasing ownership concentration. As is shown in Table 2.11, the ownership concentration changes during the last five years are explained mostly by the percentage of ownership held by the largest shareholder that declined from 50.4 percent in 1996 to 33.8 percent in 1998 to increase again in 1999 to 44 percent (Consob, 2001: 7). In fact, Consob reports a stable ownership concentration rate for nonstate quoted firms that was not susceptible to the process of privatization. Thus, among the non-state-owned firms that were listed in the Italian stock exchange during the 1990–2000 period, the average percentage ownership of the first shareholder has remained substantially unchanged with a value around 50 percent of total market capitalization (Consob, 2001: 9). In sum, high ownership concentration continues to be the main pattern of Italian corporate control where in 2000, the ownership percentage of the largest shareholder accounts for over 50 percent of ordinary capitalization for 141 firms out of the 237 quoted in the Italian stock exchange (Consob, 2001: 122).

The Italian single majority shareholder phenomenon can take several forms. Among small firms, it is typical to find absolute control by an indi-vidual (often the founder) who holds a majority of voting rights. According to Barca (1996), this control model accounts for approximately 9 percent of the activity of manufacturing firms with more than 50 employees. The ownership of quoted Italian firms is concentrated around three main models of corporate control: families, coalitions, or the state.

Ownership concentration of listed firms is usually explained by the fact that the main shareholder acts as a *blockholder*. This form is referred to as "pyramided" holding, Chinese boxes, or hierarchical group control. It is estimated that one-third of Italian firms are controlled in this fashion. A pyramidal group is formed by judicially autonomous firms (that may range from two firms to hundreds) controlled by the same entrepreneur via a chain of proprietary and control relations that are vertical and unidirec-tional (Brioschi et al., 1990; Zattoni, 1994; Barca, 1996; Bianco et al., 1996).

The main characteristic is that the blockholder controls directly through both equity or indirectly through the nonvoting shares and shareholder agreements the majority of the firm's voting rights (Melis, 2000: 348). "Upstream" firms along the chain of control directly own majority stakes in "downstream" firms which accounts for the high concentration of ownership in pyramidal groups. There exists a single strong shareholder at the top of the pyramid.

> The remaining members of the controlling group, in turn, are normally large or controlling shareholders of other companies and are sometimes involved in related industries. Shared control and minority holdings, when significant and part of a broader agreement, tend to form webs of stable inter-firm relationships. Such relationships, however, remain mostly one-directional: the law confines cross-ownership to small percentages of the capital, and a circular ownership, although not expressly prohibited, faces some obstacles. (Stranghellini, 1995: 144)

Pyramidal groups are used as a device by blockholders to retain huge corporate control of capital though spreading the voting rights of minority shareholders over a large number of firms, with little direct ownership, and dispersed risk.

Pyramidal groups are intended to allow greater separation between ownership and control, and their spread goes hand in hand with the absence of specific regulations to safeguard the interests of minority shareholders in subsidiaries. The pyramidal pattern is transforming as the rest of the economy. The average number of quoted firms in Italy that formed the top ten nonstate pyramidal groups was seven in 1990 versus three in 2000. The concentration of corporate control of pyramidal groups is illustrated by the average separation (capital under control/capital owned) which has been reduced 25 percent among the top ten nonstate pyramidal groups in the period 1990–2000 (from 2.4 to 1.8) (Consob, 2001: 8–9).

The use of nonvoting shares, an important device in the corporate governance of pyramidal groups, has also diminished from being used in 40 percent of total firms quoted in 1990 to 25 percent in 2000. Thus, the capitalization weight of nonvoting shares over total market share capitalization decreased from 14 percent in 1990 to 4 percent in 2000 (Consob, 2001: 8–9). In contrast, shareholder agreements, another mechanism to maintain the control of the company by a coalition of blockholders (Melis, 2000: 350), have increased despite the Draghi reform intended to weaken them. According to Consob (2000: 6), at the end of 1999 there were 70 listed companies – as opposed to 56 and 65 in 1996 and 1998 respectively, representing 32 percent of the total market capitalization of the Italian stock exchange. "The holdings involved in these agreements [in 1999] were equal to around 50 percent of the company's ordinary share capital on average and their market value was equal to 12.9 percent of total market capitalization of the Stock Exchange" (Consob, 2000: 6). There has, however, been a slight decrease in the percentage of share capital covered by shareholder agreements from 15.9 percent in 1996 to 12.9 percent in 1999 (Consob, 2000: 7).

Controlling owners at the top of a pyramidal group are either families, coalitions, or the state. A study of the pyramidal groups among Italian quoted firms in 1993 by Barca et al. (1994) shows that attributing control of the company at the top of the pyramidal group, to all companies of the group, 40.7 percent of the firms have family control, 18.8 percent coalition control, and 15.2 percent state control.

"Family control" is widely represented by family groups that illustrate the predominance of family-run business in the Italian economy (Bianco et al., 1996: 19). Shareholders in this model are usually the firm's founders or families of the founders also highly involved in the day-to-day management duties of the firm. Noncontrolling investors come from family links and are based on trust relationships. There is limited separation between ownership and control and strong barriers against growth, which tends to be limited by the size of existing families. This model enter into crises due to generational succession and the need for further corporate financing. "Coalition control" as in the family control model entails a trust link between entrepreneurs and investors – often through contractual or implicit shareholder agreements – and a trust based on shared values or economic experiences. This is also the case of the well-known *industrial districts*, the corporate networks among small and medium-size enterprises (Best, 1990; Pyke et al., 1990; Weiss, 1984). Finally, "state control" played a crucial role up to the mid-1990s when the government controlled a major stake in large state-owned enterprises and also allocated resources to private ailing firms. This model is tightly linked to the political environment in Italy, though it is slowly changing with the privatization process.

Table 2.11 shows that ownership concentration in Italy has decreased since 1996, although still highly concentrated, and it is certainly almost impossible to exercise corporate control measures typical of dispersed firms in Anglo-Saxon markets.

2.4.4   The role of banks

The financial model of control is basically absent in the Italian corporate scenario. A distinguishing feature of the structure of corporate ownership in Italy is the minor role played by financial institutions. When contrasted with other Continental European countries, we observe that financial institutions are not highly involved in the corporate monitoring of Italian listed firms. Although banks have a relevant stake in corporate external financing (Ciocca, 1991, 2000; Capra et al., 1994), due to the historical weak relationship between banks and industry, they do not participate in corporate governance (Capra et al., 1994). The role of banks in Italy explains why this is the case. The 1936 Banking Law enforced the separation between banking and industry introduced by (1) prohibiting banks from holding equity participation in industrial firms, and by (2) drawing a sharp division between commercial banks (specializing in short-term lending), and investment banks (specializing in long-term lending). This law was similar to the American Glass–Steagal Act, although as Magnani and Trento (2001) point out, it was never intended to relaunch the stock market and obtain a broader ownership base.

The prevalence of the 1936 Banking Law until 1993[10] banished the existing universal banks, and prevented the development of strong bank–industry relations (Zamagni, 1993; Bianco and Trento, 1995). Banks are generally not involved in the economic activities or auditing of corporate performance of their clients. Mixing of industry and financial corporations can only be found in the pyramidal groups. One of the main activities of Italian banks is lending to nonfinancial firms rather than holding stakes in nonfinancial corporations. However, long-term credit to nonfinancial corporations can only be provided by two special credit institutions or *merchant banks* (IMI and Mediobanca), and therefore short-term credit represents the dominant form of financial investment in nonfinancial firms by banks. Table 2.12 shows that in the 1990s short-term lending represented nearly 90 percent of the lending undertaken (mainly through bank affidavits and also checking-account overdraft facilities), while long-term lending accounted for merely 10 percent.

Another feature of the Italian banking system is its relatively small size (OECD, 1994–95: 73) and low concentration (Conigliani, 1990). A high number of banks survive because multiple bank lending is a common practice in Italy. According to Barca (1996: 8), firms with total debt higher than 1 million lire in 1992 borrowed from an average of five banks per firm. Borrowing from multiple banks allows industrial corporations to multiply their financing opportunities and decrease their level of dependency and corporate transparency, while banks diversify risk (Ceola et al., 1994; Bragantini, 1996). There is no evidence of bank monitoring of corporate performance due to short-term lending, the high turnover of

Table 2.12 Bank lending to nonfinancial enterprises in Italy (% of total loans)

Year	Total loans (billion lire)	Short term	Long term
1990	448,219	90.0	10.0
1991	516,370	89.6	10.4
1992	591,977	89.1	10.9
1993	632,416	88.6	11.4

Source: OECD (1994–95: 76).

bank–customer relations, firms enjoying multiple credit lines, and the wide use of collateral. In addition, "banks have in general preferred an arm's-length relationship with their customers to relational financing: while minimizing their irreversible investments in stable, long-term customer relationships, they have relied on the opportunity to discontinue credit to their clients or to forfeit their personal wealth" (Barca, 1996: 9). In this financial context, banks have traditionally developed little know-how in corporate finance, and no other financial institution (for example investment banks, fund managers, or accounting houses) has replaced the role of banks in the ownership structure and become active in the Italian economy. Initially, the state took over the banks, but the absence of other financial institutions such as pension funds is partly explained by the country's broad-coverage, pay-as-you-go pension system.

During the 1990s, partly as a result of the new 1993 Banking Law as well as the liberalization of the banking sector, Italian banks have started to merge and work to establish a national presence. Table 2.13 shows the number of banking mergers and the significant increase in the merger rate since the early 1990s, and Table 2.14 indicates the concentration in the Italian banking sector by size and how their loan composition directly related to the size of the bank.

The main exception to the eradication of the bank–industry relationship was the investment bank, Mediobanca, formed in 1946 with equity capital from three IRI banks: Banca Commerciale, Credito Italiano, and Banca di

Table 2.13   Number of bank mergers in Italy, 1980–97

1980	7
1981	8
1982	8
1983	11
1984	6
1985	9
1986	12
1987	12
1988	21
1989	22
1990	23
1991	48
1992	48
1993	42
1994	52
1995	56
1996	44
1997	34

Source: De Bonis and Ferrando (2000: Table 6, p. 28).

Table 2.14   Italian banks by size and composition of loans

	1989	1992	1995	1998
Large banks				
Number	26	25	24	24
Branches	6,426	9,132	11,464	12,566
Average total assets (billion lire)	35,095	49,995	63,684	72,730
National loan market share(%)	57.0	58.4	59.8	59.2
Loan composition(%)				
Large nonfinancial firms	42.9	42.9	43.2	41.6
Small and medium nonfinancial firms	26.5	24.1	25.9	23.1
Other borrowers	30.7	33.0	31.5	35.3
Medium-sized banks				
Number	40	39	36	32
Branches	2,742	3,356	3,964	4,484
Average total assets (billion lire)	7,480	10,533	13,963	16,564
National loan market share(%)	21.1	20.7	21.6	19.8
Loan composition(%)				
Large nonfinancial firms	42.4	44.9	44.8	47.9
Small and medium nonfinancial firms	32.6	30.1	30.4	28.7
Other borrowers	25.0	25.1	24.8	23.4
Small banks				
Number	1,057	1,000	912	862
Branches	6,401	7,523	8,210	9,577
Average total assets (billion lire)	408	562	718	979
National loan market share(%)	21.9	20.9	18.6	20.9
Loan composition(%)				
Large nonfinancial firms	31.2	32.9	32.1	34.5
Small and medium nonfinancial firms	45.5	43.9	46.9	43.5
Other borrowers	23.2	23.2	21.0	22.0
Total banks				
Number	1,176	1,073	970	921
Branches	15,569	20,011	23,638	26,627
Average total assets (billion lire)	1,462	2,086	2,802	3,365
Loan composition(%)				
Large nonfinancial firms	40.6	41.6	41.7	41.8
Small and medium nonfinancial firms	31.3	28.8	29.7	27.6
Other borrowers	28.1	29.6	28.5	30.5

Source: Bonaccorsi di Patti and Gobbi (2001), Table 2 from *Italian Central Credit Register and Bank Supervisory Reports*, p. 27.

Roma. This bank replicated the universal bank role for Italy's leading private firms, guaranteeing their stability and growth, and helping them in times of crisis (De Cecco and Ferri, 1996). Mediobanca led Italian capitalism. It was at the center of a web of directorship interlocks (Aguilera, 1999) and influences, thanks to its stakes in the main Italian financial and industrial groups and its well-connected shareholders, the so-called Milan *salotto buono.* Up to the end of the 1990s as *The Economist* puts it, "this small and secretive bank was the pre-eminent power in Italian finance" (June 23, 2001: 82–3). More recently, mostly due to financial deregulation and the privatization process, international investment banks have settled and expanded in the Italian financial market and Mediobanca's influence seems to have declined, leaving it appearing smaller, parochial, and often left behind in the main Italian financial operations. For instance, Mediobanca, relative to international investment banks, benefited little from privatizations. In addition, unlike international investment banks that headed the lists in Italian merger and acquisition operations, it ranked only sixth according to Morgan Stanley or tenth according to Rothschilds (*The Economist*, June 23, 2001: 82). Mediobanca's future role is therefore in question.

2.4.5   Stock market

Italy has a relatively small stock market that has played a minor role in Italian corporate governance. It has traditionally been described as lacking transparency, efficiency, and depth. As Table 2.15 confirms, in the 1990s there were fewer than 300 Italian companies listed and regularly traded on the Italian automated stock exchange whose administrative and operating headquarters are in Milan. In May 2001, the number increased to 352 mostly due to privatization patterns (FIBV, 2001). Table 2.16 shows that in 1996, the total capitalization of the Italian stock exchange was about 21 percent of the GDP, a percentage substantially lower than in most other OECD countries, especially Anglo-Saxon countries. Economic and institutional factors have restricted the development of the Italian stock market. According to the OECD (1994–95: 82), "besides the fear of losing control, entrepreneurs are reluctant to go public because underpricing in Italian initial public offerings is particularly high". In addition, from the small investor side, minority shareholder rights have been rudimentary, favoring the few large shareholders (Bianchi et al., 1998).

The state stunted the growth of the stock market by offering one of the largest bond markets in Europe, and the third largest in the world. This resulted in a *crowding out* effect, and one of the highest European government debts. This is particularly notorious in Italy where the government percentage of total bonds in 1997 was 83.5 percent (OECD, 2000: 86).

Despite the Italian stock market's minor role in the economy, the number of listed companies in Italy has followed a steady increase in the last 20 years and the stock market as a whole is growing. This growth is explained by several factors:

1. Approval of the Italian Stock Market Law of 1991 intended to reform the Italian public financial market under the supervision of the Bank of Italy and Consob (the supervisory agency for the public capital markets);
2. The favorable, if temporary, tax regime introduced in 1994 for companies that choose to go public (Stranghellini, 1995: 135);

Table 2.15 Number of listed domestic companies, 1989–2000

	1989	1991	1997	1998	1999[a]	2000[a]		
						Domestic	Foreign	Total
Australia (Assoc. of SE)	1,258	957	1,219	1,162	1,287	1,330	76	1,406
Austria (Vienna)	81	105	101	96	144	97	14	111
Belgium (Brussels)	184	183	138	146	278	161	104	265
Canada (Toronto)	1,146	1,086	1,362	1,384	1,456	1,379	42	1,421
Denmark (Copenhagen)	257	261	237	242	242	225	10	235
Finland (Helsinki)	78	63	124	129	150	154	4	158
France (Paris)	668	551	683	711	969	808	158	966
Germany (Assoc. of SE)	628	428	700	741	851	744	245	989
Italy (Milan)	**217**	**224**	**235**	**320**	**270**	**291**	**6**	**297**
Japan (Tokyo)	2,019	2,107	2,387	2,416	1,935	2,055	41	2,096
Netherlands (Amsterdam)	313	204	201	212	387	234	158	392
New Zealand	242	139	190	135	189	144	56	200
Norway (Oslo)	122	112	196	236	215	191	24	215
Spain (Madrid)		433	384	484	727	1,019	17	1,036
Sweden (Stockholm)	135	230	245	258	300	292	19	311
Switzerland (Zurich)	177	182	216	232	412	252	164	416
Turkey (Istanbul)	50	134	257	277	286	315	1	316
United Kingdom (London)	2,015	1,623	2,046	2,399	2,274	1,926	448	2,374
United States (NYSE, AMEX and NASDAQ)	6,727	6,742	8,851	8,450	8,504	7,274	971	8,245

[a] 1999 and 2000 data are from *Fédération Internationale des Bourses de Valeurs* (FIBV), Table 1.1, www.fibv.com.
Source: IFC, *Factbook* (1999), *Emerging Markets Data Base*, p. 23.

3. The increasing internationalization of capital markets, and primarily
4. Privatization of state-owned companies initiated in 1992.

In 1998, the volume of trading in the ordinary shares of privatized companies accounted for around 34 percent of the Italian stock market total (Consob, 2000: 12). Reform initiatives by the Consob and the Bank of Italy led to the enactment of a new law for listed companies in 1998: the Draghi reform (Legislative Decree, February 24, 1998, n. 58). This reform fostered the rights of minority shareholders by regulating listed companies on issues such as shareholders' agreements, internal controls, and public bids (Melis, 2000: 348). The 1998 legal reform also encouraged more activism in the Italian stock market, and maybe empowered minority shareholders by providing them some tools to discipline managers. Recent data demonstrate that the pattern of capital market development continues: Italian market capitalization of shares of domestic companies increased 12.6 percent between 1999 and 2000 (FIBV, 2001), and in 2000 market capitalization of

Table 2.16   Market capitalization of listed domestic equity issues at year end in selected OECD countries (% of GDP)

	1975	1980	1985	1990	1993	1994	1995	1996
Australia (Assoc. of SE)	22	40	37	37	71	67	70	80
Austria (Vienna)	3	3	7	17	16	16	14	15
Belgium (Brussels)	15	8	26	33	37	36	37	44
Canada (Toronto and Vancouver)	30	45	45	43	61	59	66	86
Denmark (Copenhagen)	11	8	26	30	31	34	33	41
Finland (Helsinki)	–	–	11	17	28	39	35	49
France (Paris)	10	8	15	26	36	34	33	38
Germany (Assoc. of SE)	12	9	29	22	24	24	24	28
Italy (Milan)[a]	**5**	**6**	**14**	**14**	**15**	**18**	**14**	**21**
Japan (Tokyo)	28	36	71	99	68	77	69	66
Netherlands (Amsterdam)	21	17	47	42	58	67	72	95
New Zealand	–	–	39	20	56	53	53	56
Norway (Oslo)	–	–	16	23	24	30	30	36
Spain (Madrid)	–	8	12	23	25	25	27	33
Sweden (Stockholm)	3	10	37	40	58	66	75	95
Switzerland (Zurich)[b]	30	42	91	69	114	109	129	136
Turkey (Istanbul)	–	–	–	–	20	17	12	17
United Kingdom (London)	37	38	77	87	122	114	122	142
United States (NYSE, AMEX and NASDAQ)[c]	48	50	57	56	81	75	98	114

[a] Italy – all Italy on a net basis since 1985.
[b] Switzerland – only Zurich throughout 1990.
[c] United States – including foreign shares in 1975.
Source: OECD (1998: 18).

the Italian stock market represented 65 percent of GDP (Magnani and Trento, 2001: 24).

2.4.6   Corporate financing

Corporate financing is an important determinant of corporate governance since it varies considerably across countries and it is a spinoff of the role of banks and stock markets (Zysman, 1983; Berglöf, 1990; Edwards and Fisher, 1994; Steinherr and Huveneers, 1994; Fukao, 1995; OECD, 1995). Several factors ranging from fiscal distortions and regulatory constraints to the features of corporate structure and control characterize Italian corporate financing. As a result of the difficulty of raising bank capital, Italian companies have relied on self-financing as a primary source of financing, followed by high levels of borrowing that enjoy a preferential fiscal treatment over equity, and on fiscal evasiveness (Bianco and Trento, 1995). Equity issues are a minor source of financing, even in listed firms (Melis, 1999). This corporate funding strategy is consistent with the political control of blockholders and with preventing threats from investors. Moreover, the highly interventionist Italian state often described as *pervasive* (Bianco et al., 1996: 6), has not prompted the need to develop alternative financial sources.

By studying the different types of corporate financial sources, we can better understand a firm's financial dependence. A study by the OECD on the Italian corporate financial structure between 1989 and 1992 states that 50 percent of the total financial resources come from self-financing, around 43 percent from debt, and 5 percent from equity issues (OECD, 1994–95: 70). Another study of 300 Italian small and medium industrial companies (between 20 and 500 employees) in 1993 offers further evidence on the patterns of financing sources (see Table 2.17) (Barca et al., 1994). Table 2.17 shows that 83 percent of financing comes from internal sources. These are to an extent composed of personal and family resources (22 percent), but the great majority come from the sale of assets and self-financing (61 percent). Externally financial resources represent a much smaller fraction of financing (17 percent), with bank debt being a main contributor. Italian firms, particularly small and medium ones, are reticent to use the stock market as a financing tool which leaves some vulnerable to acquisition.

From a comparative perspective, two illustrative indicators of a country's corporate financing are (1) the degree of reliance on debt and equity financing, and (2) the pattern of banks' on-balance-sheet lending versus direct intermediation through securities markets. Table 2.18 reveals that leverage ratios (debt/equity ratios) in Italy are higher than in other OECD countries, with the exception of Japan. This characteristic corporate funding is also discussed by Guatri and Vicari (1994). The high leverage ratio in Italy is explained by several factors. First, public authorities may be involved as financial sources, either directly as owners or indirectly via financial institutions. Second, the existence of underdeveloped debt security markets deflects the reliance on equity issues. And third, countries with small and medium-sized companies tend to have greater leverage ratios. As in Japan and Germany, corporate debt consists mainly of high levels of borrowing from banks, yet a distinguishing feature of Italian corporate financing is the wide recourse to multiple short-term bank loans, the

Table 2.17 Corporate finance resources for 300 Italian small and medium firms in 1993 (as a % of total financial resources)

Internal sources	83.0
Personal or family	22.4
Sales of assets or self-financing	60.6
External resources	17.0
Equity issue	6.7
Bank debt	9.9
Other debt	0.4

Source: Barca et al. (1994: Vol. 1).

Table 2.18   Debt/equity ratios of nonfinancial enterprises at book values, OECD countries

	1980	1985	1992	1993
Belgium	2.67	1.91	1.54	1.46
Canada	0.76	0.81	0.97	0.99
Denmark	1.73	1.36	1.27	1.19
Finland	4.01	2.57	1.73	1.76
France	2.13	3.44	1.36	–
Germany	1.75	1.53	1.52	1.57
Italy	–	**3.11**	**3.24**	**3.36**
Japan	5.15	4.40	3.92	3.88
Netherlands	1.34	1.32	1.27	–
Norway	3.98	4.08	2.79	–
Spain	–	**1.65**	**1.59**	**1.63**
Sweden	2.08	1.87	2.02	–
United Kingdom	–	1.03	–	–
United States	0.46	0.60	1.04	1.03

Source: OECD (1995: 15).

virtual absence of securitized debt, and the lack of bank stakeholders. Table 2.19 shows that comparatively the percentage of bank debt over total debt for large firms is 27.3 percent, half that of Spain and three times that of the US.

In sum, Italian enterprises continue to find it easier to resort to debt financing than to expand the number of shareholders, the result being that Italian firms tend to have highly leveraged and bank-dependent capital structures. The latter is particularly true for unlisted companies. In 1992, the average debt/equity ratio for the largest 152 private Italian groups was close to 3 : 1 (*Mondo Economico*, December 25, 1993: 251).

2.4.7   Institutional investors

The increasing role of institutional investors is a pattern of the 1990s in many Anglo-Saxon countries as well as in countries like France. Institutional investors have traditionally represented a small fraction of ownership and possessed a minor role in countries where pensions are provided by the state. The small stake in nonfinancial corporations in Italy held by institutional investors is concentrated in insurance companies and mutual funds. According to an OECD survey, "their role in monitoring corporate performance is extremely passive, since they have small shareholdings and are often owned by the industrial and banking groups representing the bulk of stock market capitalization. Regulatory constraints on proxy voting further limited their role in shareholders' meeting" (OECD, 1994–95: 79). However, the role of institutional investors has more than doubled since 1992, as shown in Table 2.20. This is explained by the intro-

Table 2.19   Bank debt as percentage of total debt in 1998

	Small and medium-sized firms	Large firms
Belgium	46.5	50.1
France	48.8	21.3
Germany	57.4	29.9
Italy	**66.4**	**27.3**
Netherlands	54.9	35.9
Spain	**66.5**	**50.4**
US	40.9	7.9

Source: Bonaccorsi di Patti and Gobbi (2001: Table 1, p. 26).

Table 2.20   Financial assets of institutional investors (as % of GDP)

	1990	1992	1994	1996	1997
Greece	6.5	8.5	18.8	28.5	–
Hungary	–	2.5	3.7	5.7	–
Luxembourg	926.8	1630.5	2170.2	2310.4	–
UK	114.5	115.3	149.3	193.1	–
Poland	–	–	1.9	2	4
Mexico	8.8	5.6	3.5	4.5	4.7
Portugal	9	17.3	31.9	34.4	31.7
Korea	48	52.3	57.5	57.3	37.2
Italy	**13.4**	**18.5**	**32.1**	**39.9**	**53.2**
Spain	**16**	**22.8**	**36.4**	**45.4**	**56.1**
Germany	36.5	33.7	44.1	49.9	57.5
Japan	81.7	78.1	84.8	77.6	75.3
France	54.8	60.5	75.6	83.1	90.6
Switzerland	119	119.4	148.6	152.4	92.7
Netherlands	133.4	132.8	157.7	169.1	183.8
US	123.8	141.3	149.7	181.1	202.8

Source: OECD (1998) *Institutional Investors, Statistical Yearbook*.

duction of financial market reforms and as part of the emerging institutional investor capitalism trend initiated in the US and the UK with highly diversified portfolios.

2.4.8   Summary of Italy

In sum, Italian corporate governance is characterized by high ownership concentration, little political separation between ownership and control, the legacy of legal constraints on bank ownership, and primary corporate control in the form of pyramidal groups, either family-owned or coalitions, and state ownership. The most striking feature is that there is no mechanism of inside (banks) or outside (markets) corporate control.

2.5   Corporate governance in Spain

Spain's industrial structure is similar to Italy's in many respects. The Spanish economy includes many small and medium-sized businesses, and a few large corporations that account for the majority of the country's GDP. Most firms are owned by the state, banks, and foreign investors. In contrast to Italy, however, family-owned large enterprises in Spain are not as predominant. In particular, since the Spanish entry into the European Union (1986), foreign capital has come to control an increasing proportion of business in Spain (Salmon, 1995: 36). For instance, the Spanish auto industry, Europe's third biggest, is entirely foreign-owned.

The Spanish economic structure has unfolded in historical circumstances that include the legacy of an autarkic and interventionist government, international economic pressures to develop, and the harmonization policies pursued by the European Union. In this section, I discuss the main features of corporate governance in Spain.

2.5.1   Corporate law and type of corporations

Legally, the internal structure of the Spanish corporation consists of shareholders, directors, and executive officers. The Commercial Law provides for one or more directors to represent and manage the affairs of the company.

The Spanish corporate law is based on the 1885 Commercial Code, and it has been updated with multiple laws (Sánchez-Calero, 1982; Uria, 1991). There are three main types of corporations: the Sociedad Anónima, SA (stock company), the Sociedad Limitada, SL (limited liability company), and Sociedad en Comandita or Sociedad en Comandita por Acciones, SC (limited partnership company or limited partnership with shares company). The SA structure is the most common type among large Spanish firms, and is strictly regulated under the 1989 Law of Sociedades Anónimas. The internal structure of an SA which consists of shareholders, directors, and executive officers has specific economic consequences for the firm (Arruñada, 1990). The SL, often found in small or family-owned businesses, "has a fixed capital, divided in equal parts which are cumulative and indivisible and are represented as non-negotiable instruments. The number of other members may not exceed 50 and their liability is limited to the extent of their contributions" (Fabregat and Bermejo, 1990: 54). Finally, SC constrains the liability of partners to the extent of their investment in the partnership. This legal form of corporation is suitable for groups of professionals.

2.5.2   Type of corporate ownership

The main shareholders of Spanish listed companies in the 1990s are family groups, banks, foreign companies, and the state. As shown in Table 2.8, in 1996 among these different types of owners, the primary shareholders are foreign institutional investors (28 percent) closely followed by individuals and family groups (24 percent). The high percentage of foreign ownership of Spanish corporations is mostly due to the openness of the economy after 1986. The high percentage of bank ownership relative to other OECD countries is also notable. As will be discussed later, this is a legacy of the historical economic development of Spain and the very particular role of banks.

The 1988 Law on Capital Markets introduced more flexibility into the capital markets which had led to a gradual change in the composition of shareholders in the stock market. Table 2.21 shows the decline over time in the ownership percentage of banks and the state, and an increase in institutional investors, foreign capital and individuals. The most remarkable transformations in the 1990s were the small representation of the state that in 1989 controlled 14 percent of Spanish market capitalization, while in 1999 is barely existent (0.3 percent), the increase in foreign ownership, and consequent decrease in domestic ownership (Galve and Salas Fumás, 1992). According to recent CNMV (2000: 59) data, foreign capital and families/individuals controlled 36.5 percent and 34.1 percent respectively of Spanish market capitalization in 1999. In addition, there is a small decrease in the overall percentage of institutional investors with respect to 1998, and a considerable increased role of nonfinancial firms such as Terra Networks.

2.5.3   Corporate control

In a comparative perspective, Table 2.10 indicates that Spain is among the countries with the highest ownership concentration, along with Italy, France, and Germany. In 49 percent of the firms quoted in the Spanish stock market in 1990, the largest owner has more than 50 percent of the capital. This percentage contrasts with only 9 percent in the US in 1986, 5 percent in Japan in 1983, and 2 percent in the UK in 1976.

Table 2.21   Significant shareholdings in listed Spanish companies(%)

	1992	1994	1996	1997
Banks	15.56	15.09	14.06	12.66
Insurance firms	3.37	2.68	2.20	2.60
Domestic institutional investors	1.65	3.04	5.02	7.55
State	16.64	13.77	10.87	5.57
Nonfinancial firms	7.72	6.80	6.90	5.58
Individuals	24.44	22.76	23.59	28.73
Foreign	30.61	35.86	37.36	37.31
Total	100	100	100	100

Sources: Bolsa de Madrid; Eguidazu (1999: 256–7).

Table 2.22 demonstrates that ownership concentration is very high among publicly traded companies in Spain, where firms are often under absolute or majority control. In the 1990s, the percentage of corporations in which the three largest shareholders hold more than four-fifths of the control has increased from 13 to 17 percent. Roughly 55 percent of the firms in the Spanish stock market in 1995 are majority-controlled (that is, the largest three shareholders held at least half of the capital of these corporations). Table 2.23 shows ownership concentration for the largest shareholder in 1997, and the main conclusion remains that there is little room to change corporate control, as in almost half of the firms in the market (48.9 percent) representing 20.6 percent of market capitalization, the largest owner is a majority owner.

2.5.4   The role of the banks

Historically, Spanish banks have been privileged by the state, concentrated, and extremely protected against competition from foreign banks (Velarde, 1969; Muñoz, 1970; Tamames, 1977; Tortella and Palafox, 1984). The state, through the Bank of Spain, encouraged bank-led industrialization, and as a result the "big banks" performed as mixed or universal banks. They were debt-holders and shareholders of industrial corporations, particularly in economic sectors defined as key for Spanish economic development (Lukauskas, 1994; Tortella, 1994; Pérez, 1997). Bank competition was limited and it was difficult to establish new domestic banks, because the

Table 2.22   Ownership percentage among the first three shareholders (k3) for Spanish quoted firms

Type of control of three main shareholders	1991	1992	1993	1994	1995
Absolute control (k3 < 80% capital)	12.92	13.75	16.25	17.92	17.08
Majority control (50% < k3 > 80%)	40.00	38.75	41.67	37.08	37.92
Minority control (5% < k3 > 50%)	38.75	41.25	35.42	39.17	37.92
Internal control (k3 < 5%)	8.33	6.25	6.67	5.83	7.08

Sources: Cuervo-Cazurra (1997) from 240 firms; CNMV (2000: 83).

Table 2.23   Likelihood of corporate control change among Spanish quoted firms, 1997

% of ownership of first shareholder	No. of firms(%)	Market capitalization(%)	Corporate control change
Less than 25	25.1	66.2	Possible
Between 25 and 50	26.0	13.2	Impossible
More than 50	48.9	20.6	Impossible

Source: CNMV, *El País* (June 18, 2000).

few dominating banks enjoyed a status quo position. The establishment of foreign banks in Spain was not allowed until 1978,[11] and even then foreign banks experienced great difficulties in entering retail banking.

Banks have been the only financial institution in Spain during much of its economic development, and therefore played a key role in corporate governance up to the 1990s, as discussed above. They are divided into state-owned banks, commercial banks, and savings banks. Savings banks, unlike the other two types, do not participate in industrial holdings, instead they are oriented to family savings and occasionally to small business customers. In contrast to many other legal systems, there are no restrictions on the participation of commercial and state-owned banks in nonbanking business. In 1993, banks held 13 percent of the shares of quoted firms, but they were also prominent debt-holders or financial intermediaries.

In the last 20 years, the banking scenario has been modified by mergers among the largest banks,[12] and the two largest banks (BSCH and BBVA) have undertaken an aggressive process of acquisition of smaller banks. Thus, while in 1990, the eight largest Spanish banks controlled 50.5 percent of market share, by the end of 2000, the four largest Spanish banks controlled 54 percent (with the two largest controlling 38 percent) (*El País*, June 10, 2001: 10). This banking concentration allowed Spanish banks to become more internationally competitive and to be able to cope with the entry of a few strong foreign banks. Moreover, financial services in Spain are in the midst of important reorganization due to the necessity to adjust Spanish banking regulations to conform with the Second Directive on Banking from the European Union, as well as the banks' interest to develop alternative financial interests with the liberalization of capital movements, the internationalization of financial markets, and other financial innovations.

2.5.5 Stock market

Historically, the Spanish stock market resembles the Italian one. It did not take off until the Capital Markets Law of 1988 which provided a modern regulatory framework. This law aimed to activate the stock market, by providing more protection to stakeholders as well as to increase transparency in stock market operations. It founded a supervisory institution, the National Securities Exchange Commission (Comisión Nacional del Mercado de Valores, CNMV), that is governed by a board appointed by the government. There are four stock exchanges in Spain (Madrid, Barcelona, Bilbao, and Valencia) that are traded continuously. The Madrid stock exchange is the largest one: it represents 97.7 percent of the capitalization, and 85 percent of the trade in 1998. The stock exchange has traditionally been narrow with only a few hundred companies quoted in the Madrid stock exchange in 1970s, surpassing 1000 in 2000 as shown in Table 2.15.

By 1992, market capitalization had increased tenfold since the early 1970s (Tamames, 1993: 461). Market capitalization of listed firms as a percentage of GDP was under 10 percent before the mid-1980s as indicated in Table 2.16, but since then it has accelerated rapidly, reaching over 30 percent in 1995, and up to 69 percent in 1998 (Torrero, 2001: 84). The main triggers of change have been economic prosperity, Spain's entry into the European Union, the rapid process of privatizations, and the emergence of investment funds.

The Spanish stock market has grown immensely as is shown in Table 2.15, surpassing the marking capitalization and number of quoted companies of Italy. Part of this high rate is due to the high level of foreign capital participation in the Spanish stock market compared to the Italian, as shown in Table 2.21. However, the Spanish stock exchange still trails those in many other OECD countries; it remains narrow and lacks transparency. Two features of its backwardness are the concentration of a high percentage of market capitalization in a few companies, and the failure of the industrial sector to reflect the real economy distribution. The top 10 companies out of the 125 in the Madrid Index accumulate 66.56 percent of the index's total capitalization, and the industrial distribution of banks, electric companies and the Spanish telecommunications firm, recently privatized, Telefónica accounts for 80 percent of the Madrid Index (Torrero, 2001: 87–9).

2.5.6   Corporate financing

In Spain, banks have traditionally played a key role due to the underdevelopment of capital markets and difficulty of foreign financing. Thus, the primary sources of Spanish corporate financing are self-financing and bank debt (Costa, 1996: 291; Salas Fumás, 1991). When comparing the Spanish case to other OECD countries as exhibited in Table 2.18, it is noticeable that the Spanish leverage ratio (debt/equity ratio) in 1993 is high (1.63), but not nearly as high as in Japan (3.88) or Italy (3.36). This is due to the fact that Spanish banks are often part of large industrial holdings, and the Spanish industrial corporations usually do business with only one bank that in turn owns shares in the firm. Unlike Italian banks, Spanish banks tend to be involved in and informed of the economic and strategic activities of their nonfinancial clients.

Table 2.24 describes corporate financing patterns for Spanish manufacturing firms for the period 1983–92. It shows a decrease in bank debt over total debt, compensated by an increase in financial autonomy. Bank debt has decreased from 54 percent in 1983 to 33 percent in 1992, and debt over liabilities has also decreased from 72 percent in 1983 to 64 percent in 1992, according to Bank of Spain data (Genesca and Salas, 1995). However, an international comparison of bank debt over total debt shows that Spanish firms (both small and medium-sized firms and large firms) still rely heavily on banks for their corporate financing, as shown in Table 2.19. The recent OECD (2001: 21) country report on Spain states that Spanish firms have increased their indebtedness, and given the turbulence on stock markets, debt/equity ratios have risen.

2.5.7 Institutional investors

In general, the involvement of institutional investors in the Spanish financial scene is limited. Investment funds are the main institutional investors in Spain. These do not influence the financial market much because their holdings are mostly composed of fixed-interest-bearing bonds *(activos de renta fija)*. Cals and Garrido (1999) point out the minor involvement of institutional investors in Spanish corporate financing, despite the rapid emergence of institutional investors as shown in Table 2.20. They also highlight the importance of foreign investment in the Spanish stock market. Foreign capital institutional investors have driven the stock exchange since 1985, with banking, electricity, construction, and chemistry being the economic sectors that have been principally targeted. An important future challenge might be public pension expenditures. As a result, governments are introducing incentives for citizens to complement public pensions with private pensions. The offering of public pensions was widely spread in the early 1990s in both Italy and Spain, but not really adopted as a saving strategy by individuals.

2.5.8 Summary of Spain

In sum, Spanish corporate governance is characterized by high ownership concentration, almost no separation between ownership and control, no constraints on bank ownership, and – since the Spanish entry into the European Union – considerable changes in the infusion of foreign capital,

Table 2.24 Corporate financial structure of Spanish manufacturing firms, 1983–92

	1983	1985	1987	1989	1990	1991	1992
Equity/total liabilities	28.06	33.88	39.04	45.09	42.10	38.99	35.58
Debt/total liabilities	71.94	66.12	60.96	54.91	57.90	61.01	64.42
Financial costs/gross	79.60	57.23	37.91	28.40	40.80	51.66	69.79
Short-term debt/total debt	68.94	69.71	72.33	73.17	72.43	70.50	68.58
Long-term debt/total debt	31.06	30.29	27.67	26.83	27.57	29.50	31.42
Bank debt/total debt	54.37	49.25	39.71	31.08	33.20	32.48	33.44
Short-term bank debt/ short-term debt	46.79	44.63	35.04	26.73	30.23	28.93	30.44
Long-term bank debt/ long-term debt	71.21	59.88	51.89	42.95	41.02	40.98	39.9

Sources: Genesca and Salas (1995: 157); data bank for the Accounts of Companies Harmonized, Central de Balances del Banco de España.

significant decrease in state ownership, and the need for financial adjust-ments to harmonize with the European Union.

2.6   A comparison of corporate governance in Italy and Spain. Where do Italian and Spanish corporate governance practices fit?

In this section, I explore similarities and differences in corporate gover-nance between Italy and Spain which are shaped by the respective chang-ing institutional environments in these two countries. I maintain a comparative perspective, reviewing these two settings relative to other countries that conform to the Anglo-Saxon and the Continental models to provide a broader picture and a thorough comparison. I will highlight six main issues that are striking in this cross-national comparison.

First, Italian and Spanish corporate laws are constructed within the tradi-tion of the French Civil Code rather than the common law tradition of Anglo-Saxon countries. As such it appears at first glance that there are few differences between them. However, different national economic attributes such as the nature of the corporation, and the relationships of the corpora-tion with the state and other external institutions have contributed to the development of differences in corporate law. For instance, during the 40 years of the Spanish dictatorship (1936–77), there were very few legal modifications in Spain's corporate legislation. In the democratic period (1977 onwards), several corporate laws were approved to modernize the Spanish corporate system. Italy experimented with a more turbulent pattern, marked by several economic crises such as the banking crisis in the 1930s, the inflationary episode in the 1960s, and the more recent interna-tional competitiveness that forced a change in Italian corporate legislation.

In the 1990s, the main thrust of change of company law has been provided by the directives of the European Community (now the European Union, EU), and its attempts to harmonize business practices across EU members. Nine EU directives that have been implemented between 1969 and 1993 deal directly or indirectly with corporate law. In addition, pres-sures to privatize the large state-owned sectors, adjust to the increasing internationalization of markets, and particularly in the case of Italy strengthen its financial system, have led to the enactment of new corporate and financial legislation.

Second, the structure of corporate ownership and control highlights the main institutions involved in corporate governance. Table 2.8 provides an overall comparative perspective on the types of ownership by showing the direct ownership of listed companies. Four observations need to be pointed out. First, among Continental European countries, Italy has a small per-centage of ownership in the hands of banks. Only 11 percent of Italian listed companies are owned by banks, in contrast to 13 percent in Spain and 25 percent in France. Second, domestic nonfinancial capital in Italy is higher than the average, while in Spain it is below average. Third, foreign ownership is very prominent in Spain (28 percent), while Italy follows the trend of the Anglo-Saxon countries in that it has low rates of ownership by foreign capital (below 5 percent). Last, while state ownership is the highest in Italy, it is surprisingly low in Spain.

Third, corporate control is measured by the degree of ownership concentration. Ownership of both Italian and Spanish corporations is highly concentrated. In almost every company, publicly or privately held, there is a controlling shareholder or a group of influential shareholders tied by strong contractual relationships. Table 2.10 specifies the level of concentration in comparative terms by measuring the ownership share held by the largest shareholder of the company. We observe that in Italy in 60 percent of listed firms, the largest owner has majority stockholdings, compared with 66 percent in Germany, and 49 percent in Spain. Ownership concentration is much dispersed in the Anglo-Saxon countries (9 percent in the US and 2 percent in the UK) and in Japan (5 percent). In sum, although Italy has a higher ownership concentration than Spain, both countries are characterized by concentrated ownership patterns compared to the Anglo-Saxon model countries.

In contrast to the Anglo-Saxon model where there is more diversified ownership, most dominant or controlling shareholders of listed companies in Italy and Spain have traditionally been directly involved in the management of the company for a long time. Families of the founders (or strong individuals in the case of Italy, and banks in the case of Spain) control each company, either by themselves or jointly with other large shareholders. Members of the board of directors in Italy and Spain have fiduciary duties with respect to shareholders. However, as Melis points out (2000: 348), traditionally the expression "shareholder value maximization" in Italy is equivalent to "maximize the value for the blockholder." This usually occurs at the expense of minority shareholders.

It is common for Italian and Spanish firms to issue nonvoting shares that are risk free for the control of the company. The Italian Draghi reform effective in July 1998 attempted to introduce modifications in the *shareholder agreements* to weaken the power of blockholders (Melis, 2000). However, Becht and Röell (1999) show that the median size of the largest voting block for industrial companies in the late 1990s is 54.53 and 34.2 percent in Italy and Spain respectively. The percentage is particularly high in Italy where the gap between ownership and control is huge. Pyramidal groups are the mechanisms to gain massive voting power when owning a relatively small share of the company. Zingales (1994) and Nicodano (1998) report how the benefits of control enjoy an abnormally high premium. Finally, disclosure rules and insider trading regulation were not enforced, and proof is that of the 51 insider trading investigations conducted by Consob in 1997–98 only one resulted in a guilty verdict (Brunello et al., 1999: 10). Table 2.23 demonstrates that an involuntary change of corporate control is only possible in 25 percent of the Spanish quoted companies due to ownership concentration. The first high profile Spanish hostile takeover attempt was in 1988 between two of the largest banks (Banco de Bilbao and Banesto). It failed. Ever since, several anti-takeover measures were introduced to prevent such controlling measures. For instance, all privatized firms in the IBEX35 (Spanish blue chip firms) have incorporated golden shares in their corporate control models which allows special owners to veto decision-making. Consequently, there have been only 111 major hostile takeovers between 1989 and 1998, 1995 and 1996 being the most active years.

A main difference in corporate control in Italy and Spain is reflected in the role of banks. In Spain, the predominant banking model is the universal bank with strong ownership ties between industry and banking. High levels of cross-shareholdings with the few existing large banks have protected managers from takeovers. Banks played a key role in the modernization of the Spanish economy during the late period of the Spanish dictatorship until the mid-1990s, by establishing exclusive, long-term debt relationships with nonfinancial firms. In addition, they monitored nonfinancial corporations by sitting on their boards (Aguilera, 1999). In the Italian case, where the legacy of the 1936 Banking Law prohibited bank ownership of industrial holdings, and separated short- and long-term lending institutions, banks do not replace the missing external markets for corporate control. The majority of Italian banks are relatively small and establish arm's-length relationships with nonfinancial corporations. Yet, there is no real financial institution substituting for the weak role of banks.

Therefore, the pattern of control in Italy and Spain leads to the conclusion that the public company described by Berle and Means (1932) and more recently by Roe (1994), where there is a sharp separation between ownership and control, does not exist in these two countries. The high ownership concentration and lack of political separation between ownership and control in Italy and Spain explain why very few companies are targets for hostile takeovers or other market mechanisms of corporate control common in the US and the UK.

Fourth, state intervention influencing corporate governance in these two countries is one of the most representative features. Up to the mid-1980s, the state was highly interventionist as an owner and saver of ailing industrial and financial firms through state industrial holdings. The liberalization and deregulation pressures from the EU led to major processes of privatization monitored by the state. However, privatized companies provide further evidence for lack of a genuine market for corporate control. There are two illustrative examples. First, the Italian and Spanish governments introduced veto power, dubbed the *golden share*, over privatized companies of national interest which in the case of Italy include a ban on wielding more than 3 percent of a company's voting capital. Second, recent decree laws enacted in both countries limit any significant foreign owner-ship in the hands of the state (for example EdF) of domestic firms (Montedison) in the recently privatized energy sector.

There exists a constant trade-off between national and supranational interests because the European Commission continues its efforts to disman-tle the golden share method. This is reflected, for instance, in the Draghi law attempt to impose some market corporate control among privatized firms. Hence, in Italy, this reform established that "the 3% voting ceiling under the privatization law evaporates if a formal offer for 100% of ordi-nary shares is made" (*Euromoney*, July 1999). Perhaps, the main exception toward an effective market for corporate control in these two countries has been Olivetti's audacious takeover bid of Telecom Italia in February 1999, with Deutsche Telekom as a white knight, the high profile involvement of Shröder and D'Alema and several Anglo-Saxon fund managers, and most importantly the exclusion of the *cozy salotto buono* (the drawing room where Italian deals have always been struck among blockholders) which brought a new reality to Italy's corporate governance scenario.

Fifth, the bulk of Italian and Spanish private industry has grown without the contribution of the public stock market, notwithstanding recent regula-tory attempts to provide incentives for firms to go public and to bring more transparency to the stock market. Table 2.16 illustrates this trend toward greater market capitalization. Yet, corporate cultural factors are changing only gradually, as individuals in Spain and Italy have traditionally preferred to make their investments in personal savings or government bonds.

A new phenomenon in Europe in the late 1990s was the launching of New Markets, à la Nasdaq, reserved for small and medium-size technology companies. The first European "Nasdaq" opened in 1996 in France, the Nouveau Marché, and was followed in 1997 by Germany's Neuer Markt, Euro NM Belgium and Euro.NM Amsterdam. In 1999, Italy and the UK caught up with the New Market, launching Nuovo Mercato and Techmark respectively. In 1999, all these markets experienced an extraordinary growth due to the high number of public offerings as well as the individual value of market capitalization. Particularly outstanding was the Neuer Markt, recording over 140 initial public offerings and accounting for more than 80 percent of all newly listed German companies, and capturing more than 60 percent of the funds raised on the stock market by German compa-nies that went public (Consob, 2000: 33). Another market of rapid growth is the EASDAQ, an independent market like Nasdaq located in Brussels that unlike the former is not linked to the respective national markets.

The Spanish New Market (Nuevo Mercado) was not launched until April 2000 with ten listed companies and a capitalization of 40.2 million euros, becoming the third largest New Market in the euro zone (Banco de España,

1999). However, a comparison with the Nasdaq undermines its speedy start, indicating that European New Markets lag significantly behind the American one. The launching of New Markets in Italy and Spain has enhanced equity culture since these markets require higher transparency and accountability than regular markets.

Six, institutional investors have been, in comparison with other countries, largely absent from Italian and Spanish corporate governance, although they are starting to become relevant. Companies have historically not relied on stock capitalization, opting instead for debt financing or self-financing. This has a dual explanation. First, pension funds have not been necessary given strong welfare state provision in these countries. Second, huge public deficits have forced the state to continually borrow capital from the public, thus attracting a large part of household savings from private capital markets and into the government's coffers.

Discussion of these six issues in Italy and Spain indicates that these two national cases are best classified within the category of Continental or insider models of corporate governance, particularly because of their under-developed capital markets, and the concentration of ownership. However, a further issue needs to be explored: the role of banks.

The role of banks described in previous sections points to the principal dissimilarity between the Italian and Spanish corporate models. While in Spain there exist "mixed banks," in Italy in general there are no close and long-term relationships between banks and industry. Thus, while Spain's version of bank–industry relations falls into the bank-led or Continental model of corporate governance, Italy's pattern of bank–industry relations is one more typical of the Anglo-Saxon model. The banking patterns of these two countries will affect their respective corporate structures. One outgrowth of the role of banks is the degree of bank borrowing. Interestingly enough, despite the constraints on bank ownership, the debt/equity ratio of Italy is much higher than that of Spain, and indeed than those of other OECD countries except Japan.

In sum, Spanish and Italian corporate governance shares many key attributes, but they also differ in important respects. In particular, we can define the Spanish case as a typical Continental model, with financial and family ownership of industrial firms, high concentration of ownership, the leading role of banks, narrow stock markets, little separation between ownership and control, and the Spanish particularity of high foreign capital participation. Italian corporate governance exhibits many, but not all, of the latter features, therefore it must be defined as an outlier (Barca, 1996; Bianco et al., 1996; OECD, 1995). As in the Anglo-Saxon model, restrictive investment regulations and corporate culture have prevented Italian commercial banks from holding a substantial stake in nonfinancial companies. At the same time, other corporate governance devices more frequently found in the Anglo-Saxon or outsider model, such as acquisitions, fiduciary duties, and financial institutions, have not developed in Italy.

This chapter shows that historical legacies such as banking laws, protectionism, and the strong hand of the state have shaped and transformed corporate governance in these two countries in different directions despite equal pressures for international competitiveness and European harmonization.

Notes

1. The author would like to thank participants at workshops at the WZB, and the "Shareholder Value Capitalism and Globalization" conference, Bad Homburg, May 2001. Their comments received in these two conferences helped to improve the chapter.
2. Also referred to as: outsider, market-oriented, common law tradition, or "New American Model."
3. Also referred to as: insider, bank-oriented, French Civil Law tradition or "Rhine Model."
4. For studies on the Japanese corporate model see: Gerlach (1992); Hoshi (1998); Dore (2000); Ozawa (2000); and Jackson (2001).
5. According to Amatori (1997: 250), in 1991 the top 100 industrial companies by percentage of sales held, accounted for 40.1 percent of sales/current manufacturing in current prices in Italy.
6. According to the Istituto Nazionale di Statistica (ISTAT), in 1996, 94.8 percent of Italian firms had between 1 and 9 employees, 4.7 percent had 10–49 employees, … and 0.01 percent had more than 1000 employees. Macey (1998: 701) suggests that "the industrial structure of the Italian economy doubtlessly can be explained by the fact that Italian firms with more than 15 employees are much more strictly regulated than firms with fewer than 15 employees."
7. This discussion of the Italian Corporate Law is based on Stranghellini (1995).
8. The recent corporate governance reforms are as follows: the establishment of the first Italian Competition Law in 1990 which instituted a Competition Authority, and the legal basis for privatizing state-owned companies with the Privatization Law of 1992. Moreover, in 1992 the major state entities (IRI, ENI, ENEL, INA, IMI, and BNL) were transformed into joint-stock corporations (SpA). Reforms in the financial markets refer to permission to banks to operate nationwide, more independence between the Bank of Italy and the Treasury, the 1991 Stock Market Banking Law, the 1992 law concerning takeover bids, the 1993 Banking Law, the opening of a primary market for private bonds in 1994, and the 1998 Draghi reform on financial markets, securities and corporate governance (OECD, 1994–95).
9. Stranghellini claims that "the high stability of the personally liable directors, who cannot be removed by a simple shareholders' vote, and the relative unlikeness of a financial breakdown of a company not involved in direct economic activity (either operating or financial), can render the form of societa in accomandita per azioni attractive for this use. For example, at the top of the Fiat group pyramid (a group with $20 billion turnover in 1994) is the Giovanni Agnelli & C. Società in Accomandità per Azioni" (1995: fn. 10).
10. This legislation reform was initiated by the so-called "Amato Law" in 1990 with the intention of accommodating the European Union Act – Uniform Code on

Banking and Credit of 27/9/93 (G.U. 30/9/93), which assimilates and puts into practice the contents of the EEC Council's Second Directive No. 89/646/CEE dated 15/12/89. The new 1993 Banking Law could have revolutionized the context in which the activity of banking is carried out in Italy (Filotto, 1995: 86), although business practices were already embedded in the corporate culture and are hard to change. See also Dermine (1990).

11. The only exceptions are the few banks that existed in Spain before the start of the Franco regime (1939). These are: Crédit Lyonnais, Société Générale, Banco Nazionale del Lavoro, Bank of London and South America (Salmon, 1995: 224–5).

12. The number of "big banks" has ranged from six (Hispano-Americano, Bilbao, Urquijo, Central, Vizcaya, and Espanol de Credito) in 1923 to five (Banco Central-Hispano, Banco de Bilbao y Vizcaya, Banco de Santander, Argentaria, Banco Popular) in 1997, to three in 2000 (Banco Santander Central-Hispano, BSCH; Banco de Bilbao Vizcaya Argentaria, BBVA, and Banco Popular).

3
Ukraine: the Newly Built State and Economic Institutions

Volodymyr Sidenko and Oksana Kuziakiv

Since gaining its state independence, Ukraine has engaged in a pro-democratic and pro-market transformation, like many societies of Central and Eastern Europe. What was different, however, from other countries considered in this book, was the necessary construction of the sustainable state/government institutions (*rozbudova derzhavy*) that paralleled the introduction of basic market principles. This combination of targets, in the context of a persistent legacy of the former Soviet Union's command economy, has determined the painful and inconsistent route of Ukrainian institutional transformation.

The aim of this chapter is to expose the Ukrainian mode of institutional change toward a market economy. Attention is mainly paid to the problem of an institutional framework for sustainable corporate governance. The authors' approach focuses on the analysis of the behavior of economic actors who have determined corporate governance in its actual shape, with clans formed around bureaucracy being at the core. Another goal is to show the role of privatization and the difficulty of the genuine growth of the private sector. Special regard is given to the way the banking sector influences corporate governance.

While the main focus of this chapter is concentrated on the micro level, the embedded political and economic environment in which governance practices have been constituted is also highlighted. The claim here is that political and economic ambience was a decisive factor for Ukraine in meeting the challenge of profound institutional transformation.

3.1 Ukrainian reforms in retrospect – the dominant tendencies

The departure point of Ukraine in its road toward a market economy, as with other Newly Independent States (NIS), was much lower than many other countries of the region that lie west of Ukraine.[1] This simple fact has brought huge consequences and has to be acknowledged in approaching the matter of Ukrainian performance.

Ukraine proclaimed its full independence on August 24, 1991. But even before this date, since the adoption of the Declaration on State Sovereignty on July 16, 1990 and the Law on Economic Independence dated August 3, 1990, the Ukrainian Republic launched the intensive building of its independent economic and state/government institutions, separated from the all- (Soviet) Union government agencies. August 1991 broke the remnants of the formal Union links and accelerated the former process, bringing with it the collapse of the Soviet Union in December 1991.

However, the emergence of the formally noncommunist, independent Ukrainian state brought to the fore the second-rank communist leaders of the recent past, who were very prompt in acquiring new, formally democratic and market-oriented raiment. In the absence of market-type legislation and with close links to the old guard of "the red directors," they were very sensitive both to the demands of the managers of huge state-owned enterprises (SOEs), and to the new opportunities derived from the combination of political power and ownership. The multiple legislative gaps were crucial in shaping the conduct of "agents of the new system" and manifested themselves in virtually every important aspect of economic life. These gaps concerned commercial banking and banking control, protection of property rights, control over state-owned property and management of SOEs in a market environment, possible instruments against monopolistic practices and abuse of dominating market position, protection of consumer rights, basic forms of business transactions, payments (especially in respect to responsibility and accountability in business), and so on.

The above circumstances, from the very beginning, determined the extremely hesitant and inconsistent course of economic reform, which in different aspects only simulated real economic transformation. Much space was left for partial temporary agreements between different clans prevailing over the formulation of nationwide, stable, and predictable rules of economic behavior. Moreover, the absence of much needed experience in independent state administration did not give Ukrainian leaders the required skills to develop and implement viable transformation schemes.

The inconsistency of economic reforms showed itself in the absence of a systemic approach to them.[2] It showed up, for instance, in asynchronous liberalization, that is the gap between a more liberal regime for price formation and external transactions, and the lack of freedom in business inside the country. In general, the pace of creating a competitive environment was extremely slow. Actually, the former monopoly of the central plan was substituted by the monopoly of vested interests distributing the most profitable business areas and budget resources. The discretionary combination of obsolete versus innovative forms of organization and principles of economic activity was symptomatic.

The rather decisive early stage of economic transformation (till mid-summer 1994) may be characterized by three major factors that affected institutional development in the whole period of transformation:

- The creation of the huge bureaucratic machine that has dominated the Ukrainian economy ever since;
- The process of informal capital redistribution in favor of the private but politically influenced sector;
- An inconsistent monetary policy.

The first factor was a certain side effect of the rapid construction of government agencies. The idea of national development was widely used at this stage for the sake of an accelerated process of bureaucracy building and replacing of the former Soviet Union agencies with Ukrainian government structures. It was justified from the perspective of development of the independent state, but in fact it followed an old Soviet pattern of bureaucratic structures, with extreme complexity, lack of transparent competencies of numerous "branch ministries," and state committees aiming at regulating narrow but overlapping segments of the economy.

The second factor produced a set of laws to regulate major sectors of the economy, including laws on enterprises, on companies, on banks and banking, on external economic activities, on investment activities, and so on. But because of the haste stimulated by the necessity of arranging the national regulative framework within a short period and lack of experience, practically all of them had serious drawbacks and loopholes with regard to evasion. These legislative flaws gave tremendous opportunities for the transfer of formally state-owned property into private hands. These practices created quasi-private entities, with little or no responsibility for their operation. Typically, various small businesses created around SOEs were a major element in this construction.

The third factor was connected with the policy of periodic credit injections intended to compensate for the profound structural distortions caused by abrupt price liberalization in early 1992 and the rupture of economic ties within the former Soviet Union. But, in fact, it had a hidden aim – to accelerate the redistribution of state-owned property through selectively addressed bank loans, which were often not paid back, and through high inflation stimulated by this type of monetary policy which provoked the lowering of the book value of state assets. Thus, in 1992, the average monthly consumer price index rise was 33.5 percent, and in 1993, 47.1 percent. Under these conditions enterprises escaped long-term decisions which prevented SOEs from doing fundamental restructuring and resulted in the prevalence of short-term adjustments. In fact, profound and costly restructuring was neither feasible nor needed by the rapidly forming economic and political clans. On the contrary, they were more interested in economic decay to depreciate the state assets on the eve of privatization.

At the same time, the newly born private firms, which were not linked to government structures and state-owned property redistribution, suffered from this type of economic policy. It prevented them from making any substantial investments, thus hindering the whole process of economic modernization. The growing understanding of this prepared the basis for "the new stage of social and economic transformation" launched in October 1994 under President Kuchma.

The main concept of this stage was to implement decisive macro-economic stabilization and radical systemic transformation (Philipenko and Bandera, 1996). It implied the priority of economic liberalization (both internal and external), strict monetary policy, and a tighter fiscal policy, as well as accelerated privatization.

But at that time, the implementation of these goals confronted the complete domination of the already "embedded" government bureaucracy, as well as widespread criminal economic activities and repetitive violation of the law on the part of the government. To this one should add the lack of competition and freedom for market entry, highly inefficient budget policy, suppressive taxation, and the lack of a market infrastructure. This resulted in the permanent struggle of two major tendencies, one of them being public pressure in favor of genuine competitive market-oriented transformation, and the other evidently prevailing tendency consisting of the formation of what can be termed "clan and bureaucracy monopolistic capitalism."

3.2   The legal forms of firms and companies in Ukraine

Among the diversity of institutional problems that Ukraine faces in its transition to a market economy, the development of the proper foundations for free enterprise is of utmost importance. Formally, the legal basis for economic organizations and their activities was introduced rather quickly in 1991 and was comprised of the two following legislative acts.

The Law on Enterprises, adopted on March 27, 1991,[3] defined legally admitted forms of enterprises, which included:

- Individual enterprise (*indyvidual'ne pidpryemstvo*) based on ownership by a physical person and exclusively his/her own work;
- Family enterprise (*simeyne pidpryemstvo*) based on ownership and work of Ukrainian citizens who belong to one family and live together;
- Private enterprise (*pryvatne pidpryemstvo*) based on ownership by a Ukrainian citizen, with the right to employ workers;
- "Collective enterprise" (*kolektyvne pidpryemstvo*) based on "collective ownership" by the staff of an enterprise, cooperative or other statutory company, public or religious organization;

- State-owned municipal (*derzhavne komunal'ne pidpryemstvo*) enterprise based on ownership by administrative and territorial entities;
- State-owned enterprise (*derzhavne pidpryemstvo*) based on ownership by central administrative entities;
- Joint venture (*spil'ne pidpryemstvo*) set up on the basis of common property of different owners (on mixed ownership), including juridical and physical persons from Ukraine and other countries;
- Enterprise based on ownership by juridical persons and citizens of other countries.

The law also introduced the notion of a small-business enterprise. Any above-mentioned enterprise belongs to this category provided its staff does not exceed certain limits (200 workers in industry and construction, 50 workers in other production industries, 50 workers in science and related services, 25 workers in nonproduction sectors, 15 workers in retail trade). The development of small businesses was very important in the aspect of the emerging Ukrainian middle class supporting market reforms. But though small-scale enterprises have constituted, since then, an important and permanently growing sector of the Ukrainian economy, on the whole their role has remained far below the standards of most developed market economies.

The law of March 27, 1991 allowed different types of voluntary enterprise amalgamations, including associations, corporations, consortia, concerns, and others acting on the basis of an agreement or statute, reserving the legal independence of their participants.

Company Law as of September 19, 1991, introduced an important innovation to the above legal scheme by adding five legal forms of companies:

1. Joint stock company (*aktsionerne tovarystvo*), with its two options:
   (a) open joint stock company (*vidkryte aktsionerne tovarystvo*) – with shares distributed via open subscription and sales on the stock exchange;
   (b) closed joint stock company (*zakryte aktsionerne tovarystvo*) – with shares distributed among its founders, and not intended for subscription or sale on the stock exchange;
2. Limited liability company (*tovarystvo z obmezhenoyu vidpovidal'nistyu*);
3. Extended liability company (*tovarystvo z dodatkovoyu vidpovidal'nistyu*);
4. Full partnership (*povne tovarystvo*);
5. Commandite partnership (*komandytne tovarystvo*).

The new classification of business entities as of September 19, 1991 did not fully comply with the principles of the earlier one (dated March 27, 1991), which was not revised with the adoption of the new classification. This ambiguity is one more argument pointing out the general inconsistency of Ukrainian economic reform policy. Only on February 4, 1998 was the Law on Enterprises amended, in order to ensure more compliance with the Company Law, and eliminate certain irrelevant forms of enterprise organization. These changes:

- Excluded certain forms of enterprises (individual, family, joint venture, enterprise based on ownership by juridical persons and citizens of other countries);
- Added some new forms (company; enterprise based on ownership of associations of citizens; government-ruled enterprise *(kazenne pidpryemstvo)* as a specified form of state-owned enterprises);
- Modified certain forms (municipal enterprises are no longer treated as state-owned but as based on ownership of a territorial community).

It is to be emphasized that the Law on Enterprises simply listed certain legal forms according to the ownership basis, but did not succeed in outlining a comprehensive and detailed regulatory framework for economic actors and their decision-making as regards each of these forms.

Among the discrepancies of the above-mentioned legal forms, those of the joint-stock company and limited liability company are the most important and widespread in Ukraine. Not only was the number of such companies rapidly growing, but they also served as a legal model for outlining management structures for other legal forms. For instance, practically all joint ventures in Ukraine function as joint-stock or limited liability companies. The bulk of SOEs have also acquired this form in the process of their "corporatization," favored by the state as an introduction to further privatization. As far as "collective enterprises" are concerned, in many cases, due to the lack of detailed legal prescriptions, they were shaped very closely to the model of a closed joint-stock company.

As far as the formal structure of the company is concerned, the main features of corporate governance imitate those existing in advanced market economies. However, there are important details that distinguish the mode of corporate behavior of Ukrainian companies.

For instance, the law, as in many other countries, allows the owner to exercise his rights of control directly or through authorized bodies. The owner may transfer his rights to an enterprise council or board *(rada* or *pravlinnya pidpryemstva)*. While there is nothing surprising in this, this legal institution was widely used by SOE directors to acquire practically full control over the enterprise from the state. In the sense of decision-making, they created their governance system to formally resemble a privately controlled company. In any instance they were controlled by private owners, avoiding full economic responsibility for their performance.

Another example, also widespread, was the selection of legal forms of the company. Both open and closed joint-stock companies exist. However, in the early stages those who went through the so-called "corporatization" preferred the latter form. It resulted in far-reaching consequences, such as blocking the entry of outsiders into company management, or weakness of the financial basis for company development and restructuring. The real significance of supervisory bodies within company structures called company councils (*rada tovarystva*) or supervisory boards (*sposterezhna rada tovarystva*), has turned out to be minor. This is due to the lack of legal provisions regulating their functions as well as the general absence of transparency related to boards of directors and the vague character of both election and monitoring procedures within Ukrainian companies.

The law of September 19, 1991 treats a company's board of directors (*pravlinnya*) as the executive branch responsible for current administration. Its head/president (*golova*) is actually the person who runs the company and takes most important decisions. Formally though, he is subject to the decisions of the company's General Meeting and "conference" of shareholders. In many aspects, however, the latter's real competence is functionally restricted in practice. In many cases, such a company's highest authority merely automatically approves decisions taken by management.

Only at the end of 1997 did an important amendment to the existing Company Law clarify internal company relations. In particular, it strengthened the authority of a company's General Meeting and cancelled the institution of the company's "conference," which had formerly enabled directors and other top managers to filter "representatives of shareholders" according to their will.

For limited liability companies, full authority is assigned to the executive participants (*zbory uchasnykiv*) and its president/head (*golova*). Subject to this is the executive branch, represented either by a director (*dyrektor*) or directorate (*dyrektorat*) headed by a general director (*general'ny dyrektor*). In fact, this structure of governance did not prevent practically unconstrained authority from being vested in the head.

Summarizing the trends in legal framework development, we may state that the formation of the structure of control within the above-mentioned legal forms was, to a great extent, left to the discretion of the dominating economic actors themselves. Actually, the regulatory gaps and dysfunctional nature of the existing regulations, because of their inherent inconsistency, not only made room for but also actually provoked and favored the old enterprise management in their efforts to introduce multiple, informal schemes of enterprise control, which served their own personal interests.

The most evident consequence of this was the rapid synthesis of former SOEs to a sort of quasi-private enterprise where formally employed directors could actually exercise full authority as if they were genuine owners. Another crucial consequence was to distort the real power structures within the enterprises and, in many cases, to cause them to deviate substantially from their legal title. Thus, the majority of Ukrainian "collective enterprises," as well as many closed joint-stock and limited liability companies,[4] are in fact privately controlled by their top management, or even their top manager alone, with the other formal owners frequently ignored.

Summing up, we can say that the legal environment for enterprise and corporate governance in Ukraine is stuck somewhere between an administrative, centrally planned economy and a market economy. It lacks clearly defined rules, and contains plenty of conflicting and vague provisions leaving much room for discretionary behavior both at the government and corporate level.

3.3   The banking system, its reform and involvement in corporate governance

The Law on Banks and Banking Activities passed on March 20, 1991 has been the stepping-stone in shaping the present two-tier banking system in Ukraine. The banking system consists of the National Bank of Ukraine (NBU), being the banker of commercial banks (the first tier), and about 200 commercial banks (the second tier). In principle, Ukrainian banking law is much closer to the American system than to the European. Legally speaking, Ukrainian banks are not engaged in control over manufacturing or retail activities.

From the formal point of view, Ukrainian commercial banks are highly independent in their performance. According to the law, they are dependent on the central bank (NBU) regulatory prescriptions and economic standards, including equity/asset ratio, maximum single-client exposure, minimum value of authorized capital, and so on. The law ceased their direct dependence on the government and branch ministries. Indirectly, however, these links are preserved, due to many commercial banks having large industrial SOEs as their shareholders. Furthermore, they extend their loans mainly to enterprises and state agencies of particular industrial and agricultural sectors from which their shareholders originate.

In general, the banking infrastructure has remained rather underdeveloped. This is stipulated by legal restrictions regarding the entry of foreign banks and the scope of their operations, usually limited to enterprises with foreign capital.

Commercial banks were formally restricted as to investments into statutory capital of joint-stock companies. This obstacle seriously impeded the flow of banking capital into the manufacturing sector in the course of privatization and, in the situation of widespread insolvency in the manufacturing sector, widened the gap between it and the financial sector. Owing to legal barriers and the closed character of corporate governance in Ukraine, commercial banks exert only a slight influence on enterprises and companies in the manufacturing sector. The credit given to this sector has been predominantly short-term loans to keep the level of circulating capital at an acceptable level. Long-term credit for investments has been extremely limited since the beginning of the 1990s, and this has resulted in the deepening separation of the banking system from the manufacturing sector and its actual needs. As a source of their income, banks in Ukraine prefer foreign exchange and purely financial deals, with government bonds having held a good share of their portfolios prior to the crisis of September 1998. Actually, they have been very slack in fulfilling the most important functions of accumulating free money from multiple private depositors, and allocating them into commercially viable investment projects.

The width of the split between companies in the manufacturing sector and commercial banks is partly illustrated by the prevailing negative attitude of the former to bank loans. Thus, two-thirds of those Ukrainian companies surveyed declared that they generally try to avoid taking on credit because of the unrealistically high interest rate despite the fact that bank loans are usually treated as something essential for their activities.

However, the mentioned separation of the banking sector from the manufacturing sector should be treated carefully. To a great extent, it is a direct consequence of the unhealthy position of the banking system. Thus, by the end of the 1990s, more than a quarter of all Ukrainian banks were in the category of "problem banks" (Yuschenko, 1999), with low capitalization and financial capacity.[5] As a rule, they have attempted to avoid the huge risks associated with long-term or even medium-term crediting of the manufacturing sector. The financial position of the latter, after years of high inflation and soft budget constraints, looks even worse (with more than half of all enterprises suffering losses). The legal provisions for debtor–creditor relations have moved far beyond the standards of developed market economies with no actual visible progress since the early 1990s.

The evident disruption between the actual needs for finance and its availability forced manufacturing sector companies to seek alternative solutions. One of them was to establish a commercial bank controlled by a group of companies. As mentioned before, in the early 1990s many Ukrainian commercial banks originated from manufacturing sector capital and still have big manufacturing sector enterprises as their shareholders. But this solution was possible only for large enterprises in the situation of an abundance of capital in that period. Another solution, currently much more feasible for companies, was the establishment of specific favorable relations with an independent commercial bank based on mutual benefits and/or services rendered on preferential terms, or mutual interest in, for instance, tax evasion. One more possibility was a sort of financial cooperation of a group of enterprises with the creation of a "financial aid fund," which provides interest-free financing. But the most widespread practice has been to seek preferential credit given or guaranteed by central or local government.

The lack of formalized institutional linkage between commercial banks and manufacturing sector companies produced the attempts to create the so-called "financial and industrial groups" (FIGs),[6] both Ukrainian and international (Plotnikov, 1995). Whatever the reasons for such linkages may be, the essence of the model of "bank–manufacturing companies" relations is to establish an individual link with a selected bank which stands out against the free credit market environment. This results in serious distortions in decision-making in the banking sector, with plenty of loans granted on a noncompetitive basis to "friendly" clients, thus preventing them from undertaking profound restructuring. At the same time, it is an explanation for the overloading of loan portfolios of almost all Ukrainian banks with bad loans.

It is clear that the Ukrainian banking system can hardly be regarded as a sustainable part of a developed market environment. It is partly the product of the commercialization of the former banking structures typical of centrally planned economies, and partly represents a conglomerate of rent-seeking institutions. The distorted corporate governance has helped to form and fix the strength of this rent-seeking. On the whole, it needs profound restructuring on the basis of a new law, with expanded banking regulations, opportunities, and incentives to invest in the manufacturing sector of the economy. The new Law on Banking and Banking Activities was finally passed on December 7, 2000. It makes the whole system of banking regulations more consistent and closer to those existing in developed market economies, and tries to eliminate some of the most evident flaws of Ukrainian banking. Nevertheless, it will require considerable effort on the part of the NBU to implement these standards in practice.

3.4   Economic actors and actual corporate governance

The economic reality of Ukraine proves that market institutions remain highly underdeveloped. This major factor determines both the types of behavior at the micro level and the pace of structural adjustment of the whole economy. In these circumstances, different informal clans have emerged around bureaucratic structures of the state machinery and exert the strongest influence. The proximity of a firm's manager to a central or local government "decision-maker" is, for the vast majority of large companies, of vital importance. In a situation where many regulations regarding the behavior of firms are still absent, and a lot of existing rules are contradictory, bureaucrats are the ones who really decide. They are able to close any firm on the grounds of "violation of the law," and, at the same time, can make any business flourish by giving it government protection and free access to government funds.

Thus, in Ukraine, there exist "government, financial and industrial (agricultural) groups" (G-FIGs) within which most principal decisions are taken and implemented, and which, in many cases, have become substitutes for legally created FIGs as instruments of capital concentration. There are several reasons for the actors involved to consolidate these relations.

Firstly, the direct involvement of the government provides security against instability and nontransparency of regulations and multiple controlling procedures. Secondly, informal business–government relationships provide preferential access to government loans, subsidies, guarantees, material and financial reserve resources, as well as vital information. This is indispensable for access to free budget financing. Friendly contacts with government officials are also vital for tax evasion or illegal transactions involving capital. Another incentive is that informal business–government relations are very promising from the point of view of participation in privatization on preferential terms. Finally, the most distorting of the institutional system is probably close relations with government officials which enable the G-FIGs to have an influence on legislative acts and government regulations. This plays an enormous role in Ukraine, often resulting in intentionally designed loopholes.

In conditions of close proximity of a firm's manager to central or local government (it depends on the size and branch of activity), government officials become vital to the firm's survival. These officials are inevitably rent-seeking. Furthermore, attempts to hide the illegal links lead to the informal character of such G-FIGs, which entangle the country's economy and suppress free and fair competition. In a broader sense, they represent the foundation of what J. Sapir called "post-Soviet neo-corporativizm," that is the dominance of large enterprises often integrated in a cartel which include financial institutions aimed at organizing production and exchanges as well as administering an important part of social life (Sapir, 1997).

Different market infrastructure institutions (stock exchanges, investment banks and funds, trust funds, nongovernment pension funds) have played a relatively moderate role. This is partly the result of generally low capitalization of the market, and partly it has become a psychological phenomenon based on the early practices of different trust funds, which became notorious for their swindling of ordinary depositors. Additionally, however, this is the direct result of the above-mentioned informal monopolization of the economy through the G-FIGs.

Formal structures designed for free exchange and competition seem irrelevant in the ambience of an administratively regulated market. It is a system of informal links which forms the real structure of control and the balance of power, and determines the actual decision-making practices in the sphere of corporate governance. The declared formal structures have to adapt to these informal relations and power networks formed by informal clans.

3.5 Institutional framework for company performance and strategy

In the course of market-oriented transformation, Ukrainian firms (by which we understand all forms of enterprises and companies under Ukrainian law) were faced with the need to adapt their strategies and behavior to the more complicated and stringent economic environment. They encountered multiple obstacles along the way. This happened for a variety of reasons ranging from huge external shocks (McCarthy et al., 1994) to internal institutional and regulatory obstacles (Siedenberg and Hoffmann, 1998; Kaufmann, 1997; Soros International Economic Advisory Group, 1996–98).

In this context, it is highly important not only to identify the set of factors that restrain positive adjustment of enterprises to the evolving market system but to expose the typical reactions of firms to certain changes in their economic environment, and to understand their reasons. In fact, the scope of Ukrainian enterprise strategies for the transition period is rather diverse, and includes:

- Strategies of internal restructuring;
- Strategies aimed at the modification of their economic environment, or moderating its negative impact on economic agents.

Initially, firms tried to avoid the first group of strategies, or at least postpone their implementation. They treated them as excessively time-consuming, expensive, and fraught with internal conflicts arising from labor and income redistribution. In addition, these strategies implied too much risk under inconsistent government economic policy. Moreover, such strategies were looked upon as somewhat redundant in the situation of soft budget constraints which were eased with regular monetary injections.

In fact, the strategies of many SOEs, especially of those producing tradable goods, were directed at the redistribution of public capital in favor of private individuals who ran these enterprises. With this aim, different schemes were employed, one of them being the use of multiple private intermediaries set up around these SOEs both in Ukraine and abroad. Sophisticated mechanisms, including multilateral barter transactions, fake commercial contracts, excessively large advance payments and commercial credit granted to customers and so on, served to illegally export capital, the total amount of which was estimated at $15–20 billion for 1991–95 (Borodiuk and Turchinov, 1999).

The new economic conditions that began to dominate in Ukraine at the end of 1994 caused certain changes in firms' behavior. But in a situation of more expensive credit, combined with the drastically reduced purchasing power of potential customers and the underdevelopment of the basic institutional foundation and market infrastructure, many firms appeared unable to fulfill the necessary positive adjustments.

In these circumstances, tendencies toward negative forms of adaptation to economic environment began to dominate.[7] Large firms started to exercise active individual and group pressure on the government in favor of protectionist policies, including higher import duties and nontariff import restrictions, and even individual tax, price, and credit preferences.

Unregistered sales and tax evasion became the most typical conduct for any firm striving to survive under the ever-growing tax burden. Attempts to acquire direct access to state budget funds were a top priority for the more powerful firms. Because of this, some of them made great efforts to acquire seats in parliament, central or at least local governments and in different consultative structures to the president and prime minister.

Many enterprises resorted to interenterprise arrears as a means to ease the problem of financial weakness. In fact, they actually acquired the role of quasi-emission centers. But the result was that the whole financial structure became increasingly precarious and open to the adverse cumulative effects of insolvency. It also drew attention to the widespread belief that the government would assist in paying off debts if the threat of bankruptcy were to arise.

The weakness of company investment activities in Ukraine has become one of its institutional characteristics, resulting not only in slow internal modernization, but also in the relative rarity of investing in other entities (acquisitions or mergers). The low rate of capital interflows has delayed the redistribution of assets and their concentration in more efficient areas. An important feature of this investment behavior is also the avoidance of portfolio investments. It reflects the widespread distrust of existing instruments of the Ukrainian capital market and the lack of financially strong and viable companies.

The external investment activity of capital allocation abroad is clearly subdivided into two unequal categories. The dominating part is associated with capital flight. There are indications that illegally exported capital is not practically allocated to areas connected with basic fields of the activities of exporters. As far as official exports are concerned, the volumes amount to only a few percent of capital flight. The low volumes of officially registered capital exports seem to indicate not only the financial weakness of the majority of Ukrainian enterprises, but predominantly the current lack of potential for successful international competition.

Slack investment activities are accompanied by the dominant reliance on enterprise self-financing, with the rather rare use of external resources. It seems to be completely abnormal that almost three-quarters of the companies involved in case studies carried out by the authors showed a 100 percent dependence on their own financial resources.

Apart from the above-mentioned trends, the financial weakness produces many adverse firm strategies including: lean inventories, postponement of investment, increased use of bartering, reductions in the labor force, and increasing wage arrears, or wage payments in kind. All these phenomena have resulted in the rapid demonetization of the Ukrainian economy.

Our case studies showed that only one-third of all firms had no wage arrears whatsoever. The average term of this debt for 300 selected industrial enterprises was equal to 5.6 months in the first quarter of 1999 (ICPS, 1999a, b). According to other data for the 300 selected industrial companies (ICPS, 1999a, b), the number of enterprises where workers received some share of wages in kind had reached 51.6 percent, and the average share of in-kind payments in salary had increased to 62 percent. For many enterprises bartering in 1990s turned into a dominant form of transaction, making them operate like natural economies but without money. Only by the year 2000, under the government of Victor Yuschenko, did Ukraine demonstrate a clear tendency to decrease the barter economy, which was backed by economic stabilization, first signs of economic growth, sound monetary policy, and consistent policy to curb nonmonetary forms of economic relations.

The structural crisis of the manufacturing sector can be attributed to a great extent to the slack pace of internal restructuring of enterprises. It is manifest in several aspects of company performance. One of them, and quite symptomatic, involves sales activity. A majority of companies have organized specialized marketing divisions. But as a rule, they are very far from being able to work out a comprehensive marketing strategy. Instruments of sales according to market segmentation, commodity distribution and promotion, public relations and feedback mechanisms that induce production pattern adjustment, are quite underdeveloped. Perhaps they are more vigorous in firms operating in new sectors of the economy (like computer industries and telecommunications), and in most successful companies in foodstuff and textile industries.

Changes in the organizational pattern are usually not too intensive. In fact, almost half of the Ukrainian companies involved in our case study testified to the complete absence of any noticeable shift in organizational structure. The most frequent changes related to work organization and wage schemes. But in many cases, the latter are only a passive adaptation, not really being a sign of positive adjustment to market conditions. "Innovations" in organizations such as payment in kind can hardly be referred to as such.

The general changes in management systems have taken place mainly in the field of management structures due to privatization and change in the legal form of enterprise (corporatization). Only in a few, mainly newly established, companies can we observe qualitative improvement in the staff and methods of management. Even to a greater extent it relates to financial management, changes in which are mainly linked to the creation of a specialized financial division.

In the overwhelming majority of Ukrainian companies, there are very modest positive shifts in the field of modernization of existing production. A company providing full modernization still seems to be a rarity. Almost a quarter of the companies we studied have not undertaken even partial modernization since 1990.

In spite of the general tendency of reduced employment, in many old companies it is evidently not the result of an employment policy aimed at higher efficiency, but rather a spontaneous process. Within it, an outflow of personnel, including qualified and highly trained staff, dismissals of workers on their own initiative, part-time work schemes and additional vacations are very frequent.

Far more noticeable changes take place in the field of the company's current commercial activities. In our opinion, this, coupled with slack investments, testifies to the dominating mode of short-term adjustment to the economic environment.

It is very important that the above-mentioned changes were induced by external developments independent of enterprise management. Thus, restructuring in the pattern of suppliers and consumers is to a great extent the result of the collapse of the former centralized supply (*derzhpostach*) system. On the other hand, it was caused by radical changes in relative prices after their liberalization and the disintegration of the Soviet Union, which caused the breakdown of many old economic ties between enterprises.

Among the factors of institutional development in Ukraine, those relating to the character of a competitive environment are, perhaps, the most substantial. Here we can find the roots of the competitiveness crisis of the majority of Ukrainian companies. In fact, the economic environment still leaves little room for genuine market competition.

The monopolistic economic structure inherited from the past period of economic development under central planning, with plenty of enterprises being sole or almost sole producers within their production spectrum, still determines the nature of economic relations. Excessive administrative regulations of the economy and multiple obstacles to market entry of new businesses are deeply rooted in the bureaucratic complexity of economic governance. Pervasive dependence on central and local government bureaucracy in current economic activities distorts competition considerably and makes it unfair. One can add to this the high level of discretionary subsidizing of economic activities, with rather vague or even no rules for granting such subsidies.[8] But, as if this were not enough, criminal activity, with plenty of nonproductive rent-seeking intermediary structures, tries to penetrate most profitable economic sectors.

On the other hand, in spite of all the above-mentioned negative factors, one should not ignore certain positive trends toward a more competitive economic environment. First of all, central and local government structures as well as SOEs are steadily losing their dominant position as a source of commercial orders to Ukrainian privatized and newly created private companies and to foreign firms. In this sense, long-term connections with government agencies have partially lost their previous significance. Long-term links with SOEs still have some importance. Yet the new firms (mainly

Ukrainian but also foreign) that emerged as a result of steadily growing market competition have become the main source of commercial links and orders.

Nevertheless, we can list a number of factors that stuck economic adjustment at the micro level, as observed in the field studies. A general lack of financial resources for the manufacturing sector is one of the most visible. Under serious financial constraints, no market strategy looks viable because the company has no financial instruments at its disposal to structure its market engagement. The majority of Ukrainian firms face a kind of a vicious circle: their structural problems and low competitiveness hinder them in obtaining the necessary financing from commercial banks and investors, while poor financial capacity aggravates their weak position in terms of competitiveness.

As a result, growing insolvency, delayed payments, and compiling enterprise arrears have become a crucial problem of economic links. In the absence of an efficient institutional framework, any nonpayment, once it emerges, spreads, multiplies, and persists.

Special attention should be paid here to the inefficiency of the existing bankruptcy procedures. One of the main factors underlying this is the widespread understanding of the weakness of the country's judicial system. There is an evident lack of trust in the courts and judicial procedures in their present form. A study of selected Ukrainian enterprises has shown that less than one-third of them actually applied to the courts to solve their disputes with debtors. At the same time, however, more than half of these companies believe that judicial procedures may, in principle, be an effective instrument under more effective arrangements.

Firms typically lack working capital. To a great extent, it was "swallowed" by a combination of the hyperinflation of the preceding years, massive outflows of capital abroad, and what is most persistent, by the tremendously unproductive use of funds and low return on investments.

High taxation further aggravates the financial situation. The contraction of the taxation base, which has developed alongside a decrease in production, has led to the tightening of tax pressures on companies, thus exacerbating their financial weakness. The *long-term economic instability* increases financial risks and, therefore, interest and insurance rates, makes money more expensive, and suppresses consumer demand.

The narrowness of the market does not guarantee the reimbursement of expenses. The contraction of consumer demand below a certain critical point enables neither the sale of old products with sufficient profits for simple reproduction, nor investment in new products and technologies due to the uncertainty regarding possible returns.

Other important factors include the inefficiency of Ukrainian legislation, corruption, high tariffs on energy, and flaws in the management of bank accounts. Directly or indirectly, via additional losses, they lead to an increase in transaction costs, thus inducing inflation and producing further disturbances in the financial sphere.

The financial weakness in the manufacturing sector of the economy, combined with huge interenterprise arrears, has seriously distorted the structure of payment and transaction methods. The field study of selected enterprises revealed that, by relative frequency of use, it may be described as shown in Table 3.1.

These data are supported by nationwide statistical indicators that point to a 42 percent quota of bartering in the sale of industrial companies (UEPALAC, March 1999). The study of 300 industrial enterprises showed that over three-quarters of them used bartering, especially in heavy industry, machine-building, timber and construction material industries (ICPS, 1999b). There is convincing evidence that bartered transactions, though they help somewhat to expand sales with the limited payment capacity of consumers, seriously distort price and other parameters of commercial deals, serve to evade taxation and ensure illegal incomes. Bartering enabled directors to receive "monopoly rent" (Lunina, 1999). That is why measures to curb bartering were at the core of the government's financial policy of the late 1990s and the beginning of the 2000s. This policy has resulted in a considerable decrease in barter. Thus, in January–February 2003, the share of barter in market sales of Ukrainian industrial enterprises reached 2.2 percent, though it remained high in weaving (25.4 percent), and ceramic products (22.2 percent), especially in ceramic tile production – 42.4 percent (State Committee of Statistics of Ukraine, January–March 2003). The share of enterprises using barter has sharply decreased from about 60 percent in the third quarter of 2000 to 28.2 percent in the fourth quarter of 2002 (Institute for Economic Research and Policy Consulting, February 2003).

On the other hand, advance payments produce serious complications with the expansion of sales and overcoming economic stagnation. Coupled with the still existing bartering, they are a comprehensive institutional problem and an urgent priority for Ukraine.

Table 3.1 Main instruments of payments and transactions (frequency of use by selected companies)

	Always	*Frequent*	*Seldom*	*Never*
Barter	+	++		
Advance payment		++	+	
Bills		+	+	
Written guarantees			+	++

++ Widely spread.
+ Rather spread.
Source: The authors' estimates based on field study.

An extremely important characteristic of Ukrainian firm behavior is that currently they, as a rule, have *no effective strategic approach to tackle their problems and ensure prosperity in the long run*. This can partly be considered as a sort of residual reaction to the discredited central planning of the past. But to a considerable extent, this is closely connected with the multiple obstacles hindering the development of an efficient long-term strategy. What really matters is, above all, a set of factors determining the absence of stable, clear, and reasonable business rules, as well as the general economic and financial instability, which leads to the lack of confidence in long-term perspectives.

Efficient privatization could have been, and still can be, a measure to break this vicious circle, but thus far it has failed to do so.

3.6   Privatization and the genuine growth of the private sector

As a political process, privatization started on the basis of a set of privatization laws passed by the Ukrainian Parliament in 1992. Initially, it was commonly believed that privatization would bring more economic freedom, private initiative, and more competition, thus resulting in rapid economic modernization on the basis of capital accumulation in the hands of those who operate more efficiently.

The basic legislative act was the Law on the Privatization of the Property of State-Owned Enterprises, now acting in the wording of the law as of February 19, 1997. The laws envisaged the so-called "small privatization" which included the sale of small SOEs, mainly in trade and services, and "big privatization."

As in many other countries, privatization was typically preceded by so-called "corporatization" or "commercialization." Both terms had the same practical meaning, that is SOEs were transformed into joint-stock companies, initially remaining under full state control. Afterwards, certain packages of their shares were designed for sale to private holders, thus launching privatization. The first result of commercialization/corporatization (or, to be closer to the Ukrainian term *rozderzhavlennya* that is "going out of state control") was simply the further relaxation of state control over SOEs. The change of the legal status offered to SOE directors extended operational freedom from direct interventions on the side of branch ministries in questions such as price formation, choosing suppliers, and distribution channels, defining the structure of production (outside the system of state orders), the distribution of profits, and so on.

There were various paths of privatization, adjusted to the size and situation of the privatized object, form of payment, and type of buyers. Among them were:

• Sales of state-owned property to any citizen for privatization vouchers and certificates;

- Sales of privatized objects at auctions, tenders, including those for privatization vouchers and certificates only;
- Sales of state-owned shares in companies at auctions, tenders, stock exchanges, and in other manner on the basis of free competition;
- Sales on competitive terms of an "integrated ownership complex" of an SOE or of a controlling share of an open joint-stock company;
- Redemption of property of an SOE according to an alternative privatization plan.

But the most widespread variant of privatization, at the early stage of this process, was the *lease of the assets of an SOE* (with further payments to the state treasury or free handover) to the specially created so-called "collective enterprises" or closed joint-stock companies with workers and management as shareholders. This method of privatization may also be referred to as "management–employee buyout," although compared to Western practices, the price of shares offered to the staff was usually very low and the purchase was often supported by some extra funds raised especially for this purpose.[9]

Since 1997 the law in Ukraine, except for small privatization, forbids these forms of privatization. Many SOEs have changed their ownership through sales at certificate auctions. As a result, shares were spread among a large number of individuals with practically no strategic investors appearing in the above-mentioned cases. Only since 1997 has there appeared to be an explicit shift toward selling privatized objects at commercial and noncommercial tenders.

The real outcome of privatization, on the whole,[10] did not correspond to the initial expectations (Estrin et al., 1997). The major factor affecting results of the process was that formal privatization in Ukraine has been widely replaced by, or subordinated to, a process of informal privatization. By the latter, we mean the situation when an SOE remains formally under state control, but informally, through extensive relaxation of economic control, is not only freely governed by its general director, but, as far as its profits are concerned, almost fully belongs to the enterprise's top management. The top management, not the state, derives the bulk of its profits while economic responsibility for losses usually rests with the government.[11] In fact, the entire process developed spontaneously on a nonlegal or quasi-legal basis.

Statistically, the relative growth of the nonstate sector in Ukraine is quite evident. In industry for instance, it has expanded from 17 percent of overall production in 1992 to 77.4 percent by December 2001, with 82.3 percent of all large- and medium-scale industrial enterprises being from the state sector (UEPALAC, December 2001). But the real impact of privatization has turned out to be quite moderate. Privatization frequently only means a change in the legal title of an enterprise. The performance of SOEs and privatized enterprises in this country does not differ significantly. Both register decreases in sales and increases in output inventories, wage arrears and the share of barter, as well as stagnation in investments. Many formally privatized enterprises have preserved their old top managers and their old modes of behavior and in many aspects resemble SOEs. They depend heavily on government subsidies and other protectionist measures.

The most significant feature of Ukrainian privatization is that it *did not give birth to new capital formation. It has remained primarily a means of public capital redistribution, with high-ranked government bureaucrats being at the top of the list.* In many cases, privatization is linked with the explicit abuse of the law and the involvement of criminals. All these circumstances have resulted in a general adverse effect of post-privatization development. This was a major factor in the decay in gross fixed capital formation which has decreased in Ukraine in the period since 1990 by more than 80 percent, and only since 2000 has it resumed an evident upward trend.[12]

Let us summarize what were the factors that sharply decreased the quality of privatization. Firstly, in the structure of privatization methods an excessive role was played, especially in the early stages, by "collective enterprise leases" with the subsequent buyout of state property and the formation of so-called "collective enterprises." The staff and, primarily, the management of the relevant SOEs played a major role in the procedure of privatization both as initiators and benefactors. That ensured the support of these influential groups for privatization, but turned out to be devastating for numerous firms.

Genuinely private Ukrainian firms, independent of state bureaucracy, played little part in privatization. The role of foreign investors was incidental. The government lacked a policy clearly addressed to these two types of investors. The survey of selected Ukrainian open joint-stock companies (ICPS, 1999b: 18–19) points to a 54 percent quota of workers as shareholders in 1997, and 47 percent in 1998, while Ukrainian companies hold 15 and 13 percent respectively, and foreign investors 1 percent.

Another factor refers to redistribution processes. Maneuvers to change the ownership structure that took place after privatization were not addressed to any external investors and were not focused on improving the prospects of the firm, but simply aimed at crowding out workers as owners by managers. Mergers and acquisitions resulting in a redistribution of private property in favor of a more efficient owner did not really follow the initial privatization. The instruments of portfolio investments have also been underdeveloped and unreliable. Only a few companies have participated in such transactions in the securities market. Cases of a more vigorous presence on the financial markets and trading in the Ukrainian stock exchange are relatively rare. Thus the famous argument of effective reallocation through privatization did not work.

Finally, as mentioned earlier, privatization procedures in Ukraine lacked fundamental transparency and for this reason did not provoke open and free competition for the productive assets, neither prior to nor after privatization. The rules of the game have often been subject to various quasi-formalized regulations and informal pressures, and were subject to specific relations within and between informal G-FIGs. This prevented the appearance of a genuine competitive owner capable of consistent and comprehensive internal restructuring.

As mentioned earlier, the involvement of foreign investors in the process of privatization has been very limited, and more importantly was formally restricted in comparison to the practices of Central European countries. Foreign investors were not able to compete openly with Ukrainian entities for privatization bids on a formally equal basis, except for a limited number of cases where such participation was directly prescribed. Interestingly, however, there are assumptions to consider such as far more serious control of some enterprises from abroad, especially from Russia.[13]

The method of privatization carried out in Ukraine with privileges for the personnel of SOEs, and lack of antitrust measures, has *hampered the development of a genuine private sector*. Ukrainian privatization practices give a lot of credence to the important statement that privatization by itself is a desirable, but not sufficient, step on the way to higher efficiency. It can even result in economic decline if it is not backed by necessary changes in other segments of institutional settings, being superficial and not creating a real owner.

Despite the relatively slow pace of Ukrainian privatization, there is a growing perception among leading Ukrainian economists that the principal mistake was its high speed, compared to the changes in other institutional segments. It has been inconsistent with the potential of the original institutional basis of the country and its further ability to create such a basis. The formal privatization process has thus been far ahead of institutional changes in management and government administration as well as the building of an adequate market infrastructure and introducing the necessary legal norms (Pokrytan et al., 1999).

It is highly symptomatic that the genuine growth of the private sector in Ukraine is much more noticeable along the lines of some newly created companies. On the whole, one can find a considerable difference between the Ukrainian sectors of newly established private companies and those nonstate companies that came through privatization. These differences may be summarized as shown in Table 3.2.

The relatively worse performance of the privatized sector, versus the newly established private sector, can be largely explained by the persistence of inertial old structures that require a lot of time and money to overcome. Another reason is that the majority of successful newly created firms operate in the fields of new products and services (computer industries, telecommunications, internet provider services, and so on), and widespread

Table 3.2   The main performance differences between privatized and successful newly established private companies in Ukraine

Performance characteristics	Privatized companies	Newly established private companies
Market competitiveness	Medium or low, not very different from SOEs	Above average, due to higher quality of products and services, better schemes of marketing and management
Dependence on government support	Old links with government structures and "friendly" officers are usually preserved, subsidy dependence is frequent	Usually do not require government subsidies, oriented at lobbying market-type laws
Innovation ability	Strong tendency to preserve old structures	Rather high, though in many cases due to imported innovations
Organization structures	In many cases, obsolete, inflexible, and closed to outsiders	Much more flexible, internationalized, with many elements resembling Western companies
Employment	Usually overstaffed	Rather compact, with many young people (under 40) in the staff
Financial and payments discipline	Medium or low (like SOEs), wage and payments arrears are frequent	Above average, in spite of substantially higher payments on wages

Source: The authors' estimates based on field studies.

consumer goods production with rapid capital circulation (foodstuffs, beverages, textiles, and clothes).[14] Besides this, there has emerged a completely new sector aimed at meeting the high-standard needs of newly rich consumers (construction or reconstruction of private houses and premises up to European standards, supply of costly exclusive goods). In all these markets, aggregated consumer demand has remained relatively high with customers' expectations also high and selective. This has favored a competitive environment in these markets with entry barriers usually lower than in other sectors.[15]

It is the sector of newly established private enterprises that may become the leader in forming the foundations of an efficient private sector in the Ukrainian economy. But its size is not yet sufficient to overcome the inertia of the old sectors. Thus, more freedom for market entry in different areas of economic activity is vitally important for the acceleration of transition to an efficient market system.

To summarize the real influence of privatization in Ukraine, we can say that it has brought the intensive withdrawal of enterprises from direct state control, usually substituting this with methods of informal control. Thus, it has meant the dismantling of central planning, while fostering intensive informal bargaining between businesses and bureaucrats. On the whole, Ukrainian privatization has not led to the emergence of new institutional market arrangements suitable for capital accumulation and investment; on the contrary, it has often provoked capital flight and the unproductive spending of money.

Nevertheless, an important subeffect of privatization in Ukraine has been the widespread understanding that a new approach is needed in order to drastically change its adverse impact on economic development. This new approach, based on a much more *competitive approach to privatization,* will be pursued with respect to the most important entities on the privatization list. It is hoped that privatization tenders exclusively on cash terms would bring genuine private owners and strategic investors which, it is hoped, will become the engines of economic growth in future. However, it is too early to judge whether these new hopes can become a reality within the distorted and corrupted framework of Ukraine's central and local government administration.

3.7   Informal institutional framework for corporate governance

It is quite typical in Ukraine that, in spite of the existence of boards of directors (*pravlinnya*), it is solely the director or company's other top manager who is the main actor shaping decisions. Although it seems peculiar, it is also common that companies' supervisory boards (*naglyadova rada tovarystva*) are, as a rule, not important actors in decision-making. They play more of a decorative role, being typically composed of workers and managers from the same company. Representatives of external Ukrainian or foreign companies and banks as well as government representatives are usually not present in such managerial structures.

The formal influence on decision-making of external actors who do not directly belong to company management is generally limited. But this is only a superficial vision. Practically all the top managers stress the extremely high significance of their personal contacts with authorities, banks, and partners. It means that, at least indirectly, external actors retain their important role in shaping decisions in the firms, but this is not reflected in the formal governance structure of the company.

We can also point out the decreasing impact of workers on any decisions in the firm. That is explicit in newly created private firms. Though it is more hidden in SOEs and former SOEs, the marginalization of workers is common. Formally speaking, there are instruments available for workers' participation in decision-making through both shareholders' meetings and meetings or conference of the collective (*zbory aktsioneriv, zbory, konferentsiya kolektyvu*). Formally possible topics addressed here may refer to virtually all important decisions, such as new major fields of business activity, organization of production, product quality, investments, problems related to social security and social infrastructure, and so on. But in fact, the theoretically possible influence of workers is watered down through informal managerial practices.

The same may be said about trade unions, which, in the overwhelming majority of companies, claim to exert some influence mainly through collective bargaining. But it looks as if their real impact on strategic decisions remains very limited. Trade unions tend to approve all major decisions taken by management and avoid confrontation. This mode of conduct may be attributed primarily to the huge disparity of power between management and labor. In situations when the discrepancy of incomes between managers and workers has become extremely high, the loyalty of trade union leaders to management is simply remunerated. But in essence, the law on labor relations can be almost openly neglected due to the social disintegration and poor enforcement of the law, affected by the questionable independence of judicial system.

What is crucial, however, for the long-term formation of new market institutions, and not so easy to address in an empirical study, is the question of managers' motivation. It is evolving and not entirely consistent, but also influenced by both certain objective parameters of the economic environment and strong newly spread public stereotypes. Especially in the first period of transformation, quick individual success and a vision of "Western-type" personal prosperity were the dominant motivation for individuals. The reaction to the quite suddenly increased economic freedom was to use it at full extent to get higher profits in a short period, and to reach a new quality and better standard of personal consumption. That is quite an important part of the explanation of why profits were not redirected to the modernization of companies, rather feeding current consumption. Weak formal constraints on the part of government were not sufficient to limit these motivations. Wide gaps in legislation made it possible to play a game with almost no rules, or, to be more exact, with rules permanently changing depending on the person who was in charge of the relevant branch ministry and of the relevant territory.

Later, under President Kuchma's policy of macroeconomic stabilization and at the outset of structural reforms, the space of unconstrained economic freedom of firm managers shrank considerably due to curbed monetary expansion and the generally more difficult environment. But instead of purely financial and market-type constraints, the managers returned to dependence on government decisions, although in an informal way. A number of factors severely diminished the scope of maneuver of managerial decisions and tightened political loyalty to political bosses and high-ranking officers in government structures as a rule of the game for enterprise survival. There were a number of measures in officials' hands that reoriented managerial motivation. From a true avalanche of new regulations, very often contradictory and not transparent, through the tightening of tax pressure alongside the needs of the state budget, to the discretionary decisions on different government preferences, exemptions, and privatization deals.

It turned out that the slack pace of enterprise restructuring in Ukraine reflected not the inability to reform, or lack of willingness to transform, but first of all the internal contradiction within the system of economic motivation among all major economic actors. One should not oversimplify the involved actors' motivation. Many of them were vitally interested in the well-being of the firms, or localities, or regions and some were sincerely identifying themselves with the enterprise. But the system of existing institutions has not been able to work out a comprehensive structure of motivations and keep it relatively stable for a longer time.

The actual corporate governance remains poorly institutionalized, thus with little space for working out any consistent strategy of the firm, focusing on temporary adaptations to current economic and political circumstances. In these circumstances, different types of enterprises adopt various strategies of economic conduct depending on their ability to "improve" the adverse economic environment. As mentioned earlier, the informal proximity of the management to central or local authorities plays a substantial role in selecting the strategy. Interestingly, a contradiction between large and small firms could be observed in the field studies. The large firms relied primarily on their "political capacity" to build their policies in relation to a larger political net. By contrast, small or medium-sized businesses, which are very limited in their capacity to influence even the local government, relied on any political links being cut off, assuming that any likely contacts with bureaucrats might only damage the business. Thus, they first of all used diversified ways of escaping government control, and often ducking into the shadow economy. The latter accounted for about 60 percent of GDP in Ukraine, and it seems to be a direct result of excessive administrative regulation (Kaufmann, 1994).[16]

There is also a certain difference between large, medium and small-scale enterprises, the latter being much more flexible and adaptive in their strategies. However, the above characteristics are not to be treated as completely uniform. We can see, for instance, a growing difference between those large-scale enterprises, which originated as monopoly structures within the former centrally planned economy, and those private entities that have grown under a more competitive environment. Unfortunately, these more successful entities still do not play a key role in the Ukrainian economy and are still rather exceptions to the rule.

To sum up, the whole structure of corporate governance in Ukraine retains much from the former system of central planning, with closed and, in many aspects, autarkic (self-sustaining) corporate structures, the absolute domination in decision-making of the enterprise's top manager, and widespread government interference and paternalism. These obsolete structures, as a rule, are essentially unable to play an active role in economic strategy formation, resulting in the domination of merely short-term adjustment.

3.8   Conclusion

The painful road to economic transformation in Ukraine gives much insight for theoretical generalizations and practical policy solutions. We can draw the following main lessons from the tendencies described above.

Lesson 1. Of great importance to the outcome of market transition is a consistent and clearly defined policy of macroeconomic reforms, which forms the general economic environment for enterprise restructuring. The vagueness and lack of consequence of macroeconomic measures provoke ambiguity of microeconomic adaptive reactions, thus leading to their pathological character. That is why we witness the "half-market" behavior of enterprises, with plenty of residual elements from the former economic system based on central planning, administrative regulation, and informal relations between managers and bureaucrats.

On the other hand, the pace and shape of reforms at the enterprise level form the foundation for macroeconomic policies. Without success at this level, any macroeconomic achievements, including monetary stabilization, would not be viable.

Lesson 2. The tight monetary policy and not excessive fiscal policy are to be complemented with active institutional policy which plays a decisive role in successful transformation. It should aim at the emergence of all necessary market institutions which are to replace discretionary government interference in economic activities.

Much attention in government policy should be paid to general development of institutional infrastructure, providing fair conditions for positive adjustment to a more competitive environment and hard budget constraints. In this context, one cannot overestimate the role of a healthy judicial system, as well as consistent Civil and Criminal Codes, bankruptcy law, antimonopoly law, corporate law, and other segments of legal foundation for fair competition.

Lesson 3. The Ukrainian experience stresses the significance of clear and understandable rules of the game for all economic actors. This conclusion emphasizes the vital importance of a systemic approach in their formation, preventing the existence of sizeable institutional gaps or conflicting arrangements, as opposed to the immediate dismantling of earlier institutions (such a task looks completely unrealistic).

Any "quick-fix" approach may easily lead to dysfunctional legal arrangements that provoke deviations and informal configurations of power/influences. They lead to an explicit substitution of publicly embedded institutions with temporary clan compromises, which ruin the institutional framework and determine far-reaching degradation at the enterprise level.

Lesson 4. A powerful and healthy financial sector is a sine qua non for restructuring of the manufacturing sector. At the same time, legal and economic provisions to facilitate interactions of commercial banks with manufacturing companies may turn out to be important for successful restructuring and sustainable adjustment to market environment. However, the informal government–financial–industrial groups (G-FIGs) that came into existence in Ukraine were not able provide long-term strategies at the micro level. The direct links between the banking and manufacturing industries can bring positive results only if the financial sector itself is first restructured on a sound market basis.

Lesson 5. A consistent (but not hasty) policy of privatization aimed at the emergence of efficient owners is a general foundation for successful market-type transformation at the enterprise level. Privatization is to be looked upon as a necessary, but not sufficient, prerequisite for efficient restructuring. In the absence of a clearly defined *competitive approach to privatization*, and the dominance of specific informal links between business and government, formal privatization quickly creates distorted and noncompetitive economic structures, lacking real private owners who would be able to bear full economic responsibility for their actions. More emphasis on easing market entry and providing a sound basis for genuine private firm development is needed. A more robust expansion of a genuine private sector may compensate for the deficiencies in the activities of old privatized enterprises.

The old privatized sector, with the dominating role of large companies, needs large investments. But only on the basis of thorough-going internal company restructuring will it be feasible to reverse the decline in investment activity. These two processes are two sides of the same coin and should not be treated separately. Substantial effort is needed to normalize the financial aspects of enterprise activities on the basis of harder budget constraints and less subsidizing, alongside a considerable decrease in tax pressure. Without these measures, Ukraine's companies will not serve as a promising object for intensive investment from outsiders, including commercial banks and institutional investors, both Ukrainian and foreign. More sound and stable financial indicators of manufacturing sector enterprises are the decisive condition for decreased financial risk in their financing, and thus, for the general lowering of market interest rates.

Lesson 6. Decisive action is needed to reverse the persisting tendency of Ukrainian companies to operate as economically closed, autarkic, and "monarch-type" entities (strong domination of insiders in corporate control – although under informal constraints from the outside – the reliance on self-financing and "self-sustaining" performance, absolute power in hands of the top manager in internal relations sometimes neglecting legal provisions).

Such an internal structure makes them extremely resistant to possible inno- vation. The essential enhancement of the role of boards of directors and shareholders' meetings coupled with the introduction of economically efficient outsiders is essential for a genuine market transformation at the company level.

It is now more important than ever that the whole process of further institutional development of Ukraine be closely linked with its obligations under the Partnership and Cooperation Agreement with the European Union as of June 16, 1994. Namely with its Article 51, which calls for the compatibility of Ukrainian laws with European ones in such fields as: customs, company law, banking, accounting and taxation, intellectual property, labor protection, financial services, competition rules, govern- ment purchases, environmental protection, technical regulations and standards, and so on. It is evident that the implementation of these obliga- tions could be a major factor in fostering Ukrainian transition to a genuine market economy and genuine sustainable development as an integral part of the European economy.

Notes

1. The analysis of the case is also, in some aspects, a more difficult matter, com- pared with Central European and even Baltic countries, due to the absence of many data and still inadequate statistical information needed for empirical study.
2. In this sense, it is very difficult to speak about any country model which Ukraine tries to pursue in its reform policy. Though in some aspects, for instance in banking regulation, it tends to converge toward the Anglo-Saxon model.
3. Though it was adopted prior to full national independence, it was actually the Ukrainian, not all-(Soviet) Union legal act.
4. In Ukrainian statistics, they are also referred to as forms of "collective enterprises."
5. The total capital of the Ukrainian commercial banks was equal, on March 1, 1999, to $1.2 billion, and their total assets only about $5.6 billion (Suhonyako, 1999). On January 1, 2003, the total capital of the Ukrainian banking system reached $1.9 billion, and its assets $12.7 billion (Baranovsky, 2003).
6. They were intended, first of all, for branches with diversified cooperation links, like aircraft, agriculture, machine building, and so on.
7. Here and later on in all cases, which contain no references to other sources, we rely on the data obtained during the field study of 21 Ukrainian companies located in Kiev, Kharkov, Lvov, and Odessa. This field study was carried out under the RRS project.
8. As far as subsidies are concerned, their estimates differ. For example, according to Inna Lunina and Volkart Vincentz (Siedenberg and Hoffmann, 1998), in 1997, direct budget subsidies to Ukrainian enterprises were equal to 7.4 percent of GDP, while indirect subsidies (tax preferences, arrears in taxes and budget payments) were 12.7 percent of GDP, in total 20.1 percent. UEPALAC (June 1999) estimates direct subsidies as 3.2 percent of GDP, but on adding to them indirect subsidies (postponement of tax payments, privileges in foreign trade,

preferential bank loans or those guaranteed by government, government purchases at excessively high prices or with the aim to clear the commodity stock which would not sell otherwise), the indicator rises to 20.73 percent. Of course, such extremely heavy subsidizing cannot but essentially distort competition and weaken stimuli for enterprise restructuring and positive adaptation to an economic environment.

9. In Ukraine, a much smaller role was played at that time by voucher privatization, which ran counter to the experience of many other post-Soviet states. Voucher privatization was the primary method: in Georgia, Moldova, and Russia relying on the system of concessions to insiders, and Kazakhstan and the Kyrgyz Republic providing equal access to all voucher-holders. In addition, sale to outsiders was used as a secondary method in Kazakhstan, Moldova, and Russia. And management–employee buyout served as a secondary tool only in Georgia and the Kyrgyz Republic, and as a tertiary one in Russia (EBRD, 1997).

10. Of course, certain positive exclusions do exist, for instance in the food or textile industries, or other areas where competition was higher due to the initial absence of monopoly structures.

11. S. Djankov (1999) is right in referring to Ukrainian privatization practices as the process that favors incumbent managers.

12. Now, it still amounts to about one-third of the 1990 level.

13. Unfortunately, it is extremely hard to evaluate this influence in quantitative terms because of their informal and predominantly hidden character. But one can refer here to the growing penetration of Western companies into some sectors of the Ukrainian economy, for instance confectionery and beverages, and the tobacco industry. Recently, some proof of interest in the energy sector enterprises appeared, and many of the regional power-distribution companies are claimed to have been privatized with noticeable participation of capital coming from abroad. As far as informal privatization procedures are concerned, we find some examples of penetration by Russian companies in the Ukrainian gas sector. There is evidence that the Mykolaiv Alumina Plant has come under the control of Syberia Aluminium Co. from Russia.

14. In this respect, we may point, for instance, to such leaders of the Ukrainian market as "Kvazar-Micro" and "MDM-Service" then called "e.verest" (computer industry), Ukrainian Mobile Communications (UMC), "Obolon" (beverages), "Svitoch" and "Kraft Jacobs Suchard Ukraina" (sweets and chocolate).

15. The privatization of local energy supply companies, in contrast, has produced not higher efficiency but a severe energy crisis, because it could not overcome the deep structural monopolization in this sector, and only complicated the management of this basically integrated system.

16. In later publications, we find the estimated 48.9 percent of unofficial activity in Ukraine for 1995, which was obtained on the basis of the electricity consumption method (Friedman et al., 2000).

4
Bulgaria: the Rise of Capitalism and Actors' Rationality
Douhomir Minev and Maria Jeliazkova

4.1 The framework

4.1.1 Social context

Corporate governance inevitably reflects the social and economic environment in which the main actors play. Different types of social changes shape the functioning of corporate governance, regardless of formal structure. This chapter deals with this relationship. More specifically, it examines the relationship between the transformation of social structures and the economic behavior of corporate actors. One may distinguish three types of changes performed in the name of socioeconomic transformation: (a) replacement of top figures of the sociopolitical structure with no considerable structural change; (b) gradual transformation of the social institutional order but within the same basic social configuration, including configuration of major political forces; and (c) the evolution of a basic social configuration and institutional social order. The Bulgarian transformation presents a mixture of the first and second types of change; yet only the third type is the one where real social development (in the Weberian sense) takes place (Schluchter, 1981). The fact that social change in Bulgaria was only partial influences the nature of corporate governance and corporate behavior, and contributed to the long-lasting domination of political logic over economic relations. As the result, the main actors at the corporate level continue to be under the pressure of the predominating sociopolitical configuration. We call this durable structure the "basic social configuration," and see its persistence, despite a formally democratic environment, as a critical point of explanation of why the economic transformation in Bulgaria has been incomplete and slow.

On the one hand, corporate governance was formally reshaped by some institutional–legal changes. On the other hand, however, it reflects a not so transparent means of privatization, which has been undertaken by leading political forces, and thus is affected mostly by the old and lasting sociopolitical configuration. In that sense, one can get a much better understanding of economic relations through a recollection of the basic characteristics of society before the reform, in which the political elite were able to exercise complete control over society. For that very reason the main problem of transformation is whether and to what degree the structure of political (formal and informal) control, as a basic configuration of the former social system, is likely to weaken. What are the chances of making a transition from "absolute power" of a given interest group toward an open society and balanced influence of different social groups? To what extent can the new normative and institutional framework provide it?

This thesis thus suggests that the formally democratic political institutions are a necessary but insufficient condition for enabling economic transformation. The "basic social configuration," with its power relations typical of the past period, dominates economic relations, including real corporate governance, and severely limits people's economic activity and initiative. The depoliticization of economic relations and competitive markets is not likely to succeed without a more vigorous democratic and civic environment.

Bulgaria did not take a significant step toward civil society despite the strong public striving for democracy and the market. Although the high rate of participation in the parliamentary and presidential elections of 2001 may be interpreted as a sign of people's longing for change, there is still a long way to go from this initial expression of a general public will, to a transparent and well-functioning institutional system, including corporate governance, in which genuine economic actors would be ready to legally defend their authorized interests. This chapter describes the fuzzy boundaries of actual corporate governance and the distorted roles of corporate actors that resulted from politically controlled privatization and the still significant presence of the state in microeconomic performance.

4.1.2 Discussion of the transformation

The "basic social configuration" of pretransitional social order has been supported through the lack of a developed sense of citizenship and political democracy, and through the specific normative framework of a centralized "planned" economy. Thus, the change of the basic configuration may only be exercised by restricting the discretionary power of the political elite though the development of civic structures, political democracy, and new normative design together with market institutions. What we experienced in Bulgaria, at least in the first phase of transformation, was a partial reform in the sphere of market institutions, with not much change in the sociopolitical background. Only a comprehensive set of political and social mechanisms may underpin economic transformation. When we look at advanced societies and economies, these mechanisms have also played significant roles in their economic development over the last 50 years. By contrast, in the initial trajectories of post-communist transformation, the democratic and civic evolution was mistakenly treated as a secondary issue, which should give way to macroeconomic stabilization and rapid privatization.

The Bulgarian experience clearly shows that the basic social configuration of the prereform period has been able to keep its vigor and has to a large extent captured the new "market" institutions. This was possible because the democratic and civic activities came to the point of genuine development only when major pieces of the pie were distributed, while some new economic institutions were already distorted, promoting the status quo rather than a competitive environment. These mechanisms are still weak and not effective enough to ensure the rise of a new configuration of actors in society and the economy. Although the recent democratic and civic development seems to be more promising, the earlier settings still hamper genuine activity, limiting new possible sources of growth.

In a sense, the whole idea of a corporate type of economic activity, which in principle makes it possible to put together various financial and social resources to create new economic value, is not really implemented in corporate practice. The corporate actors rather try to protect their position which they acquired in the first (wild) period of transformation than look for new possibilities for the development of enterprise, as these new capacities might challenge their own influence. In order to explain this, it is necessary to analyze the nature and type of corporate actors who emerged in the course of economic transformation in Bulgaria.

Before doing this, let us briefly evoke some theoretical beliefs that unintentionally supported the suboptimal trajectory of economic transformation, in which the "basic configuration of the social order" was able to craft economic institutions in an exclusive way, focusing on its own survival rather than on economic development.

(a) Some authors had a special opinion on political democracy during the transformation. The democratic system has never been directly attacked but there was a strong belief, among both Bulgarian and international experts, that democracy could introduce difficulties for radical economic reform. Supporters of such a theory argued that it would be hard to consolidate reforms under conditions of impoverishment in a genuine democratic environment. This point of view does not meet the post-communist reality, that is clearly reversed: the more political the democracy, the more consistent are economic reforms and less extended over time (Hellman, 1998). Despite extensive empirical evidence, these outdated ideas still reappear in scientific and political circles. In fact, such a belief made it easier for the rulers to avoid standards of transparency and establish exclusive practices in a formally democratic shell.

(b) Even though almost everyone agrees that one or another form of market economy is a necessary and desired outcome of transformation, there are still discussions "for and against" the market at a (too) general level, ignoring the regional context. One of the strategies used to reject the "market" is connected with the vagueness of the concept of market itself. Sometimes this leads to considering markets as "empirically empty conceptualizations of the forums in which exchange costlessly takes place. The legal system and the government were, for example, relegated to the distant background" as pointed out by Demsetz (1982: 6). At other times the following argument is stated: we do not know what a market is and that is why we cannot create a "market by design." The other form is undisguised opposition to the market. A widespread statement is that modern capitalist economies should not be reduced to one of their elements. As Hannan and Freeman emphasize, markets are but one of multiple coexisting coordinating mechanisms in modern capitalism. Transformative schemes that rely on an exclusive coordinating mechanism do not so much emulate existing capitalism as echo the implementation of state socialism. Thus they carry the danger of sacrificing the dynamic efficiency and flexibility that depend on the diversity of organizational forms (Hannan and Freeman, 1989).

Our point is that these intellectual debates on the nature and content of the market do not take into account a post-communist context at the time of transformation after a long period when the market was ideologically rejected. In fact, in domestic politics the questioning of the market economy served mostly as a substitute for a real debate on the concrete shape of market–legal institutions. In the context of virtual market nonexistence as a mechanism of legally granting economic coordination, social efforts to reform were wasted, giving free rein to the discretion of policymakers. The domestic and international debate regarding adequate legal and institutional constraints was initially rather weak. However, those who support the market as a transformation device were aware of necessary social and political determination, expressing a simple argument that "markets can emerge and quickly – but only if all actors are legally and institutionally constrained to accept that there is no other alternative" (Amsden et al., 1994: 206).

The last quotation rightly suggests that all discussions about the market should be to a greater extent discussions concerning the significance of the normative and institutional framework that can help establish the necessary constraints that bind both policymakers and corporate actors. This is also the way to set a proportion between the market and other types of coordination (Chavance and Magnin, 2000). If we do not accept the market in a deformed way, as shown by Demsetz (1982), then we will have to look at it as "patterned interrelations." This would inevitably mean creating certain norms, which prescribe models of behavior, and sanction deviations from them. At the same time, the existence of institutions empowering norms by socially embedded normative sanctions against deviations is necessary.

That is why the market is not only a question of a mechanism of coordination. It is a question of a socially legitimate order. This normative nature of transformation toward a market economy was neglected at first, yet decisively pursued for the next ten years or more in the period of post-communist change. While the disputes of the market as a dominating coordination mechanism meant an indirect contest of market-related legitimate order, pleading for "various organizational forms" meant in fact giving a free rein to economic and social anomie. Instead of a "right proportion" between market and non-market types of coordination, by weakening pro-market transformation, it contributed rather to pathological forms of privatization. The partial and inconsistent trajectory of economic reforms, which we classified at the beginning of the chapter as the first and second types of transformation, prevented the third type, which is essentially the change of basic social configuration that eventually leads to a new, socially legitimate order. By questioning the market and neglecting its normative component, it helped to marginalize genuine market agents and favored the political (old and new) elites. This is how we understand the background of the crisis of 1997 in Bulgaria.

The notion of "anomie" is of particular importance here. Anomie is manifested most visibly in the specific type of politically distorted privatization, but may also be applied in a more general sense that refers to its Durkheimian origins. The post-communist social anomie, with its strong political and economic connotations, consists in a lost social sense of a normative framework that in general enables social organization. In restoring the sense of a normative framework, both democratic political reforms and market economic reforms (together with international assistance for both), could have played a decisive role. But in Bulgaria they did not reach a critical point until the severe economic and political crisis of 1997. The rhetoric of democracy and the market was not accompanied by normative content.

By the normative content of reforms we do not just mean a set of norms and rules of the game, which typically shape the institutional framework. What is also important is a sense of basic values that underpin democratic and market-oriented social order, such as individual citizenship rights, economic freedom, free access to information, and an independent juridical system. Without the clearly normative meaning of these values one cannot expect new institutions to embed in social practice, and without a transparent (for the public) correlation between norms and everyday practice a new legitimate order is not likely to emerge. The contrast between Western and Eastern Europe is that these normative structures are taken for granted in the former (sometimes not even acknowledged by their citizens), while in post-communist environments they are the subject of endless political maneuvers, reducing them to formal labels with little social content.

Sigurt Vitols identifies similar problems (Vitols, 1996), when describing two models of restructuring: (a) "public order," which is based on an empowered normative framework and (b) "private order," which is based on individual employers' decisions that are almost unrestricted by social norms. Our study demonstrates a high degree of coincidence between the main characteristics and consequences of the "private order" and Bulgarian transition. Anomie is an important characteristic in both cases.

This anomie strongly affected corporate governance, directly through privatization schemes and inconsistent laws, and indirectly by an easy deviation of the typical roles attributed to the actors of corporate governance, such as owners or managers. Additionally, the slow pace of reforms throughout the 1990s maintained the feeling of lack of stability and shortened the time perspective of any business activity. The partial changes of the first and second type did not create a favorable environment for adequate economic restructuring. More importantly, they did not promise much in terms of a new and more dynamic configuration of factors of economic growth. This is how the type of social transformation determines the type and scope of economic reforms. If privatization and governance are simply understood as distribution of power among old and new elites, and not as an important part of a larger socially (and legally) embedded order, the result inevitably manifests itself in distorted corporate governance, short time perspective of the involved actors, and weak moves toward restructuring.

There is also an international aspect to the problem. The more the social changes occur in the trajectory of the first type, the more unsuccessful the integration of the national economy in European economic structures. This is because the domestic "basic social configuration," which ensures control of the political elite over the economy, is not interested in a real internationalization of economic relations at the expense of its own influence. Partial institutional change, without a transparent normative component, cannot target domestic "low level equilibrium" (Greskovits, 1998). As a result, the "nationally oriented" economic relations, including privatization that restricts foreign actors (investors) from taking part in it, contribute to isolating the national economy instead of looking for new possibilities for economic development.

4.1.3   Distributive coalitions – a key problem of post-communist transformation

The legitimate order on the macro level – the regulative reforms, citizenship, and democracy – have important effects on the micro level. They outline the "figures" of the main economic actors, defining their rights and responsibilities, and at the same time determining their rational action. If some of the mechanisms in question are absent, these "figures" deform, and individually rational behavior does not bring positive results. More precisely, individual conduct is guided more by "distributive coalitions" than by general rules. The notion of distributive coalitions, although elaborated some 20 years ago, is quite useful in understanding the duality of contemporary economic life in Bulgaria. This is the duality in which the formally independent economic actors practically have to be a part of an informal structure that binds them more than the legal settings.

The analysis of Olson (1982), regarding the groups he calls distributive coalitions, is related to some economic actors who appear during the transformation in anomic crises. He describes these distributive coalitions as groups/organizations that aim at providing a higher share of the social product for their members. He notes that there are no restrictions to the social price that these organizations (today we would rather call them "networks") would force on society to pay in order to get a larger part of the social product. The consequences are devastating for the national economy. Olson's main interest was in the reasons for stagnation in developed countries. However, the discussion of distributive coalitions gives his analysis a much wider validity. Olson emphasizes that the countries where these distributive coalitions have been weakened or suppressed by a totalitarian regime or by an outside occupation seem to develop quickly after a free and stable lawful order is established. Suppression of both conflicts and gains in group privileges partially explains, according to Olson, the postwar economic miracles in Germany and Japan.

The analysis of distributive coalitions corresponds somewhat to the recent concept of "state capture" (Hellman, 1998), worked out in the context of post-communist countries. According to Hellman, the progress of economic reforms is largely determined by the capacity of state institutions to avoid capture by local political elites for their particular interests. According to Olson, relations between the state and distributive coalitions determine whether a certain country belongs to the "first," "second," or "third" world. Nowadays, using the language of some 20 years ago, the "second" (post-communist) world lies more than ever between the "first" and the "third," and the result of economic transformation greatly depends on the political capability of the country to effect the suppression of domestic distributive coalitions. Unlike in the Olson diagnosis, in the post-communist context, there is no conceivable dictatorship able to do that. Rather, as Hellman (1998) suggests, the more democratic the regime, the less captured the state.

In summary, in Bulgaria, with remote prospects for European Union accession, the first and most influential phase of transformation, as far as corporate governance is concerned, has shaped a dual anomic configuration. On the one hand, some partial legal reforms and privatization itself introduced typical corporate actors such as private owners and professional managers. On the other hand, the distributive coalitions achieved even stronger control, binding the key economic actors and exercising their power on the basis of unclear legal solutions and opaque rules of appropriation that established new owners. The existing dual configuration, one of "visible" economic actors and another of distributive coalitions that remain "in the dark" but still have decisive roles to play, makes any formal distinction between "private" and "public" ownership irrelevant. The "captured" ownership, regardless of whether it is formally granted in private property rights or not, may be under question and does not provide a sense of stability to the owners. The distributive coalitions try to keep the status quo, and by doing so are perhaps the most powerful factor hampering the consolidation of a comprehensive new order, maintaining the "basic social configuration" of the past. This is how we see the key problem of transformation. In our research we examine the role of typical corporate actors in the context of the distributive coalitions that they are forced to belong to. We were interested in the way in which the dominating transformation trajectory in Bulgaria has influenced the "figures" of the corporate actors, their behavior, interactions, and the outcome of their conduct in terms of real restructuring.

4.2 Corporate actors in the context of specific transformation trajectory

4.2.1 Distributive coalitions, corporate actors, and macroeconomic context

One of the most sticky aspects of transformation in Bulgaria is that it did not create authentic economic actors ruled mainly by economic rationality. This is not to say that they behave irrationally, but rather that the complexity of the environment that they have to respect does not allow them to maximize corporate profit and optimize long-term prospects of the company. Their rationality is not easily measurable by economic means. The delineation of the role of the owner, as well as of manager, is blurred, mixing the standard attributes of these "figures." This also affects any specific decision-making in which they take part.

Above all, the actors are involved in two different interacting configurations: one typical of corporate structure in its formal shape, and another called (after Olson) "distributive coalitions." The latter plays a main part in the overall configuration of influences. This duality is of special significance for the behavior of economic actors and for corporate governance. We put "coalitions" in the plural due to their multiplicity and changeable nature; it is not possible to identify just one relatively stable coalition. The distributive coalitions are specific vertical structures in which the managers and the owners of enterprises, the representatives of local and central public institutions, and the political parties are included. The coalitions connect central bodies of public power, especially the executive and the legislature, to micro-level economic entities. This obviously changes considerably the very configuration of actors that one has in mind when discussing corporate governance.

As a consequence, the coalitions affect not only decision-making, but also the whole sense of rationality and actor behavior. Thus, a specific "system" is formed which connects through strong organizational/network ties, actors who formally are not corporate actors but who should be autonomous and independent. Additionally, typical corporate actors lose their autonomy. Inevitably, organizations/networks that are best built vertically with clear hierarchic levels and links among them, begin to play leading roles in decision-making, especially in those decisions that are related to any kind of distribution, and also those affecting strategic thinking. The structures involved are mainly of two types: public administration and major political parties. These two types ("individual" and "collective") of actors appear to be the main protagonists in the distributive coalitions. Their position allows them a permanent mixing of rationalities and goals, which is nothing but a restoration of the old "party–public–economic" relations. The difference, in comparison to the old regime, is that there is more than just one influential political party and the parties have to compromise their realms. This is not to say, however, that existing distributive coalitions clearly reflect political cleavages. On the contrary, to some extent their economic interests make them mix political affiliations and remain within various circles.

Thus, the key aspect of this development is the combining of economic and political power. In everyday practice, this combining occurs, as our interlocutors call it, either by the "business entering" political parties, or by the "political elites' entrance" to businesses (which is usually, but not quite adequately, interpreted as corruption). It is not easy to determine whether and in which particular cases the political side dominates business or vice versa. Nevertheless, the distributive coalitions tend to act as strict hierarchies. This is of particular importance. On the one hand, they are able to cross both organizational boundaries of the enterprises and the borders outlined by the ownership. On the other hand, they mix public bodies of local and central administration with the vertically built structures of the political parties. In the long run, it leads to erosion of property rights in spite of their formal reestablishment.

There are two additional factors at play here. One is that involved actors, especially from outside the firm, are highly motivated by their possible direct incomes. This is an important factor hampering investment, even if some of the corporate actors see investments as necessary and rational. The second is that distributive coalitions have emerged in macroeconomic environments of undoubtedly "soft budget constraints." The dominant logic of their existence and conduct was built on their access ("entering") to the state resources as major sources of individual income. In this context, privatization became one more opportunity of distributing assets and influences. As mentioned, in spite of some bargaining on the political scene, often in one and the same distributive coalition representatives of different political parties were included. This is of particular importance because it hindered a group of reformers from developing real alternatives for macroeconomic policies until serious financial crises occurred and even afterwards.

4.2.2 Owners

The Bulgarian transformation shows the evolution of the economic figure called "owner," but does not reach a full definition. At the starting point of this evolution, economic actors who negotiated contracts on behalf of enterprises were often interested in deriving incomes from state-owned enterprises (SOEs). Surprisingly, the new owners in many privatized enterprises continued with a similar perspective on acquired assets. That is why we use the term "quasi-owners." Typically, quasi-owners opposed the development of the firm. Explaining such unusual behavior is the most important part of understanding corporate governance and its prospects in Bulgaria.

The unwritten assumption of transformation was that the new owners, even if they started their businesses as "quasi-owners," would enforce sound governance in their own interests. In this sense, a second phase of transformation was supposed to develop the figure of the "real owner," either individual or institutional, whose interest would be to increase the economic value of the assets of the firm. Relying on this assumption, one would expect that new owners would possibly engage in strategy building for the development of the firm, or at least that the interests of the owner would coincide with firm development. This is still rather questionable. Of course, there are some indications of positive change, but these special features of quasi-owner behavior are still present in privatized as well as state and mixed sectors. "They [the owners] behave as if they were not owners," a manager from a large privatized plant in Sofia said.

It is not possible to explain the strange behavior of owners without referring to the above features of the economic environment. When considering a larger context, however, it seems that the evolving actors who played the roles of owners have been avoiding investment even after acquiring property. There are several aspects of the new owners' conduct. Firstly, in many cases they have accumulated their financial resources during the first phase of transformation, before privatization, by means of the well-known scheme of "draining" public enterprises. At the end of this phase they acquired some of the firms, but there was no point in investing in the same enterprises that had been drained before. The method of accumulation of these financial resources had obviously aggravated the state of the enterprises. Secondly, the whole process was extended over several years. Over time, not only "draining" but also "aging" of the material assets reduced the enterprises' capacities. Especially when confronting potential international competitors, the desired investments would have to be very large in order to enter the market successfully. The new owners typically did not have adequate financial resources. One could reasonably ask why they acquired the property of a drained firm, with no possibility of adequate investment for its profitable functioning.

The third and most important aspect, looking at the poor results of many privatization cases, may be distributive coalitions. These are not stable hierarchies/networks which would be able to coordinate the action of multiple actors and provide them with a predictable framework for their rational decisions. In that sense, any easy analogy with Far East organizational design is highly misleading. On the contrary, the functioning of the distributive coalitions is mostly based on managing the current opportunities, with a strong feeling of lack of stability. Individual actors involved in the game cannot reasonably predict/plan their possible engagement in the medium term. Belonging to the "coalition" gives them temporary opportunities that in fact they must take; otherwise they would risk exclusion from the game. Being marginalized in the hierarchy/network is the biggest risk for the individual player. By contrast, acquisition of an enterprise does not bring any significant risks. Even if the enterprise is not profitable it may still have some valuable assets, and the acquisition, comparing the price, is still interesting. Our interlocutors from the Privatization Agency pointed out that the big players did not play for the production activity of a firm. They played mostly for its major durable assets, such as buildings, land, and to a smaller extent machines (which were often resold). The distributive coalitions have created and coordinated (managed) "taking opportunity" activities, and the scope of opportunities relied mostly on current, rather temporary constellations among the most influential players.

The activity described cannot be classified as a market game, although a kind of market vocabulary was often used. More surprisingly, however, it is also not accurate to classify the conduct of distributive coalitions as a political game. Looking at the political results for the involved parties, one cannot see clear political strategy and coordination behind a massive "taking opportunity" activity. The informal "coalitions" that spread in a post-communist context became overlapping and linked various groups, organizations, and political factions. Their shape reflected mixed attempts of erratic reduction of uncertainty, while looking for unprecedented opportunities, rather than a guided coordination, even if certain efforts to coordinate their action were undertaken.

The microeconomic results of the game between distributive coalitions, in regard to privatization and corporate governance, may be well characterized by a case study. A large enterprise in Sofia, producing mechanical equipment at the beginning of the 1990s, was profitable, enjoyed good recognition in Bulgaria, and had access to some international markets. The economic indicators worsened sharply after the signing of unfavorable contracts with newly established wholesale and retail companies (in other words, the profit was transferred to some new firms). In 1997, the owners of the new companies bought the enterprise, but they did not start to invest in it. Rather, they continued the previous scheme of income distribution. Soon the new owners entered into conflict. As a result, one of them stopped investing in the domestic firm and financially engaged in establishing a chain of shops in Austria. Another owner forbade the rest of the owners from entering the firm.

The case quoted shows how weak and delayed the possible positive effects of privatization in a typical scheme of erratic distribution of property "coordinated" by informal coalitions can be. Nevertheless, the "quasi-owners" are not irrational. Simply, the politically driven opportunities for property acquisition have given them experience of a highly unstable atmosphere, where almost anything may happen overnight. As individuals, they would certainly be interested in reduction of uncertainty and stable rules for corporate governance. However, individually they are not in a position to engage in adequate institutional reforms. On the one hand, they have little legitimacy to ask for such a change, and on the other, actively engaging in such reforms might even increase their individual risk of losing support of the "coalition," without which their business could easily be stopped.

The existing research does not allow us to say how frequent the cases of malpractice regarding property rights are. There are of course many positive examples. However, by referring to a negative case from our field study, we want to suggest that malpractice, even if not widespread, occurred in many sensitive nexuses of the economy, where likely profits might have fed economic development. A slow process of privatization, with many cases of intermediary private ownership delaying emergence of strategic investors, in the absence of a transparent normative environment provoked massive deterioration of material substance and economic performance.

The process described above is not easily measurable in economic terms. One can imagine two general indicators of the economic outcome of the game over property. One is the ratio between the resources, which have been accumulated by draining enterprises, and the amount of investment that the enterprises would need to restore their position. It is not, of course, easily calculable. Nevertheless, according to our interlocutors, based on concrete cases, that ratio might be roughly estimated to be 1 : 5. Briefly, resources that have been accumulated by draining activity are not enough to restore the economy. The new owners were aware of that disproportion and tried to escape from the uncertain environment and find a more secure place for their investments. That is why they placed their capital mostly outside acquired firms. But generally, such a ratio gives an impression of the "efficiency" of distributive coalitions as a "reallocation mechanism." The second indicator, related to the first, might show the ratio between inflows and outflows of financial capital. The problem of financial outflows from the country is often discussed in the context of economic transformations in Russia. It is present in the Bulgarian economy as well. Estimations of this ratio are even more difficult than of the previous one. Just to amplify possible figures, we may quote that the inflow of the FDI to Bulgaria, from the beginning of the transformation until 1998, reached $1.7 billion. In contrast, some economists estimate that the outflows only in 1992 reached $3.2 billion. We cannot really verify the rate of outflows, but the cases examined perfectly exemplify the rationale behind exporting money out of an unstable domestic economy. The "return" of these investments, from the national economic viewpoint, is problematic.

4.2.3   Managers

One of the distinctive features of the change in Bulgaria relates to the disempowerment of managers. Unlike in other transforming economies (Szelényi et al., 1996), Bulgarian managers cannot be seen as major "winners." In the first stage there were some analogies between managers' positions in Bulgaria and in other countries. Soon, however, the distributive coalitions were able to seize and subordinate the role of managers. Only a few of the managers could reach higher levels in the informal hierarchy of distributive coalitions. The coalitions were dominated by "domestic outsiders" who came mostly from politics or administration, possibly with ties to the secret police, and not from the private sector. Even if some of these people were involved in private business, their initial position in the coalition was not a function of their business activity.

On the surface, managers enjoy almost limitless power, but this is power only in relation to workers, power that they need in order to be able to follow the instructions of agents who are external to the enterprises and who quite frequently do not possess any formal property rights. The continuous replacement of managers, usually arising from changes in the governing political group, can be regarded as one of most significant factors in the deprivation of managerial power. In this regard, the position of managers of SOEs under the previous regime was much more secure. The directors of SOEs typically had to respect the will of the main political group (sometimes two competing groups) within the ruling party, but in fact they were relatively autonomous in managing everyday enterprise performance. During the initial stage of transformation the managers seemed to retain significant independence and power. The reason was the "sleeping partner" – the state. As a consequence, a large spectrum of possibilities for appropriation of part of the firm's income was at the managers' disposal. Due to this relatively comfortable position, managers mostly made attempts to oppose restructuring of power through privatization, trying rather to maintain the status quo. This changed, however, over time. On one hand, growing tensions at the highest level of the political scene with permanently changing constellations, and on the other, financial incentives/temptation, lured more individuals and groups into the game of enterprise incomes. Together with reestablishing more or less coordinated informal interest group action, the role of managers was seized and controlled by outsiders. Within the distributive coalition, managers were forced to direct part of the income of the enterprise toward one or another external agent, either before or after formal privatization.

Some field studies from the first half of the 1990s indicated malpractice by managers. From a 12-year perspective we know that this was only the tip of the iceberg, the hidden part of which was made up of complex relations. The owners, potential future owners, or other agents stood behind managerial decisions often unfavorable for the enterprise. Sometimes, managers tried defending the enterprise against the external agents of the coalition. It is not to say that the coalitions themselves were totally "external" to the enterprises. The managers were a part of both the firm and the "coalition." Nevertheless, they often were not major benefactors, and their interest was closer to the well-being of the enterprise than other interests in the "coalition." In fact, managers had limited scope for maneuver. The study enabled us to identify the two main tasks of managers after privatization: first, "to put the enterprise in order" after an undetermined period, and second, similar to the preceding period, to "consult" over the process of decision-making within a larger network of agents. Clearly, the managers avoided taking important decisions by themselves. Interviewed, for instance, about the investment plans for the firm, they usually described many possible variants, but rarely talked about concrete projects or achievements, or even their own will and plans. It is a well-known opinion about Bulgarian managers spread among their foreign counterparts that "the Bulgarian managers are afraid of taking decisions" (as expressed by a businessman in the weekly *Capital*, July 3–9, 1999). But they are not often aware of the complexity of "the net" that the Bulgarian managers deal with.

As we can see, the role of management has evolved over the past 12 years. At the beginning, managers typically covered part of the role of owners. Over the past few years, the new owners have strongly intervened in management. However, it would be misleading if one tried to imagine owners' interventions in management in the way that is experienced in the genuine development of a private firm. In such a regular case, the owner executes everyday management as a founder and the main actor of business activity. Then, together with the firm's growth, the owner steadily delegates managerial functions to hired staff. Eventually, he/she often keeps only selected strategic decisions, leaving all the rest to executive management. In the end, the executive management engages in raising new corporate capital, and new owners/shareholders often are not interested in decision-making. This is how the issue of corporate governance emerged and such a typical picture is often behind the mode of thinking of possible problems that it may represent in a privatized firm. But this picture may be misleading. In the privatized firms the relations between managers and owners strongly depend on the manner of acquisition of the firm. In order to understand the evolving corporate governance in the course of economic transformation in Bulgaria, one has to observe the evolution of the (mostly informal) relations not only between managers and new owners, but also between managers and all external agents. Again, the notion of distributive coalitions is very helpful. The owner's position in this coalition does not change dramatically at the moment of formal privatization.

Indeed, managers in SOEs were quite independent and not controllable, whereas over the last few years in privatized firms the new owners have had tight control over them, and managerial decisions were subordinated to owners' interests. These two contradictory stages might appear to be very positive developments. What is important, however, is what occurred between these two opposite stages that occurred in the long and rather slow emergence of new owners. The recent past still negatively affects owners' capacity to specify and follow their strategic interests. The owners' current interests are often still remote from the firm's prospects for development. The distributive coalitions provided a mechanism for eventually establishing ownership relations in a significant (and lucrative) way in the economy, but that was not their original and primary goal. Initially, they simply put together influential actors, including SOE directors, who on the one hand tried to minimize the current uncertainty of erratic changes, and on the other sought to profit from the ongoing opportunities on an unprecedented scale. The hierarchical structure of these organizations/networks was powerful enough to minimize external (to the net) control of potential transparency standards or open access to the game, but was not able to ensure its real internal coordination. The constellations of coalitions changed and were in permanent internal conflict. Finally, the major gains were not provided simply by draining enterprises, but rather by draining the state through these enterprises. This anomic performance obviously affected future owners' capacity to engage in any strategic thinking and develop a long-term perspective that would be adequate for the real challenge of firm restructuring and new market development. The role of managers as figures in corporate/coalition governance was reduced to a "consulting body" and keeping the enterprise "in order."

4.2.4   Workers

Under the previous regime, in SOEs, state employees' interests to a large extent coincided with those of managers. In a sense, both managers and workers represented the state (as owner) in corporate structures. In good and bad, the interests of managers, of the "owner," and of workers were often not distinguishable within the old institutional framework. The enterprise was controlled from outside by the administrative and political structures, but the SOE managing director tried to increase enterprise autonomy, sometimes using the argument of worker attitudes and expectations as a shield. In this game, the workers remained quite influential through their relatively strong informal bargaining position. In fact, state employees in Bulgaria tended to support the status quo of state property.

Together with the political and economic reforms of the early 1990s two contradicting tendencies occurred: pro- and anti-worker positions, potentially influencing future settings in corporate governance. The second turned out to be stronger. The first tendency aimed at legal and organizational underpinning of workers' interests and making them explicit. The law on collective bargaining of 1990 authorized strikes, which seemed almost revolutionary at the first stage of transformation. The legislative acts were preceded and paralleled by significant organizational changes in Bulgarian labor unions. First, the new independent union Podkrepa was established and tried to expand its action all over the country. Second, the old unionist structures tried to quickly abandon the "transmission belt" legacy of the past and internally reform in order to become more sensitive to workers' interests. Also, a number of smaller unions emerged. Finally, the law on tripartite commission was passed relatively early, compared with other transforming countries. All these changes, in spite of temporary problems, looked quite vigorous (Iankova, 1998). However, they occurred mostly on the national level and turned out to be not really embedded at the micro level.

Within the enterprises, the directors continued to navigate between paternalistic and authoritarian styles of management, although less on the paternalistic side. With a few exceptions, unions of all kinds were not strong within enterprises. In relation to workers, managers enjoyed almost limitless power with very vague legal constraints. Together with financial problems of the enterprise, labor costs and social provisions were first to be cut. These cuts were much more drastic than in the countries of Central-Eastern Europe. The formerly strong bargaining position of workers did not encourage active attitudes toward protecting labor interests. Also, the former coincidence of managers' and workers' interests did not evoke any structures of consensual problem solving. Certainly the "Work Councils" established in 1986, with some exceptions, did not provide such a structure, but even they were soon liquidated. For most of the workers the ongoing attempts to reshape the labor unions were somewhat external to their enterprise and their current problems. The tripartite commissions were not embedded at lower levels, and national level talks were mostly influenced by the current needs of the government.

Summing up, our thesis is that the workers were deprived of any influence during the economic transformation. From the economic point of view, one can reasonably ask whether that had positive or negative effects on the transformation. Quite often, especially among economists, the dominant opinion is that workers' interests should be suppressed in order to give way to deep restructuring. This position focuses on the necessity of a painful process, which inevitably targets concrete interests, mostly those of workers, but in the long run brings positive results and eventually offers more to labor. There are some implicit assumptions in this statement. First of all, it is strongly believed that managers and/or owners are able to build a comprehensive vision of the future of the firm and that they themselves are obviously interested in its future prosperity. Second, they are supposed to formulate a concrete strategy for overcoming current difficulties and subordinate all action to this strategy, which was hardly the case in our research. Looking at redundancies, for instance, they have almost never been related to a larger restructuring plan. Finally, it is often supposed that workers themselves can hardly bring valuable inputs to the problems of deep restructuring, because their perspective is dominated by current needs that naturally oppose restructuring.

We do not want to engage here in a general and often too abstract debate on worker contribution to decision-making in corporate governance. We are simply considering the concrete situation of the Bulgarian transformation. The most striking aspect is that the transformation after the communist period did not occur in the clear context of the well-established sense of property rights, socially and legally embedded role of the owners, and professionally experienced managers. As was shown in previous sections, not only corporate structures, but also the specific roles of corporate actors had to be formed. That happened over a long process of reshaping the informal power structure called distributive coalitions. The eventual owners of former state assets, in the end, are probably more similar to typical owners than those who drained enterprises. However, their property now has often not much in common with the initial stage of the enterprise. In the meantime, workers' interests were apparently closer to the future well-being of the enterprise than those of many outsiders.

Our thesis is that the weakness of organized labor made possible the completely discretional practices of the distributive coalitions in their devastating conduct. No formal structure at the national level provided effective support for those workers who were ready to protect assets at the level of enterprise. Without the support of workers, those managers who were interested in effective restructuring and improving of enterprise conduct were easily replaced by coalitions.

4.2.5   Banks

The behavior of banks is important for two reasons. One comes from a standard belief that banks may play a special role in corporate governance, at least by monitoring investments. The other relates directly to post-communist reality and indicates that the banking system provides a clear example of the detrimental role of distributive coalitions and their influence on the interests, behavior, and interactions of economic actors.

Looking at the development of the banking system, two stages may be discerned. Stage 1 consists of an "unconstrained expansion," and stage 2 is characterized by growing control over banks, and monetary constraints. What clearly divides the two stages is the serious financial and banking crash of 1996/97.

The first stage saw typical phases. In the initial phase, the rapid mushrooming of a large number of banks looked like a "rush on banks," but not a rush of customers, rather the rapid movement of influential agents of distributive coalitions taking advantage of new opportunities. In many cases it was related to legal infringements, mostly because of fictitious subscribed capital. This particular phase was then followed by an exceptionally vigorous credit expansion of the banks, which tended to extend significantly the amount of the loans. The data indicate that Bulgaria was among the countries with the most rapid and extensive credit expansion in the first half of the 1990s. As in the Slovak Republic, the amount of credit to the nonfinancial sector reached almost 70 percent of GDP in 1993 and exceeded 50 percent in 1994, dropping to 41 percent in 1995, which still was almost double compared to that of transforming countries which avoided a banking crash. In Bulgaria, the bad credits soon started to accumulate in banks' portfolios and in 1996 the banking system collapsed.

What is interesting and important to reconstruct about the logic of distributive coalitions in the period of credit expansion is that the money flows were rarely linked directly (explicitly) to privatization of SOEs. This activity was dominated not so much by SOE acquisition as by pulling financial capital out of the public sector. There is a widespread but misleading thesis that the large volume of bad credits resulted from subsidizing of loss-making state enterprises. However, more than a half of all credit was directed to the private sector, and that took place in a period when the "private" sector was insignificant compared to the state sector. Another important feature of crediting can be found in the fact that it was concentrated in a very small number of individual credits, which were of substantial amounts. As foreign observers commented: "there are clear indices that the commercial banks have distorted incentives and that they by themselves have actively participated in the growth of the bad credits" (OECD, 1997b: 7). There is an analogy between the mentioned distorted incentives of banks, and distorted incentives of (quasi-) owners in the nonfinancial sector. The banking sector illustrated the nature of unconstrained activities of distributive coalitions in a most spectacular way; nevertheless there was no clear distinction between agents from financial and nonfinancial sectors within the coalitions.

As far as credits to state enterprises are concerned, there are grounds for believing that the credit expansion of stage 1 was employed in part, again, for provision of gratuitous funding to (selected) private companies. The rhetoric used by politicians often evoked the vocabulary of state intervention and support for "national/public" enterprises, but, in fact, during that particular period, the incomes of SOEs were transferred to private firms. Similarly, banking credits were transferred to the private nonfinancial sector whereby SOEs served as "intermediaries." Eventually, it became a part of strategy to achieve control over material assets of the SOEs by new owners, and agents of coalitions.

Therefore, huge enterprise debts toward banks accumulated. And this also meant that external (from outside coalitions) investors willing to buy enterprises would be expected to pay for SOE liabilities that had arisen from the ample and uncontrolled funding of private satellites. No doubt this resulted in the low interest shown by foreign investors in Bulgarian enterprises.

In a crisis situation, the government was still unwilling to declare the insolvent enterprises bankrupt so that their debts to creditors would become redeemable. The credits extended to SOEs contributed to the insolvency of the banks rather than of the enterprises. Obviously, the government policy of remittal of SOE debts stimulated inflation, but even more importantly, it contributed to social anomie by extending the scope of normlessness. The Bulgarian National Bank was not able to exercise control over the other banks, and the government did not oversee necessary regulations. Instead, it tried to continue with ad hoc measures in response to the situation.

Stage 2, however, in a medium-term perspective brought a certain improvement of the general business atmosphere. As a consequence of the crisis of 1996/97, the government became involved in active measures aimed at consolidation and stabilization of the banking system, coupled with privatization of banks. One-third of all banks immediately disappeared from the economic landscape, and the others were subjected to financial constraints. The credit expansion policy of the banks ceased. Instead, new banking practices went to the other extreme, strongly limiting credit. As a result, the banks started to dominate the firms by imposing one-sided crediting conditions. Yet banks had far from real control over industrial firms.

The banks themselves still considered that they had no potential and experience to interfere in management so they clearly avoided it. In our study, there was no bank declaring that it had a systematic approach and formulated policy toward clients in this respect. This is a good example indicating that the will for control contradicts expertise. The banks initiate some activity only in cases of long delay of payment, but even in such cases the banks do not engage in improving the management of the client firm.

The conclusion is that the banks are neither very interested nor sufficiently prepared to play a significant role in the governance structure and to stimulate long-term prospects for companies. The stabilization that occurred after the crisis, together with financial constraints, improved economic relations. It imposed certain norms on informal coalitions and significantly weakened their access to fresh financial capital. The social anomie, however, affected relations between banks and firms and decreased the potential for further development of corporate governance. On the whole, the links between banks and enterprises are unstable and both sides refer to each other with mistrust.

4.3   Conclusion

Distributive coalitions are important for explaining the dynamics of economic transformation in Bulgaria. The informal and politically oriented coalitions affected not only property transfers but also distorted the very nature of evolving corporate actors and structures of governance at the micro level. The scale of distortion goes beyond typical observations such as those of violation of minority shareholders' rights. Actually, as we can see in this volume, minority shareholders' rights are not perfectly respected in many advanced economies, not only in the emerging markets. Although we can expect some improvement of corporate governance resulting from the strengthening of minority rights, the deeper reasons for distortion of the incentive structure are more critical. Certainly, the question of legality and law enforcement (Pistor, 2000) is at the core of the problem, but it also needs a broader context.

Explaining the evolution of corporate governance and privatization in Bulgaria, we refer to social anomie understood as a crisis of socially embedded norms. In the transformation after the communist regime, however, the crisis of norms should not be confused with a Western feeling of the "end of modernity" paradigm that has been a subject of hot debate among academics in the last decade but only vaguely touched economic and political life. The normlessness in Bulgaria had concrete forms of law violation that deeply undermined the social sense of justice. The normlessness was used and produced by informal coalitions at the time of intensive distribution of property and income. It affected social and economic life in the period when the new (normative) order was expected to establish foundations on political and economic freedom, equal opportunities, free access to information, and a clear sense of property rights. Instead of founding a new socially embedded order, it contributed to the devaluation of all these values.

Our study led us to two concluding theses on informal networks. The first thesis points to the double face of informal networks, negative and positive.

The double face of informal networks simply means that there are two very different principles behind the emerging networks of influential actors. The first, which we mostly exposed in the analysis, uncovers the attitude of greedy acquisition of assets or profits in times of unprecedented and very temporary opportunities. It aims at maintaining these opportunities, with little respect for social legitimacy and lawful conduct. The most important features of this restructuring are: the lack of regulation; the reduction of labor costs; the "low profits–low investments" trap; weak competitiveness in the international markets. In addition, the distributive coalitions have continued the practice of "soft budget constraints." The cost of this restructuring is extremely high in terms of lost capital, lost opportunities for investments, and lost time.

Networking is a regular and well-known reaction to the great complexity of changing environments all over the world, and Stark and Bruszt (1998) exposed this positive aspect when they claimed that neither markets nor hierarchies but networks might have helped transformation. However, in some transitional patterns, the networking occurred in the strong context of the "other face" of coalitions, predominantly aiming at distributive control, with blurred political affiliations, a hint of secret police involvement, and surprisingly strong informal hierarchies reemerging from past relations. That is why the socialist elite, or clans, did not transform into "deliberative associations" but rather into Olson's "distributive coalitions." Those who joined the coalitions mainly or exclusively to cope with the complexity of the changing system had to respect their hierarchical, yet unstable rules, which were determined mostly by those interested in distribution. For this reason the efforts to reduce uncertainty (economic and social risks) for them turned out to increase the uncertainty for nonmembers. In terms of privatization and corporate governance, the coalitions produced quasi-owners who significantly delayed and deformed restructuring.

The second thesis claims that quasi-owners could take their expected roles as regular owners in stable environments do. For this aim the influence of the distributive coalitions should be significantly reduced. This is a very complex and difficult change, requiring above all a reform of the juridical system, strengthening of the democratic political institutions and authentic civil society organizations.

5
The Czech Republic: the Case of Delayed Transformation

Marek Havrda

5.1 Introduction

Corporate governance, in a broader sense (that is not limited to the principal–agent problem), is an opportunity to describe and analyze the successes and failures in 12 years of efforts aimed at overall institutional change, the transformation of the economic system and its outcomes for the whole economy. The notion of corporate governance enables us to identify actors as stakeholders in the transformation process (state, banks, enterprises, managers, trade unions, and other institutional actors) and to trace their motivation. This broader understanding of institutional and formal relations among shareholders associated with companies and understanding of networks created by these actors can contribute to formulating and identifying their strategies. Moreover, the influence of institutional changes on strategy formulation at the enterprise level, including enterprise restructuring, can be discussed in the framework.[1]

This chapter addresses the question of how it was that a well and proficiently started institutional rebuilding of a market-oriented economic system, together with flourishing development of the new private sector from scratch, did not ensure sustainable and long-lasting growth. Why was a kind of a "test by recession" necessary to instigate the strategic decisions of completion of institutional change? It touches on a very sensitive aspect of the systemic development in the Czech economy. It is to be stressed that all generalizations of this type must be considered, while bearing in mind the complexity of the economic system, influenced by historical, political, social, and cultural circumstances.

The aim of transformation has been to change the economic system from a command (planned) economy to a market economy. The goal of the transformation was to change the very basis of the system rather than the improvement of the inherited economic system, as with all changes and reforms before 1989.

Programs in the social and environment area accompanied systemic and institutional changes. A social safety net was established. Macroeconomic stabilization and maintenance of social peace were considered inherent to the process. These issues and the total collapse of the economic links in the Eastern bloc made the transformation very complicated. The split of the Czechoslovak federation enhanced many of these complex economic and political problems, especially in their international dimension.

Although there have been many problems, the state succeeded in maintaining macroeconomic stability through the stabilization policy. Except for the price jump after the introduction of price liberalization, the inflation rate has been around or lower than 10 percent and the unemployment rate has also been comparatively low. The introduction of a new negotiation mechanism by institutionalizing the so-called "tripartite" forum – government, unions, and employers' associations – contributed to the maintenance of social peace (there have been virtually no strikes in Czech industry).

The main systemic changes were:

1. Price liberalization (abolishing of administrative pricing);
2. Liberalization of imports;
3. Introduction of currency convertibility (current account convertibility);
4. Macroeconomic stabilization policy including anti-inflation policy, policy of social guarantees and social protection;
5. Introduction of a new tax system;
6. Liberalization of exports (abolishing of export monopoly of former foreign trade companies);
7. Wage deregulation;
8. Fast and broad privatization at the microeconomic level.

In the first stage of systemic change, the reforms were supported by significant fiscal discipline (except for budgets of municipalities), which contributed to the stable macroeconomic environment. Furthermore, the growth of a genuine private sector positively contributed to the development. Although these reforms brought about positive results in the second stage of transformation, it is now obvious that there are some serious deficiencies in the institutional regulatory framework. There has been room for managers and large shareholders to abuse their positions, the bankruptcy mechanisms have not functioned effectively, the major nonprivatized banks have been under political pressures, and the rights of creditors have not been strengthened sufficiently.

In the 1990–92 period, there was a widely accepted societal and political consensus to remove socialism and build up a Western-type democratic state. The main political forces were not parties but movements: Občanské fórum (Civic Forum) in the Czech Republic and Verejnost' proti nasiliu (Public against Violence) in the Slovak Republic. During that time, the scenario of economic transformation was also accepted and started to be applied. This included the successful liberalization of the majority of prices. Before the elections in 1992, new political parties were created based on factions in the political movements. The elections were won by Klaus's ODS in the Czech Republic and Mečiar's HZDS in Slovakia. Thus in the Czech Republic, a right-wing coalition of the ODS and two smaller parties was created. After the partition of the Czechoslovak federation, the economic reforms gained speed in the Czech lands where the right-wing coalition had the majority support of the Czech Parliament. Small- and large-scale privatizations were carried out in this period.

The pace of the reforms slowed considerably after the elections in 1996. Although the same coalition formed the government, it was a minority government and later depended on the voice of a "nonpartisan" member of parliament. At the same time the Czech economy experienced its first crisis (see Table 5.1) triggered by external instability and resulting in the devaluation of the currency and a switch from a basically fixed exchange rate to a floating mechanism (no longer maintaining the exchange rate within a certain limit). The reaction of the government was to introduce two "packages" of measures of generally restrictive fiscal character. The economic failure and scandals around the financing of political parties caused the breakup of the coalition and creation of the bureaucratic government led by the then governor of the central bank, Tošovský, who prepared, but stopped short of, completing further transformation steps. The government led the country until the early elections in 1998, won by the social democrats and resulting in the formation of a single-party minority government

Table 5.1   GDP growth in the Czech Republic

	GDP change (%)
1990	0.3
1991	−11.6
1992	−0.5
1993	0.1
1994	2.2
1995	5.9
1996	4.8
1997	−1.0
1998	−2.2
1999	−0.8
2000	3.1
2001	3.6
2002	3.1[p]

p = prognosis.
Source: Patria Finance.

of social democrats with tolerance for their largest rival, Klaus's ODS, signed in a so-called "Opposition Agreement." The government has continued with the privatization of banks, and prepared and launched a so-called "revitalization program" for large companies experiencing serious problems.

The argument raised in this chapter is that the rapid change in the first period of the transformation of the Czech economy was not accomplished in a comprehensive systemic manner. As a result, the incoherent institutional environment of manufacturing enterprises did not force them to restructure. Individual actors who were interested in restructuring did not get much support from institutional actors whose interests were elsewhere. In such circumstances, a temporary strategy of rent-seeking dominated over vast parts of the economy, especially those controlled by large organisms with ownership structures interlocking the manufacturing, financial, and state agents. Such a delay of comprehensive institutional change, covering all important segments of the economy, eventually led to a slowdown in economic growth, and to a vulnerability to external pressures. Thus, since the financial crisis of 1997, a "test by recession" has shaken the political elite of the left and right and pushed them toward more comprehensive institutional change. However, it turned out to be much more difficult than it would have been if the necessary changes had been undertaken in the first part of the 1990s.

The key process of the Czech trajectory of transformation was the way in which the massive property transfer took place. This chapter starts by examining the general results of privatization. Then, because banks play a very important role in the Czech system of corporate governance as remote owners and the main providers of finance, the banks' institutional position and performance are discussed, together with some political background of their delayed privatization. In that context, the next section will analyze corporate governance in more precise terms, pointing to the differences between the formal setup and practical use of it. In the critical approach of the essay, some positive actors of firm behavior are also presented, to show that they have actually paid a high price for delayed reforms, by suffering a necessarily restrictive environment despite their development potentials. The concluding remarks return to the interests of institutional actors and show their inconsistent attitude toward restructuring.

5.2   Privatization

Privatization is the main difference between reforms and systemic transformation. Macroeconomic stability and price liberalization may be included in the reforms of a planned economy, but it is only massive privatization that brings or increases the efficiency of markets of both production factors and capital. Therefore, privatization is definitely one of the most important aspects of the transformation process. Privatization created a completely new structure of ownership, thus changing the very nature of the economy. It brought about new actors as well assigning new and often very strong competencies to them. However, some of the key actors, such as the Ministry of Privatization, ceased to exist.

It is possible to divide privatization in the Czech Republic (former Czechoslovakia) into various cases of:

1. Restitution to the original owners (sometimes called natural restitution);
2. Transformation of agricultural cooperatives;
3. "Small-scale privatization" – usually in the form of auctions;
4. "Large-scale privatization" – including direct sales to domestic and foreign investors, voucher privatization, and any possible combination of the above.

The restitution process returned property to its original, prenationalization owners. The cutoff date of the restitution was set to the year 1948. Throughout this process, the state returned houses, shops, and firms to their former owners or their descendants. The term "small-scale privatization" applies to the privatization of small and medium-size enterprises (32 billion CZK of net income to the state budget, 36 billion CZK of gross income) (Ježek, 1994: 13). The main mechanisms of this method were auctions – direct sales. This privatization method was socially problematic, because the public felt that only people who had acquired money through gray activities or as a part of the former nomenclature had a chance to participate in the process (foreign investments were not allowed and bank credits were in general not available).

However, the most important was the "large-scale privatization" of factories and some utilities (state property of total price of 976 billion CZK). This was based on the privatization projects prepared by potential new owners. The competing privatization projects (on average five for each business according to Buchtíková, 1996) were evaluated by the appropriate ministries and the final decision was made by the Ministry of Privatization. Many of these projects included the voucher privatization method, which was the most important means as regards the total amount of privatized assets, of which 27.5 percent were direct sales, 58.6 percent were distributed free of charge and 13.9 percent remained in the NPF (National Property Fund) (Ježek, 1994: 14). Out of the 58.6 percent of those distributed free of charge, 82 billion were given to municipalities and 407 billion were privatized using the voucher method. (For a comprehensive study of Czech privatization, see Mejstřík, 1997.)

Often partial restructuring accompanied privatization. Although the rationale behind the privatization–restructuring issue was that restructuring should be carried out by the new owners, the implemented privatization projects often broke up local monopolies. One of the main goals of the designers of privatization was to receive different competing projects and finally adopt the most suitable one. This goal was not always completely achieved. However, many "Molochs" were consciously split by the privatization plans. Therefore the state played a conscious role in the beginning of restructuring. This fact contrasts with Pistor and Turkewitz (1994), who claim that the state was not able to play any sensible role in the restructuring and that the impact of state ownership on firm-level restructuring was just a result of its complete passivity (Pistor and Turkewitz, 1994: 24).

After the final decision by the Ministry of Privatization and the approval of the privatization project, the firms were moved under the jurisdiction of the NPF, which was responsible for the execution of the aforementioned project. The privatization projects specified the portions of the total assets to be freely distributed (by voucher privatization), as well as the fractions to be sold and remain in state ownership. Three percent had to be put into the restitution fund to be used later in outstanding restitution claims. However, the state retained about 43 percent of shares of the financial sector. After the second wave, voucher privatization was ended.

Voucher privatization was politically successful in its initial stage due to the huge advertising campaign carried out by the investment privatization funds (IPFs). Eligible citizens received, after paying a 1000 CSK registration fee, privatization vouchers for free and became DIKs (holders of investment vouchers). DIKs could invest their vouchers directly in the firms or in the IPFs that then invested acquired vouchers in the firms. IPFs succeeded in the task in which government failed, that is to express the value of the vouchers in monetary terms. In the first period, IPFs offered to pay around 10,000 CSK after a period of a year after a DIK invested all his vouchers in the fund. DIKs could also split the vouchers among different IPFs or even among IPFs and privatized firms. Later some funds even offered immediate payment after investing.

In October 1991, the Ministry of Finance launched its own advertising campaign in order to inform the public about opportunities to profit from voucher privatization. The response from the public was limited, and the deadline for registration had to be extended. In November 1991 the polls showed that only 25 percent of eligible citizens were interested in participating in voucher privatization (Coffee, 1996: 123–5). However, after the start of the advertising campaign by the first fund, Harvard Capital and Consulting (HC&C), the public responded quickly. This huge campaign resulted in over 98 percent of eligible citizens participating in voucher privatization.

The privatization funds obtained over 70 percent of all available vouchers. Although there were about 400 IPFs, the seven largest obtained 46 percent of all vouchers distributed on the market. Each bank created several IPFs, and among the largest investors in that sense were Česká spořitelna, Investiční banka (later Investiční a poštovní banka, IPB) and

Komerční banka (the three largest banks). The rules of compulsory distribution of the IPFs' portfolios resulted in at least one of these giant investors being present in every privatized firm. Therefore the concentration of ownership became a serious issue. Except for the Harvard Investment Group, all the other top six funds were associated with Czech (and Slovak) financial institutions. Nevertheless, the banks were prevented from investing in their own shares. However, it must indeed be asserted that the funds were not controlled by transparent hierarchical relations but by nontransparent cross-ownership relations creating a special kind of network or even a web (see Mejstřík, 1997).

According to the Law on Investment Companies, an investment fund could not invest more than 10 percent of its assets in the same company. In addition, an investment fund could not own more than 20 percent of the shares of one company. This limit was lowered to 11 percent in July 1998. According to the former Minister of Finance, Ivan Pilip, this was in accordance with governmental policy to shift the IPFs to the position of portfolio investors not playing the role of active monitors of companies.

The legal framework specified that banks were allowed to own shares of companies. However, their direct representation was not very frequent. They were much more preoccupied with their role as creditors and they used their influence through the IPFs funded by bank-sponsored investment companies. Banks could also own shares of their IPFs. They could acquire these shares from original individual shareholders that invested their vouchers in IPFs. It is estimated that more than one-third of IPF shareholders sold their shares by 1995 (OECD, 1996). It is often supposed that banks used their influence in IPFs not to govern and monitor companies, but to gather information for their creditor activities.

In 1996 some IPFs decided to transform themselves into holding companies due to worries about forthcoming stringent legislation which would prevent such a transformation. Although the main aim of the IPFs was to escape regulation and supervision, it can be argued that this step contributed to ownership concentration since the limits diversifying the portfolios of IPFs did not apply to the holding companies. On the other hand, it was a clear violation of small shareholders' rights, completely lost in the transformed IPFs, which were founded as joint-stock companies from the legal point of view. Moreover, this step together with nontransparent transactions on the capital market destroyed the credibility of the Czech capital market and questioned the credibility of privatization itself. The legal structure of investment funds is very important in order to protect investors' money. However, the legal framework enabled operations that were in fact stealing the investors' money. This insecurity is a warning legacy and endangers the further development of the Czech economy.

The regulatory framework of Czech capital markets in the post-voucher period was rather light in order to facilitate and speed up the process of secondary trading that would lead to the concentration of ownership rights. Secondary trading was intensive and eventually led to concentrated ownership structure. However, this concentration was achieved with heavy losses, including the loss of credibility of the capital market itself since the deals were often nontransparent ("over-the-counter" sales) with possible price manipulation. [2]

As Table 5.2 indicates, real concentration ownership was the result of secondary trading. Owners owning over 30 percent are most probably strategic investors or holding companies since IPFs and mutual funds cannot own over 20 percent of shares. However, this regulation may be bypassed by the diverse holding of several funds within one financial group. Most significant is the group of companies having a majority owner (over 50 percent), which rose from 1 percent in 1993 to 38 percent in 1997. However, it should be noted that a much smaller percentage of shares can usually assure an actual majority in voting at a general meeting of shareholders. (For detailed analysis see Mejstřík, 1999.)

5.3   The outcomes of privatization in the context of corporate control and firm strategies

Voucher privatization proved to be successful as a means of fast transfer of state property into "private hands," but its results in general are much less clear. It was successful in the sense that voucher privatization did not impose further debts on the corporations as would have happened in the case of companies privatized by management buyouts (MBOs) or employee

Table 5.2   Ownership concentration in listed firms (%)

Largest owner's share	Over 50	30–50	10–30	5–10	Under 5
Czech Republic					
1993	1	6	85	6	2
1994	4	8	73	12	3
1995	10	16	62	9	3
1996	23	27	43	5	2
1997	38	35	22	4	1
France	55	21	16	5	2
Germany	66	14	9	7	5
Sweden	42	31	12	11	4
UK	5	29	27	30	9
Japan	5	15	25	30	25
US	9	29	10	29	23

Source: Benn Steil, 1996. Quoted in The European Equity Markets, Aspekt. In *Czech Republic: Capital Market Review*, World Bank Country Study (Washington, DC: World Bank, 1999), 48.

buyouts (EBOs). The expectation was, as already mentioned, that the owners would restructure the companies. In a broader sense it was the interplay of new owners, bankruptcy law, a transparent and functional stock market, and the punishment of debtors that would eventually force the restructuring. The observed results differ from the government expectations in fact. Indebtedness increased and virtually no bankruptcies occurred.

One of the problems of privatization was that after the end of the voucher method some IPFs expressed their clear intention not to take part in corporate governance. They were concerned merely with maintaining their portfolios. Therefore, their main activities were trading on the capital markets and especially over-the-counter deals. They suggested that they were not capable of taking a more interventionist approach with respect to the firms that they eventually privatized.

A further drawback of the noninterventionist approach was that the incumbent managements were left in place and there were no procedures set up to remove inefficient staff and replace them with more competent professionals. (For more concise evaluation of mass privatization see Gatsios, 1996.)

The lack of an interventionist approach of the IPFs caused a lack of efficient pressure on management. Managers did not feel obliged to undertake extraordinary efforts toward restructuring, since the IPFs and banks lacked sufficient commitment to change the status quo. There were two more factors that contributed to the behavior of firms. Firstly, due to the existing legislation, virtually no bankruptcies took place. Secondly, debtors were not being punished. These facts greatly contributed to the increasing moral hazard that managers faced. It is difficult to find out how much the designers of voucher privatization counted on such a huge participation of the IPFs. However, the result was that almost overnight the managers of the IPFs owned a great number of the privatized assets without investing any cash except, of course, the money invested into advertising activities in order to persuade DIKs to invest in that particular fund.

Thus voucher privatization brought about serious problems. The fact that the majority of trading took place outside the capital markets (stock exchange, RM-System) reduced credibility for foreign investors and led to suspicions of deceiving small shareholders. In addition, there was the issue of execution of property rights of the state in both SOEs and partly privatized firms. The initial idea was that the state should not be involved in the execution of its property rights, because in any case it was not capable of such activity. Privatization was expected to be so rapid that the state would not need to engage in the execution of its property rights. Indeed, although privatization in the Czech Republic was relatively fast, in the majority of cases it was not fast enough (and could not have been so) to make the execution of property rights by the state completely unnecessary. Therefore, the state has had to care for its assets, and in fact did so in a nonsystematic way.

It is to be stressed that since the beginning of the privatization process, the Czech Parliament publicly proclaimed no interest in taking care of state assets. Also, little interest was shown in the privatization process itself. Although the Large-Scale Privatization Law was passed, it only named the firms to be privatized, but did not put any guidelines on the procedures. This gave great freedom to the government. The government took up this opportunity and privatized with the highest possible speed, where it decided to do so. This was not the case with banks and some large enterprises, utilities, and so on. As a result, rapid institutional changes in some segments of the economy were not backed by adequate changes in other segments.

The ethical aspects of privatization have been very important. Up until the very last moment the government neglected violations of the privatization laws. In many cases the new owners did not pay the NPF for the privatized property and disposed of that property. Furthermore, many contracts without sanctions against nonpayers were signed. This was the price to be paid for speed.

In the second half of the 1990s we witnessed the so-called tunneling of privatized firms. Major shareholders moved the healthy parts of the companies and their assets to existing or newly created firms, thus leaving just an empty shell of a company for the other shareholders. These and similar processes were carried out right on the edge of the law. The state was not able to make sufficient moves immediately to prevent such processes. So the overall result was serious discrediting of privatization and the stock market in the eyes of the general public. Moreover, this factor was one of the strongest sources of distortion of firm strategies. If one can make money by tunneling, others will also deviate strategically toward "short-termism."

Thus, a high moral hazard was involved in the whole process. Since the most frequent method of privatization was free transfers or MBOs covered by privatized assets, the new owners were obviously less risk-averse than if they had acquired their property for cash. It would be naïve to believe that "owner" means the same thing in all circumstances, especially regarding the environment of badly shaped and incomplete contracts.

Moreover, there is a competing explanation for the adoption of voucher privatization. The stated goal of ensuring economic efficiency by transferring the property to private hands should be analyzed within the political timing of the program. The first round of voucher privatization started in the week of parliamentary elections in 1992. Thus the government's interest in the voucher method might also have been of a political nature.

On the other hand, voucher privatization was not the most important method of privatization of large companies. These were mostly privatized in the "Czech way" (including, for example, Poldi Kladno, Škoda Plzeň, Chemapol Group, ČKD Holding). The companies (or the decisive shares) were sold to small managerial companies (owned completely by Czech managers) with very small equity capital, thus merely using bank loans without foreign capital. Thus, further debts were imposed on the companies. Not only were there no finances for crucially needed restructuring, but not even just for the operation of the companies. Moreover, it is obvious that the "new" owners favored their own personal interest, which was in contrast with improving the financial situation of the privatized companies. Thus, again, the moral hazard was enormous. This caused the gradual deterioration of the quality of companies, resulting in a situation where formerly would-be interested foreign investors no longer had an interest in investing. Moreover, the role of the capital market as a monitor of companies completely failed, the managers-owners having the decisive voice over a company were not replaceable in face of the pressure of declining share value. The only factor that could force them out was in fact the virtual bankruptcy of the company. The agony was prolonged by the non-private banks, which chose to support such companies until the very last moment. Thus, the "test by recession" multiplied the transaction costs for the replacement of inefficient management.

The sentiment expressed by the opposition and government benches against selling the "family silver"[3] to foreigners, also contributed to the adoption of this privatization method. On the other hand, in smaller companies this method of privatization was often successful and brought about the stable development of enterprises. However, the dream of large powerful firms that would be domestically owned aggravated the problems of the economy and banks in particular. Again, we are faced with the overestimation of the abilities and moral qualities of domestic managers of large enterprises and banks.

One of the elements contributing to the detrimental effects was the uncontrolled intention of expansion. Companies often made large acquisitions of firms, not only in their own sector but also well outside their industry, almost always financed by credits. Thus the credit burden exceeded the potential of the companies to pay back. The question why banks provided such credits can be answered partially by political imperatives: the state would not let the largest enterprises fail because of the necessity to maintain social peace (too big to fail phenomena). Therefore, the largest enterprises seemed very good clients to the banks. In addition, there were direct political pressures on banks' management to provide further credits to these companies. As soon as this kind of financing was reduced the companies started to lack operational capital. Once again, it should be stressed that the loans were in general not used for the much more urgent task of restructuring, but for further expansion (and/or further acquisitions). We can hypothesize about the incentives behind the fact that bigger firms enjoy a better negotiating position with the state when subsidies or risk of failure are involved.

However, it is difficult to evaluate the results of privatization in terms of corporate governance and restructuring. It is almost impossible to compare the initial differences among enterprises before the privatization process had started. Moreover, it is obvious that foreign investors were interested in the best companies having the most favorable potential for development. Often the investors were even supported by the state, as in the case of Škoda Auto Mladá Boleslav or Czech Telecom (state guarantees of a different nature and the revenues from its privatization did not go to the NPF as usual but to Czech Telecom itself). Thus the privatization method and resulting corporate governance are not the only factors that can explain the difference among the companies.

Although the ownership issue is just one of the factors influencing restructuring and strategic firm behavior it is the most important one. It shapes, together with the labor market (and its regulations), financial constraints and finance availability, and the corporate code (together with bankruptcy law), the very basic framework and boundaries of firm behavior.

The most serious implication of the privatization process is that the state remained the most important large owner of firms (although indirect) through the banks that had not been completely privatized to the end of the 1990s. In spite of the fact that state ownership was three steps removed (the state owning shares in banks, banks owning their privatization funds, IPFs having shares in the privatized firms), the state had its shares in virtually every firm privatized by a project including the voucher privatization method! However, it is to be stated that today the number of firms with total direct state ownership is already insignificant. It can be argued that many of the problems were caused by extended state ownership, or at least, that state ownership contributed to that development. Even though state ownership was indirect, the managers and owners, and all other stakeholders, considered it as an important factor in their decision-making (state umbrella).

5.4   Problems and dynamics of the Czech banking sector restructuring

The crucial problem of mass privatization schemes is to find a concerned strategic owner. Banks can play a key role in this search. Even though not allowed or able, for example for capacity reasons, to become strategic investors, they can intermediate in finding such an investor. In this way they can contribute to more effective corporate governance of enterprises. Banks should be considered as one of the main actors of restructuring since only they, besides managers, have access to insider information through their existing credit relations. Moreover, it is they who must impose tight budget constraints on enterprises. However, to fulfill these crucially important tasks the economy needs an effective banking sector.

Privatization of the main Czech banks has been a question of ideology. In the first period of transformation the original justification for retaining large stakes in banks was for the state to provide a minimum degree of economic stability (Pistor and Turkewitz, 1996: 227). At later stages it can be identified as a classical example of a lock-in mechanism of the state caused by particular interests (resistance against privatization in the banking sector as well as on the side of the state). Although the parties of the political right subsequently recognized the importance of rapid privatization, not many steps in this direction were actually taken while they formed the government. The absence of privatization in the banking sector was caused by the intention of the government to exercise a type of industrial policy through the bank ownership of many companies. Even as late as November 1998, Václav Klaus publicly stated that the nonprivatization of banks was intentional in order to assure credit for companies. He did not mention that this credit was in fact a subsidy for nominally private enterprises. Thus, we can identify the incentives behind the existence of a so-called "banking socialism." This "transformation strategy" resulted in an accumulation of bad debts in portfolios of all large banks and at the same time the important pressure on enterprises to restructure was reduced. On the other hand, the Social Democratic Party, although it agreed that privatization should proceed, claimed, especially during its political campaign, that it should not be rapid in order to allow the state to prepare it properly and thus receive larger revenues! During the 1997–99 recession, there was a legitimate argument that the banks would be sold most easily and with the largest revenue to the state budget if they were sold when the economy reached an expansionary phase. But it is obvious that the longer the period of negative growth in the Czech economy, the more serious the problems of the banks would become. The large number of companies having serious difficulties worsened the balance sheets of banks by turning credit into bad credit. This, of course, also decreased the potential sale price of banks to be privatized. In other words, the value of the Czech banks rapidly decreased, and the state had to clear their portfolios through its own Consolidation Bank (today's Consolidation Agency), as it did in many cases. Thus, it was the taxpayer who paid for delayed privatization, and the burden of taxation contributed to the slowing of economic recovery.

To sum up, it was not only the Social Democrats who hindered the process of bank privatization. The Klaus government intentionally nonprivatized, although proclaiming a completely different ideology. This was obvious when Tošovský's government, between the Klaus and Social Democrat administrations, took over and in a very short time undertook significant steps toward initiating serious bank privatization. It is a great example of how political (here we could even say populist) interests may have hindered the process of systemic change, and the costs to be paid are extremely high. The political elites (on both sides of the political spectrum) were not able to accept responsibility for this important segment of systemic change, and it had to be the recession that caused the serious fall of the value of the "family silver" and thus forced the state to act. The story of large enterprises privatized in the "Czech way" is a good analogy. We can talk about the so-called test by recession.

However, the reasons why banks favored providing credit to large enterprises might be more complicated than pure political pressures. As Gatsios argues, they too might have considered their debtors to be too big to fail and thus they would eventually have to be rescued by the state. This consequently created an interlocking network of banks and large enterprises, which indeed might have been too big to fail and thus the liquidity had to be redistributed from viable to unviable firms.

At the same time, the old management often overestimated the financial institution that it managed as well as overestimating its own skills. However, it was also the state that overestimated the banks' capacity, or maybe ill defined the banking problem. This could explain the fact that, although having the majority of shares, the state did not in many cases replace the management of ill-functioning banks.

An important role of the banks is the role of monitors of enterprises in the corporate governance framework. Banks play an important part in the Czech corporate governance setup, since they are the largest owners of privatized companies. Thus, in a situation where the banks were not private, they were not pushed to exercise their ownership rights in companies. Therefore, banks did not fulfill their roles of monitors to whom the managements of companies would be accountable. Hence the pressure to carry out painful steps of restructuring was insufficient.

As far as the monitoring functions of banks are concerned, we could broaden Diamond's argument (Diamond, 1996) that due to the costs of monitoring and enforcement of credit contracts it is better to use an intermediary for investing. This argument is obviously valid for banks as well as direct investors in companies (often through their investment funds), that is when intermediating in the investments of small investors.

However, the problem has one more layer, that of "who monitors the monitor." Diamond argues that it is the threat of bankruptcy and liquidation that makes the monitors act responsibly; however, this is not sufficient in an economy where bankruptcies are very inefficient, capital markets can hardly provide reliable data, and the monitors are owned in a decisive way by the state.

Moreover, to complete the privatization of banks it is important to cut off the banks from direct political influence. It was necessary to stop "banking socialism," in which the managers of banks are pushed by government (since they could be recalled by the majority owner) to provide credit to larger enterprises for purely political reasons. Thus the behavior of two main Czech banks, Česká spořitelna and Komerční banka, was very different from the conduct of the earlier privatized Živnostenská banka, which was much more cautious in providing credit and thus did not experience the first recession so painfully. Since the major banks were partially privatized in the first stage of privatization, by putting the pressure on banks to finance nonfeasible projects and provide credits to nonrestructured enterprises, the state was actually stealing from other shareholders.

To sum up, at least till the end of the 1990s the role of banks as economic actors in the Czech economy had been distorted, having a state umbrella for their inefficient lending activities on the one hand, and being inclined to follow political pressures on the other. Today when all major banks are in private (and foreign) hands the circumstances are much more favorable for finishing restructuring. However, it should be stated that the privatization of banks, although necessary, has not cured all the problems of the Czech economy. One of them has been the question of actual relations among formal actors of corporate governance in the exact sense of the notion.

5.5 Legal framework vis-à-vis corporate governance in practice

The most important legal form from the perspective of privatization and corporate governance is the joint-stock company (corporation). The Czech Commercial Code defines the structure of the statutory bodies of the joint-stock company and their interrelations as follows. There are three statutory organs of a joint-stock company: the board of directors (*Představenstvo*), supervisory board (*Dozorčí rada*), and the general meeting of shareholders (*Valná hromada*). The board of directors and supervisory board are elected by the general meeting of shareholders, which must meet at least once per year. The general meeting of shareholders also recalls both boards. Alternatively, there exists a possibility closer to the German system, that is that the general meeting elects the supervisory board and the supervisory board elects the board of directors. However, this arrangement is rather rare in practice. No person can serve on both boards at the same time, and the members of boards are subject to special conflict-of-interest provisions.

The board of directors then elects and recalls its chairperson (*Předseda představenstva*) who is the top official of the corporation. According to the Commercial Code, the board of directors is the main executive body of the corporation that directs the company's activities and acts on its behalf, except for the functions defined in the Commercial Code that are reserved for the general meeting.

However, besides the formal structures (board of directors, supervisory board, general assembly), Czech companies have management consisting of a general manager (*Generální ředitel*) and his/her deputies responsible for particular areas, such as finance, marketing, production, and so on. These managers have everyday control over the company. The general manager (who partly corresponds to the CEO) and other top managers are appointed by the board of directors. In practice the general manager has often been appointed as a member or chairperson of the board of directors. Other members of the board are usually representatives of other stakeholders such as banks, IPFs, other top managers, and external experts.

The supervisory board has, in most cases, a similar structure to that of the board of directors, that is, it also includes representatives of management, owners, banks, and so on. The Commercial Code requires that at least one-third of members of supervisory boards are representatives of employees. In reality, those employee representatives are often managers (even top managers). According to the Commercial Code, the supervisory board consists of at least three members. This is often the size of supervisory board in reality. The board of directors usually has at least twice as many members.

The executive management of a company has an information monopoly over the company. Therefore, the executive management has a greater chance to persuade the board to accept its proposals. Thus, it can be stated that the management retained its superior position in corporate governance in the Czech Republic. This seems to be reality even vis-à-vis important actors such as owners, employees, creditors, customers, and so on. This applied especially to companies privatized by the voucher method before the concentration of ownership reached its current level. On the one hand, the influence of management increased after privatization. On the other, the influence of banks increased as well, as they acquired a twofold role in the companies. Firstly, they retained the role of main creditors. Secondly, they became the owners of privatized companies (through IPFs). So some analysts refer to this development as a managerial and banking revolution (Mertlík, 1997: 53).

The voucher privatization method created dispersed ownership and allowed management to retain control over the companies' assets. Thus, in a sense, we can talk about managerial continuity, where the plan of the command economy was to a certain extent replaced by the pressure of banks performed especially through their role as the sole providers of credits. This continuity of strong position or revolution on the other hand was basically possible because of a complete lack of any actors that would take over the role of real concerned owners, which was also the case of companies privatized in the "Czech way."

At the same time there is a striking similarity between Mlčoch's upside-down pyramid, where the management of enterprises in a planned economy had an information monopoly and thus were the most important actors, and the situation after privatization. However, this information asymmetry exists everywhere, including advanced economies, but the problem is the unity of actors having a stake in the enterprise. This means that the most important aspect for the effective functioning of the monitoring system is the existence of a unity of interests of management and IPFs and/or banks as the owners of enterprises. The actual setup of corporate governance should help to resolve this agency conflict. In contrast, the result is a system of low transparency and accountability.

While the board of directors is supposed to be the main controlling body of the company, the Czech Commercial Code does not use any term such as "management" ... However, these powers are often moved to the top managers, who do not have to be the members of the board of directors. It is common practice that the statutes of the company define the top management as the superior controlling body that manages the company in accordance with the formal decision-making process such as general meeting, voting procedures, and so on.

In this setup the board of directors takes on rather the role of a supervisory board, while the supervisory board itself becomes a redundant body, sometimes called a "declining institution" or "useless body" (Coffee, 1996). Often the important issues of the company are not discussed by the supervisory board because of the legally grounded presence of employee representatives. On the other hand, the supervisory board serves as an important channel of insider information about the company.

External members of the board of directors usually cannot meet often. They are typically rather passive. Yet, the Commercial Code requires the members of the board of directors to carry out everyday management. Thus, the widespread practice of selecting the board members from outsiders of the company may even cause a conflict with the law. The state institutions and agencies use this practice as well. The lack of an active approach of the members of the board of directors can be explained by the reluctance to undertake any risk. Indeed, the external members of boards, being involved in many other activities, are not only unable to carry out day-to-day control over management, but also are reluctant to contribute to strategy building in the company (Mertlík, 1997: 55).

5.6   Managers, decision-making, and firm strategies in a distorted environment

As Lubomír Mlčoch stated, in the centrally planned economy managers played a very important role in the game with political authorities (Mlčoch, 1992), which is often underestimated. Their power even increased in the preprivatization period when only the top manager had to be approved by the sector ministry, but all other decisions, including those on personnel matters, depended on the top manager. In order to reduce many potential losses caused by the fact that managers had rights as owners, the Act 92/1991 was approved, which froze the momentary state of affairs in the

SOEs. Thus, all larger transactions such as mergers, joint ventures and sales of real estate were not allowed from summer 1991 until the company was privatized. The managers had the most favorable position in the privatization itself, and as analyzed above, they were usually able to maintain their control over a formally privatized enterprise.

However, one should distinguish ambiguous cases of privatization among large and extra large companies (both voucher and "Czech way" MBO privatization), from numerous quite positive cases of small and medium SOEs (of roughly 50–1000 employees), and sometimes even larger ones. The latter were not necessarily the subject of interlocking ownership, political pressures, or tunneling. Their managers were typically interested in survival, and managed to be relatively effective. The point of view of managers of relatively good enterprises on their day-to-day practice and problems may help to explain the dynamics of the Czech economy.[4]

Typically the top managers have been affiliated with their companies for a long period of time. They often started in lower managerial posts and were promoted to higher ones, sometimes having spent some time either in a ministry or some other state institution. Thus, the managers have little or no foreign management experience and retain certain personal links with the structures of the state.

Among manager motivation factors, it is possible to include the feeling of power, the chance to manage people, a feeling of being the savior of a company, and last but not least, high financial remuneration. The other important factor is a chance to be able to take a leading part in the systemic changes of transformation, to influence the process. They want their company to be comparable to similar companies in the world and the best possible. They claim that the image of a stable well-run company attractive for investors is an important goal for them. Hence, according to themselves they managed to find a unity of interests of their own and those of the company, and to identify themselves well with the company. Still, reality often differs, considering that one-shot game rent-seeking has been a widespread strategy.

Nevertheless, all examined cases have undergone a substantial restructuring of their internal organizational structure. The structures of relatively independent business units have been applied in many larger companies. The changes encompassed increasing stress on the change of corporate culture, which included a customer-oriented approach. Companies have reduced the absolute number of employees and at the same time changed the structure of the employed labor force toward employees with higher education. The clear focus on quality has also been quite apparent; some companies have managed to acquire certification such as ISO 9002. In addition, companies were often getting rid of formerly accumulated overcapacity, particularly through the sale of unused real estate. These have been major lines of restructuring strategies of relatively successful enterprises.

They did not suffer serious financial problems, which was contrary to the vast part of the economy (where we can talk about deep undercapitalization). Thus, they have been able to pay for goods and services provided, as well as to repay credit on time. However, as was stated, this is quite exceptional in the Czech economy as a whole.

For many companies the main source of uncertainty was the state, with no clear rules for regulation (pricing in still regulated sectors such as gas and electricity distribution). Thus, not knowing the further steps of the government, managers were quite limited in decision-making about further development. The exchange rate volatility was also an important source of uncertainty. It is obvious that in an environment of weak exercising of ownership rights, the performance of the company depends to a large extent on the abilities and moral features of managers. Public control, although sometimes considered, has severely limited power. The same is true about bottom-up control by worker representation. In general, trade unions do not have any direct influence on the decision-making in the company except for some incidental actions in the mining industry. On the other hand, in companies where the union leader has managed to become a member of the supervisory board their role is much stronger.

However, unions have some impact through the Tripartite Commission. They conclude sector-wide collective agreements, which are mandatory for all companies in the sector. There are about 30 such agreements in the country. These collective agreements include the increasing of wages, which is usually stated as an absolute figure, for example 5–7 percent, and does not reflect inflation nor is it dependent on a real increase in productivity. The Ministry of Labor and Social Affairs can withdraw a particular company from such an agreement. The decision is based on current conditions in the company. This practice may have a very negative influence on the economic system.

In the eyes of the managers interviewed, the Czech economic environment was undoubtedly market oriented and markets are the main coordination mechanisms. However, the state often intervened in private economic conduct in a nonsystemic way, and major economic relations were still quite linked to the political arena. The state sometimes intervened directly, not necessarily through the semistate banks. One of the main problems felt by managers was the inefficiency of bankruptcies, which distorted their relations with insolvent contractors. In addition, managers were very skeptical about the quality and efficiency of the Czech court system. Managers also see the need for further liberalization of prices, in particular utilities (Czech Telecom, CEZ) and rents.

In more practical terms, an incomplete institutional environment imposes financial limits of development on firms. The main sources of financing for investment activities of companies are bank loans. These were directed mainly to large and extra large companies. The capital market, with a few exceptions, does not serve as a mechanism providing any financial sources. In that situation, smaller enterprises with no political significance have to rely on their own resources, or on relatively expensive and very scarce credit. A kind of "low financial ceiling" for development is precisely the way through which smaller enterprises (both privatized and genuine private) pay the cost of delayed reforms and subsidies to large conglomerates with interlocked ownership. Even relatively successful firms might have been constrained in their market expansion by the scarcity of capital.

5.7   Conclusion: actors in corporate governance and the question of restructuring

The Czech governments adopted the so-called bottom-up concept of restructuring. Thus the state relied on improving competition and lifting the barriers to entry, including the liberalization of foreign trade. At the same time, the state decided not to intervene directly in the restructuring of enterprises. However, it directly or indirectly provided capital to selected corporations, provoking and maintaining cross-ownership structures with significant state involvement, which was in fact a hidden intervention in restructuring policy leading to a large degree to failure. The results in the overall economy structure were an even stronger position of heavy industry.

The banks played a very special role in the transformation process. Their main interests were to keep and increase their profits by maintaining good clients and reducing the impact of bad credit developed before and throughout the process of transformation. With regard to the role of banks as remote owners of enterprises via "their" IPFs, it seems that banks used these opportunities more for their credit business than in order to run the enterprises efficiently.

The IPFs' main interest shortly after the privatization process had been completed, was to obtain enough cash to be able to fulfill their promises to buy back shares from their shareholders since the latter, in general, favored liquidity over long-term investments into funds. This is applicable to sole individual investors in voucher privatization, where it is assumed that the vast majority have already sold their shares. Further, IPFs wanted to clean their portfolios. These new actors on the scene were often not interested in controlling companies.

The position of management in restructuring seems to be of highest importance. It can be observed that management acted spontaneously. In the first stage of privatization management decided on a purely economic basis whether to privatize the company by MBO or use some other privatization method. In case MBO was not feasible, usually due to high interest on credits, management opted either for finding a strategic foreign partner or for the voucher privatization method. However, MBOs were quite rare since their political acceptance was rather low. In the case of the voucher method, management expected that the dispersed ownership structure would create inefficient corporate control and thus the management would keep its position, which was actually its main goal in every case.

To sum up, except for companies having a majority foreign owner or smaller companies privatized as MBOs, the results of power games among the interests of different actors and stakeholders were not very favorable for the real restructuring of enterprises. Theoretically, in the MBOs the division between ownership and management does not really exist and thus the restructuring is in the best interests of managers. However, we witnessed a completely different development in the larger companies privatized in the "Czech way," offering large assets to small managerial corporations with practically no capital and no related risks. In other words, the actors of restructuring were missing. The story of foreign direct sales is somewhat different. Foreign investors were able to supply their new ventures with technical and managerial expertise and a clear system of corporate governance. They often brought a net investment enabling restructuring.

In general, the shareholders were in favor of nonrestructuring or "restructuring as little as possible." Since considerable downsizing is an important part of restructuring, it is obvious that employees as one of a group of stakeholders would not support restructuring. A similar interest can be identified with the policy of the government, which would not support restructuring because of the immediately associated social costs. At the same time the banks, having the potential loss of clients in mind, preferred to keep the status quo than to enforce restructuring. This was often accompanied by pressures from the largest bank owner – the state – to keep many companies afloat. Considering supplier–producer relations, suppliers were not often interested in their partners' restructuring, because it could bring about a potential loss of customers or a need to restructure themselves. Moreover, as already stated, IPFs were more interested in their portfolios than in the conduct of companies in which they owned shares. The overall strategy could thus be described as short-termism at least till the moment when the majority of banks were privatized.

Thus each actor behaving rationally did not positively contribute to restructuring. If we employ a broader notion of corporate governance to identify the major actors of firm strategies and their motivations, we see a lack of actors interested in real restructuring, except for some goodwill managers. In other words, the institutionally grounded pressure toward restructuring produced by the key actors on managers was not strong.

One of the most important findings is that new private owners do not often act as concerned owners according to theory. This could be called "the real owner problem." Hence, the quality of privatization is the most important factor influencing corporate governance and enterprise restructuring. As a result of the Czech privatization scheme, new owners were often not capable of, and not really interested in, restructuring newly acquired firms. The rational behavior of the owners was based on taking advantage of temporary, and to quote Mejstřík, unrepeatable opportunities in the environment of imperfect regulation and incomplete contracts.

When this kind of "successful rent-seeking," often quasi-legal in nature, becomes a norm in the economic system, it will generate the strongest negative incentive for other companies to reevaluate their positive long-run strategies in the framework of "learning by watching."

The lack of actors interested in firm restructuring influenced the state – where only partial restructuring has taken place – but not in the necessary scope and quality. In other words, the results of power games played among stakeholders did not produce efficient corporate governance, and thus the results of privatization differ from those driven from theory. That is why systemic change is far from being completed and some further institutional steps need to be identified.

However, there are striking differences among enterprises. For example, in general the enterprises privatized by majority foreign owners have proceeded the farthest on the road of restructuring. Whereas many large, even core companies, either not privatized or privatized via the "Czech way," demonstrated the least success and often ended up being tunneled by their quasi-owners. The political background contributed to such results.

The inadequate protection of minority shareholders' rights seems to be one of the main deficiencies of the privatization process vis-à-vis its real outcome for the economy. Thus the discredited capital markets did not play any further significant role in the Czech economy.

Although the privatization of banks has been virtually completed, there is still a lot of room for improvement. Making the bankruptcy mechanism effective is a crucial step. The capacity of banks to handle the problem of debtors by increasing the rights of creditors in the Czech economy must be enhanced. In addition, improving the efficiency of the courts will enable business disputes to be solved faster and thus will contribute to the improvement of business morale. In addition, liberalization of still regulated prices will decrease the distortion in the markets.

Furthermore, the state should promote strategic investors to take on their roles. One step already undertaken was the approved measures for support of foreign direct investments including tax holidays for such companies. The foreign investors will also bring capital and, last but not least, the professional expertise so much needed for the restructuring of Czech companies. Recent developments seem to be encouraging. The level of foreign investment has increased, which has contributed to the recovery of the Czech economy. However, it is obvious that further reforms toward complete institutional settings for sound corporate governance depend, to the largest extent, on the political will to do so.

Notes

1. Data used in this research come from various sources. Along with published literature, Pavel Mertlík generously provided his data gathered for the Czech part of the international research project *Enterprise Restructuring at Different Stages of Ownership Transformation: the Czech Republic and Poland,* which was supported by the "Action for Cooperation in Economics" (ACE) program of the European Commission (a part of the Phare program, research grant No. 92-0223-R). The sample consisted of ten medium-size enterprises (between 500 and 1000 employees) in food-processing and textile and garment industries. Of course, the sample is not representative for the whole population of enterprises (not even for sectors). Nevertheless, more general conclusions might be drawn from those case studies, because the mode of privatization was more or less the same in all other parts of Czech industry.
2. During the first period after privatization the majority of stock deals were conducted between the two parties at the counter. The dealers did not have an obligation to publish the price on which they agreed.
3. For rational and as well irrational reasons, at the beginning of the transformation process the Czech public did not support sales of "family silver," that is old well-established mostly manufacturing firms such as for example Skoda Plzen, to foreign investors.
4. In addition, in order to obtain data on opinions of top managers of positive cases (companies with no serious financial problems), four in-depth interviews with CEOs of selected larger Czech companies (Czech Telecom a. s., Středočeská plynárenská a. s., Pražská energetická a. s., and IPS Holding a. s.) were conducted by the author in 1999 solely for the purposes of this research. The data obtained are the main source of information for this section.

6
Poland: Worker-driven Transformation to Capitalism?

Michał Federowicz

6.1 Introduction: corporate governance, a case of deep institutional change

Corporate governance is an important part of the economic system. It links micro-level performance with the economic institutions of the most important segments of political economy: finance, and industrial relations. The problem of corporate governance begins with a distribution and delegation of property rights in a corporation, but it goes beyond the classic "agency problem" which points only to the relations between owners (investors) and managers. Other actors involved may also contribute to the governance structure. Property relations are not the only factors that affect and constrain strategic decision-making. Each country builds up its own constellation of formal and informal rules of the game, and types of involved actors.

Beside the complexity of rules, country-specific formal institutions, and distribution of power, the issue of emerging structures of corporate governance after a period of communist-type economy (party–state-controlled economy), raises additional problems. In general, these problems originate in a deep and quite radical institutional change in the political and economic spheres, where the old and new institutions mutually interfere, often provoking high uncertainty for the actors participating in the game. Corporate governance is affected by more than an unclear combination of old-transformed, new, and new-distorted institutions. It is also under the pressure of new owners, and old and new managers, who may perform surprisingly different roles than those usually assumed by governance theories. The same confusion arises from the behavior of creditors and other financial institutions. Thus, what is beyond the agency problem in countries rebuilding capitalist relations after a period of planned economy is not only a question of a more inclusive definition that would encompass more than two actors of decision-making: managers and owners. It is also a need for a broader analytical framework that could help to interpret atypical and sometimes surprising individual strategies. These strategies are provoked by a nontransparent and unstable combination of institutions in a period of deep change.

When looking at emerging corporate governance during the past 12 years in these countries, two major factors were key for both the institutional arrangements and the roles performed by the actors. First is the process of rapid capital formation after a period of "undercapitalized" economy, and second is the unprecedented impact of the state on the process of capital formation. Privatization created the main context for the process of capital formation, but the existence of genuine growth in the private sector was essential. Besides privatization and the inner processes of capital formation, foreign direct investments, often combined with privatization, strongly intervened in corporate governance, not necessarily through the transfer of home country arrangements, but by trying to straighten out the processes of the creation of laws and enforcement. Without the significant contribution of external agents, privatization based on domestic actors, irrespective of their being insiders or outsiders, often provoked irregular individual strategies, and a formal institutional setting insufficient to constrain or consequently predict such strategies. The second factor that shaped the specific post-communist combination of institutions and actors comes from the deep involvement of the state in all stages of capital formation. It is not so much a direct legacy of the former system, where the state was present in the majority of microeconomic decisions. In the Polish case for instance, this general attitude was relatively easy to remove. Of much more significance is the state's major role in setting formal institutions. In practice, this process is subject to strong interest group pressure. But perhaps the most notable aspect of the state's dominant role is visible in the privatization itself and in the capital flows from public funds to the newly formed private capital.

Thus, rapid capital formation and the deep involvement of a weak state are the most specific features of the emerging systems of corporate governance, and more generally, of the emerging capitalist relations after communism. This environment may distort the formally existing incentive structures of all parties to the game, including foreign investors. However, in time this changing environment may improve together with the progress of transformation, despite being damaging in its initial stage. The nature and actors of such dynamics are the focus of this chapter which explores the Polish case. Corporate governance change is just a part of a broader process of deep institutional transformation.

One of the theses on the dynamics of corporate governance change in the Polish economy is that in spite of a legal framework universally applied to the whole economy, there are different outcomes in terms of the dominating governance structure in different sectors of the economy. This segmentation is mainly the result of different types of interactions between the actors actively participating in the process of privatization.

In more general terms, and this is the second thesis, this segmentation is an outcome of the institutional arrangements of the final stage of the previous system, and of the initial period of deep transformation that followed after 1989. Notably, the previously existing institutions of worker representation played an unexpectedly important role in privatization. They did it in an organized way, which was unique for Poland among other economies in the region. Specifically, given the unparalleled strong position of worker councils and the support from trade unions at the grass roots level, labor was able to enter the game for corporate control in the most sensitive period of transformation. Yet, worker representation, and specifically worker councils, did not manifest itself with equal strength across the various segments of the economy, contributing to the differentiation of the outcome.

Worker councils were not the only collective actor that intervened in the emerging governance structures, and they were definitely not the most powerful. In general, worker councils only moderated the strong impact of the managerial networks and the state. However, they were embedded strongly enough at enterprise level to generate an "inside market" for corporate control. Worker councils turned out to be quite influential in those enterprises where outside investors were weak or absent. They significantly reduced or modified the power of previous managerial networks. However, they did not have an equally strong impact across all segments of the economy. Worker councils were sometimes passive, or simply not part of the game.

The third thesis of crucial importance for the understanding of institutional change in Poland is that in spite of the impact of initially influential actors and institutions, the nature of the emerging system depends on the capacity of concrete institutions and types of actors to reproduce themselves in a changing environment. In this context, the question of the nature and reproduction of the managerial networks themselves is quite important, central to the development of all countries in the region.

This chapter will search for explanations of the dynamics of segmented corporate governance, seen as a general outcome of the particular ways in which the incorporation of existing assets and further capital formation proceeded. It will first look at the initial formal arrangements, pointing to what was specific for Poland. Then, privatization in the manufacturing sector will be considered, while discussing the most important aspects of alternative governance structures, and taking into account the contribution of FDI and the development of a genuine private sector. Finally, the evolution of the banking system and the question of banks' engagement in corporate control will be analyzed.

6.2 Legal foundation of the change of corporate governance

The major legal act that regulates the formal governance structures is the Commercial Code – the core of the Central European tradition of regulation in this domain. The two most common legal forms of economic activity for large and medium-size enterprises are the joint-stock company (*Spółka Akcyjna*) and the limited liability company (*Spółka z Ograniczoną Odpowiedzialnością*). The formal governance structure of a joint-stock company (corporation) is organized at three levels: the general assembly of shareholders, GAS (*Walne Zgromadzenie Akcjonariuszy*), the supervisory council, SC (*Rada Nadzorcza*) elected by shareholders at the GAS, and the board of directors (*Zarząd*) usually appointed by the SC, or sometimes directly by the GAS. The board of directors is typically composed of two to five full-time executive managers, with the chief executive manager at the top, called the president of the company (*Prezes Spółki*) who represents the company in external relations. The top executive manager (president of the company) is responsible for both everyday management and strategy formulation, the latter being the subject of SC discussion and approval. The SC meets not less than once a year, but usually much more often, four to six times a year or more. The general assembly is usually held once a year. The three-level structure of corporate governance could be a standard case of the agency problem. However, not all the parties that are important for corporate strategy are reflected by the ownership structure. For instance, creditors very rarely hold shares in the companies. Their representatives may be present in the SC, but rather as "invited" members whose positions do not have a basis of real executive power.

In the limited liability companies (LLCs), corporate governance does not necessarily reflect the formal structure either. In a genuine private enterprise the agency problem hardly exists in an LLC, because the number of owners is rather small and the major owners often take on the role of everyday management. The relatively small size of the LLCs, as compared to joint-stock companies (JSCs), makes the owner–agent relation quite manageable. However, this is not necessarily the case in privatized entities. Especially during the initial steps of the privatization process, when the economic environment was quite far from what markets entail, the legal form of LLCs was often applied to quite large companies, and the ownership structure partly reflected the previously existing managerial networks. The use of the LLC form, instead of a JSC, was intended to provide dispersed capital engagement and poor disclosure standards imposed by the Commercial Code, but it did not often correspond to a large scale of controlled assets.

More generally speaking, for both LLCs and JSCs, the implementation of the Commercial Code, although usually correct in the literal sense of the law, did not necessarily follow the spirit of the law. This was especially true for the first period of privatization when there was practically neither a market for corporate control, nor a functioning bankruptcy law. A good example of such a discrepancy between the "technical" use of the Commercial Code and the intentions of its advocates was the frequent use of numerous nonstandard solutions included in the Code. Although these solutions were originally designed for rather exceptional cases, in the late 1980s and early 1990s this became a regular practice. For instance, for a long time various types of privileged shares reflected more an underlying power configuration that often did not correspond to the structure of ownership existing in the books. Only when a more vigorous market for corporate control started to manifest its force in the second half of 1990s did the regular use of "exceptions" begin to play a less significant role, but the process of clarification of power relations in companies has not seen its end.

Thus, the circumstances under which the Commercial Code and other legal acts are implemented are at least as important as the formal regulations themselves. Not only do current circumstances matter, but so does their recent history. It is, for instance, quite meaningful that the Commercial Code from 1934 was unexpectedly revived in 1987 after 40 years of abolition, and that it was not substantially changed until the year 2000. In addition, some other acts that may seem remote from the question of corporate governance of a private entity, play a role in the dynamics of corporate control. In the Polish case, these are first of all acts on state-owned enterprises (SOEs), but also acts on privatization and the financial restructuring of banks and enterprises. The evolution of the banking system itself was of major importance as well. The focus of this section is on the most specific aspects of corporate governance regulation in Poland, that is, the two acts on (SOEs) and self-management.

The point is that the legal foundation of SOEs established in 1981 during the Solidarity period, and partially adjusted in the early 1990s, established a new type of actor that later contributed to the first period of the privatization process. These were the worker councils (or employee councils/*rada pracownicza*) in the SOEs who not only modified actual corporate governance in a significant portion of the privatized economy, but also affected the law on privatization. One should not be confused by a substantially different phenomenon in other countries of the region, from Hungary to the Soviet Union and then post-Soviet states. Equally misleading would be the reference to the German works' councils. Neither manipulated eastern councils, nor codetermination, mirror the worker councils in the Polish SOEs of the 1980s and 1990s.

The recent history of the councils demonstrates their strong embeddedness in a genuine social movement which tried to compromise between the labor and managerial perspectives on industrial enterprise. The result of this negotiated compromise was expressed in the idea of employees' self-management. Established from 1980 to 1981 and legally acknowledged in 1981, the councils quickly mushroomed among manufacturing enterprises (Lewandowski and Szomburg, 1985). The imposition of martial law in December 1981 dramatically stopped their activity, later to be reactivated, but with a radically weakened position. Yet martial law was not able to modify other basic laws which provided councils with formally very extensive rights of comanagement, placing them in an equal position with the managing director for all strategic decisions. Every two years in almost all manufacturing enterprises the workers democratically elected their councils, with an average turnout of 70 percent (Osiatynski et al., 1985). Despite restrictions, a number of worker councils in important SOEs remained very active during the entire decade of the 1980s (Jakubowicz, 1989), protecting their legal status within the framework of enterprise comanagement, and actually being engaged in some managerial decisions. They manifested their independence from external pressure in various ways, including court trials against unlawful decisions of ministers. They also contributed to the public (or rather quasi-public) debate on economic reforms. In 1986, when the government attempted to recentralize its control over the economy, the active councils strongly opposed it and none of the 11 bills prepared by the government were passed (Federowicz, 1994).

Soon after the failed attempt of recentralization in 1987, the communist authorities decided to reestablish the prewar Commercial Code, and a more open discussion on property rights began. The councils, with their activity growing at high pace, entered the new debate as the most vigorous and well-organized actor, also establishing a Self-Management Forum – an informal institution strengthening the interenterprise links and debate. When political change came about in 1989, it resulted in the extremely active position of the councils toward participation at both levels of their activity – nationwide and within enterprises. The latter (to be discussed in the next section) was to directly affect a large number of privatization projects in the years to come. The former, together with self-management activists elected to Parliament in June 1989, created a strong lobby at the time of the preparation of the first privatization bill which was passed in July 1990.

The legal framework of the governance structure of formally state owned enterprises (1981) was completed by an amendment in early 1990. It made clear that it is the worker council's responsibility to appoint and dismiss the director, by respecting the formal procedure of open competition for managerial positions, and with the passive acceptance of the ministry. This amendment was passed at the same time that the neoliberal reformers in the new government were trying to reduce or liquidate the impact of councils (Federowicz and Levitas, 1995).

Under the influence of the IMF, a regular practice of CEE governments in the early 1990s was the commercialization of the SOEs as the initial step toward privatization. More precisely, this was a "corporatization" which meant the removal of an economic entity from the legal framework offered by the law on SOEs and its operation under the Commercial Code as a JSC or LLC with 100 percent of shares in state hands. In Hungary or the former Czechoslovakia a general "corporatization" of SOEs took place almost overnight. In Poland, however, the vigorous worker councils consequently blocked such a move, because it was equated to the liquidation of their existence. They generally accepted privatization, which also ended their existence, but they opposed "commercialization." Thus, they were able to keep control over privatization projects, as they were empowered by law with the right to approve any substantial property shift or change in the organization of "their" SOE. Although councils were not generally promoted by "Solidarity" at the national level, they received much support from Solidarity within enterprises, as well as legal advice from Solidarity's regional offices.

One of the hottest issues of the first period of privatization was the question of mushrooming quasi-private satellite enterprises around SOEs. In the Polish case it started some two years before the political turnaround. Since 1989 and especially in the period 1990–93, both the councils and trade unions have reacted against this quasi-privatization. This was not a unique pattern of reaction, but in general, it reduced the scope of so-called "nomenclatura privatization," and to some extent modified the working of preexisting networks.

In the Polish way toward clarified corporate governance, worker councils played a quite significant role, especially in the period 1989–93, and thus they contributed to the segmentation of corporate governance. Having played this role, they gradually vanished in the course of privatization, being neither powerful enough, nor sufficiently interested in finding a new place in the growing private sector. Even the regulation on one-third participation in the SCs in companies, which was easily introduced into the Commercial Code, has never been seriously considered in Poland. Only after the "corporatization" of SOEs, where the state still remains the owner, does the SC have a mandatory composition of one-third of representatives elected by the employees. When the share of the state goes below 50 percent, this regulation no longer applies.

Paradoxically, the initial very strong position of worker councils and their managerial nature prevented them from establishing a new form of institutional representation in the private sector. Yet, there was still another factor that contributed to the final suppression of the councils. That was the widely held consensus among reformers of all political orientations, that the Commercial Code from 1934 should not be submitted to any substantial modifications before the privatization process reached a critical point. Otherwise, the practice of the extensive use of "exceptional solutions" offered by the Code, as well as a practice of establishing new private or quasi-private entities on the edge of the law in order to minimize economic risk to the founders, could have initiated pressure on lawmakers for endless amendments to the Code. That would have weakened the Code's internal coherence, perfectly designed a few generations ago. Nothing like that happened, but on the other hand, Poland made no changes to the Code for the whole decade of transformation. The Code was finally modified in 2001.

6.3   Privatization and segmentation of corporate governance

From the very beginning there were a number of controversies related to privatization. On the one hand there was a large consensus among reformers and society at large that privatization was unavoidable. Furthermore, public opinion polls showed a rapidly growing support for ownership change economy-wide. On the other hand, concrete scenarios of privatization and real dilemmas related to the methods were continuously provoking strong disagreement. Experts' opinions also often contradicted each other. Even after a few years of this ongoing process, evaluation of its results was far from being unanimous. For instance, quite substantial amendments in the state sector in the same period (Dąbrowski et al., 1993a; Pinto et al., 1993) may have suggested that privatization itself did not bring as much as expected. On the other hand, privatization contributed to a substantial change in the business environment. In the open question of whether the major factor of change was privatization or marketization (Chavance, 1997; Chavance and Magnin, 1997), the general outcome of relatively successful transformation economies shows a kind of synergy of the two, rather than clearly pointing to just one factor. A precise empirical investigation of the real outcome of privatization in an econometric sense has been practically impossible. Too many factors affected the changes in both the privatized and the state sector, too quick were the changes, and too high the uncertainty faced by the economic actors.

The most important outcome of privatization is not necessarily visible in a direct output measurable in econometric terms. It is first of all a change of corporate governance. But going further with this statement, a new corporate governance does not necessarily result from "finding a concrete owner," as was strongly believed in the initial period. Corporate governance, aiming at sound decision-making, links various institutions that affect corporate performance. It is a sensitive nexus linking the perspective of microrationality of the individual actors with the institutional environment that determines capital flows, industrial relations, and the involvement of the state. Thus the relations between owners and managers, specified in the Commercial Code, constitute only one aspect of the actual governance structure.

When interpreting privatization as a substantial change of corporate governance, as compared to SOEs, it becomes clear that removing an enterprise from the legal regulations of an SOE and placing it under the Commercial Code is not enough to achieve a real change of governance. Surprisingly, this is often not enough even if the share of the state in a privatized company drops below 50 percent, or even 25 percent. The result depends on the configuration of owners, managers, and the constellation of other actors who may affect capital flows. An apt definition of corporate governance showing the agency problem from the perspective of investors says that: "Corporate governance deals with the ways in which suppliers of finance to corporations assure themselves of getting a return on their investment" (Shleifer and Vishny, 1997: 737). But corporate governance may also be interpreted from a managerial perspective. If the manager wants to develop the company, he/she usually has to attract external capital. In case the new owner does not have enough financial capital for development, as is often the case in CEE, both the owner and manager have to look for other sources. It is not surprising that the manager looks for financing at a lower price. Usually this originates from more or less hidden state contributions. The point is that these resources typically come from somewhat privileged relations between managers and public funds and (state-controlled) banks, regardless of their formalized role as investors. If this is the case, the real governance structure goes beyond the formal relations defined by the Commercial Code and is not necessarily reflected in the ownership structure or by the SC. A weak financial position of new formal owners opens the way for networks of managers and owners of various legal entities, as well as politicians and other actors who try to keep control, or at least maintain their influence over companies.

The essence of the change lies in the fact that these networks are not always the same. Their nature and capacity for reproduction depend on the nature of the economic and political environment they face. It also depends on the presence of entrance barriers to other actors who might start the game from outside the existing networks. The internal game on the one hand, and the nature of the economic and political environment on the other, determine the dynamics of institutional change and also, to some extent, the dynamics of the change in identity of the actors involved. It also reshapes the constellations of actors participating in the game for control.

Privatization, not only in manufacturing but also in the financial sector, is a major process confronting the actors trying to keep or gain control over assets. The widely spread mainstream opinion of experts repeatedly expressed from the beginning of transformation, and even more loudly by the time of the Czech and then Russian crisis, were that the speed of privatization, rather than the way and quality mattered (for example see EBRD, 1996). This turned out to be very misleading. The way and quality of the process have been important for the maintenance of minimal standards of transparency to reduce corruption, the need for which was quite obvious, but which was not easy to achieve. Moreover, the methods of privatization have been important for the type of actors and incentives that were likely to shape the actual structure of corporate control, before and after formal privatization.

The segmentation of corporate governance, in the sense explored in this book, draws attention to the various constellations of actors who fill in the formal structure of corporate governance, providing different outcomes in terms of corporate control and its further development, as well as in terms of firms' capacity to restructure. In the Polish case of systemic change, the segmentation results from the degree of intensity of the internal market for control in the enterprise before privatization on the one hand, and from the intensity of inflows of FDI on the other. A third factor contributing to a less significant, yet quite important extent, consists in the genuine development of private firms, sometimes able to grow to the size of the largest privatized enterprises. As the intensity of the internal market for control has depended on the size and type of SOE, we will first discuss the privatization of manufacturing enterprises and its main variants in Poland. Then, the problem of large economic entities resulting from both privatization and genuine private development, and finally the dynamics of the FDI impact will be discussed. We will leave out banking sector involvement, which will, necessarily, be considered in the next section.

6.3.1 Main line of privatization in the manufacturing sector

As mentioned earlier, the strong position of the worker councils was institutionalized by the law on SOEs (1981), and was socially embedded in a large movement with the ethos of independence from the state authorities at its core. It enabled councils to persist in their vision of an autonomous enterprise with internal social control during martial law and a comeback of authorities' recentralizing efforts, by the time of a new decentralizing wave and then, political change (1989). There was not much support for worker councils by the Solidarity trade union at the national level. However, within enterprises the potentially strong position of councils was often used by the reemerging Solidarity to win democratic election to the worker council. At the beginning of 1990, an amendment to the law on SOEs made it clear that councils were to appoint and dismiss the enterprise director, and they made extensive use of this right in the following years. Nevertheless, in the national debate over the privatization law, worker councils achieved much less than they had demanded. Before the passing of the Privatization Act in 1990, the Parliamentary Commission had worked out a compromise between the new, neoliberal government, and workers' expectations expressed mainly by the councils. It made room for certain "unconventional" methods of property transfer and for certain insiders' privileges during the process of privatization. Such privileges were greater then in Hungary for instance.

In this way the councils entered the game for a stake in the privatization of SOEs. They were equipped with the right not only to replace a managing director, but also to approve the enterprise project of privatization. To the extent that labor representatives were able to mobilize employees, a fact strongly dependent on the reputation of the members of a given council, they could also control the major steps of management. That provoked a series of conflicts and internal "wars," but was also compromised by inside actors. According to some estimates, more than 70 percent of directors were replaced in period 1990–92 (Pańków, 1993). However, quite often old directors were skilled enough in talking to labor to be readmitted to their managerial position. In the end they kept control over privatization and made extensive use of the privileges addressed to all insiders, including managers. Sometimes, councils appointed to a managerial position a director who had been dismissed by the ministry in the past. But also, many leaders of the councils, with managerial ambitions and skills, were able to take up managerial positions themselves. They then played a major role in privatization, often being the first to suppress the impact of worker representation during restructuring.

It is without doubt that the strength of the councils opened new channels for managerial careers, and it occurred at a time of intensified preparations for privatization at the enterprise level. This resulted in a kind of internal market for control. How much of a market, and how much politics was involved, is more of a contextual question related to every concrete enterprise. At the national level "Solidarność" rejected worker councils as a potential device of its own policy. At that time, union leaders strongly rejected a unique party, and centralized involvement in microeconomic decisions. Besides Solidarność, no other national force was able to affect worker councils' decisions. At the enterprise level all scenarios were possible, from revenge against some old *nomenclatura* members for their political past, to open competition for new projects for enterprise development, and to the strengthening of the position of some other *nomenclatura* managers because of their experience and useful international contacts.

However, purely political attitudes of the internal actors were marginal. Typical of the internal game for power, both before and after formal privatization, was a kind of "internal quasi-politics" as termed by a Hungarian economist "politicking within the enterprise" (Antal-Mokos, 1998), with not much reference to external politics at the national level. The market-type concern in this internal market for control was dominating, being radically emphasized by a hardship of economic environment created by Balcerowicz's stabilization program. Together with macroeconomic measures that dragged down domestic demand, enterprises faced a drop of real turnover, accompanied in the majority of cases by labor force downsizing. Redundancies were generally accepted by all kinds of worker representations, being only a subject of quarrels over the details of labor reduction schemes. The councils often played the role of mediator between managers and unions to reach final agreement on redundancies prior to privatization. "Enterprise egoism" did not exist as a notion in Poland, because there were no arrangements above enterprise level, but an economic perspective on the enterprise definitely dominated the inside game (Dąbrowski et al., 1991, 1993a).

For the emerging new corporate governance, the internal market for control with likely replacement of the managing director significantly modified the previously existing managerial networks. It also enhanced the disclosure of enterprise information to other actors. One of the hot issues was the "tunneling" of enterprise assets, especially financial capital, to artificially founded, external, quasi-private companies. Quite often the councils' and unions' impact helped to reduce and marketize the enterprise relations with these satellite companies. Those that survived became economically rationalized and were confronted with open, external competition. The "satellitization" of SOEs started even before the political change, and the number of such companies has been significant (Błaszczyk and Kamiński, 1999). However, the bottom-up mechanism of control turned out to be extremely important in putting privatization on a more lawful track. In the search for viable privatization projects, the old and new managers, quite often together with the councils, looked for external investors both domestic and foreign, depending on the size of their enterprise. As a result, insiders did not necessarily dominate the new ownership structures. This was especially the case with larger entities, where, despite some privileges, insiders' financial capacity did not cover the minimum requirements established by law.

This is not to say that the internal mechanism for control brought only positive results. The enterprises have actually faced a lot of internal tensions and open conflicts, even strikes. There were cases where councils replaced the director almost every year. In other cases, bottom-up control significantly delayed privatization, in disregard of the drop in the value of the enterprise. This was one of the reasons for the sluggish privatization in Poland (Błaszczyk, 1997). Paradoxically, the most successful councils led more effectively to relatively quick privatization which consequently induced their dissolution, but offered better prospects to the enterprise. In general the presence of labor representation at the enterprise level prevented many firms from being involved in cross-ownership or tunneling, phenomena so typical for post-communist transformation. Thus they contributed to the clarification of the ownership structure of the privatized companies and to the marketization of their relations with temporary satellite firms (Gardawski, 1998; Pańkow and Gąciarz, 1998). Bottom-up control did not manifest itself with equal intensity in the entire manufacturing sector, and cross-ownership schemes did appear and often persisted, but to a lesser extent.

The scenario of the involvement of worker councils as described above was mostly present in manufacturing enterprises with typical size varying between one thousand and a few thousand employees. In smaller SOEs, despite similar formal settings, the social tradition of labor mobilization was rather weak and a real capacity for worker representation was rarely present. Labor's position was easily suppressed by management as a result of often quite large, but necessary redundancies that sometimes went down to 40 or even 20 percent of previous employment levels (Federowicz et al.,1995). But these relatively smaller SOEs did not actually manifest many of the corporate governance problems. After privatization, they turned into typical medium-size LLCs, controlled by managers or by managers and some external domestic capital of comparable size.

Acute governance problems have manifested themselves in large and very large SOEs, before and after privatization, and worker councils were able to reduce them through the temporary mechanism of the internal market for control. However, that mechanism could hardly continue to exist in extremely large firms employing a few thousand workers or with huge asset values. There, outside interests related to the firm were too strong to leave room for a bottom-up mechanism of control. Besides the size and (potential) value of the assets, another important criterion was the exposure to competitive markets versus protected monopolistic positions. In the latter case councils were practically eliminated from the game by external actors whose interests could have been threatened by them. Those facing competition, and often financial problems, were more willing to submit to the internal control of councils, and then to that of external investors. Market pressure from foreign and domestic competitors was in place soon after the initial stabilization and liberalization processes, and grew stronger during the 1990s (Krajewska, 1999). Yet there were some important sectors holding a somewhat privileged position in the domestic market.

6.3.2   The problem of large organisms and the role of FDI

As already pointed out, not all enterprises took advantage of the kind of internal market for corporate control on their way to healthy corporate governance and restructuring. Large company size, high value of assets, and delayed exposure to the competitive environment were among the factors hampering restructuring. However, there were also entities that benefited from avoiding the internal game for control and any labor-driven impact. These were mostly firms involved in international trade in previous decades. They were not numerous, but turned out to be very influential on the threshold of the new economic reality. Some of them came to be among the biggest companies in Poland, while others practically went bankrupt or shrank to a marginal size.

In the past, these enterprises were founded as exporting and importing entities specializing in a given, often quite narrow, field. They practically monopolized the foreign exchange of a given segment. For that reason they were under strong criticism from short-lived vocal wings that favored decentralization. That was the case in 1980–81, and then from 1987 and up to the restoration of the Commercial Code. When the Commercial Code was restored, enabling the SOEs' legal status to be changed, foreign trade enterprises were the first to take the legal form of a company, thus removing the employee council from their governance structure. The new ownership structures of these companies reflected preexisting links among various SOEs related to foreign trade, or expected to provide new financial inputs. In the early 1990s, the privatization of these companies did not attract much public attention despite the fact that privatization, as a general issue, was more than ever a subject of heated debate. What seemed more important at that time was quick liberalization, opening access to international transactions for all enterprises. The former companies that specialized in international trade lost their monopolistic positions, but they did not lose their experience and contacts. They also maintained their informal domestic networks, freed from any formalized control from outside the net. At the start of the privatization process, most of the companies possessed some financial capital in hard currency, the value of which jumped almost threefold overnight in terms of domestic purchasing power. This was a result of the initial devaluation of the Polish zloty as decided by the stabilization program of 1989/90.

Under these circumstances, and contrary to other cases in Poland, the privatization of international trade companies went rather smoothly, free from public concern and with easily reached agreements between them and corresponding state agencies. The new ownership structures aimed at a clever construct, seeking to reconcile two contradicting purposes: to provide more financial capital in the coming years, and to maintain autonomy. There were two potential sources of capital: the state, and foreign investors. Typically both these sources contributed capital. Cross-ownership in a group of privatized entities was to protect investors from a possible direct intervention of state agencies in the case of unfavorable political developments. It was also intended to prevent potentially hostile takeovers by much stronger foreign investors. The newly privatized companies in this segment turned out to be able to attract some important foreign investment and credit, and at the same time to access public capital flows. There is a certain analogy between these evolving business groups and industrial conglomerates in the Czech economy for instance. As in other countries in the region, there were public rumors that key figures in some of these rebuilding organisms were involved in the activities of the former secret police.

Capital coming entirely from private sources was initially very low, but it increased quite rapidly later on. After being privatized in the ways just described, many companies soon started to contribute to the privatization of other firms. The law prevented all state-controlled enterprises, agencies, and financial institutions from acquiring privatized SOEs. Yet, those companies already privatized, with less than 50 percent direct state participation, were allowed to buy shares in the newly privatized firms with no restrictions. The trade companies have used this opportunity extensively, steadily building large holdings. They were usually interested in the acquisition of manufacturing firms within their old branch of specialization (Romanowska et al., 1998). However, especially in the early 1990s, some of these companies were buying whatever firm was for sale at a low price, demonstrating the weakness (or lack) of a real strategy (Dąbrowski et al., 1993a). Unlike the Czech economy, such actions did not affect the Polish economy in a major way. In the Polish case buyers were not numerous and their economic weight was not so significant. But seemingly, only a few years later a necessary clearing of their portfolios followed, together with the first serious financial problems for these companies (Federowicz and Jasiecki, 1998). In this sense, as in the case of other countries, the "test by the crisis situation," although not accompanied by explicit recession, proved to be equally important to Poland as well.

The financial capital for acquisitions was to a large extent provided by bank credit. Before starting to diversify their policy a few years later, banks offered credit quite easily to these companies, claiming that they were among the most reliable clients (Boguszewski et al., 1993). Financial resources also came partly from the raising of corporate capital, with growing engagement of both foreign and domestic investors. Political involvement in this process has certainly been important as well. Links between these firms and politics and politicians are not an easy subject for scholarly investigation, yet a few hypotheses seem quite plausible. First of all, in the Polish case, "the networks of corporate control" constituted themselves mostly in the period between 1987 and 1992, and people involved in this process were perfectly aware of the necessity and/or inevitability of market competition for their companies. It is equally true that they were aware of the scarcity of financial capital for the development of their companies. In the initial period the only source of capital could be the state. From that perspective the involvement of state institutions and representatives in the networks was inevitable for ensuring financial inflows for business activity from public resources. Yet, in the majority of cases, the managerial elite of these networks wanted to reduce or even get rid of the political impact on their businesses. However, not everybody was equally devoted to a purely managerial vision, or was equally successful in getting away from politics. A continuum of managerial strategies may be identified, from deep political involvement (the case of a large company Universal, which was eventually expelled from the Warsaw stock exchange for low disclosure standards in 1999) to cutting off political links when the first opportunity presented itself and actual removal from the initial type of networking (the case of a bank established in 1988 and then very quickly expanding, and four years later privatized with a serious German partner). Politicians, on the other side of the story, were interested in getting back some financial inflows at the most sensitive moments of their own careers.

The most important thesis is that the nature of the economic environment has been the most important factor in management's selection of corporate strategies. In other words, in a less competitive environment, the more "politicized" strategies were more likely to ensure successful corporate development, while in a more competitive environment, the least politically affected firms were more likely to survive and develop. However, the borderline between these two contradictory circumstances is hardly visible. In the long run, the most successful companies were those whose managerial staff were able to foresee the growing pressures of the competitive market, and to reduce their political involvement early enough by giving up the potential political benefits. Thus, the economic environment and the managerial capability in strategy building are the most powerful explanations for the growing diversification of corporate structures among large companies. After all, these "domestic economic empires" suffered continuously from a scarcity of capital. Some of them were rather greedy in their acquisition of other companies during the privatization process, and devoted their resources to that activity, while some others were more careful with their internal restructuring and the restructuring of the firms controlled by them. In this sense, the "taking opportunity economics" was not always a good starting point for long-term strategy building.

Additionally, in the Polish case, the thesis on economic environment interferes with an important change on the political scene in 1997. The ruling coalition (1993–97) of two post-communist parties, the SLD (the Democratic Left Alliance) and the PSL (the Peasants' Party), mostly identified with the preexisting managerial networks, lost power to a new coalition of two post-Solidarity parties, the AWS (Solidarity Election Action) and the UW (the Freedom Union). This shift in government happened at the time of a series of financial crises in various parts of the world. In Poland, the earlier clearing of the banking system, and radical cooling of the economy, prevented a nationwide crisis, but the years 1998–2001 tested the capacity of large and small businesses to survive in a period of serious economic slowdown. For the large companies analyzed above, the growing complexity of the domestic political environment played an important role as well. A kind of hidden "political competition" for control over some large businesses occurred, mainly between the AWS and the SLD. It is difficult to clearly distinguish the economic and political factors in this game. Surprisingly however, although the two kinds of competitive pressures placed companies under strain in the short run, they were rather favorable to more transparent economic relations, and thus contributed to the clarification of owner-ship structures and the relations between owners and managers, leading to more sound corporate governance.

Beside firms that formerly specialized in international trade, some financial institutions (except large banks), as well as some enterprises in manufacturing and services followed a similar pattern, but they were not numerous and not necessarily equally successful in terms of acquiring capital. Their general pattern of development and a delayed confrontation with competitive environment persist. For instance, the insurance com-pany Polisa, which was deeply linked to politicians and had a "politics-dependent" strategy, faced a rapidly worsening financial condition at the time of the "external test" and finally went bankrupt in 2000, while other companies with interwoven ownership, with much bigger distance from politics were able to survive in the same market. A sign of the changing political environment is also visible in the newly created markets such as that of pension funds. As usual, the push for political control has been quite strong, but tensions among all political wings were increasingly mutually counterbalancing each other. In this situation it was much easier for the reformers to keep the floor open to foreign capital, and to keep the regulating state agencies resistant to direct political maneuvering. The result was that there was practically no room for lack of transparency in the case of interwoven ownership structures.

The most politically vulnerable remain the not yet privatized very large companies, such as the copper company in the raw materials industry, or petrol companies with delayed exposure to international competition, or telecommunications in the infrastructure sector. It seems reasonable to expect that the perspective of European integration will play a significant role in the restructuring of these industries.

The other trajectories toward a sound decision-making structure oc-curred in the genuine private sector. Typically, private firms developed outside of former managerial and political networks. They mainly used a quick turnover strategy for rapid accumulation of capital, expanding from local to domestic markets, and so often avoiding bank credit. However, the largest domestic fortunes originate from more heteroge-neous sources. There was a continuum of their relations to politics, ranging from overall rejection to deep involvement and mixing with old and new networks. When the latter slightly modified the networks, the former showed an alternative strategy. Interestingly, genuine private business people who kept a sound distance from politics and public money inflows, although not leading in terms of controlled assets, came to play a dominant societal role (Federowicz and Jasiecki, 1998; Jasiecki, 2001). Nevertheless, the most important phenomenon, which reflects the business environment in Poland, is that these genuine private firms, with no political involvement, were able to expand their size to levels comparable to the largest domestic companies. Often a quite important source of capital for their development came from the Warsaw stock exchange, or the international financial markets.

The role of foreign investment is fundamental in the evolution of corporate control in Poland. Undoubtedly, the agent that most helped the clarification of corporate structure has been FDI. As mentioned earlier, foreign investors did not necessarily transfer all the solutions typical for their countries of origin. They rather needed transparent relations based on domestic legal arrangements in order to be able to gain control over the structures of corporate governance. For that reason they usually avoided legal ambiguity. However, they were not necessarily interested in improving domestic laws by using, for instance, a dominant position against minority shareholders. One should also distinguish between stable foreign investors, who usually follow their general worldwide strategy when they enter a new market, from smaller and sometimes ad hoc composed international capital, often interested in short-term gains only. The composition of capital inflows originating from these two different kinds of investors probably depends on the business and political environment in a given country. The impact of FDI on structures of corporate control is underinvestigated; however, it is not an easy field for empirical studies.

Summing up, segmentation of the methods of evolving constellations of corporate governance came from a variety of economic and collective actors who contributed to institutional change. In the last few years, foreign investors have often played the role of "last resort" in this process. But serious foreign capital did not rush into Poland on the day after the Balcerowicz stabilization plan was introduced. In the first five years of systemic change, FDI inflows were marginal. The GDP growth achieved since the third year of transformation came mainly from genuine private sector development. That would not have been possible in the absence of an earlier dismantling of the old industrial structures. The dominant course of privatization hampered the easy reconstruction of the old networks, in large part due to the mechanism of bottom-up control initiated by social collective actors such as the workers' councils and the internal market for control they had set up. However, some old/new networks were able to expand through the intensive acquisition of privatized firms, but were later submitted to the external test of market competition. At the same time, genuine private corporations were formed and established themselves among the biggest domestic firms.

6.4   Involvement of the banks

The picture would not be complete without an assessment of the involvement of banks. Over the past 12 years, banks have never been seriously interested in maintaining a portfolio of enterprise shares, and were hardly interested in getting involved in enterprise restructuring. In the first period, like all state-controlled entities, they were simply not eligible to acquire shares in privatized SOEs. Having hardly worked on improving their basic functions in the past, and starting to build up new banking activities that they had never practiced before, banks remained mainly focused on their internal problems. For the most part, they tried to avoid any kind of direct involvement in the nonfinancial sector. Yet, their own performance, financial conditions, and ownership status were quite important for the development of the corporate control of industrial firms.

The first important step in building a market-oriented banking system was taken at the very beginning of 1989, on the eve of political changes in the country. In order to build up its actual role as a central bank, the National Bank no longer played a "commercial" function. Nine new commercial banks were created, covering nine regions of the National Bank's earlier activity. Beside these nine banks, there were three other commercial banks and one large savings bank, all of them in state hands. The legal act that introduced the reform of the banking system opened the way to create new banks by other economic actors (at that time mainly state controlled). There were extremely low entrance barriers for the new banks, and small, new banks started mushrooming. By 1992 there were some 80 new banks, almost all small or extremely small, with a mix of capital coming primarily from other state entities.

Despite that initial step, the reformers somehow neglected the banking system. They believed in a steady improvement resulting from increased competition. Yet the nine "post-national" commercial banks covered more than 95 percent of the credits to industrial firms. The newly created banks were not able to threaten their position, and the "big nine" did not compete among themselves. The openness to international banking competition resulted in a rather symbolic presence of a few important banks, which covered all together only about 1 percent of the domestic banking activity (Kloc, 1993). In the years 1990–92 the banks suffered the biggest outflow of financial capital, usually on the edge of the law, if not altogether illegal. The same period was the most damaging in terms of bad debt accumulation.

Only in late 1991, after a series of banking scandals triggered by the press, was a new board nominated to the central bank which took more seriously its function of control over the quality of the banking system's activities. The central bank started to impose stricter norms of secure transactions, focusing on EEC standards. That put pressure on the smaller banks to merge. At the same time the government realized that eventual privatization of the largest banks, mostly with foreign capital and know-how, was inevitable. The first privatization occurred in 1992 and two others followed in 1993. Also, a legal act on the restructuring of qualified credit, specifying the precise procedure to be followed on a case-by-case basis in the negotiations between in-debt enterprises and creditors, and offering financial instruments for those debtors able to work out a new plan for restructuring, was passed by Parliament in 1993.

Soon after, the privatization of the next banks became one of the hottest political issues, dragging on the process for a few years. Public opinion was stirred up by some politicians fighting for a "national character of the banks." The coalition coming to power (1993–97) forced the vision of domestic bank consolidation rather than case-by-case privatization, and dismantled the reformist team dealing with the banking sector in the Ministry of Finance. However, the consecutive versions of possible consolidation were repeatedly rejected by the most important state-owned banks, the boards of which were perfectly aware of the political bill they implicitly included. They were ready to consolidate, but not necessarily under a political umbrella (Silitski, 1998). Finally, only one merger out of four larger banks took place in 1997, with the privatization of the group coming just the next year. The other banks preferred a strategy of direct foreign investment, with no illusion that they might build a healthy and powerful domestic banking group. Presently, with a background of more than 70 percent foreign control of banking capital, the openness of the domestic banking market to international competition was mainly inevitable. This perspective was also fostered by the policy of the Polish central bank that was able to maintain its political autonomy established at the beginning of the reform and confirmed in the new Constitution of 1997. The policy of the central bank aimed to reach EU standards in the whole banking sector in as short a time as possible.

The history described here explains why banks tried not to be involved in industrial restructuring. Even the law on the financial restructuring of banks and enterprises (1993), which aimed at stimulating the banks' active role and at offering them stock options, did not really result in significant property relations between banks and firms, although individual negotiations between banks and firms were performed in about a quarter of industrial firms (Krajewska, 1999). Banks used this legal measure to reduce or get rid of bad debts, but not for taking an active role in terms of property relations. They definitely preferred, and were forced by the evolution of banking markets, to focus on developing new types of banking services, when tough international competition was more likely to come.

In this way, one can say that banks were not a source of dynamism for evolving governance structure in the nonfinancial sector. Apart from a few cases of small and rather unsuccessful banks, the two sectors, financial and manufacturing (together with the commerce and nonfinancial services sectors), stayed away from one another, each with its own problems. More importantly, however, banks were not able to fully control their creditor policies in the first years of transformation, or perhaps, hardly had any policy. In this way they contributed to a significant distortion in corporate decision-making and strategies. Further improvements were also rather slow, until they finally understood the danger of competition coming from outside. In this sense the real privatization, with foreign banking capital, of the majority of large banks would inevitably improve the financial environment of industrial firms.

6.5   Back to the theoretical context

It is not necessary to point out that the transformation could not aim for an initially "targeted" model. Equally true, however, is that it needed a concrete design to be able to orient the change in one clear direction, otherwise reforms would not have any consolidating tendency (Federowicz, 2000). During the entire time, two contradicting tendencies were clearly competing from the beginning of the process. One tendency was based on a neoliberal reform package, while another was based on opposing the majority of these measures. There are many detailed controversies in classifying the steps taken by reformers (not only declared by them) and in evaluating reforms according to their theoretically "too much" or "not enough" liberal tastes. The tension between the mainstream approach and those opposing it creates an overwhelming context (explicit or implicit) for any research perspective on transforming economies. This context is also visible in a broad field focusing on the convergence–divergence debate in the contemporary world (Berger and Dore, 1996; Hall and Soskice, 2001). One cannot neglect this debate when dealing with institutional change in the economy. Let us find a place for the empirical evidence on corporate governance in Poland in the time of systemic change, not ignoring a more comprehensive, critical evaluation of the neoliberal design, while not entirely embarking on it.

On the part of neoliberal reformers, the implicit assumption was that "finding a real owner" would automatically lead to sound corporate control and restructuring with a clear grounding of the owner's position in the Commercial Code. There was not a precise model of corporate governance in the reform design. Nevertheless, the key steps taken, such as low entrance barriers, withdrawal of the state, and, first of all, efforts to establish and foster the role of the stock exchange as a main segment of the market for corporate control, clearly suggested a desired US style of governance (Balcerowicz, 1995).

A sizeable complaint came from enterprises not only about financial hardships that they faced, but also about cutting industrial links and cooperation between firms, as well as about vanishing R&D activity. Many academic researchers supported the attempt of a bottom-up rejection of neoliberal reforms. The most advanced models of the issue evoked the Japanese, or Korean solutions (Amsden et al., 1994). The major argument was that neoliberal measures atomize enterprises and make them more vulnerable to external competitors. Thus, the reform design should help to develop links between economic actors and not damage them.

If the critics of any superficial and often just nominal property shift in privatization accurately showed the weakest aspect of transformation, the dream of Polish *chebols* was equally nonrealistic compared with the core assumption about "real owners" participating in quick and large-scale privatization. Both of these scenarios neglected the political involvement of large entities, which grew up in the past with a very different logic, where proximity to the political decision-makers was decisive for an enterprise's prospects.

In this regard, however, the atomizing pressure on enterprises by macro-economic measures and the exposure to a growing competitive environment was more enhancing for internal restructuring than the opposite strategy.

Nevertheless, none of the existing models could correspond to the complexity of decision-making in the severely unstable institutional environment. A meaningful empirical exercise has been provided by the Czech economy. Some part of the international audience was willing to see it as taking from both the American and the German models in developing a quite original solution. Coffee was probably the first to question such a picture. He pointed out that financial markets and banks did not correspond to US standards (Coffee, 1996). This statement applies to Poland as well. Even if banks finally engaged themselves in carrying out their own restructuring, the expectation of their playing a more significant external role was not realistic. In the same vein, even if the Warsaw stock exchange provided convenient capital for a few dozen expanding companies, it did not change much in the dominant business environment.

Stark and Bruszt noted that the search for a targeted model was pointless and should be replaced with a venture that relied on the specific strength of each post-communist country (Stark, 1996; Stark and Bruszt, 1998; Grabher and Stark, 1997). However, their concept that neither markets nor hierarchies, but networks may play a role in the founding of new economic relations, neglected the nature of post-communist economic actors. The problem is not whether or not to focus on networks, but on the kind of conceptualization that may open the way for an empirical diagnosis of the actual role of networks in transforming economies. In the post-communist context, the initial choices were not "between markets and hierarchies," but rather between market-oriented and politically oriented networks. These are very different types of networks. If in the former, the involved actors, regardless of how well they are installed in the network constellation, are eventually tested with external criteria; the latter has been an arena of much more fundamental fighting between two different organizational logics. One is trying to open preexisting structures while the other one grew up under no risk of external evaluation and tries to maintain its status.

The thesis here is that the nature, constitution, and role of networks depend on the type of environment with which they deal. Furthermore, their capacity to reproduce themselves varies together with constraints and opportunities arising from the environment. The success of systemic change from communist to democratic and market type of arrangements lies with a move from a monopolistic to a pluralistic type of relation in both politics and in the economy. Competition as a systemic mechanism is one of the few devices available to break the monopolizing attitudes of a group of interests that have typically hampered development over the decades prior to systemic change. The environment, which determines the networks' reproduction, is mostly characterized by the combination of monopolistic protection and competitive pressures. The latter appear together with the openness of both political and economic arenas to potential and actual newcomers. The same statement may be expressed from a different perspective: the monopolistic (closed) versus competitive (open) environment determines to a large extent the changing identity of economic and political actors and their networks. The more competitive the environment, the more likely the shift toward market-type networking. The concept of networks cannot be understood in the absence of a specific context.

6.6   Conclusion: models ahead?

From a Russian perspective, Shleifer and Vishny (1997) realized that all of the advanced economic models of corporate governance, despite having many contradicting elements, have one common feature of fundamental importance. They are all built on the assumption of lawful attitudes of the involved parties, as well as the institutional capability of law enforcement (Shleifer and Vishny, 1997). Even if the problem of poor legal systems and poor law enforcement in transforming economies is widely known nowadays, this general remark shows how different the starting point in these countries was from any model of advanced capitalism. The question of models is not about a "targeted" model, but a "transforming" model. In other words, it does not need to make a "final" outcome concrete but rather provide the tools and the capacity for deep institutional change. But such a concept has to take into account the nature of real actors who are present in the game, as well as those who may potentially enter it. The same is true in considering how to achieve minimum standards of law and lawful attitudes in order to talk about any kind of functioning corporate governance.

In the Polish case, it is clearly visible that the dynamics of institutional change not only depends on the quality of legal settings and their enforcement, but also on the nature and changing constellations of social, economic, and political actors who both create, fill in, and reproduce the institutional arrangements.

The trajectories of evolving corporate governance provoked segmentation in terms of different intercompany relations and intercompany control. Worker representatives were active in executing their legal rights to intervene in managerial projects of privatization, but they quite often led to a partial cutting of the previously existing informal links, which were not justified by the new economic activity of the enterprise. Sometimes too many conflicts hampered the real restructuring, but usually initial tensions between insiders eventually led to a compromise and equilibrium at a higher-quality level for the firm, quite often with the contribution of a domestic, genuine private investor. Such a scenario was likely to occur in medium- and larger-sized SOEs, but not in very large and extra large ones. The latter were much more politically involved and often not privatized at the time. If they were financially lucrative, which was the case in a few of them, they had been targeted by politicians from all political wings. Some other trajectories appeared among those medium and larger SOEs that were not successful in improving their financial condition, no matter whether worker councils were active or not. These firms often went to the program of mass privatization through the so-called National Investment Funds (NFI).

The program of mass privatization, however, played a marginal role in Polish transformation. Altogether, capitalization of the NFIs did not reach the level of even one successful company developing from scratch or expanding from former activity in international trade. A few genuine, private, and very large companies provide good examples of positive outcomes of initial decomposition of industrial links and of atomizing pressures provoked by macroeconomic hardship. The smaller the protection of old industrial ties, the more room and capital there were for genuine private expansion. Companies/holdings/groups that originated in the past monopolistic position in Polish export–import activity exemplify the networking style of business activity. Under the growing pressure of a competitive environment and political turbulence, they were reshaped by external forces, or sometimes they reshaped themselves, or were eliminated. Preoccupied with their own survival under real competition, after an uncontrolled engagement in the first years of transformation, the banks have been interested in keeping their distance from nonfinancial sectors.

Together with the tightening control of the banking system by the politically autonomous central bank, this attitude prevented the emergence of large-scale and uncontrollable financial–industrial groups. However, there are some cases of dubious bank ownership structures, where large contributions from the state still persist. Parliamentary control over public funds is still not transparent. Some important industries are still in the state's hands, provoking endless political bargaining. If this kind of informal bargaining was hidden in the past, over the last few years it has become more open and visible to the public, while subordinated even more to current political tactics.

Nevertheless, the 12-year transformation has fundamentally changed economic relations. During this period, the first four years were decisive for the whole process. With a certain vision of liberal economic relations, there was no concrete model of corporate governance to start with. Central European countries relied on their prewar legal tradition, but the actual dynamics of institutional development did not have much in common with prewar commercial relations. In the absence of a coherent and realistic model, actual corporate governance depended on many intermingled tendencies such as: weak but slowly improving exit mechanisms, variation in the access to public money through political channels, as well as the different origins of managerial careers, and finally the significant impact of foreign direct investors.

What is specific for Poland is that before the serious entry of foreign capital occurred, worker participation contributed significantly to the game for control. That is not to say that the corporate structures nowadays are more oriented toward workers than elsewhere; rather the contrary. The point is that in Poland, workers' participation was not only a feature of a typical labor movement. It was also a relatively vigorous manifestation of civic activities, with structures supporting the disclosure of information to the public and to potential channels for individual careers of people from outside earlier establishments. Like well-performing mass media in developed civil societies, the worker organizations at the bottom level (institutionalized as both unions and councils) contributed to the clarification of the rules of the game in the most vulnerable period of property transformation. That was a temporary substitution of market for corporate control. It worked not only because of its social underpinnings but also because of clear macroeconomic constraints imposed in the initial period of transformation by the stabilization program. If the social support provided some new actors with a "voice," the hardship of the economic environment, together with anticipated privatization, oriented that voice toward more businesslike behavior.

When talking about "dynamic" models of deep institutional change, three general factors seem to be at play. First is the mix of economic, political, and social actors that are likely to participate in the game. Second is the macroeconomic environment and its stability. This element clearly contributes to shaping actors' orientations and strategies. And third is the strength of democratic and civic institutions, which provide "voice mechanisms" in times of intensive shaping and reproduction of economic institutional settings. If the second factor received much international attention, the understanding of the first came with a significant delay. The third factor, at least in official statements, has never been explicitly attributed to the economic reforms, yet it is one of its fundamental conditions.

7
Ownership and Corporate Governance in the Hungarian Large Enterprise Sector

Éva Voszka

7.1 Introduction

The privatization of post-socialist economies, including the transfer of state assets to other proprietors, new start-ups, and greenfield investments, has produced a wide variety of ownership structures in Central and Eastern Europe (CEE). One of the main questions discussed in recent years concerns the basic characteristics of post-socialist ownership. Are the new structures unique as compared to recent Western market economies, as several researchers argue (Stark, 1996; Earle and Estrin, 1997; Andreff, 1998)? Is the dominant form some kind of recombinant property, that is, a mixture of state and private ownership, dominated by interorganizational (corporate) shareholders (Stark, 1996; Stark and Kemény, 1997)? Or do we face a model of managerial capitalism, as Szelényi et al. (1996) suggest?

This chapter analyses the Hungarian case that seems to be rather special in comparison to other post-socialist countries – but not peculiar in comparison to some other market economies. We will argue that the basic features of the ownership structure in the large enterprise sector are not dominated by specific institutional solutions. If there are some specific features, they mainly include quantitative aspects (such as the concentration of assets, outputs and ownership positions, the predominance of foreign investors) rather than qualitative ones.

We have to stress that these hypotheses have been formulated and tested in the large enterprise sector or, more precisely, the largest 100 Hungarian firms as ranked by sales. Of course this group is not statistically representative for the economy as a whole, but its performance is decisive for macroeconomic indicators such as growth and balance of trade. The "top 100" firms accounted for more than a third of sales and profits and half of exports in Hungary in 1997 (*Figyelő*, 1998).[1]

This chapter first gives a picture of the Hungarian formal ownership structure in general and in the "top 100". The next section describes the origins of this structure and interprets the recent situation as a consequence of the conditions during inception, economic policy, and privatization methods applied. The following section goes beyond the quantitative features and tries to sketch a picture of some corporate governance issues. A somewhat narrow concept of corporate governance is applied based on the principal–agent approach, concentrating on the relationship between owners and managers. In summing up the findings, we outline some hypotheses about the main characteristics of the Hungarian ownership structure.

7.2 General features of the Hungarian post-privatization ownership structure

As privatization came to an end in the late 1990s, the basic characteristics of the enterprise sector, such as strong concentration, a high proportion of foreign investors, and the marginal role of "special" owners, seemed to form a stable ownership system. This did not mean, however, that there was a lack of changes at the level of individual firms, including mergers and split-ups, or further concentration of shares.

The first criterion in describing post-socialist countries is the change in the role of the state as a proprietor. Throughout the last decade, the proportion of state assets was reduced significantly. The private sector in Hungary expanded via greenfield foreign investments, domestic start-up firms, and privatization. Nor was the selling of state-owned firms confined to strategic sectors. Private shares in telecommunication, banking, and energy sectors (oil, electric power plants, electricity and gas suppliers) grew to a high level even by West European standards.

As Table 7.1 indicates, the proportion of private ownership in registered capital reached 80 percent by the end of 1998 in the group of firms that practiced double bookkeeping. Slightly more than half of this was foreign investment. The largest group of domestic owners consisted of domestic companies. Insiders in the form of ESOP (employee stock ownership programs) organizations and cooperatives owned 0.4 and 1.6 percent, respectively. The 20 percent of state ownership covered central government (with 10 percent), local government (with 7 percent) and other organizations – including nonprivate social security funds, state development bank, foundations, and so on – with 2.4 percent.

Thus, the first characteristic of the Hungarian ownership structure is a relatively small proportion held by the state and a high stake held by foreigners in comparison to other CEE countries. The second main feature is that the role of indirect state ownership (parastate institutions) is not widespread. Most Hungarian firms recorded by official statistics as privatized are actually in the hands of individuals or privately owned companies. The main exception to this rule is foreign investment which is considered by Hungarian statistics as private, although several foreign firms themselves

Table 7.1   Ownership structure of companies (% in registered capital)

Owner	1992	1993	1994	1995	1996	1997	1998
Hungarian individual	9.8	11.9	12.3	12.4	11.6	11.3	12.0
Domestic company	12.4	14.2	17.1	19.9	20.5	24.1	27.2
Cooperative	2.8	2.6	2.6	2.0	1.8	1.6	1.6
ESOP organization	0.1	0.3	0.9	0.9	0.8	1.2	0.4
Total domestic private owners	25.1	29.0	32.9	35.2	34.7	38.2	41.2
Foreign owners	10.1	16.1	18.9	28.4	31.5	35.3	39.1
Total private ownership	35.2	45.1	51.8	63.6	66.2	73.5	80.3
Central government	58.9	48.4	40.4	29.5	22.4	15.8	10.4
Local governments	5.1	5.8	6.6	5.9	10.2	8.9	6.9
Other	0.8	0.7	1.2	1.0	1.2	1.8	2.4
Total state and other	64.8	54.9	48.2	36.4	33.8	26.5	19.7
Total	100.0	100.0	100.0	100.0	100.0	100.0	100.0

Note: Firms with double bookkeeping.
Source: Pitti (1999).

were state or municipally owned at the time of their investment, mainly, but not exclusively, in the energy sector.

The second question concerning ownership structure is the concentration of shares. The Hungarian ownership structure cannot be evaluated as a dispersed one. Analyzing a sample of firms with 100–2000 employees, Ábrahám (1996) and Tóth (1998) found that in 80 percent of the population there was one majority owner holding more than half of the shares in 1995 (Table 7.2). In another sample of big firms (with more than HUF 200 billion turnover) Kovách and Csite (1999) found that 85 percent of firms had one majority owner in 1997. Thus, in most companies there is one dominant owner or block shareholding.

The ownership structure of the "top 100" is similar to the general picture in several respects. Analyzing the big firms, we found six groups of owners: foreign investors (firms and institutions, not including financial ones), state organizations[2] (central and local governments and others like state social security funds,[3] Treasury), domestic corporations, financial institutions, individuals and employees-management.[4] Foreign investors were the main players within these six ownership categories, holding a stake in three-quarters of the big firms. The state was placed second with 37 percent and domestic corporations third with 27 percent (Table 7.3).

The ownership structure of the "top 100" is highly concentrated. Table 7.4 shows that there is only one owner in 50 percent of firms. On the other hand, there are more than 3 shareholders in 44 percent of firms, but in 18 of those there is also only one majority owner. Thus, nearly three-quarters of the firms are dominated by one shareholder.

Table 7.2 Big and medium-size firms[a] according to number of owners and majority ownership, 1995 (%)

Number of owners	Proportion of firms	Proportion of firms in the given category which have majority owners[b]
One	19.0	19.0
Two	31.0	29.0
Three	25.2	19.0
Maximum three	75.2	66.2
More than three	24.8	14.8

[a] Number of employees between 100 and 2000.
[b] One owner with a stake more than 50%.
Source: Ábrahám (1996).

Table 7.3 The presence of different types of owners in "top 100",1997

Owners	Number of firms	% of firms (N=100)
State[a]	37	37.0
Foreign investors[b]	75	75.0
Domestic corporations[c]	27	27.0
Financial investors	12	12.0
Individuals	30	30.0
Employees and management	14	14.0
Total		100.0

[a] If there are several representatives of state organizations (central government and local governments) in one company, they are counted only once.
[b] If there are several representatives of foreign owners (companies and financial investors, excluding banks) in one company, they are counted only once.
[c] Not including banks.

Table 7.4 Number of owners and the presence of majority shareholders

Number of owners	Number of firms	% of firms (N=100)	Number of firms with one majority owner[a]	% of firms with one majority owner (N=100)
One	50	50.0	50	50.0
Two	5	50.0	5	5.0
Three	1	1.0	0	0.0
Maximum three	56	56.0	55	55.0
More than three	44	44.0	18	18.0
Total	100	100.0	73	73.0

[a] With more than 50.1 % of shares.

Having an overview of owners and the concentration of their holdings, let us combine these two dimensions.[5] Presuming that a "single player" ownership situation (with more than 90 percent of shares) might have special consequences for corporate governance, we have made a distinction between *majority* being: (a) near 100 percent stake and (b) between 50 and 90 percent stake. According to these considerations, we define six ownership types: subsidiaries of foreign firms (where the owner holds more than 90 percent of the shares), foreign-dominated companies (where the owner holds 25–90 percent of the shares with a dominant role), state-dominated firms, "cross ownership" with the dominant position of another domestic firm,[6] dispersed ownership (with no investor holding more than 25 percent of shares), and employee-management ownership.

As Table 7.5 indicates, the ownership structure of the "top 100" in 1997 was dominated by foreign companies.[7] The largest group of large Hungarian enterprises consisted of subsidiaries of multinational firms (44 percent). The portion of domestic corporations as dominant owners was rather small (9 percent), comprised mainly of state-owned units. Although state ownership had decreased dramatically during the past decade, central and local governments as majority shareholders were still present in 14 percent of the "top 100". Special types of owners (such as parastate owners and employees-management) did not play a decisive role.

Our data on the big enterprise structure differ from David Stark's results on several points. Considering that the two basic elements of the concept "recombinant property" are intercorporate holdings (networks, cross-ownership) and some combination of state and private control (Stark, 1994; Stark and Kemény, 1997), let us show the differences according to these two points.

Stark found the presence of domestic firms as shareholders in 40 percent of the largest 200 firms and 25 banks in 1993, with a majority position in

Table 7.5   Ownership types of "top 100" according to the owners and ownership concentration, 1997

% of ownership stake/ type of dominant owner	25.01–50.0% as a dominant stake	50.01– 90.0%	90.1– 100%	Total	% of registered firms (N=100)
Foreign firm	13	6	44	63	63.0
State	0	3	11	14	14.0
Domestic firm	3	1	5	9	9.0
Employees and management	3	3	0	6	6.0
No dominant owner				8	8.0
Total	19	13	60	100	100.0

half of them (Stark, 1994). In the second stage, working with the data from 1996, the presence of other firms as shareholders expanded to 77 percent, and in 40 percent of these cases, all (top 20) shareholders were other firms. Both proportions continued to grow in the two-year period examined (Stark and Kemény, 1997).

Several publications had already questioned the dominance of this ownership structure, showing the high proportion of isolated firms (that is, companies not owned by and not holding a stake in any other company), the limited role of domestic firms as majority shareholders and that of ownership networks among big Hungarian enterprises,[8] similar to our data on the "top 100".

The picture is much different if we put all corporate shareholdings in one group, covering both domestic and foreign firms as owners, as Stark and Kemény did at the second stage of their research. In this case, the proportion of firms in the "top 100" with at least one domestic and/or foreign company on the list of owners is 90 percent holding majority position in 71 percent of these firms. As we have seen, however, most of them are foreigners.

As for the role of the state, governmental and municipal organizations are present in more than one-third of the "top 100", but mainly in minority positions. This is partially rooted in privatization laws and methods. Local governments received a fragment of shares in privatized firms as a result of legislation and the Hungarian Privatization and State Holding Company (HPSHC) often putting its shares on the market in smaller packages. State ownership is decreasing steadily. Three firms with dominant state ownership in 1997 were privatized the following year and minority shares were also sold on the stock exchange or to strategic investors. Foreign investors are especially active in this field. They tend to buy up to 100 percent shares whenever possible.[9]

Before turning to the question of the differences in corporate governance according to ownership type, let us see how and why this ownership structure emerged.

7.3   Origins of the ownership structure

On one hand, the characteristics of the recent Hungarian ownership structure are influenced by the inherited economic and social structures, and on the other, by the economic and privatization policies applied during the last decade.

Although economic reforms under a planned economy were neither consistent nor unidirectional (for details, see for instance Antal, 1985), some of their consequences proved to be favorable from the point of view of transformation. Firstly, private activity had been allowed in Hungary as early as the 1960s, mainly in agriculture. From the 1980s on, new legal and regulatory frameworks gave impetus to the expansion of small private business, albeit restricted in both size and field of activity. The mushrooming of small entrepreneurship proved to be important, not so much from the point of view of accumulating capital as accumulating experience and business contacts.

The second factor is the formal and informal position of state enterprises. The basic idea of Hungarian reforms beginning in the 1960s, was to increase firms' autonomy. The process meant the gradual decentralization of property rights from central bureaucratic organizations to enterprise management. After the abolition of compulsory plan targets, several groups of firms achieved an informal, but strong bargaining position against governmental organizations in setting targets and improving their financial position, independent of market performance. The last step of decentralization was the introduction of self-governing forms in 1985. The enterprise councils, established in two-thirds of economic units, consisted of insiders only and were practically dominated by the management. These controlling bodies obtained the rights to determine the organizational structure, to appoint the chief executive, to decide on mergers and splitting up and to found joint ventures with other companies involving state assets. Thus, the inheritance of the planned economy in Hungary was not a strong and stable state ownership, but a dispersed model where property rights were divided between enterprises and party–state organizations.

Thirdly, several market institutions had been introduced before the political turnover along with significant liberalization and deregulation. The possibility of foreign investment dated back to the 1970s. Administrative control over founding joint ventures was loosened and preferences were extended in several stages during the next decade. As a reform of taxation, personal income tax was introduced, the system of turnover tax simplified and profit tax became uniform for all firms. Social insurance was (at least formally) separated from the central budget. In the late 1980s, the government cut subsidies sharply, liberalized foreign trade, and eased the rigor of price and wage regulation. A new company law was enacted in 1988, giving a legal framework for share companies and other limited liability firms. In this period the monobank system was abolished by allowing foreigners to open branches in Hungary and by founding state commercial banks. The law on reopening the Budapest stock exchange was passed in early 1990.

The last government of the one-party system tried to introduce a decisive change in economic policy in order to harden the budget constraints of state firms. In the late 1980s it drastically cut budgetary subsidies. The first signs of the Comecon crisis, the recession of the domestic market, and the quick liberalization of foreign trade shrank the market and sharpened competition for most firms to an extent never experienced before.

The widening possibilities, along with growing pressures, created the motivation and compulsion for enterprises to look for their own ways of survival without the help of the government. The way out for many of them was spontaneous privatization. Enterprise management, the legal basis of self-governing forms, and new company law initiated this. With their markets lost, debts spiraling and state subsidies cut back, several dozen big enterprises broke up into groups of companies. The intention was to separate loss-making units, to give a chance for the rest to find new owners and markets or to offer debt–equity swaps to banks and other creditors. As a general rule, at the first step the enterprise center remained the majority shareholder of the new companies formed from the factories of the big firm. Although these enterprise centers often called themselves holdings, they preserved the traditional socialist enterprise form and remained in state ownership. With a lack of private capital involved, this basic type of "spontaneous privatization" was not real privatization. It was rather a change in organizational form (called "corporatization" or "commercialization"), that might be considered as the first step toward selling the shares.

The first freely elected government continued with liberalization and deregulation but intended to stop "spontaneous privatization" and reestablish stable state ownership. Having centralized privatization decisions to the central privatization agency, the government concentrated all ownership rights in 1992 in the State Property Agency (SPA). The method was the compulsory transformation of all state enterprises into company form in 1992, and this meant the abolition of enterprise councils.

On the other hand, the government stuck to the intention of its predecessor to harden the budget constraints of state-owned firms. Privatization policy claimed that the best method of state asset management was selling the enterprises without any prior centrally financed restructuring.

Neither concentration of ownership rights and privatization decisions, nor tight fiscal policy proved to be of consequence during the last decade. The managers of state companies maintained their influence on the forms and timing of privatization and sometimes even on choosing the owners (several examples are given for instance in Antalóczy, 1999; Mihályi, 1998; Voszka, 1997). This informal influence turned into formalized channels in some special programs. State subsidies and preferences did not disappear either. As well as the case-by-case bailing out of certain firms, several packages of restructuring were introduced, such as the preferential treatment of the "dirty 13" big companies and the waves of credit, debtor, and bank consolidation. This last measure alone cost 400 billion HUF before 1994, more than all the privatization revenues up to then (see Várhegyi, 1998; Balassa, 1996; Karsai, 1993). Following the second parliamentary elections in 1994 redistribution continued, partially from the state budget and partially from the central privatization agency, in the form of increasing capital and credit from the owner. In 1996–97 the HPSHC, the legal successor of the SPA, spent 15–35 percent of all privatization income on reorganization, just as in the first half of the 1990s. In 1998 these expenditures jumped to an unprecedented high, exceeding privatization revenues.[10]

Nevertheless, old-fashioned redistribution of income in favor of the large enterprise sector as a comprehensive mechanism of state corporate governance was not reestablished. Under these circumstances, the way out for most state companies from shrinking markets, spiraling debts, and the need for reorganization was the involvement of new owners.

The initial stage of selling state firms on a case-by case approach proved to be very slow. Of the 20 firms listed in the *First Privatization Program* in 1990, only two were sold during the first year and a half. Having realized the failure and the pressure of different political and managerial groups, governmental policies turned in two directions in 1992–94: toward the decentralization of decision-making mechanisms from a previously centralized approach, and toward the free or preferential distribution of assets instead of selling for cash.

The first intention was reflected in the self-privatization program. Involving nearly 500 small and medium-size enterprises in this special project, the SPA reserved only controlling functions and delegated rights and responsibilities of selling to the consulting firms. These firms had well-defined incentive schemes. Their fees depended on the price and speed of selling. As a result, most enterprises involved in the program were privatized. There was an opportunity for the employees to buy their firms, mainly in an ESOP construction, financed with preferential credit.

Free distribution and preferential selling in 1993–94 were aimed at strengthening the financial autonomy of several institutions (local governments, social security, churches, several foundations) and at creating a broad and vigorous proprietary middle class in Hungary. Instead of maximizing revenues, the government gave priority to social and political goals, taking into account the forthcoming parliamentary elections.

The main method of free distribution concerning certain groups of individuals was restitution, a specific mode of reprivatization in Hungary. Compensation notes to the value of 220 billion HUF were given to 2 million citizens, deprived of their properties or specific human rights during World War II and the decades of socialism. The freely tradable notes could be used in auctions for agricultural land, could be converted into shares of state firms on the stock exchange or used as a substitute for cash in the purchase of privatized companies.

Existence loans were the most widespread tool for preferential selling. Long-term credit with a five-year grace period and an interest rate much lower than inflation could be used only for buying state assets from the SPA. Existence loans played a role in more than 400 transactions to the value of 68 billion HUF contributed to employee and management buyouts between 1990 and 1998. Besides that, employees of all enterprises could buy shares in their company on preferential terms of up to 10 percent of the assets, even if the firm was sold to outside investors. Other preferential methods were rarely used. Privatization leasing, for instance, appeared in 27 cases to the value of 6 billion HUF.

The Small Investor Share Program was implemented as an attempt to provide quasi-free distribution to every citizen, similar to the Czech coupon system. The first phase of the program, started just before the parliamentary elections in spring 1994, involved only two companies. The new government did not continue the project and, moreover, announced a new privatization policy, reflected in a new privatization law passed in spring 1995.

The main motivation in the turnover in goals and methods was the unavoidable introduction of a stabilization program. The balancing of the central budget required not only cutbacks in expenditures but also increased revenues, including privatization incomes. Considerable sums could be expected from selling firms in the energy and infrastructure sectors. Within one year, majority shares of 13 firms (gas and electricity suppliers along with power plants) were sold to foreign strategic investors for more than 400 billion HUF, nearly double what the total cash privatization revenues had provided up to that point. In addition, the first share packages of the largest retail bank were introduced on the Budapest stock exchange. This was an overture involving private capital in the banking sector. By 1997, the proportion of the state in the registered capital of banks decreased to 21 percent, while foreigners owned more than 61 percent (Várhegyi, 1998).

The success of the stabilization program improved conditions on the stock exchange for privatization. Initial public offerings played an increasingly important role in the sale of state shares involving foreign and domestic capital, as well as institutional and small investors. Besides well-performing companies, the privatization agency tried to get rid of big loss-making, subsidized firms as well. Some of them were sold far below their nominal value, with the obligation of the buyers to repay debts or increase capital. In the second half of the 1990s, privatization went on with centralized, case-by-case selling, mainly for cash.

To sum up, privatization methods, targets, and priorities, as well as legal and institutional frameworks, changed several times during the period from 1989 to 2000. Hungarian privatization may be characterized as an unstable and mixed process. In a final evaluation, however, it is distinguished in the CEE context by the predominance of standard selling methods rather than special solutions or free distribution.[11]

This privatization approach directly explains the specifics of the recent ownership structure in CEE in comparison to some Western European structures. Because of the predominance of selling methods as opposed to distribution, there are real, personified owners, who, as a general rule, have risked their own financial resources. Because of the lack of mass privatization in

Hungary, there are significantly fewer parastate owners and quasi-privatized firms than in other post-socialist countries. Investment funds or mutual funds are not present as owners. Parastate institutional investors such as local governments or social security funds are not listed as private owners, and in many cases have begun to put their shares on the market to cover their current expenditures.

Other beneficiaries of free or preferential privatization behaved similarly. These methods helped accumulate domestic private capital, but not on the intended scale and not necessarily for the social strata targeted. As it turned out soon, many of the beneficiaries were either unable or unwilling to maintain the owners' position in the long run. Most primary holders of compensation notes sold the papers well below the nominal value. Hard-pressed either by lack of additional capital or by debt, the new entrepreneurs, like ESOP organizations, often sold their shares to outsiders.[12] This process might be interpreted as competition for ownership positions and market selection of the proprietors.

To sum up, the scarcity of domestic capital, along with the priority of selling for cash, resulted in the dominance of foreigners in the big enterprise (and banking) sector. Most Hungarian citizens and firms could become shareholders of large companies only on the stock exchange, and only in a minority position.

The attitude toward foreign capital has been one of the most stable elements of Hungarian economic policy. Foreign firms and individuals have been welcomed as greenfield investors and have been allowed to participate in all privatization transactions.[13] Nevertheless, the successful attraction of foreign investors goes beyond the scope of privatization policy. It is due to the rather stable political environment, the relatively developed legal framework and the increasingly promising general economic situation. Foreign direct investment exceeded 20 billion USD in 1999. This capital, along with new markets and management skills brought in by multinational firms, contributed to the restructuring and increasing competitiveness of the economy. After several years of recession, the growth of GDP in Hungary exceeded 4 percent between 1997 and 1999. Deficits of foreign trade, balance of payments, and state budget were moderate, while inflation and (registered) unemployment decreased (for more details see for instance Financial Research Ltd, 2000).

7.4 The impact of ownership structure on corporate governance

Having outlined the origins and the main characteristics of Hungarian ownership structure, we now turn to the question of how this structure works. Based on the results of empirical research of the "top 100",[14] we can formulate some hypotheses about the influence of ownership structure on corporate governance. The investigation focuses on five issues, namely the representation of owners in the firms, the interests of the owners, the formal position and interest of the management, the incentive mechanisms, and decision-making and control.

7.4.1 Owners and their representatives

All members of the "top 100" are organized as public (share) companies (*részvénytársaság, rt*) or limited liability companies (*korlátolt felelősségű társaság, kft*). According to Hungarian legislation, share companies have a dual board system. Boards of directors (*igazgatóság*) are composed of delegates of shareholders and may include the managing director (CEO) or some other members of management.[15] Boards of directors are supposed to prepare decisions and control the managers, and they may also be authorized to make certain decisions. Supervisory boards (*felügyelő bizottság*), consisting of the deputies of shareholders and employees (the latter group in minority position, involved only in large enterprises), exercise general control, without executive rights. In limited liability companies there is only one body, called the supervisory board.

Boards of directors in our sample are outsider-dominated without exception, but the executive director (CEO) is a member of the board. In four cases (one in state hands, two widely held, one management dominated) one or two other representatives of management are also involved. If the dominant shareholders are firms or the HPSHC, they often delegate their employees on the boards. In widely held companies, owners such as investment funds might also be present on boards, but most members are independent persons.

The formal decision-making power and the real influence of boards of directors cover a wide range even in our small sample. The committees have to discuss business plans and market strategies, and evaluate their fulfillment and the performance of the management. They often decide on major investments and organizational changes as well. Moreover, they may interfere in day-to-day decisions and act as management bodies. The frequency of board meetings may be considered as an indicator of the real influence of the committees. The most widespread practice in firms is the monthly meeting, reflecting a medium strength of the board. In one extreme we found a state-owned company with serious financial, organizational, and management difficulties, where the board sat every week or fortnight. The other extreme is the management-dominated firm, where board members meet "a few times a year."

In these cases, boards can hardly control the management. It is even more widespread that members of the board are in two minds, confused about whether they represent the interests of the owners or those of the firm. As some interviews indicated, they often tended to become agents of the management (or the firm), instead of controlling them.

This might be one reason to simplify ownership representation. One method is to dissolve the board of directors even in share companies, as happened at a big firm in our sample. The other solution is to choose the more simple limited liability form, designed originally for smaller units: 34 of the "top 100" were organized in this way. As the bulk of them (28 firms) are subsidiaries, we presume that this framework serves as a tool to avoid setting up the board of directors, and also to eliminate one hierarchical "agency" level in order to avoid the involvement of outsiders.

Besides formal bodies, in at least three cases in our sample there were informal representatives of the owners, called "coordinators" or "traveling consultants." They were not in a superior position in the hierarchy but had a decisive role in running the business.

Another solution to owners' representation by intermediaries is the establishment of a special organization for controlling several investments in Hungary. The two holdings of this type in our sample took over the ownership rights, including the delegation of board members to the affiliated firms, from the mother company. In the other version of funding new hierarchical levels, Hungarian subsidiaries might be acknowledged as regional holdings. As a subsidiary company of a multinational firm indicated, this arrangement entailed the owner having direct controlling rights over other subsidiaries in CEE.

State ownership has some specialties in this respect. According to an interview with a prominent personality in the HPSHC, the state shareholder's representation has become more organized during recent years. The votes of delegates to the general assembly are prescribed in detail by the board of the HPSHC. The board members appointed by the holding company, partially influenced by direct political considerations, have a free vote but they tend to follow the official "guidelines" in order to keep their position. They regularly consult the person in charge of each company who holds permanent contact with the management and has the most information about the firm. In the case of majority stake, the managing director of HPSHC responsible for the firm often visits the board meetings of the company and the CEO-president of the holding company meets the CEO of the firm regularly.

The system of corporate governance on the local level is even less structured. The ownership rights are divided between the general assembly (the Parliament of the local government), the mayor and his deputies, the ownership committee and other committees and the several departments of the apparatus. This constellation makes instruction of the board members rather confused. The parties involved in local government appoint representatives of local governments and the proportion follows their prevailing power relations (one of the important reasons why the number of board members increases in many companies after elections).

7.4.2 Interests of the owners

The main owners' interests, as formulated by them and interpreted by the managers, seem to be more independent from the ownership structure rather than owners' representation. The ultimate goal for every type of shareholder is gaining and increasing profit.

The concrete formulation of targets is closely related to the starting conditions of the investment. If shareholders purchased a company in poor financial condition, as was often the case in privatization transactions, the first goal was to minimize losses. In order to turn the company around, new owners started reorganization with considerable additional investment, including the repayment of loans or raising capital as well as restructuring production, market, and organizational frameworks. The latter usually meant concentration on core business, outsourcing of peripheries, reducing hierarchical levels inside the firm, and introducing new systems of accounting and controlling (through the State Property Agency, SPA) in order to increase transparency and to adopt the standards and procedures of the mother company.

As for most greenfield investments, the first aim was to introduce the trademark and increase market share. This was sometimes put as "achieving a dominant market position," and sometimes catching up with the market share of the mother company or other subsidiaries.

Having taken these steps or in cases of originally well-functioning firms, "owners are interested in the right bottom corner" of the balance sheet. Profit before taxation or profit per income is the most common task, precisely defined in yearly business plans. Shareholders of listed companies are interested in good preconditions for exit, that is, high prices on the stock exchange. The aims, declared as increasing quality or meeting customers' demand at the highest level, are to be interpreted in the context of increasing turnover and incomes. The profit task, formulated on a general level, however, opens the field for discussion with managers about the appropriate methods to be applied.

There is only one type of owner whose openly declared interests are more complex than profitability. State majority shareholders on governmental and local levels alike, might consider special issues.[16] Our interviews do confirm that the traditional approach of "responsibility for supply" (well-known in planned economies) has not disappeared and mainly concerns public services in a monopoly position. In most of these segments, prices are controlled, sometimes by the owner itself. High quantity and quality, no subsidies, and low prices or, as a manager summarized it: the task of the local government should be "zero profit and peace." In several other cases, state ownership is maintained in order to achieve goals such as controlling the strategic points of the economy or reserving some elements of natural, industrial, or historical heritage of the country. These considerations may obviously involve cross-profitability. The differentiated and conflicting targets leave wide room for maneuver for the state firms' managers.

7.4.3 Position and interests of the top management

The key figure in management in the corporate governance context, independent from the ownership structure, is the chief executive (or managing director). This individual is the "main agent" of the owners, supposed to mediate their interests in the organization. At the same time they are the representative of management, often sitting on the board of directors. In addition, they should act on behalf of the firm as a whole, enforcing their personal interests as well. Standing in the focus of multiple interests, the CEO *per definitionem* has to fulfill a delicate role.

Most directors interviewed formulated the main goal of management as the stability and constant development of the company. Concrete aims differed according to the firm's position, ranging from overcoming current financial crises to creating a regional multinational firm.

Growth of the company in terms of assets, market share, or turnover seems to be a general goal of management. "If the moon is not waxing then it is waning," explained a CEO. In some cases not only financial or small investors, but also strategic owners may consider management's growth plans hazardous. Nevertheless, the opposite case seems to be more widespread. Taking profits and returns as a starting point, owners urge quick growth, while management prefers moderate, steady rates. "We are like squeezed oranges", commented a director on the decision of the owner of the firm to halve the period for returns. The intention of managers is to minimize risks and effort.

Conflicts of interest concern not only the rate but also the preconditions of growth. Management fights for more resources and investment and in the case of multinational firms with numerous subsidiaries in several countries, this conflict often appears as competition among daughter companies or the conflict of interest of the individual firm and the group controlled by the same owner. The reallocation of incomes and investment funds inside the group may involve the basic task of profitability at the level of individual firms.

The other typical disagreement, determining dividends, has not been very sharp up till now. The reason is obviously the indisputable need to reinvest profits into new operations or state enterprises acquired before reorganization.

The interviews confirm the general aspiration of managers to increase room for maneuver and for autonomous decisions. This may concern the value limit of underwriting, the number and location of new units, the selection of business partners, the organizational structure of the firm, and so on. Centralization of decision-making rights throughout the multinational group, including the Hungarian subsidiary, proved to be a reason for the divorce of one of the CEOs interviewed.

During the past few years, changes in top management (chief executives and their deputies) affected nearly half the companies in our sample. Positions were preserved for long periods, sometimes independently from ownership changes, if the firm's performance was good. Former professional contacts and reputation also played a part. The position of directors seems to be the most unstable in subsidiaries. According to general assumptions, dispersed ownership gives less chance to change the guard, but it may also happen under these circumstances. At one of the biggest listed companies the shareholding structure did not protect either the chairman (and several members) of the board or the CEO. Considering the presence of the state as a minority, but relatively large, shareholder and the timing of the firing, direct political influence should not be excluded. Minority shareholders are also able to form a coalition against the incumbent management. In a widely owned firm with employee-management domination, market and financial crises first led to debt–equity swapping, then to banks' domination, and then to the changing of management.

In this latter case, the Hungarian CEO was succeeded by a foreign national of domestic origin, a person well-known as a former top manager in another "top 100" firm. The change from foreigners to Hungarians seems to be more widespread, however. The "import of managers" at the start of an operation is due to a lack of sufficient information about possible domestic candidates and special targets in the period of founding or acquiring the firm. Having set the new framework and become acquainted with the domestic market for managers, however, foreign directors are often replaced, at least partially, by Hungarians. The replacement is partially motivated by the attitudes of the visitors, since "they always have an eye on their home country." Additionally, domestic directors seem to be rather well-trained. Out of the ten companies in the sample where foreign owners were present, in at least five, Hungarian directors had had experience with other foreign firms and/or had some formal or informal training abroad. This included postgraduate studies as well as working at other firms of the same owner in several countries.

The general impression from the interviews was that directors were reserved in declaring their aims or the interests for the firm, which were different from those of the owners.[17] The reason behind the general carefulness is obviously the unstable position of directors and consequently loyalty to the owners. There is sharp competition in the market for top managers in Hungary. It is difficult to get inside the circle and there is too much to lose in terms of income, prestige, and other forms of compensation.

7.4.4   Incentive mechanisms and compensation

The main tool at the owners' disposal to solve the principal–agent problem, that is, to induce management to act according to shareholders' interest, is the system of incentives and sanctions. Some of the firms visited, mainly subsidiaries, had no well-defined incentive scheme to begin with. The salaries and bonuses of directors were not connected to any indicator. This meant uncertainty for the CEOs and probably a rather ineffective solution for shareholders. By the second half of the 1990s, all firms in our sample had applied some sort of calculable incentive mechanisms.

The compensation system usually consists of three elements: a fixed monthly salary, a bonus or premium, and noncash compensation. The flexible elements include comprehensive indicators such as the fulfillment of a yearly plan, the volume or rate of profits, and the level or growth of turnover, often supplemented with more detailed tasks such as decreasing costs or stock, or introducing new standards.

The proportion of fixed and sliding elements varies widely in our sample. The most common solution is the bonus ranging from three to five months' salary. At one extreme, this goes up to one year's salary in a state-owned company. At the other extreme, at a privatized firm with a dominant foreign strategic investor, the original system of combining the two factors is replaced with a fixed salary only. The consideration of owners might be that the responsibility of the subsidiary's manager is the fulfillment of the business plan under strict control, thus special incentive mechanisms are superfluous.

A relatively new attempt to fit managers' tasks to those of the owners is share options. Both widely owned and quoted companies in our sample applied some kind of share option. One firm bound the system to a medium-term increase in share prices in order to overcome the problem of price fluctuations independent of the firm's results. Another took into account as a basis of comparison the average stock exchange index (BUX) and the trends of other companies in the same sector, listed on leading financial markets.

The third package of compensation is the noncash form including cars, insurance, pensions, and healthcare contributions. An important element of these forms is "the prestige of the company," the chance to work with a large, often global firm. As a general practice, commitment is strengthened by the owners by inviting the subsidiary's management to the headquarters or the annual meeting of directors, often in exotic places. "These meetings have the atmosphere of celebration. Not all top managers are invited, only those who have deserved it. Anyone who is not present on these occasions, may not feel favored by the owners." The rather widespread attitude of directors employed by multinationals shows the dominance of hierarchy and respect of authority that holds mainly for young experts.

The specialty of state ownership in compensation mechanisms is rooted in differentiated goals with contradicting elements. In order to cope with this difficulty, state proprietary organizations attempt to set as detailed goals as possible. CEOs often have a new management contract every year, including numerous qualitative and quantitative targets and bonuses connected to them. It is well-known from the period of compulsory targets, that the more concrete the indicators are, the better the chance to fulfill them at the expense of neglecting other fields not included in the contract.

After many years of confusion, the HPSHC is now working with well-defined categories and rules concerning management compensation. Companies in majority HPSHC ownership are thus categorized according to their size. This serves as a basis for ranking salaries of the CEOs. As some directors indicated, the upper limit of salaries is influenced "by the envy of state bureaucrats": incomes of industrial managers have to correspond to those of civil servants. The upper limit of bonuses is officially capped at 50 percent of yearly income. Local governments have less general rules as they tend to set up incentive schemes for the firms individually. Both local owners and managers of enterprises tend to keep an eye on practice and income level applied by central state organizations.

7.4.5   Decision-making and controlling systems

The central element of decisions and control, just like that of compensation schemes, is the yearly business plan. It is approved by shareholders at the general assembly, but management also takes part in its preparation. Drafting the plan is the most important period for enforcing interests of both sides in terms of bargaining between owners and executives.

Empirical evidence shows intensive communication in the preparatory period between owners' representatives and managers, mainly on an informal level, or by the board of directors. Boards dominated by independent members do not make real decisions due to the asymmetry of information. Board members are also aware of their constraints, thus they tend to be rather cautious. "They often postpone decisions, indicating that they do not have sufficient information. We handle this problem by personal negotiations before or after meetings with each board member," one CEO told us.

Major decisions not included in the yearly plan are generally divided between owners, boards, and managers. The allocation is often formulated in terms of value limits and in most cases, limits for CEOs go up to 100 million HUF. At one extreme we found two subsidiaries with autonomous decisions of 10 million, on the other, a state firm with 500 million. As a general tendency, higher sums are affiliated with widely held and employee-management dominated companies, with low limits to subsidiaries and other foreign-owned firms.

The main method of control, applied in all firms visited, is a regular report regarding the fulfillment of the yearly plan. Reports differ according to frequency and content. In three cases (two subsidiaries, one state owned in crisis situation) detailed documents have to be produced every week. In more than half of the sample, management writes monthly reports. They may include some important indicators such as turnover, income, expenses, or 15–20 tables reflecting all fields of activity including non-financial indicators. Companies on the stock exchange are obliged, and other widely owned firms are usually allowed, to report their performance every quarter of the year.

Frequency and content of regular reports seem to be a sensitive indicator for the centralization of decisions. There are examples of loosening control at some subsidiaries and firms owned by another domestic company, mainly after stabilization of their performance and good personal contacts with the management. The main tendency, however, was strengthening control over the past few years. This is the first reaction of owners in critical situations, but it may reflect acquisition by new owners or the overall change in the mother firm's controlling system. In one of the subsidiaries, quarterly reports were changed to weekly ones, following the centralization wave all over the multinational group.

Similar steps are being taken by the HPSHC. Concentrating more on asset management than on sales and intending to establish comprehensive methods of exercising ownership rights, the holdings set up a new controlling system. Companies held in majority by the HPSHC now have to send a detailed report every month instead of every quarter. A stake of between 10 and 50 percent means the obligation of quarterly reporting, while firms with less than 10 percent state shares have to present their yearly balance sheet. The controlling department compiles a summary of reports every three months, drawing the attention of boards and directors of the holding company to firms in trouble.

Most managers interviewed complained about frequent and detailed reporting. It meant a lot of paperwork but owners often did not use the information collected. Thus, reports might be more or less formal, nevertheless they give an opportunity for shareholders' representatives to intervene (or exit) at any time. Owners, however, have to be (and state owners certainly are) aware of the fact that more centralization on the formal level does not necessarily mean increased effectiveness of control.

This is one of the reasons why many owners tend to supplement written sources with personal presence. In several cases this means regular visits by the owners or their representatives. At one company recently acquired by another Hungarian firm, the managing director of the latter is always present at the subsidiary. At listed companies, investors' analysts come to see the firm daily. "Business discussions" and "informative meetings" even abroad are held regularly, just like "phone conferences."

As a contact person, a "person in charge" is delegated to all companies in majority ownership of the HPSHC. This individual is thus in a position to obtain daily information about the enterprise, and thus to advise bosses and colleagues in the controlling department or on boards of the firm. Nevertheless, they tend to become representatives of the companies after some time. This is partly because specialists in the departments concerned are replaced rather frequently, even though this results in the loss of information and experience.

Besides reporting and personal presence, several owners have introduced organizational changes in order to strengthen control. As we have indicated before, one of the methods is setting up a holding company to control all investments in Hungary. The other method, applied at several multinationals, is a "functional directorate." In this system directors and departments of the subsidiary are directly subordinated to the people in charge at headquarters. (For instance, the Hungarian financial director reports to the financial director of the mother company abroad.) Under these circumstances the role of the subsidiary's CEO becomes marginal.

7.5 Conclusions

To sum up the lessons from the empirical analysis, some elements of corporate governance seem to be basically independent from ownership structure. They include the formulation of managers' goals and the owners' interests (with the exception of the state as majority shareholder). Other elements investigated are more or less influenced by the type and position of the proprietors.

First of all, firms with strategic investors in a stable majority position tend to minimize formal intermediaries of owners' representation. They choose the limited liability form lacking a board of directors, or even dissolve these bodies in share companies. Where boards do exist, they are composed of a few members, mostly delegated by the mother firm. The principle of "being as close to management as possible" is sometimes reflected in the setting up of Hungarian holding companies or building up informal but stable channels of personal presence at the subsidiary. On the other hand, both state-owned and widely owned companies tend to have large boards of directors with many independent members not employed in the shareholders' apparatus. State ownership involves political criteria in nominating committee members and often shows informal influence on different levels. Firms with dispersed ownership often have a board containing more than one representative of management. This is also characteristic for employee-management dominated firms where the board of directors tends to be a formal controlling body.

Second, the position of management is stable, even independent of ownership changes, if the firm's performance is satisfactory. Former professional contacts and the reputation of the directors also play a part, mainly in firms owned by other domestic companies. Deteriorating results or financial crises lead to firing even in widely owned (listed or employee-dominated) firms. In addition, political considerations are also important in the case of state-owned companies. The position of directors seems to be most unstable in subsidiaries, often independent of firm performance.

Third, the level and proportions of the three main incentives, monthly salary, bonuses, and compensation, differ according to ownership types. In subsidiaries and foreign-dominated firms, the level of income is higher than in state and other domestic-owned companies and the bulk of it is fixed salary. Sliding elements are connected and follow general indicators to some degree. Average bonuses range from three to five months' salary but may go up to one year's salary as well. Higher figures are characteristic of state-owned and widely owned companies. Share options are also present in Hungarian firms, mainly in the case of listed companies.

Fourth, the centralization of decision-making and controlling mechanisms might be characterized, among other things, by the preparation of the yearly plan, the frequency and content of reporting, limits to autonomous decision-making by top management, and channels and organizational frameworks of control. According to all indicators, subsidiaries and other foreign-dominated firms show strong centralization. All of them consider themselves as strictly subordinated units of the owner companies. There are widely owned and employee-management dominated companies where owners vote by exit or coincide with executives. Firms owned by other Hungarian companies fill up the middle of the scale, together with state-dominated units. The need for restructuring, along with crises, induces more centralization in all types of ownership structure.

According to our limited empirical evidence, most elements of corporate governance are similar in subsidiaries and other foreign-dominated companies. Thus, in contrast to our hypothesis, having a close to full stake does not make a big difference. If owners of this type have a stable majority, they tend to behave as exclusive proprietors even if there are several minority shareholders. Nevertheless, they often intend to increase their ownership stake. Consequently, even formal shareholding structures tend to get closer to each other, resulting in highly centralized governance systems.

On the other end of the scale we find management-employee dominated and widely owned companies, where the most important decisions are made by managers. From the point of view of strength and method of ownership control, two groups of companies stand in the middle: firms dominated by the state or those dominated by other domestic companies. Their controlling system and decision-making mechanism are much dependent on preconditions other than ownership structure, such as performance of the firm and the importance attributed to it by the proprietor, personal contacts between the owners' representatives and managers, the intended durability of shareholding position, and so on.

What are the consequences of these findings for the specialties of the Hungarian large enterprise sector, first of all on the decisive role of managers and the dominance of "recombinant property"?

Although employee-management ownership means the domination of management in all decisions (see also Boda and Neumann, 1999), the bulk of big companies were not legally owned by management in the second half of the 1990s. Moreover, this group of Hungarian "top 100" has shrunk considerably.[18] The wider concept of "managerial capitalism" may include the informal position of the executives and their decisive influence on the firm's operation independent of the formal (legal) ownership structure. We found that this kind of influence does exist but it is not a general feature for all big firms. The autonomy of management is strongly influenced by the ownership type: its degree is high in widely owned and state-owned companies.

Similarly, the concept of "recombinant property" defined by David Stark also holds for a smaller group and in a special sense for the late 1990s.

The differences in the basic data shown in section 7.2 are partially due to the period analyzed. The first formulation of the concept goes back to the early 1990s when several dozen state enterprises transformed themselves into groups of companies, with majority shares of the former enterprise remaining in state hands. "Recombinant property" describes these special structures insightfully. During the last decade, however, many of the conglomerates shrank or disappeared. Because of the critical fiscal and market positions and the restricted favorable effect of the transformation method applied, most firms fell into pieces and/or were closed down completely. Enterprise centers were forced to sell or swap their shares in order to cover debts and finance shrinking production. Thus firms lost their big enterprise status, were privatized piece by piece, or liquidated.[19] In other cases, when groups of companies were sold to a single investor, new (mainly foreign) owners usually started to simplify the organization by selling the units with noncore production, outsourcing several activities, or abolishing the legal entity of smaller units. These steps often put an end to networks and the coexistence of state and nonstate property within one company.

The second questionable element of Stark's analysis, as other researchers (Tóth, 1998) pointed out, is the registration of the presence of different shareholders without considering their ownership stake. Thus, even complicated networks might prove "empty." Minority or even marginal shareholders, such as state organizations or domestic companies, in many cases do not exercise an influence on the firm's portfolio.

The third and decisive reason for the divergence in the findings is the difference (and the shift) in the content of "intercorporate holdings." Stark's first analysis concentrated on the role of domestic firms. In the second stage of the research Stark and Kemény (1997) put domestic and foreign companies in one category. Considering the dynamics of privatization, it is the increase of foreign investment which explains why the proportion of companies in shareholding position jumped between 1993 and 1996. According to our empirical results, however, Hungarian and foreign companies as proprietors belong to different groups in terms of their corporate governance.

As a consequence, "recombinant property" as a network structure holds for the largest companies in a special sense. Most big Hungarian firms now belong to international networks: they are subsidiaries of multinational companies (combination with the state is not characteristic for this ownership type). This means that the "special" post-socialist networks, characteristic of the late 1980s and the early 1990s, were replaced by the dominant role of "intercorporate holdings," based on foreign ownership.

This model, as a result of acquisition or other forms of FDI, is well-known all over the world. It is not a special Hungarian or post-socialist arrangement. The new ownership structure of big firms might be characterized as a version of the Continental model, with few listed companies and the dominance of intercorporate holdings. Its specialty is a high concentration of ownership stakes, but contrary to France or Germany, also a high proportion of foreign investment. This structure is rooted partially in economic and privatization policies and partially in the trade of shares resulting in changes of ownership type. Considering that these changes are due to the market selection of proprietors, indicating that less effective owners (like post-socialist enterprise centers, other parastate owners or employees-management) are replaced by their competitors, this tendency might occur in other CEE countries as a "secondary privatization" process.

Notes

1. The starting point of the analysis is the list of "top 100" published by the business weekly *Figyelő* for the year 1997. David Stark, whose analysis of the Hungarian case is the most insightful and perhaps the most well-known, also draws his conclusions on "recombinant property" from the top 200 companies (and 25 big banks).
2. State ownership is defined here as direct involvement in the ownership structure. Indirect ownership via publicly owned firms or financial institutions is not registered in this category. We will show later that this type of shareholding is not really widespread among the "top 100".
3. Emerging private pension and healthcare funds have a marginal role in the Hungarian capital market recently. They are authorized to trade shares of firms listed on the stock exchange, so they might become minority owners of companies. Their investments are included in the category "domestic institutional investors" or "other units with legal entity."
4. In order to interpret our findings correctly we have to admit that the list of owners obtained is not equally detailed for all firms. In several cases we have categories like "domestic investors," "domestic individuals," or just "others." All these owners are typically in minority position, each with a marginal stake. The imperfection may influence the data on the presence of different types of owners in the population, especially the role of individuals, employees, and domestic corporations. In all cases where we had "other Hungarian legal entities" or "domestic investors" in general, we presumed the involvement of domestic firms and in the latter case the presence of Hungarian small investors as well. Nevertheless, the data concerning minority positions, included in this

kind of table (first of all Tables 7.3 and 7.4) can be interpreted as minimum proportions.

5. In Table 7.5 we first introduced an additional category of majority ownership. If an investor holds less than the half of the shares but it is the largest owner of the firm concerned, its position is similar to the formally majority shareholder and might be considered as a dominant owner. We also added a category of majority shareholders besides the three groups analyzed before, namely employees-management. They are dominant shareholders in only six cases; nevertheless, they are present on the screen.

6. Here we follow the categorization of David Stark (1994). This definition does not mean a real "crossing" in ownership structures in all cases, that is the shareholder company is not necessarily owned by the firm in its portfolio at the same time.

7. According to estimations, the weight of foreign capital in the big enterprise sector might approximate 70–80 percent, while it was 35 percent for all units with double bookkeeping.

8. Tóth (1998) found that 77 percent of all firms with double bookkeeping were isolated in 1995. The list of owners included at least one domestic company in only 15 percent of the firms. In a sample of larger firms (with 100 to 2000 employees) the proportions were 50 and 27 percent, respectively. Most of these contacts, however, represented minority shareholdings.

   Analyzing the ownership structure of the 500 largest Hungarian firms, Vedres (2000) found that nearly three-quarters of them were isolated in 1997. Although domestic companies stood in second place if we only count their presence among the owners, in most cases they were minority shareholders. (One-third of their investments did not reach 1 percent in capital.) They were in majority position in 23 percent of big firms, including 6 percent where they held 100 percent; 14 percent of the firms may be considered as members of ownership networks, forming six groups in the population.

9. From 1997 to 1998 four foreign investors reached majority position and another ten increased their ownership stakes in firms where they had already been dominant owners before.

10. This was the consequence of one consolidation measure, concerning a partially privatized commercial bank.

11. This is reflected in the structure of privatization incomes: more than the three-quarters was cash and 60 percent of the total sum was paid in foreign currencies. The proportion of compensation notes was 11 percent and preferential existence loans did not reach 5 percent.

12. As Table 7.1 indicates, the proportion of ESOP organizations in the capital decreased sharply during recent years.

13. The exception to the rule is the so-called small privatization, the sale of retail trade, shops, and restaurants. This was the only program applying market restrictions: auctions were not open to foreigners.

14. I gratefully acknowledge the support of Research Support Scheme Grant (No. 1588/1042/1998) for the empirical research. Having formed the six ownership types, according to the nature and concentration of the shareholders, we chose a random sample of firms, representative for ownership types in the "top 100." The sample consists of 15 companies with different fields of activity. We held structured interviews with leading personalities, chief executive directors, or their deputies. To reveal the behavior and attitudes of the owners went beyond the scope of the recent research. The only exception is the group of state

194 Corporate Governance in a Changing Environment

owners (central and local governments) where we collected information even at this stage.

15. The last modification of the Company Law made it possible not to set up this body at all share companies. 'Board' without any attribute will refer to board of directors in this chapter.

16. State organizations in a minority position of majority privatized firms may be interested first of all in profits or share prices, similarly to other owners.

17. The exception to the rule were the CEOs socialized under the planned economy, some of them still working in state enterprises. They are more used to this type of research situation and more willing to criticize their bosses.

18. From 1997 to 1998 only two out of six firms with employee-management domination preserved their position. Three others fell out from the "top 100" and one had to make a debt–equity swap, resulting in banks' domination in the ownership structure.

19. We do not have comprehensive data on these types of transformation. There are data on only about 49 big firms, the group of the so-called preferred under socialism enterprises. Of them, 19 formed a group of companies and 11 former enterprise centers did not hold any shares in subsidiaries by the mid-1990s. In 3 of these 11 cases almost all production was closed down; however, in the remaining 8 at least some of the independent new organizations survived as medium-sized firms. Big enterprise status, however, disappeared (see Voszka, 1997).

8
Revisiting the French Model: Coordination and Restructuring in French Industry in the 1980s and 1990s)[1]

Bob Hancké

8.1   Introduction[2]: Francosclerosis?

To many it has become a well-known refrain: France is the problem case in the European Union. Whereas German industry makes the country an export powerhouse, the flexibility of the Third Italy has secured the survival of technologically less sophisticated companies, and the labor market deregulation in the UK under the Thatcher regime created the preconditions for economic growth and employment successes, the French economy seems to be caught in the worst of all worlds, and utterly incapable of doing anything about it. Companies remain organized in a top-down manner at a time that flatter hierarchies are presented as recipes for success; many small companies who are the engines of growth in other countries, are financially weak and technologically underdeveloped; the main corporate strategy is price-based competition; and the few attempts to deregulate the labor market seem to have given way not to less, but more unemployment. Reform attempts inevitably lead to large-scale conflicts, organized by small groups who refuse to give up their privileges. And in the background of all this looms the heavy shadow of the French state, at a time when governments in other OECD countries are rapidly withdrawing from the economy.

This image of France is wrong. While the above picture may describe a world that was, in the last two decades the French political economy has gone through dramatic changes, that have fundamentally changed the internal operations of businesses, their market positioning, and relations with the French state. The endemic conflict in the workplace has, despite occasional and highly publicized outbursts of protest, all but disappeared: French strike figures are currently among the lowest in the OECD, and workers' skills are put to good use by many companies. With the support of their large customers, small firms have been able to upgrade their operations substantially. Cost competitiveness remains important to French industry, but most firms now combine that with quality and flexibility. And, despite the strong presence of the state, its role is considerably smaller today than it was in the past.

The most remarkable thing about these changes is not that they have taken place – after all, the entire postwar economic history of France consists of profound change (Boltho, 1996; Kindleberger, 1963; Sicsic and Wyplosz, 1996) – but that the state has not been the main actor in the process. Even today, analyzing industrial modernization in France means understanding how the state pulls or pushes society out of its deadlock. However, the adjustment process alluded to above took place at a time when the state attempted an orchestrated retreat from the economic scene (Boyer, 1997). After a nationalization spree in the early years of the first Mitterrand presidency, many banks and companies have been (re)privatized, the credit system liberalized, and the central planning apparatus devolved into a more decentralized support system for local companies. In short, whereas before the state was the central player in the French political economy, it is very hard to keep on seeing it as such today.

This chapter will argue that the changes in the French political economy are best understood as a reorganization of the basic configuration of the French political economy, not a fundamental shift to another production regime on a Germano-Japanese or Anglo-Saxon footing. For most of the postwar period, the French state was indeed the central actor, which used large firms to assure that modernization took place according to its plans. The state set technological goals for them, provided them with credit, and organized their labor market for them. As a result, during the postwar period, the large firms were in fact the state's instruments in these policies. Today, this situation is reversed. The large firms have gained autonomy from the state, and instead of being instruments of state policies they are increasingly exploiting those policies for their own strategies.

This outcome was the result of the particular French mode of coordination, which encompassed elites in the state, business, and finance (Bauer and Bertin-Mourot, 1995; Bourdieu, 1989; Suleiman, 1979), and how this fed into the corporate adjustment path in France. Corporate adjustment is therefore seen, as in the other contributions to this volume, as a process embedded in wider institutional and structural frameworks.

The remainder of this chapter starts with a short review of the most important changes in the French production regime between the mid-1970s and today, a discussion of how the contemporary literature on the French political economy has understood this and what an approach based on coordination can offer in addition to those analyses. Section 8.3 will present the story in full: how the crisis of the French production regime challenged the basic parameters of the French model, how the state and the elite reacted, and how these reactions led to a new organization of the French production regime. Section 8.4 concludes by summarizing the main points and by asking questions about the viability of the new French model.

8.2   Explaining adjustment in France

Comparing stylized pictures of French industry in 1975 and in 1995 gives an idea of the degree of change in the French political economy. In the mid-1970s, workplaces were highly Taylorized, where low-skilled workers performed extremely narrow tasks (Crozier, 1964). As late as 1982, almost 60 percent of all workers in France were semi- or unskilled (d'Iribarne, 1989). In comparative perspective, France not only had a much higher supervisors to workers ratio (Maurice et al., 1986, 1988), but also employed, controlling for all the usual variables, simply more people (Lane, 1989). Labor relations were highly conflictual, and unions were important obstacles to organizational change. Suppliers were small firms, more interested in their own survival than in the conquest of new markets and therefore perennially underfinanced and technologically backward. The large firms treated them as extended workshops rather than fully independent firms. The corporate governance system, finally, was a mixture of direct state control via ownership, indirect state control via the credit system and the planning apparatus, all run by a small group of meritocratic elites (Shonfield, 1965; Zysman, 1983).

The picture in 1995 is fundamentally different. Workplaces still have a strong Taylorist flavor, but instead of isolated jobs performed by unskilled workers, the shopfloor in many companies is made up of teams of polyvalent workers (Benders et al., 1999; Duval, 1996, 1998). Labor unions have by all accounts become irrelevant in the contemporary French political economy. Only some 9 percent of the workforce is organized today, and in the private sector alone, the organization rate has dropped to 5 percent. Despite their monopoly in works councils sections, labor unions have lost the works councils to independent lists (Daley, 1996). In comparative perspective, France has become a low-strike country: between 1980 and 1990, strike rates were converging on the low German one, and diverging from the much higher rates in Italy and the UK (Boltho, 1996). Small firms and their relationships with large firms have changed as well. More than half of small firms make a substantial share of their turnover as suppliers to large firms: between 1980 and 1990, the proportion of subcontracting SMEs rose from roughly 40 percent to roughly 55 percent (Duchéneaut, 1995: 199). In order to be able to keep these customers, they have had to become much stronger technologically and organizationally: almost without exception suppliers are certified according to the prevailing international ISO 9000 quality management standard and as a result, they now are an active partner to their customers among the large firms while counting many international companies among their customers (Casper and Hancké,

1999). The corporate governance system, too, has changed in character: between 1986 and 1993, many formerly state-owned companies have been privatized, the system for industrial credit has been transformed around the stock market, and as a result of its increased autonomy, management is considerably more immune from state intrusion.

How should we understand these changes? Both the literature on economic change in advanced capitalism and the more narrow debate on the recent evolution in France in particular, have produced two broad perspectives to understand the transition reflected in these data. According to the first interpretation, which has been developed in many studies of the postwar French growth miracle, change as such is nothing new. Postwar economic development, captured in the phrase of the *trente glorieuses*, primarily was change orchestrated by the state. Through the industrial policy apparatus, the planning mechanism, and ownership of strategic sectors of the economy, the French state succeeded in creating the conditions for a profound transformation of the French economy from a largely agricultural society to a modern industrial power (Berger, 1972; Estrin and Holmes, 1983; Hall, 1986). This same policy-making apparatus, slightly modified to meet the challenges of the new situation, was also at the basis of recent developments. The state conceived policies that the main economic actors had to follow, and then used the industrial policy and economic planning apparatus as well as the broader legislative process to induce the latter to do so.

This interpretation explains how, as a result of direct state intervention, the French car industry rebounded after a profound crisis that led the two national car producers into virtual bankruptcy (Hart, 1992). It understands the reorganization of the French steel industry after its own succession of crises since the late 1970s as a result of state policies that helped companies restructure and corporate and labor union interests converge on a new industrial plan for the industry (Daley, 1996). This argument is also at the basis of an account of the process of privatization in France after 1986 and how it contributed to a profound restructuring in many industries, and led to a substantial difference in management styles and orientations (Schmidt, 1996).

However, these accounts do not tell the whole story. The equally dramatic failures of some of the state policies in other industries, for example in the computer and machine-tool industries (Ziegler, 1997; Zysman, 1977) should raise questions about the *omniscient* and *omnipotent* French state. Precisely at the moment, for instance, that the machine-tool industry required higher skills and more flexible forms of work organization in order for companies to position themselves in more quality-oriented and less cost-sensitive markets, the French state attempted to modernize the industry by imposing policies copied from the large firms that competed in mass markets (Ziegler, 1997).

The state-centred argument also ignores an even more important policy development of the 1980s. What probably characterized French economic and industrial policy most during that period, were the attempts by the state to retreat from direct economic and industrial policy-making. After a nationalization wave in 1981, governments have put considerable energy into privatizing the state-owned companies. Labor relations were organized in such a way that the state played a smaller role, and unions and employers were presented with the opportunity of negotiating change on their own. And in a dramatic attempt to reorganize the state apparatus, a series of decentralization laws was passed that aimed at creating new regional and local partnerships for economic development. All these policies were informed by what has become known as "Toquevillian liberalism," which implied a simultaneous reduction of central state involvement in policy-making, and a devolution of power to local and regional societal actors – in short, the opposite of a state-centred, *dirigiste* policy.[3]

An alternative interpretation builds on the reduced state role in contemporary France. What explains the transition in this view was that firms were subjected to new forms of competition, a process in which the state actively participated. By deregulating the environment of companies – in capital markets with the financial deregulation of 1984, and in labor markets since the mid-1980s – competition in these areas was intensified, and economic actors, that is, banks, companies, and workers, were forced to cope with this new situation. This interpretation has strong adherence in France itself, mainly among progressive Gaullist and left-wing observers (Comm. Général du Plan, 1996; Bourdieu, 1989), who deplore the grip of international capital markets on the French economy and how globalization jeopardizes the traditional, mainly state-organized bonds of solidarity (Hoang-Ngoc, 1998; Lipietz, 1998; Todd, 1998).

Without denying that economic adjustment in France has had disruptive social consequences, it is hard to see how this could have been a direct effect of deregulation and increased competition. By all accounts, industrial concentration has increased in France during this period: in response to the crisis that the large exporting industrial companies faced in the first half of the 1980s, the restructuring of industrial sectors frequently entailed a further reduction of the number of large firms in these sectors. In the automobile industry, for example, two firms – Renault and Peugeot – who are roughly equal in size (in terms of turnover and employment) dominate the sector. The steel industry, which was made up of a few large and many small producers before, was consolidated into one gigantic steel conglomerate in the mid-1980s. And the government used its ownership of the chemical industry to restructure the industry into a few complementary rather than competing firms. Overall, in most industries, one or very few large companies accounted for over 50 percent of turnover in 1994 (INSEE, 1996). In fact, detailed econometric evidence on the 1980s (Amar and

Crépon, 1990) demonstrates that the increase in industrial concentration during this period has been a major factor in increasing the competitiveness of French exporting industry.

In fact, the abrupt and far-reaching deregulation of the financial sector – perhaps the main instance where a policy was introduced which aimed at increasing competition – did not result in a competitive capital market characterized by a high merger and takeover activity, but in a highly orchestrated system of hard-core cross-shareholdings, which were formed precisely in an attempt to prevent rampant competition (Bauer, 1988; Maclean, 1995; Morin, 1995). In short, none of the outcomes conventionally associated with a market-led adjustment process can be found in France.

Understanding adjustment in France over the last two decades does require going beyond the state–market opposition that is central in political economy, and bring in firms – in the case of France the large exporting companies in particular – as the key actors. The modernization of the French economy over the last two decades was not a state- or market-led process, but a firm-led one, whereby firms used public resources on their own terms and for their own adjustment, and then induced other actors, through power, competition, and cooperation, to act in a congruent manner.

Anybody familiar with the postwar French economy will hardly be surprised by the central role of large firms in the adjustment process. The entire Gaullist modernization program was constructed around them as the engines of economic development, and after the arrival of the left in office in 1981, the nationalizations of the same year announced themselves as the logical continuation of the Gaullist strategy. In this situation, however, the large firms were – with only a slight sense of exaggeration – instruments for broader social, economic, technological, and regional development goals pursued by the state. In exchange, the state provided them with an institutional infrastructure in labor relations, regional development agencies, and technology transfer systems that offered them stable growth. Today, however, large firms have considerably more autonomy in designing their goals while relying considerably less upon state initiatives in their implementation. Instead of being objects of state policies, the large firms had become the agents of a profound modernization process.

The organizational basis for this shift toward a large firm-led adjustment model was the mode of coordination in France, which is based on a particular configuration, different from both the German associational model and the Anglo-Saxon market model of economic coordination discussed in the first two chapters in this volume. It entails a system whereby the state, banks, and large firms are intertwined through a complex elite network. In the course of their education, the "best and the brightest" of a cohort are selected through a series of difficult exams, after which they go on to study at the *grandes écoles*, and from where they are recruited into the top of the state administration. After a career in the state apparatus, these people then move into other areas as top managers in large companies or banks, and almost invariably start, with several years' intervals, moving between these three spheres (Birnbaum, 1994; Bourdieu, 1989; Suleiman, 1979; Suleiman and Mendras, 1995). In the 1980s as much as in the 1960s and 1970s, most CEOs in France have, in fact, followed this typical career path from the *grandes écoles* into the state apparatus and the government and then into finance or business (and back, when duty called) (Bauer and Bertin-Mourot, 1995).

This mode of coordination relies upon several mechanisms. The first is the meritocratic selection mechanism, which imbues all participants with an elitist ethos, producing a relative autonomy, on the basis of educational credentials (Bourdieu, 1989), of management. Different studies in different eras demonstrated that the social distance between top management and the rest of the company (who have not followed this elite education trajectory) is vast in France (Crozier, 1964; Hofstede, 1980). The meritocracy also socializes the members of the elite into one basic worldview. Empirical studies of the financial elite in France, one of the pillars of the system, show, for example, that the educational background in the *grandes écoles*, more than political convictions and similar experience, provides the social cement for interaction among this group (Kadushin, 1995). The final element deals, after this initial period of socialization, with the monitoring and sanctioning mechanisms within the elite. As a result of the relatively small size of the group, the track record of individual members who pursue a career is in principle knowledge shared by all in the elite, and forms the basis for further career advances. The individual reputation in this elite network, with its roots in the state, is therefore the currency used among the financial, economic, and bureaucratic elites in France.

In the early 1980s, a profound crisis hit the French production regime, and this elite coordination structure became the organizational framework for the subsequent adjustment. It filtered the effects of both the financial deregulation of 1984 and the privatizations of 1986 and thus allowed a reorganization of the corporate governance system. Deregulation and privatization could – and were designed to – impose a regime of intense competition upon CEOs, which included detailed scrutiny by investors. In fact, however, the elite coordination mechanism led to the opposite situation: it allowed for a large sphere of autonomy for top management, by shielding the CEOs of large firms from outside influences – both the state and capital markets – during the process of internal corporate reorganization. Because of this relative insulation, CEOs were now able to pursue their conception of competitiveness and profitability with considerably more vigor than under the state's aegis.

However, as the literature on the inertia of the French model predicted, firms could not simply move out of the old situation by CEO fiat. In order to pursue their internal adjustment, the companies relied heavily on public resources. The firms used the panoply of regional government agencies, technology institutes, and training centers, as well as the different laws and administrative instruments that dealt with the labor market, as instruments to fill the holes in their own adjustment capacities. By doing so, they also ended up inducing the other relevant actors – small firms, labor unions, and workers – to act in a manner congruent with the path they took.

The remainder of this chapter will develop this argument, first by showing how exactly top management increased its autonomy, and then by detailing how companies restructured internally by reorganizing their ties with workers and suppliers.

8.3   The French political economy in the 1980s

The reorganization of the French production regime followed a profound crisis in the early 1980s. The key ingredients of such a reorganization were the restructuring of the firms' internal operations, that is, workplace reorganization and suppliers' links. However, such restructuring had traditionally proven to be very difficult because of the endemic inertia in the French model (Crozier, 1964, 1970). Given the crucial role of the state in French industry, a reorganization of the corporate governance system was a necessary condition, so that top management was allowed autonomy from the state and labor unions. This section is built around that logical sequence. It starts with an analysis of the crisis of the early 1980s, and then moves on to the reorganization of the corporate governance system and how precisely it created the conditions for CEO autonomy. The final two subsections then discuss the substantive changes in the workplace and how the links between large firms and their suppliers were reorganized.

8.3.1   The crisis of the French production regime

Between 1980 and 1985, the French production regime experienced two separate but mutually reinforcing crises. The first was an internal crisis of the large firms in the first half of the 1980s; the second a crisis of the supporting macroeconomic policy regime. Despite the mass production strategies based on economies of scale – which themselves were relatively successful, since many large firms became leaders in European markets in the early 1980s – the companies posted dramatically low profits in this period: aggregate profitability in France was among the lowest in the G7 (Glyn, 1997). Moreover, as a result of the implicit soft budget constraints for many among them that resulted from the state's willingness to finance their growth, their expansion had led to a situation where they found themselves with an extremely high debt burden, the highest in the OECD

(Hall, 1986). Third, labor productivity was low by European standards. Detailed comparative assessments of car production, for example, demonstrated that the French automobile industry, at that moment a market leader in Europe, was less productive even than Fiat: Peugeot calculated that it produced 8.3 cars per worker per year in 1983 (down from 9 in 1979), Fiat almost 12 (up from 10) cars and Ford-Europe 13.2 (up from 10.4) (Loubet, 1998). Finally, massive social conflicts in those sectors that spearheaded the French economy exacerbated the internal problems: semi-skilled workers refused the organization of work and the concurrent lack of career perspectives that came with it. Combined, these four elements led to a profitability crisis of gigantic proportions in French industry. Table 8.1 presents a picture of French industry in the early 1980s.

A profound crisis of "external" conditions accompanied this internal crisis. The expansionary policies pursued by the left-wing government after May 1981, rapidly gave way to serious problems. International capital markets began to speculate against the franc, and the government was increasingly running into budgetary problems as a result of the macro-economic expansion and the nationalizations (which cost over Fr130 billion). In March 1983, the government therefore decided, after serious debate (Cameron, 1996; Halimi, 1992), to leave the "socialism in one country" policy and adopt a more restrictive stance (Hall, 1986). The political decision to stay within the ERM, and thus reorient French economic

Table 8.1   Financial results of large firms, 1981–85 (in billions of francs)

	Accumulated results 1981–85
Sacilor	−25.30
Usinor	−25.00
Renault	−27.40
CDF-Chimie	−6.50
Péchiney[a]	3.90
Bull	−2.80
CGCT	−2.30
Thomson[b]	1.90
EMC	−0.60
SNECMA	−0.02
Matra	+0.40
Aérospatiale	+0.80
Dassault	+1.90
Saint-Gobain	+2.50
CGE	+2.60
Rhône-Poulenc	+3.00

[a] Excluding capital grant to PCUK (Fr 3 billion).
[b] Excluding capital grant to Thomson-Télécom (Fr 1.1 billion)
Source: Schmidt (1996: 108).

policy in order to strengthen the franc by fighting inflation, provided the broad macroeconomic background for the crisis of the French production regime.

The macroeconomic policy adopted after 1983, which was given the euphemistic name of "competitive disinflation," had two goals. The first and most important one was to create the domestic economic conditions for a stabilization of the franc after the devaluations of 1982–83. The instrument was straightforward wage restraint by imposing inflation targets on wage negotiations. As a result, France became, after Portugal and Greece, the country with the lowest real wage growth in the EU after 1985 (Taddéi and Coriat, 1993). The second goal followed from the first and was an attempt to emulate the hard currency environment that had been so beneficial to German industry: unable to rely on competitive devaluations for export success, the argument went (Albert, 1991), German industry was forced to search for competitiveness in quality rather than price.

These macroeconomic policies radically changed the broader environment of companies. In the short run, the *franc fort* policy raised French interest rates to the highest level in the OECD, while, more structurally, the adherence to the ERM (later EMS) also implied an acceptance of the broader framework of competition rules regarding subsidies for ailing companies within the EU. The high interest rates hit companies at the worst possible moment: not only did they raise the price of productive investments, but highly indebted companies were severely punished by this situation: for some of them debt servicing reached over 15 percent of annual turnover! Finally, budgetary constraints and adoption of EU competition rules, moreover, led to a structurally new situation: the well-known option of having the state finance the losses until the business cycle picked up again was increasingly becoming impossible as a viable option.

8.3.2 State-led corporate survival

Despite the restrictions on state involvement, the government played a crucial role in the first phase of the adjustment process. Having assumed ownership of many large firms after the advent to power of a left-wing government, the government could now shelter the large companies from bankruptcy and foreign takeovers.[4] While nationalizing the industry and the credit sector in the first year of the Mitterrand presidency were actions primarily couched in anticapitalist terms, broader strategic objectives, evoking the Gaullist program of maintaining a strong national industrial basis as a precondition for political *grandeur*, were never very far away. Mitterrand expressed this idea powerfully when he presented the nationalizations to the public in September 1981, and explained that if nationalizations did not in fact take place, "these companies would rapidly be internationalized" (quoted in Cohen, 1996: 227).

By the time they were hit by the crisis, many of the large companies were therefore state-owned, which allowed them to become recipients of massive state aid: combined, the companies listed in Table 8.1 received over Fr64 billion in subsidies, three-quarters of which went to the steel companies Usinor and Sacilor (subsequently nationalized, merged, and restructured) and Renault alone (Schmidt, 1996: 108). Importantly, however, in all cases, the subsidies were accompanied by the negotiation of a detailed business plan.

The goal of the business plans in the different industries was invariably a rapid restructuring in order to redress the dramatic financial situation by means of a massive cost-cutting program. The first effort in this regard was the negotiation of a series of social plans to rapidly reduce the workforce in the companies. Between 1984 and 1987, Renault thus reduced its total workforce by almost 30,000, or 20 percent (Freyssenet, 1998). The Peugeot group did the same: between 1980 and 1987, 57,000 workers were laid off (23 percent of the workforce) (Loubet, 1998). The steel industry, where the crisis had set in a few years earlier, reduced employment in the sector by 45 percent between 1980 and 1987 (Daley, 1996). Overall, the large companies shed 20 percent of their jobs in the 1980s (Berger, 1995; INSEE, 1993; SESSI, 1997).

Since hard layoffs were (and are) very difficult in France – in contrast to the Anglo-Saxon economies – the large firms were forced to search for other ways to reduce employment. These were found in the wide array of state programs that were made available to workers for early retirement and the measures that were associated with more restrictive immigration policies (Guillemard, 1991). More than half of the workforce reductions in the car industry were financed by these measures (and for the remaining ones, the companies relied upon other state programs for industrial conversion), the massive workforce reductions in the steel industry were almost entirely state-financed through the early retirement system (Daley, 1996), and even the SNCF managed its workforce restructuring through reliance upon the state (Cauchon, 1997).

The second big cost-cutting move by the large firms was a rapid extension of subcontracting by means of outsourcing production and services. Between 1979 and 1985, for example, the vertical integration rate of Renault and PSA fell from 26 to 19 percent for the former and from 35 to 26 percent for the latter. Électricité de France, the large state-owned utility company, did the same: instead of hiring new workers, the company hired subcontractors for the maintenance of its nuclear plants and network, and for local customer service. EDF workers that were hired, furthermore, were hired with regular labor contracts, no longer on the civil servant statute typical of EDF workers.

These subcontracting operations had the advantage of rapidly clearing the balance sheets, since many of the supporting activities associated with the subcontracted tasks were eliminated as well: product development, process engineering, training, quality control, and so on. And in assembly industries subcontracting also implied just-in-time delivery of parts upon demand, which had the additional financial advantage of reducing capital tied up in the inventory of parts to a minimum. Between 1984 and 1987, for example, Renault used these plans to reduce its stock of cars that were made but not yet sold by 55 percent, and despite the increase in outsourcing, reduced its purchasing/turnover ratio by eight percentage points between 1984 and 1988, due to the renegotiation of prices with suppliers (Freyssenet, 1998).

Through a reorganization of the production and service chain, and as a result of dramatic cuts in their workforce, the large firms in France thus managed a serious reduction of their immediate production costs. The most remarkable example of such a turnaround is probably Renault: whereas the company lost over Fr11 billion per year in 1984 and 1985, from 1987 onwards, it posted high profits (and continued to do so for the following ten years). The same happened in other large companies. After the crisis of the early 1980s, for example, the French steel industry, now concentrated in Usinor-Sacilor, became one of the most profitable on the Continent (Smith, 1998), and EDF managed to turn structural operating deficits into an operating surplus despite the government's claims on its revenue. In short, by 1987, and as a result of the cost-cutting measures, the large firms had secured their financial survival.

8.3.3   Elite coordination and corporate adjustment

While these restructuring plans solved the short-term cost problems and thus helped stabilize the French political economy in the short run, they created a series of entirely new challenges for the large firms. Sustained profitability, which had become the main goal by the mid-1980s, was only possible through a series of organizational innovations that increased productivity. Two areas were, given the existing weaknesses of French organizations, of crucial importance: workforce skills and the organization of work, on the one hand, and subcontractors and suppliers, on the other. The post-mass production era required broadly trained teams of workers instead of unskilled workers as well as sophisticated suppliers to address the volatility of demand (Piore and Sabel, 1984).

Yet these were precisely the type of reorganizations that had traditionally proven to be difficult in France. Despite the "presidentialism" of French management and the relative weakness of labor unions, corporate reorganizations were difficult, because of a number of reasons: the state kept a close watch on the social policies of large firms, French workers were insufficiently trained for them to be deployed flexibly, structures for workers' participation on the shopfloor did not exist, while unions managed to mobilize possible sources of discontent in shopfloor reorganization and thus thwart shopfloor adjustment strategies. Moreover, increased outsourcing was certain to raise union resistance, because of the job losses they implied. In short, a reorganization of work could succeed only if management proved able to neutralize both the state and the labor unions.

Suppliers, on the other hand, had traditionally been treated as simple executors of large firm orders, and were technologically unsophisticated without proper innovation capacities as a result, and therefore simply incapable of dealing with any new demands from large firms. Since any reorganization of the supplier networks of large firms would entail a dramatic restructuring of the small firm sector, which included dropping some altogether and reorganizing the others through technology programs and mergers. Governments would be hard put to accept the social consequences of such a reorganization. Again, a strategy based on technologically well-equipped small firms could only succeed if management had a free hand in restructuring its supplier base.

The autonomy of top management from both the state and the stock market thus became a necessary condition to pursue internal reorganizations. Autonomy from the first was necessary to be able to drop a broad social and political dimension from management decisions and concentrate solely or at least primarily on profitability; fortunately, that was also the Fabius government's message to CEOs in the midst of the crisis of corporate France in the early 1980s. Yet being shielded from the immediate impact of the stock market was equally important, since corporate reorganizations announced themselves as a relatively long-term process, which required patient capital; without protection from the short-termness of the stock market, many companies would have been unable to survive the financial pressures they were exposed to under an open capital market.

The elite-based coordination mechanism, which tied the large firms to the state, provided the conditions for management autonomy from both the state and the stock market. As discussed before, the setup was one in which top management was sealed off from the rest of the company, but tightly linked to the administrative apparatus. The privatizations of the 1980s and 1990s grafted themselves upon this system, but led to a profound change in the way it operated. Because of how the privatizations took place, they created a protective circle of core shareholders, giving the CEO more autonomy from the state while protecting the company against takeovers. If the state was able to directly influence decision-making in large companies before, the changes in ownership structure made it much harder in the future. The hard core of investors that grew out of the privatization process simultaneously became the central point of reference for management action, and offered protection against invasive initiatives by the state.

Understanding how this happened requires going back to the end of the 1970s and early 1980s, before the reforms dealing with finance were implemented. The core of the relationship between industry and the banks in France was the vital importance of long-term debt for the financing needs of large firms. As late as 1980, French firms were the most highly indebted companies in the OECD, which put the banks in a position of serious influence over the affairs of industry; and because most of the debt was medium to long term, these banks generally took an active interest in the production and marketing strategies of the firms they supported in order to safeguard their investment (Cohen et al., 1985: 47; Hall, 1986).

Most of these credit institutions were specialized banks who, combined, collected and disposed of two-thirds of all deposits in the French banking system. In addition, there was a set of public investment funds, administering several billions of francs, that was used for joint projects with private banks and as a discount fund for their loans (Hall, 1986; Zysman, 1983).

The main problem in the system was that, by discounting the loans, the government in fact ended up assuming the risk and as a result, banks were, despite the close relationship between finance and industry, especially poor at long-term monitoring (Goyer, 1998). In order to deal with this issue, the government's aim was to reorganize the financial system in two ways. The first was to dismantle the sectoral credit monopolies by allowing most banks to become universal banks, thus installing competition for loans and deposits between them. The second was to liberalize the system of industrial credit through a series of fiscal regulations that made investing in stocks more appealing to households. As a result of these reforms, households had a variety of ways to save, and companies a variety of ways to obtain (a variety of) money: they could rely on long-term bank financing, issue shares to investors, and rely on retained earnings for investment.

The financial reform of 1984 was followed by the privatizations (under the right-wing government after 1986) of many of the companies brought under the state's control only a few years before. The formal goals of this reform were simple: selling off the nationalized large firms using the new tools that had become available after the financial reform and thus create a popular capitalism of the Anglo-Saxon kind (Goyer, 1998; Schmidt, 1996).

However, the privatizations took place in a profoundly different way. Instead of being sold to a wide collection of potential owners, the companies were sold to five categories of investors only: the first was a hard core of stable shareholders, the so-called *noyau dur*, the second the workforce, the third, quantitatively most important part, to the public at large (that is, using the financial instruments that were born out of the financial reform), and the fourth and fifth to French and foreign institutional investors (Cohen, 1996: 237–8). The privatizations were designed so that employees were given a preferred shareholder status by reserving up to 10 percent of shares for employees and giving them discounts on the purchase (Schmidt, 1996: 156–7). Furthermore, in many cases the government limited the maximum number of shares that individuals could buy, thereby assuring that ownership was not concentrated. And in order to avoid speculative bursts and unwanted swaps, shares that were not sold for a longer period (up to 18 months) were rewarded with an extra share or tax advantages. These hard cores consisted of groups of banks, insurance companies, and industrial companies that acted as long-term institutional investors and were supposed to help govern the company and protect it from takeovers (Schmidt, 1996: 157–63).

As a result of this gigantic financial engineering operation, two stable groups of cross-shareholdings emerged, each constructed around a giant utility company, a holding company, a major bank, and a large insurance company. The first had Lyonnaise des Eaux, the holding company Suez, the Banque Nationale de Paris (BNP) and the Union des Assurances de Paris (UAP) at its core, the other Générale des Eaux, Paribas, Crédit Lyonnais, Société Générale, and the insurance company Assurance Générales de France (AGF) (Morin, 1995). Together, these financial cores had direct and indirect controlling stakes in each other and almost all publicly quoted large companies. For example, the UAP–BNP core held 8.8 percent in Air France, over 15 percent in Saint-Gobain, 9.2 percent in Elf, and 7.5 percent in Péchiney. The AGF–Paribas group held 20 percent in Aérospatiale, 20 percent in Usinor-Sacilor, 14 percent in Rhône-Poulenc, and 7.2 percent in the oil company Total.

Because of the particular corporate governance structure in France, where small shareholders are neither directly nor indirectly represented (something the proxy voting system in Germany allows), this particular mode of privatization should have amounted to an extraordinary control over industry by these hard core investors (Morin, 1995). Yet the opposite was the case. Shareholders did get a better look at the inside of the companies – a result of the publication and accounting requirements following the opening up of the capital market – but that did not imply more control over management. Instead of reducing management autonomy, the reorganization of the corporate governance system opened the way for the management of large firms to construct a broad sphere of independence from outside influences.

The privatization package included a set of rules on the selection of members of the board of directors, which gave the CEO the right to appoint most of the board members and of the hard core of investors more generally him- or herself. Since the companies that these people represented were frequently entangled in complex cross-ownership arrangements with each other and with the company on whose board they sat, control was, if it took place at all, far from tough. Secondly, more management autonomy also implied more financial freedom. As a last and extremely effective safeguard against unwelcome surprises, many CEOs thus created or took control of subsidiaries that allowed them to buy back their floated shares. Even if the representatives of those companies on the board took their job seriously, they were, needless to say, more than careful in pressing too hard for control. Their career depended, after all, on the CEO that they formally controlled (see Schmidt 1996: 374–7 for full owner-ship details). François Morin, one of the most prominent observers of the restructuring of French capital, aptly calls this setup "self-management by management" (Morin, 1995).

Large firms used their own privatization to construct a situation in which they were able to pursue internal reorganizations without being burdened by traditional social policy, regional development, and other nonfinancial considerations. Thus, this situation sheltered firms from hostile takeovers during the crisis years, while it assured the companies of the capital needed for the necessary restructuring. Secondly, this holding structure also created a situation of autonomy in relation to the state and the labor unions (who often depended on the state): it allowed firms to be reorganized through massive layoffs if this proved necessary, since the state was no longer the only (socially conscious) owner. In other words, the large companies were able to pursue more relentless workforce reduct-ion policies, and increase subcontracting and outsourcing as a way to cut direct production costs. It also allowed, where necessary, international corporate alliances, as in the case of GEC–Alsthom or the planned merger between Renault and Volvo. In sum, the internal reforms – which fre-quently entailed a brutal externalization of costs onto workers and small firms – could be pursued without state intrusion and against the will of the labor unions.

The following two sections detail two critical areas of internal reform: the labor relations system writ large, and the supplier system. Both areas were at the heart of the initial restructuring to stop the crisis in the early years: massive layoffs and rapid externalization of immediate production costs. A thorough redefinition of the French production regime, however, required more than a simple reorganization to cut costs. Without the organizational prerequisites for a move into more flexible mass markets (combining high volume with high quality and product differentiation), the crisis of the French model was bound to repeat itself, probably no later than during the next downturn in the business cycle.

8.3.4 Restructuring the labor relations system

A redefinition of the French production regime critically hinged on shopfloor restructuring, and that, in turn, required a reorganization of the broader labor relations system. Such a reorganization implied solving two types of (different) problems. The first was related to the basic configura-tion of work organization and skills. French firms were traditionally highly Taylorized, as a result organizational structures were inefficient (in large measure because they employed too many people), and they incorporated a wide array of obstacles to change. Repositioning in new market segments implied a profound overhaul of the work organization system. The second, related, issue is union politics. French unions are radical, and mirroring the workplace relationships based on distrust, they are unwilling, and most likely unable, to take reform proposals, even by progressive management, seriously. However, because of their de facto capacity to block changes, a reorganization of the workplaces depended either upon the labor unions' goodwill (which was not forthcoming), or upon a strategy that sidelined them.

The reorganization of the internal labor market followed very rapidly after the first measures that secured the survival of the companies. Since the early 1980s, the goal of official government policy has been to assure that by the mid-1990s, four out of five young people had a certificate of completed secondary studies – until the age of 18 or 19, the *baccalauréat* or *bac*. In effect, by 1995, around 75 percent of the age cohort passed the *bac* exam, up from some 40 percent in 1984 (Courtois, 1995). As a direct result, higher education also increased tremendously: almost half the students of the 1975 cohort (aged 18 in 1993) went on to some form of higher education: 22 percent to university, 8.5 percent to the *écoles supérieures*, and 16 percent to short-term higher education (the so-called *bac* +2, a technical–commercial degree) (Courtois, 1995).

Alongside this quantitative increase in education, the contents of the vocational and technical training programs were reorganized as well, with France attempting to emulate the German dual training system. As was to be expected, this attempt fell considerably short of its stated ambitions, since – as the French discovered along the way (Möbus and Verdier, 1997) – many of the institutional preconditions that made the German training system work, such as strong unions and employers' associations, were simply not present in the French context. However, in their implementation, "curriculum reforms" echoed the actual needs of large firms. Some of the firms even managed to have new technical diplomas created and sanctioned by the Ministry only for them (Verdier, 1997).

While it was an important step, the revision of the vocational and technical training programs did not solve the workplace reorganization problem. The educational system may have been producing skills that were considerably more attuned to the needs of the large firms, but many of the older workers who were relatively ill-equipped for the new forms of work organization, remained in the factories. In response, most large firms accelerated their existing workforce reduction programs – this time, importantly, not to cut costs, but to qualitatively adjust their workforce to the new product market strategies they were adopting. Thus, as elsewhere in Europe (Kohli et al., 1991), the French government funded these layoffs by including many of the older workers in early retirement programs, the so-called *Fonds National de l'Emploi* (FNE) and the *Fonds Industriels de Modernisation* (FIM). They kept their income but disappeared from the factories without showing up in the unemployment statistics (Guillemard, 1991). Most importantly, it allowed the large firms to replace relatively old and underskilled workers with younger, better-trained workers (Béret, 1992; Midler and Charue, 1993).

Thus, the basic parameters in the human resources policies of the large firms were fundamentally changed. The evolution of the educational system raised and customized the skill basis of young workers, creating a large skills reservoir. These skills were not – and cannot be, given the initial situation – of the "deep" technological kind that the German system produces (Soskice, 1997), but involved general skills such as mathematics, languages, and their application in industrial and commercial activities, software and computer knowledge, and a large set of "social" skills, enabling the exchange of information between workers, production units inside the company, and the company and suppliers. In other words, they included a wide variety of skills peripheral to most production processes – administrative skills for low-level personnel and inventory management, as well as the skills required for quality control and interaction between different units inside the company – but that were essential to the large firms, since they allowed a restructuring of tasks and a reorganization of work. The early retirement packages, then, made sure that these younger workers could replace the older ones. Relying on the institutional resources provided by government measures, large firms were therefore able to integrate a series of tasks that had been outside the purview of production workers into their jobs, which allowed them to pursue entirely novel, more sophisticated product market strategies, away from classical mass production (Salais, 1988, 1992).

It is important not to misunderstand this outcome. French workplaces are still highly Taylorist (Linhart, 1991). In fact, a survey of workplace practices (Duval, 1996) emphasizes that between 1984 and 1990, the central period in workplace restructuring, the number of workers in the French engineering sector who said they performed repetitive work, where the working rhythms were imposed by machines (typical characteristics of Taylorist mass production), increased by almost a third. Yet that was exactly the point of the new education programs and the way they articulated with the new workplaces: they left the core contents of the job largely untouched, but provided employees with skills for the administrative tasks *surrounding* the actual work. Since historically these had been exactly the types of jobs – control, administration, supervision, and maintenance (Lane 1989; Maurice et al., 1988) – of which French companies had disproportionately many more than companies in other countries, reorganizing those tasks offered serious potential productivity increases, while the possibility to engage broader skills bases allowed for an increase in product and process complexity.

Copying practices that already existed abroad, large firms thus reorganized the production process in such a way that small groups of workers reappropriated many of the peripheral tasks: such teams of workers now perform primary maintenance tasks, low-level personnel administration (for example: job rotation, holidays, and so on), quality control, inventory management, and sometimes on-line contacts with suppliers. It may still be Taylorism, but it has a different form.

Workplace reorganization was intimately tied up with the labor relations system, because of the capacity of the labor unions to block far-reaching changes. Thus, restructuring workplaces also required installing forms of workplace communications that circumvented the unions. To create these, firms redeployed a series of institutional innovations in the labor relations system proposed by the left-wing governments of the early 1980s to their own advantage.

In 1981 and 1982, the government proposed a series of laws, the Auroux laws, which introduced new methods of direct workers' participation on the shopfloor that were no longer monopolized by the labor unions. Whereas the unions usually regarded government initiatives with a mixture of defiance and suspicion, for these reforms, both the communist CGT and the left-socialist CFDT, the two main unions at that moment, dropped their radical rhetoric and attempted to make the reforms work. The local union people, however, who were meant to implement the reforms, were incapable of playing this novel role. Since unions had been highly centralized prior to the reforms, the local union sections had in fact little or no experience with the type of "social-democratic" workplace union activities that the Auroux laws had carved out for them (Eyraud and Tchobanian, 1985). Thus the fundamental discrepancy between local union capacities and the new requirements of the situation, made the unions (almost) collapse under the weight of the new situation.

Employers' positions developed in a parallel way. The Auroux reforms initially appeared as the fifth column to them, and it therefore came as no surprise that the employers' association, the CNPF, and most managers resisted their introduction (Weber, 1990). Gradually, however, employers began to see the advantages of the new institutions for shopfloor workers' participation that the laws created (Morville, 1985). This was related to the structure of the Auroux reform project itself, which in fact consisted of two very different reform projects, one hidden underneath the other, almost like Russian dolls: the first project was a blend of "German-style" social-democracy and self-management ideas carried over from the 1960s, while the second was "Japan-style" workers' integration (Howell, 1992). With the unions, the necessary ingredient for the first project to succeed, helplessly standing by the side, the second scenario, the flexible workplace, revealed itself. As soon as the boom of expression groups was tapering off, French industry thus witnessed an explosion of management-led quality programs and shopfloor teams: from roughly 500 in 1981, the year of the Auroux reforms, to over 10,000 in the summer of 1984 (Weber, 1990: 446). In their search for an internal reorganization, large firms thus simply picked from the labor relations policies those elements that allowed them to neutralize the labor unions. In other words, what was initially a worker-oriented reform package became a management tool that helped defuse the conflict-ridden formal industrial relations institutions and allowed for a participative management model integrating workers' skills into the production system without integrating unions in the corporate decision-making structure. In sum, in their search for competitiveness, the large firms had simply deployed the existing policies that dealt with the labor market and labor relations in such a way that the measures ended up serving *their* needs, almost regardless of their initial intentions.

A similar argument helps understand the reorganization of supplier relationships. Here as well, management of large firms exploited the effects of government policies for their own purposes, and used them to raise their suppliers' general technological and organizational capabilities.

8.3.5 Reorganizing supplier networks

The changes in the supplier relationships of the large firms have to be understood in light of the dramatic financial problems they faced in the early 1980s. Gigantic losses, high debt, and high interest rates put serious cost pressures on the large firms and, in order to clear their balance sheets, large firms attempted to externalize as many of the costs as possible. The most convenient way to resolve the financial problem was to drastically reduce in-house inventory, because it eliminated the capital costs required to carry the inventory while imposing a new mode of production, which assured that these costs never reappeared. The answer was therefore the forced introduction of just-in-time delivery systems in French industry.[5]

Very soon, however, large firms realized that their suppliers were unable to meet the kind of demands that these new, considerably more fragile systems imposed. The causes of these adjustment problems are historical: the upshot of the Gaullist-inspired large firm-led development model in France (Kuisel, 1981) was that small industrial firms were neglected in the modernization plans, if not downright eliminated (Ganne, 1992). Despite lip service to the small firms, industrial policies were, in fact, almost exclusively oriented toward the large firms.[6] As a consequence, by 1980, when adjustment relied on closer relations between large and small firms in a subcontracting relationship, the industrial landscape in France in effect offered the opposite of what was needed for the reorganization: the engineers of the large firms detailed the specifications, delivery times, and work processes, and the SMEs diligently carried out the orders (Rochard, 1987; Veltz, 1996: 24–9). When, as a result of their own internal reorganization, the large firms imposed the new complex organizational arrangements nonetheless, the suppliers suddenly faced high costs for the externalization of inventory associated with just-in-time (JIT) parts delivery – so high, in fact, that the adjustment process of the large firms itself was endangered by the SMEs' inabilities.

Again, the large firms appealed to existing policies to fill the gaps in their own capabilities. The goal of economic decentralization policies passed by the first left-wing government was to create a vibrant tissue of small and medium-sized firms in the regions. While this reform failed miserably in that goal (Levy, 1999), it had the inadvertent effect of providing the large firms with a wide array of regional institutional resources that they could tap into in order to modernize their suppliers' networks.

These reforms were geared toward regions which had, as a result of the regional development program of the 1960s, in fact become industrial monocultures: and even today, in almost all of the 21 regions outside Ile-de-France, one large firm dominates the region in terms of output and (direct and indirect) employment (see the data per region in Quélennec, 1997). As a result of their weight in those regions, the large companies were easily able to use the institutions created by the decentralization programs of the 1980s to their own advantage: they were, in fact, the organizational interface between the regional institutions created or mobilized by the government, and the small firms that the policies were meant to address.

In the late 1980s, for example, Peugeot PSA used the local engineering school in the Franche-Comté region, in the east of the country, to help its steel suppliers upgrade their technologies and products to meet the new corrosion standards that the car manufacturer was adopting in its next generation of cars (Levy, 1999: 180ff.). A similar rearrangement of regional resources took place in the Marseille area, where the steel company Sollac, again the largest local company, drew on the regional training funds to adapt the skills of its workforce to the technological turn that the company was taking (Hildebrandt, 1996). In cooperation with the central Ministry of Education and a local training institution, the company first created two new industry-specific technical diplomas and then used its own training center to organize the courses – financed by the public authorities. The same center was also used to retrain the suppliers' workforce, again mainly funded by the regional authorities. Aérospatiale in Toulouse, Citroën in Brittany, and chemical companies around Lyon have adopted a similar strategy of appropriating public resources for their own adjustment: local schools and training programs, regional technical universities, and the battery of local employment agencies, regional offices of the ministries of industry and regional development as well as the Foreign Trade Office were used to help the small firms upgrade organizationally and technologically and then support them in finding new markets.

Importantly, however, all this attention on suppliers has not led to an increase of their power in the relationship with the large firms. Despite their technological capabilities, they are rarely closely involved in product development. Product design remains heavily centralized in the large firms' product development departments, who design new products as a collection of discrete, standardized, and in principle independent modules (Ulrich, 1995). The gains of this product development method for the large firms are obvious: they offer the benefits of advanced design and flexibility without losing control over the process as a whole. Despite the increased sophistication of the suppliers, the situation remains structurally biased in favor of the customers (Hancké, 1998).

The new supplier policies of the large firms, and the increased reliance of the large firms upon their suppliers for system development and JIT logistics for production, thus eventually ended up reorganizing French industry into a series of regional production networks, constructed around one large firm, dominating the region in every aspect: employment, output, regional investment.[7] Increasingly, France began to resemble a collection of quasi-autarchic regional economies, in which the SMEs subordinated themselves to the exigencies of the large firms' local plants, by being integrated technologically and organizationally. The regional network that thus emerged was, in turn, subordinate to the strategies conceived and developed in headquarters, usually located in the Paris area. In embryonic form, this multiple-layered hierarchical structure had always existed, but after the crisis of the early 1980s, it became a building block for the large firms in their reorganization.

8.4   Conclusion: political economy of corporate adjustment in France

French industry went through a dramatic adjustment phase after a profound crisis in the early 1980s. At the end of this process, French firms – derided as "lame ducks" only ten years earlier – had become among the most profitable in the OECD, able to survive even the tough 1992 recession (Glyn, 1997). During the first years of the 1980s, large firms in France were forced to search for rapid measures to rebalance the books and then set out to reorganize their internal structures to secure competitiveness. This internal reorganization was conditional upon increased management autonomy, especially from the state. The internal reorganization that followed, allowed French firms to pursue new human resources policies, introduce new methods of supplier integration and generally position themselves in new markets.

The central role of the large firms in the adjustment process heralds a profound continuity with the postwar large firm-centered French political economy. However, the wider context within which management operates is different. Under the old regime, large firms were policy instruments for the state; it is precisely that configuration that is fundamentally different today. Instead of a state-led path, the French adjustment trajectory was a firm-led one. Despite some *dirigiste* attempts in the 1980s, the French state today plays a considerably smaller role in the economy than before, and has lost much of its capacity to direct industrial and economic adjustment. However, and equally important, the gap that emerged was not filled by the market, but by a mode of coordination which included elites in the state apparatus, large firms and *haute finance*, who ensured that large firms were able to construct a novel institutional environment for their own adjustment and then induce other relevant actors – the state, labor unions, the workforce, other companies, and the financial world – to act according to their preferences.

This novel perspective on France – firm-led instead of state- or market-led adjustment – not only helps make sense of the developments since the early 1980s, it also sheds new light on an old theme in the study of France – the *société bloquée*. According to this perspective, reforms are difficult to implement in France, because they are conceived with strong societal actors in mind (in recent years because they were technocratically copied from the successful German experience), but the actors are in fact too weak to be able to become the social bearers of the policies. The result is policy failure – and a more general fundamental unreformability of the country's political economy. The financial deregulation, for example, led to elite-controlled cross-shareholdings instead of popular capitalism (Bauer, 1988; Maclean, 1995), because the banks were incapable of playing the new monitoring role designed for them (Goyer, 1998). The Auroux workplace reforms resulted in weaker instead of – as intended – stronger labor unions, because the unions were incapable of turning the institutional innovation into advantages for themselves (Howell, 1992). And the decentralization of policy-making led to an increased dependence on Paris instead of the construction of new policy-making systems in the regions to support industrial development, because the regional associations were unable to provide the type of interface between the firms targeted and the regional institutes that were supposed to serve them (Levy, 1999). Reforms turned into failures because the social actors that were critical to their implementation, were too weak.

Changing the perspective to the large firms as the central agents in the French political economy puts these apparent failures in a fundamentally different light. The large firms used the institutional resources provided by these policies and then deployed them on their own terms in their own strategic adjustment. The financial deregulation allowed large-firm CEOs to construct a broad sphere of autonomy; the Auroux laws provided large firms with institutions to defuse perennial workplace conflict; and the decentralization policies offered the large firms instruments to upgrade their regional supplier base. In short, by shifting the perspective to strategic adjustment by the large firms, policy initiatives that are documented as dramatic failures, take the shape of institutional resources for the large firms – a very different idea indeed than what is offered by the *société bloquée* and one which suggests that this notion is up for reevaluation (Suleiman, 1995).

While this interpretation certainly allows for optimism regarding corporate change – put bluntly, if even French industry can shape its own future and reorganize its institutional framework to do so, then the degrees of freedom for others must be larger than thought as well – careful comparative analysis is needed to discover exactly under which "hard" constraints managers were operating, and which led to them using their increased autonomy for adjustment rather than simple rent-seeking. After all, as the other essays in this volume testify, management autonomy appears to have increased almost everywhere, but it did not always lead to the beneficial outcomes documented for France. More concretely, how important was the search for macroeconomic stability by the governments since the mid-1980s in setting signposts for management? Was the existence of a healthy banking system, however archaic it may look from a Western perspective, a condition that managers in many CEE countries lack, and which makes them much more vulnerable to equity markets? How crucial was the exposure of French firms to foreign competition even before, but certainly during, the adjustment process discussed here? Finally, how important were the internal constraints on autonomy? After all, the elite system is not just a mechanism to coordinate action; it is also a sanctioning device for its members: punishment in the case of failure, rewards in the case of good results. As this suggests, the reinterpretation of the French case proposed here offers interesting avenues for comparative research on the institutional context of corporate governance, both in the advanced capitalist economies of the West and the emerging markets in the CEE.

Notes

1. An earlier version of this chapter appeared in Peter A. Hall and David Soskice (eds) *Varieties of Capitalism* (Oxford University Press, 2001).
2. Thanks go to Peter Hall, Michał Federowicz, Horst Kern, David Soskice, Eric Verdier, the participants in the workshop on Varieties of Capitalism in July 1997, as well as workshops at GATE-CNRS (Lyon) and LEST-CNRS (Aix-en-Provence) for their comments on earlier versions. If, despite all this help, mistakes remain, they are entirely my responsibility.
3. These government initiatives ultimately failed: neither the labor unions nor employers were strong enough to carry through the reforms, and the regionalization hit very poor soil in the regions, where no local actors could be found (or created) to provide an underpinning for the policies. Whether they failed or not, however, is not important for the purposes of this argument. What matters is that they were attempts by the state to disengage itself from these different fields of economic policy-making. See Levy (1999) for full details of these policies and their failures.

4. Even though failures happened. See Cohen (1989) for details.
5. The first mention of KanBan delivery systems in the car industry is 1982–83 (Labbé, 1992); other industries followed suit rapidly and by the end of the 1980s, JIT was generalized in France (Gorgeu and Mathieu, 1993).
6. The French state was careful, of course, to further small artisanal firms because of their role as a political reservoir for the right, and the numerical flexibility they provided for the mass-producing large firms (Berger and Piore, 1980), but not with targeted industrial policies.
7. For a graphic representation, see the map of the geography of France in Quélennec (1997: 19). Relevant data are found in that volume, and in SESSI (1997).

9
The Specificity of Corporate Governance in Small States: Institutionalization and Questioning of Ownership Restrictions in Switzerland and Sweden

Thomas David and André Mach

9.1 Introduction[1]

For a long time, the literature on corporate governance has been dominated by analyses of the relations between shareholders and management and was concerned with very restrictive issues, such as the way shareholders could monitor management to act in their interests. However, recent studies have increasingly adopted a broader view. In this new perspective, corporate organization is not only determined by an efficiency logic (minimization of transaction or agency costs) but also by institutional factors (Jackson, 2001). Corporate governance is thus embedded in national institutions and can be broadly defined as the interactions between the central actors of companies (owners, managers, and workers), codified in some regulatory framework (company law, financial market regulations, and labor law) produced by the state or by collective actors.

Moreover, this new perspective tends to adopt a historical viewpoint in order to understand how and why corporate institutions differ across countries. However, it focuses mainly on large countries and tends to neglect small ones. One of the main arguments of the present chapter is that small European countries have specific corporate governance mechanisms: concentration of ownership, high density of cross-shareholdings and interlocking directorates, which are often interrelated, and the establishment of various forms of "selective protectionism" concerning the market for corporate control (distortion of voting rights or "pyramidal structure," which allow control over subsidiaries).

In the first part of this chapter, we will highlight the common characteristics of corporate governance mechanisms in Switzerland and Sweden, and the way in which they have been institutionalized. We will put forward the historical construction of these defensive instruments. In both countries, these mechanisms were consolidated in the 1930s or just after World War II.

In Sweden, they have been an important element of the "historical compromise" between capital and labor, which has characterized this country since the end of the 1930s, whereas in Switzerland these corporate governance mechanisms were only established progressively through self-regulation in the corporate sector. Despite a very different national political configuration, Sweden and Switzerland resorted to similar mechanisms of selective protectionism that distinguish small European nations from larger ones.

Secondly, we will analyze the recent changes undergone by Swiss and Swedish corporate governance systems. Due to the interaction of external (liberalization of financial markets, increasing multinationalization of production) and domestic pressures, such as the rising importance of institutional investors and the changing preferences of decisive actors (banks in particular), the traditional functioning of corporate governance has been called into question. In both countries, the trend has clearly been toward a more liberal orientation, characterized by more transparency, the increasing power of institutional investors, and the growing importance of foreign shareholders.

9.2   Two models of corporate governance, and a third one?

During the last 20 years, characterized by the increasing liberalization of markets, especially of financial markets, corporate governance has become a central topic studied by economists, legal experts, and even political scientists. It has been common to distinguish between the two major models of corporate governance: the Anglo-Saxon (or market-centered) and the Continental European (bank-centered) models (see La Porta et al., 1999; Hall and Soskice, 2001; Streeck, 2001). Whereas the Anglo-Saxon model is characterized by large and liquid capital markets and an active market for corporate control, where outside shareholders can dislodge poorly performing management by way of takeover bids, the Continental European model can be described as a network-oriented system, where large corporate groupings (banks, insurance, and industrial companies) are in an intricate structure of cross-shareholdings, which has generated relative managerial autonomy from financial interests. The management was thus more able to balance the claims and interests of the company stakeholders (suppliers, banks, workers, and large communities) (Block, 1998).

Comparisons of corporate governance system have underlined particularly that these two models mainly differ in the way firms are financed and controlled. The ownership of shares by banks reflects this distinction between the two systems. In the Anglo-Saxon countries, banks do not hold shares in industrial concerns. In the US, the holding of shares in industrial companies is strictly limited and in the UK, institutional investors (pension funds and insurance companies) dominate holdings in industrial companies, not the banks (Walter, 2000: 114–16). In Continental Europe, there is a long tradition, dating back to the nineteenth century, of banks being involved in the management and the development of industrial companies as shareholders (and creditors).

This classification of corporate governance into bank- and market-centered models is not the only distinctive factor of their mechanisms. Economists recently highlighted another element, which distinguishes Anglo-Saxon countries from Continental Europe. The concentration of ownership is much higher in Continental Europe and the Scandinavian countries than in the UK and the US (La Porta et al., 1999; Becht and Barca, 2001).[2] By these two criteria (bank-centered and the importance of owner-ship concentration), Switzerland and Sweden thus clearly belong to the Continental model.

In Switzerland, the strong interrelations between universal banks and industry make its corporate governance system resemble the German case and contrast with the practice in Anglo-Saxon countries. In the early 1990s, banks in the UK and the US held less than 1 percent of the shares of the quoted firms, against 4.7 percent in Switzerland and 10 percent in Germany (Birchler, 1995). Swiss and German corporate governance structures share another characteristic: the system of proxy voting, which allows banks to cast votes for other shareholders. Private shareholders authorize banks that hold their shares in custody to represent their interests at the annual general meetings of the companies.

The interrelation between big banks and industries is strengthened by the role of the former in company financing.[3] Between 1973 and 1990, bank loans were an important source of financing for most Swiss cor-porations, even if self-financing remained the main source of capital: the contribution of internal funds to the financing of industrial companies is around 50 percent, bank loans account for around one-third and corporate bond issues represent 15 percent of the financing (Birchler, 1995: 269). From an international perspective, it seems that the role of banks in the financing of corporate activities is high in Switzerland: at the beginning of the 1990s, the indebtedness of Swiss firms was higher compared to that of US, UK and (to some extent) German firms (Hertig, 1998: 813). Thus, Swiss management has often been able to get external financing, thanks to private transactions with banks and other lenders without using the capital market, thus circumventing the pressure of capital markets on manage-ment performance.

A second feature of Swiss corporate governance is the extent of ownership concentration: at the beginning of the 1990s, 23.1 percent of all owners held 75 percent or more of the shares of the 614 largest companies (Table 9.1). According to Windolf and Nollert (2001), only Germany had a higher degree of ownership concentration. The concentration of ownership is closely related to the extent of individual/family ownership. Schröter (1993: 194–200) already mentioned this point when describing multinational companies in the small European countries on the eve of World War I. This characteristic is still present nowadays (Hertig, 1998).

In Sweden, there is also a close relation between banks and manufacturing industries, which goes back to the end of the nineteenth century. Due to the introduction of full freedom of trade for joint-stock banks with limited liability in 1864 and the rapid industrial growth during the last third of the century, private commercial banks established tight links with industry. Postwar deflation intensified these relations. In order to recoup outstanding credit and to keep industrial companies solvent, banks were forced to involve themselves more deeply in the administration of the latter (Lindgren, 1987).

In the 1930s, an important change occurred. It was no longer the banks per se but rather investment companies that played the banks' industrial role. In 1934, in the aftermath of the Kreuger crash, a law was passed which prohibited the banks from acquiring and holding shares. The major banks therefore founded investment companies (Lindgren, 1994). Two business groups have symbolized this interaction between the banking and manufacturing sectors: the Wallenberg group, the largest one, and the Handelsbank group. In the mid-1990s, these "bank-centered corporate group combinations" controlled corporations representing more than 50 percent of the stock value of the firms listed on the Stockholm stock exchange (Collin, 1998: 726). However, there is one important difference: the Wallenberg empire is a family group, whereas the Handelsbank group is much more nebulously based. On this point the Wallenberg group is no longer representative of Swedish capitalism. While family ownership was predominant until the 1960s, the situation was very different 20 years later: institutional ownership had replaced family firms, the latter having sold their shares or having gone bankrupt (Isaksson and Skog, 1994).

Deteriorating conditions for household/private ownership in the postwar period were in addition accompanied by increased concentration of private ownership in the largest firms (Henrekson and Jakobsson, 2003a).

Table 9.1 Ownership concentration in some developed countries, early 1990s

Proportion of stock owned (%)	*CH*	*NL*	*GER*	*FR*	*UK*	*US*
0–4.9	17.8	23.7	9.5	37.3	48.6	95.0
5–9.9	17.6	30.0	7.8	14.2	31.0	3.5
10–24.9	17.9	9.6	17.8	15.1	10.5	1.4
25–49.9	15.6	10.1	13.9	9.4	2.6	0.1
50–74.9	8.0	6.8	12.9	8.1	2.4	–
More	23.1	19.7	38.1	15.8	4.9	–

Source: Windolf and Nollert (2001: 64).

The ownership structure of Swedish listed companies is very concentrated by international standards (Agnblad et al., 2001: 234). This tendency has even increased during the 1970s and 1980s: in 1978, the largest single owner accounted for 20 percent on average of equity in listed firms; by 1985 this share had increased to 29 percent (Berglöf, 1994: 314).

Beyond their classification among the Continental European countries, Switzerland and Sweden distinguish themselves from larger European countries on one important point: the introduction of mechanisms preserving national control over companies against foreign takeovers.

9.2.1 Preservation of national control in Switzerland and Sweden

Small European economies share common specific characteristics in their corporate governance mechanisms: the high density of interlocking directorates and the existence of national regulations shielding their companies against the risk of foreign takeovers. Before we go into more detail regarding these characteristics of corporate governance in Switzerland and Sweden, we shall begin by showing how these characteristics are embedded in the general functioning and economic trajectory of these small open economies.

Katzenstein (1985) has argued that small European states, largely because of the small size of their domestic market and the early extroversion of their economies, developed some specific traits to cope with their international environment, which can be summarized as follows: international liberalization, domestic compensation, and flexible adjustment to fluctuations in international markets through corporatist institutions. Whereas Katzenstein, focusing on industrial policies, underlined the importance of corporatist institutions and domestic compensation in the strategy of small European states to cope with the pressures of international markets, we argue that it is also plausible to identify specific characteristics of corporate governance mechanisms (for more details, see David and Mach, 2001).

Two elements seem particularly important to explain the specificities of corporate governance mechanisms in small European states: the small size and the high degree of cohesion of the business community and the combination of a free trade policy orientation with elements of "selective protectionism." Small European states are thus characterized by a high density of intercorporate networks of the business elites, and the establishment of regulations concerning company law or financial markets that tend to preserve national control over the large export-oriented companies. These two elements are structural characteristics of the functioning of corporate governance in small European countries.

Firstly, from an economic historical perspective, Schröter (1999), focusing on cartels in small European economies, underlined the close links between economic elites in these countries. This led him to speak of "co-operative capitalism in small European nations":

> In each nation they developed a *manière de voir*, or what could be defined as a mentality as to the proper way of doing business, and a social consensus on how to proceed in economic matters. Such *manière de voir* very much included a role for the state, for as scholars have pointed out, in small nations "private and public sectors have had to find ways to collaborate" even more intensively than in a case of larger nations. Such collaboration encouraged economic concentration and cartelization. (Schröter, 1999: 192; for a similar argument on Sweden: Collin, 1998)[4]

This analysis helps to explain the density of interlocking directorates and of business networks in small European nations.

Secondly, in line with the argument of Menzel (1988) and Senghaas (1985), small European countries, despite their preference for a liberal trade policy because of their export orientation, introduced various elements of "selective protectionism." In the words of Menzel and Senghaas, their strategy toward international markets was "associative–dissociative": associative, because of their dependence on international markets for exports and imports, and dissociative, because these countries also introduced different measures to reduce the pressures of world markets on specific economic sectors, such as import-substitution policies, state intervention, subtle forms of protectionism or public subsidies for some economic sectors. This argument has often been used to explain the "dualist structure" of small European economies, with on one side the export-oriented sectors, very competitive on international markets, and on the other side, sectors producing mainly for the domestic market, largely sheltered from international competitive pressure through subsidization (agriculture or fishing industries), technical norms, or cartels by domestic producers.

Our argument is that these forms of "selective protectionism" also prevailed for the export-oriented sectors and their larger companies through the establishment of specific regulations concerning company law and financial markets, which are at the heart of the functioning of corporate governance. These regulations, such as complex voting rights structures or "pyramidal" forms of control, allowed small European economies to preserve national control over their large export-oriented companies and to avoid the risk of foreign takeovers, which was particularly high in small European states.

Thus, small European economies combined a large degree of openness with elements of selective integration and domestic compensation, which were the result of the high degree of cohesion and the cooperative dimension prevailing in the political and the economic fields. The two general characteristics of small European states (the small size and the cohesion of the business community and the introduction of some forms of "selective protectionism") are particularly salient concerning corporate governance mechanisms. From a more general perspective, it is also possible to draw a parallel between the regulations produced in labor and product markets and in the market for corporate control.[5] In all these different fields, small European economies tended to establish regulations, produced either by the state or by collective actors, which distort the pure functioning of market mechanisms: highly coordinated industrial relations and corporatist institutions in the labor market, as shown by Katzenstein (1985), a high degree of cartelization in the domestic product market[6] as underlined by Schröter (1999), and the rules governing corporate governance, as we shall see below.

On the basis of Bebchuk et al.'s (2000) conceptualization of *controlling-minority structure* (CMS), it is possible to distinguish between three major mechanisms allowing a shareholder to control a firm while holding only a small fraction of its equity:

1. The first defensive instrument is the differential voting right: a firm issues two or more classes of stock with differential voting rights;[7]
2. "Pyramiding" is the second mechanism. A CMS "can be established with a single class of stock by pyramiding corporate structures. In a pyramid of two companies, a controlling-minority shareholder holds a controlling stake in a holding company that, in turn, holds a controlling stake in an operating company. In a three-tier pyramid the primary holding company controls a second-tier holding company that in turn controls the operating company" (Bebchuk et al., 2000: 298);
3. Finally cross-ownership or interlocking directorates reinforce and entrench the power of central controllers.

In Continental Europe, CMSs are more common in small than in large nations. Thus, for example, from an international perspective, Sweden and Switzerland, followed by the Netherlands, are the countries where the magnitude of deviation from one-share-one-vote through shares with differential voting rights is greatest (Table 9.2). Moreover, pyramiding is also used in Sweden, but much less in Switzerland.

Small countries are also characterized by the centralization of their "intercorporate network," which is much higher than in large countries. Windolf and Nollert (2001) showed that the centralization of the interlocking directorate network is strongly related to the size of the national economy. In these countries, a small number of companies can form the entire national network. In his study of business groups in Sweden, Collin (1998) also underlines that in such a small country with many large companies and accordingly with many management positions to fill, competent management is a scarce resource. From this perspective, the density of

Table 9.2   One-share-one-vote distortion in some developed countries, 1995

Japan	20.00
Spain	20.00
United Kingdom	20.00
Belgium	20.00
France	19.99
United States	19.19
Germany	18.61
Italy	18.04
Netherlands	15.00
Switzerland	14.18
Sweden	12.62
Average	18.56

Note: The table refers to the minimum percent of the book value of common equity required to control 20% of the votes. The average refers to a sample of 27 countries.
Source: La Porta et al. (1999: Table IV).

interlocking directorates is related to the small size of the "managerial" labor market.

9.2.1.1   *The Swiss case: the predominance of self-regulation by the business sector*

The close relationships between banks and industry explain the fact that bank representatives can be found on most important companies' boards: "Swiss boards have specific institutional features. In a comparative perspective, it is important to note that they have always been and still are clearly dominated by outside members. Among them, bank representatives are probably the most important category" (Meier-Schatz, 1993: 310; see also Hertig, 1998). Network analyses conducted by sociologists revealed the system of interlocking directorates and the high density of the network of cross-holdings in Switzerland: representatives of the banks sit on the boards of directors of the nonfinancial companies, but, conversely, industrial firms also delegate representatives onto the boards of directors of banks (Rusterholz, 1985; Nollert, 1998). This closely meshed network implies a high degree of autonomy and self-regulation in the corporate sector, and this permits long-term cooperation and control over their markets.

The concentration of ownership, and more generally the high degree of cohesion of the business community, combined with the early extroversion of the economy, favored the adoption of "selective protectionist" measures concerning the control of national companies. The regulation called *Vinkulierung* constitutes the main instrument of this policy of selective protectionism. The term is codified in the Swiss Company Law and was first introduced at the end of the nineteenth century. The law was later re-inforced in 1936. It refers to the limitations of the transferability of Swiss registered shares:

> The Swiss Company Law recognizes three categories of participation paper: bearer shares, registered shares and dividend right certificates. . . . Registered shares differ from bearer shares mainly in the way they are transferred from seller to purchaser. As far as the company is concerned, it recognizes as shareholders only those whose names are registered in the stock ledger. To achieve entry, the registered share must be endorsed by the seller. The buyer has to prove that the share has been correctly transferred. . . . The company has the right to restrict or refuse entry in the stock ledger on a great variety of grounds. Registered shares, whose transfer is restricted in this way are said to have been *"vinkuliert."* (Kaufmann and Kunz, 1991: 5)

For a long time, registered stocks were only held by (domestic) investors accepted by the management. Foreign investors could only trade freely in the bearer shares. Both held voting rights (generally one vote per share). However, due to these restrictions, the price of registered shares is usually lower than the bearer stock. More votes can thus be controlled with the same capital by buying registered stock rather than bearer stock (Loderer and Jacobs, 1995: 318ff). The capital structure of Nestlé in 1988 throws light on the advantages of registered shares (Table 9.3).

Nestlé was not the only firm to resort to this practice of *Vinkulierung*: in 1990, out of 112 companies, 57 percent had registered shares (Kaufmann and Kunz, 1991: 15).

The high degree of autonomy and self-regulation in the corporate sector (due to the weakness of the central state and the early organization of business interests) and the strong interrelations between banks and industry largely explain the institutionalization of the process of *Vinkulierung*. The

Table 9.3   Nestlé's capital structure on November 15, 1988

	Voting bearer shares	Nonvoting bearer shares	Registered shares
Number of shares	1,073,000	1,150,000	2,227,000
Par value per shares	CH Fr 100	CH Fr 20	CH Fr 100
Percentage of votes	32.5	0	67.5
Price per share	CH Fr 8,790	CH Fr 1,280	CH Fr 4,310
Percentage of total market value of equity	46	7	47

Source: Loderer and Jacobs (1995: 321).

Swiss Code of Contracts of 1881 and the 1936 revision of the Company Law enabled the restriction on acquiring registered shares (Kaufmann and Kunz, 1991: 5). This left the business world with large room for maneuver and represented the legal translation of the delegation of the state's functions to the private sector, allowing the latter to self-regulate this field.

This process went a step further in 1961. Following a decision by the Swiss Federal Court which allowed a share to be split into membership rights and asset rights and which represented a weighty threat to the protection against foreign penetration, the Swiss Bankers' Association and the public companies concluded a "mutual assistance agreement":

> Companies practicing Vinkulierung on registered shares now attempted to design the application forms for stock ledger entry in such a way as to defend the indivisibility of a shareholder's right. The obligation to state nationality and domicile as well as the signing of an unequivocal declaration that the registered shares had been acquired genuinely as the buyer's actual, legal and financial property and not just as fiduciary property, virtually excluded front men. To supplement these measures, the banks made sure that registered shares subject to restriction did not change hands if the company's requirements for entry into the stock ledger could not be fulfilled by the purchaser. (Kaufmann and Kunz, 1991: 6)

This gentleman's agreement was clearly intended to avoid the intrusion of public authorities. Thus, *Vinkulierung* protected Swiss shareholders against the threat of a foreign takeover (for more details, see Kläy, 1997).

The practice of *Vinkulierung* helped to reinforce and stabilize the concentration of ownership. This system allows a small group of owners, very often family owners, to retain control of the firm and the right to determine their strategy independently, even when they float their companies on the market to raise funds from the public.

9.2.1.2 Sweden: a compromise between social democracy and business interests

The predominance of the two national business groups (Wallenberg and Handelsbank) and the scope of ownership concentration were made possible largely thanks to one legal instrument: dual class shares (Agnblad et al., 2001). Table 9.4 illustrates the extent of this practice:

> . . . a handful of very large Swedish companies have managed to retain voting right differences of one to 100 and even one to 1,000 through grandfathering, and may continue to issue shares with these voting rights. Shares with differentiated voting rights are very common among publicly traded shares in Sweden. In January 1992, unequal voting rights existed in nearly 90 percent of the companies on the Stockholm Stock Exchange. (Isaksson and Skog, 1994: 293; see also Berglöf, 1994)

Table 9.4   Voting right differentials between classes of
shares in Swedish listed companies, 1992

Voting right differential	Number of companies (202)
1 : 1000	3
1 : 100	1
1 : 10	165
1 : 5	6
No differential	27

Source: Isaksson and Skog (1993: 294).

The Wallenberg family has been able to maintain control of its industrial empire partly through these dual class shares. At the beginning of the 1990s, it was thus estimated that if the dual class share was abolished the influence that this group enjoyed in Electrolux would be reduced from 95 to 16 percent of the number of votes (Reiter, 2003: 109). It is interesting to stress that AB Investor, the investment company of the Wallenberg group, also resorted to a system of preferential or weighted voting rights (Lindgren, 1987: 9). The Wallenberg family has thus been able to control a major portion of Swedish industry through a pyramidal structure of control.

Pyramiding also allowed Swedish firms to protect themselves from hostile takeovers (Berglöf and Sjögren, 1998: 805; Collin, 1998: 738–9). Moreover, up to the mid-1980s, acquisition of Swedish shares by foreigners was limited by exchange controls and by legislation, which prohibited the inflow of massive foreign capital in Swedish companies without government approval. An upper limit for foreign acquisition of shares and votes in Swedish companies was introduced through the distinction between restricted and nonrestricted shares, with only Swedish citizens being allowed to acquire the former (Reiter, 2003: 108; Isaksson and Skog, 1994: 291). Until the end of the 1980s, less than 10 percent of Swedish listed shares were owned by foreigners (Henrekson and Jakobsson, 2003a: Figure 1).

As in Switzerland, there were selective protectionism mechanisms in Sweden, which allowed firms to protect themselves from any foreign threat. However, the institutionalization of these mechanisms, in particular the dual class shares, differed considerably in the two countries. As we have seen, the introduction and the reinforcement of the *Vinkulierung* process in Switzerland can be explained by the high degree of autonomy and self-regulation in the corporate sector, due in part to the weakness of the central state. In Sweden, the situation is completely different: "The traditional distribution of ownership and influence – hence the system of differentiated voting rights – was a building stone for the corporatist model that characterized Sweden from the interwar period onwards" (Reiter, 2003: 119). The growing political strength of the labor movement, following the election victory of the Social Democratic Party in 1932, then led to the "historical compromise" between capital and labor at the end of the 1930s. This compromise was underlain by a division of economic and governmental power between opposing classes. Having gained political power, the labor movement could influence the distribution of economic growth (development of the welfare state; active labor market policy) while business elites, as part of the compromise, enjoyed favorable conditions for investment and expansion (Korpi, 1982).

The mechanisms of selective protectionism, in particular the system of dual class shares, should be analyzed from this perspective. Even though the possibility of issuing dual class shares was abolished in 1944, the companies which already had dual class shares, in fact almost all the large-scale Swedish enterprises, were allowed to retain the old system. Despite political controversy on this issue since the 1960s, the Swedish social democratic government never challenged it. For the government and the labor unions, these dual class shares had two important purposes. Firstly, they contributed to consolidating a concentrated ownership structure. The investment companies, which controlled the large Swedish multinational enterprises, offered the state a counterpart in economic policy-making in the area of industrial policy. As one government report states, "the presence of a strong owner [could] facilitate the work of trade unions" (quoted by Reiter, 2003: 108). Secondly, the dual class shares and restriction concerning foreign ownership were also considered instrumental in order to retain the control of these large firms within Sweden:

> While Swedish investors had the freedom to invest anywhere in the world, foreigners were carefully screened so that control of domestic assets and manufacturing could be kept in the friendly hands of Swedish capitalists. It should be noted that this protectionist rule offered a reprieve to both Swedish firms and Social Democrats – tax rules would have been considerably less effective if many firms had been owned by non-resident transnational corporations with their capital mobility and diverse interests. (Kurzer, 1993: 129; see also Collin, 1998: 738–9)

The government also used other policies, such as capital-market and savings policies, to favor large companies and to stimulate institutional ownership (Henrekson and Jakobsson, 2003b). The Swedish tax system had the same function: tax rates were very low for large Swedish companies by international standards and thus encouraged the concentration of economic power (Lundström, 2001).

9.3   Traditional corporate governance systems under pressure

The increasing liberalization of product and financial markets during the last 20 years represented a profound change in the external environment of small European states. In this new economic context, the financial sector became increasingly important with the emergence of new financial actors, who developed more aggressive strategies to increase the return on equity of their portfolio investments. Moreover, it also drove "traditional actors" (banks notably) to change their preferences and strategies.

This internationalization of capital markets puts increasing pressure on traditional corporate governance systems of European nations. The increasing influence of investors, emphasizing financial liquidity, shareholder protection, and accounting transparency, tends to threaten the defensive mechanisms that separate capital contribution from control. Since the end of the 1980s, due to the liberalization of financial markets and their growing importance, some authors have argued that a converging trend is under way, in which the Continental European model is undergoing profound transformations and is beginning to look like the Anglo-Saxon model.

9.3.1   Liberalization of financial markets and changing strategies of domestic actors

The internationalization of capital markets represents the most important change in the political economy of the developed countries over the past three decades. The breakdown of the Bretton Woods system (1971) stimulated this financial liberalization, which is characterized by the significant growth of foreign direct investment (FDI), especially since the mid-1980s (Table 9.5).

For small countries, transnational investment reached a new dimension. In Sweden and Switzerland, outward FDI stocks accounted for more than 50 percent of GDP in 2000. The two countries have also witnessed a sharp

Table 9.5   Outward and inward FDI stocks in some developed countries, 1985–2000 (% of GDP)

	1985		1990		1995		2000	
	Out	*In*	*Out*	*In*	*Out*	*In*	*Out*	*In*
Sweden	10.7	5.0	21.5	5.4	31.6	13.4	53.8	36.1
Switzerland	27.0	10.8	28.9	15.0	46.3	18.6	95.1	34.2
Germany	8.6	5.3	9.2	6.8	11.1	6.9	25.2	24.1
UK	21.9	14.0	23.4	20.8	27.4	18.0	63.2	30.1
United States	6.2	4.6	7.8	7.1	9.9	7.6	13.1	12.4

Sources: UNCTAD (2000) and UNCTAD database.

increase of inward foreign investments, on an altogether different scale from what occurred in large countries. In Sweden, this rapid increase of inward FDI followed the liberalization of financial markets embarked upon at the end of the 1980s.

This internationalization process was even more impressive with regard to portfolio investments (stocks, bonds, and bank loans), which have grown more rapidly than FDI since the breakdown of the Bretton Woods system. The evolution of market capitalization is an indicator of this trend (Table 9.6). The huge growth of market capitalization since the beginning of the 1990s is due to several factors: the liberalization of financial markets, low interest rates, the aging population and the larger needs for pension provisions, but also the increasing popularity of share investments.

Since the beginning of the 1990s, the picture has changed considerably for small countries. In Switzerland and Sweden, the stock market capitalization, which was already substantial in 1990, was similar to that of the US or the UK at the end of the decade. In these small countries, the liquidity of the stock market is largely concentrated in a small number of large companies. In Sweden, equity finance by the public market was insignificant in 1975. Thereafter, in particular since the 1980s, the situation changed. Market capitalization levels are now close to those of the US. The government played an important role in this development through the adoption of various measures designed to improve stock market efficiency, to stimulate public interest in shares, and to increase public confidence in the market (Lindgren, 1994).

Globalization has two important consequences for companies in small countries. Firstly, the multinationalization of production reaches an unprecedented level. Secondly, the growth of the market capitalization seems to indicate the increasing importance of stock markets as capital providers for companies, a growing role of institutional investors in controlling companies, and a less important financing role of banks as well as less internal generation of capital. Thus, the liberalization of capital markets may destabilize the "old equilibrium" (Coffee, 2000: 7) and the control by traditional shareholders.

Table 9.6   Evolution of market capitalization as a percentage of GDP, 1975–99

	1975	*1980*	*1985*	*1990*	*1995*	*1996*	*1997*	*1998*	*1999*
Sweden	3	10	37	40	75	95	116	123	156
Switzerland	30	42	91	69	130	136	225	260	268
Germany	12	9	29	22	24	28	39	51	68
UK	37	38	77	87	122	142	156	175	198
United States	48	50	57	56	98	114	137	157	181

Source: OECD Financial Market Trends (various issues).

However, the potential impact of the current trend of economic globalization on small countries' corporate governance is also related to other factors, such as the influence of the US financial center and the progressive dissemination and imposition of American corporate governance criteria, such as new accounting standards as well as the efforts of the EU to harmonize company law (for more details see David and Mach, 2001).

Furthermore, corporate governance mechanisms may also be affected by the changing preferences and strategies of domestic actors (banks, institutional investors, pension funds, and multinationals) in this new economic context. Domestic actors may thus be interested in modifying the traditional functioning of corporate governance systems. The rise of institutional investors (insurance companies, pension funds, investment companies) which has taken place in Europe since the 1980s is particularly relevant since they might threaten the traditional corporate governance systems in three ways. Firstly, they have contributed to the development of an "equity culture" through the institutionalization of savings, which could weaken the concentration of ownership (Blommstein, 1998: 56). Secondly, institutional investors have enhanced their corporate governance role in the form of an increase in market and direct control through equity and debt (Blommstein, 1998: 62ff). These investors, searching for higher returns, have tried to favor shareholders' interests.[8] Thirdly, banks have changed their attitude toward share ownership as they saw themselves competing for deposits with these financial intermediaries (Block, 1998: 11). Thus, banks now have stronger incentives to support higher returns on financial assets. They therefore promote financial liquidity rather than financial commitment. One consequence could be the weakening of bank–industry linkages. Lazonick and O'Sullivan (2000) have shown that with the rise of institutional investors the maximization of "shareholder value" has become a central principle of corporate governance functioning in the US.

What about the corporate governance systems of our two countries? Is there a convergence process toward the Anglo-Saxon model and the progressive disappearance of ownership restrictions or are these nations able to keep their main traditional corporate governance features?

9.3.2 The destabilization of the "fortress of the Alps"

The general pressure, briefly outlined above, induced several changes in the traditional functioning of Swiss corporate governance. These changes resulted from the liberalization of financial markets at the international level, which imposed new constraints on large Swiss companies, and from the emergence of new domestic financial actors (investment funds) and the changing attitude of the largest banks (for more details, see David and Mach, 2001). We will now outline these major changes.

Firstly, the "process of *Vinkulierung*" is tending to disappear (Anderson and Hertig, 1994: 525). The decision of Nestlé to allow foreigners to hold registered stock in 1988 was followed by other major companies.[9] There is also increasing pressure on the companies on the Swiss Market Index (which includes the 30 largest companies) to introduce a "single share." In 1989, only 13.1 percent of the companies listed on the Swiss stock exchange had a "single share." In 2001, this proportion reached 70.7 percent (out of 198 companies) (Figure 9.1). This does not mean, however, the end of family ownership and the victory of minority shareholders. There are still other measures which allow Swiss corporations to channel the evolution of their shareholding structure: they may fix ceilings for voting rights at the shareholders' meetings or introduce a percentage limit for each individual shareholding (Anderson and Hertig, 1994: 526; Meier-Schatz, 1993: 315).

Secondly, until the 1980s, Swiss firms were dominated by a policy of secrecy and confidentiality. The obscure presentation of accounting and the accumulation of hidden reserves were a manifestation of this attitude. The need to attract (foreign) investors and thus to give them precise financial information provoked a change in this position. Under the pressure of institutional investors, large companies are increasingly adapting their statutes by adopting more transparent accounting standards.

The deregulation of financial markets, the increasing weight of institutional investors, the relaxing of the *Vinkulierung* process, and the priority given to the equity market largely explain a third feature of the last 20 years: the increasing number of mergers and acquisitions (see Figure 9.2). Three elements should be underlined. Firstly, not surprisingly, the proportion of foreign firms acquiring Swiss firms almost doubled between 1983 and 1999. Some symbols of Swiss industry changed owners: the shoe firm Bally was bought by the investment fund Texas Pacific Group in 1999, the same year that the watch companies Tag Heuer, Ebel, and Zenith became part of the French concern LVMH (Louis Vuitton-Moet-Hennessy) (*Handelszeitung*, 2000: 5ff.). Secondly, the sharp increase in mergers and acquisitions also resulted in huge mergers between some of the largest Swiss multinationals, threatened by potential foreign acquisitions: Ciba and Sandoz into Novartis, UBS and SBS, Crédit Suisse and Winthertur insurance. The third element that is worth mentioning is the foreign expansion of Swiss multinational companies through mergers and acquisitions. In 1983, the proportion of these activities in the total number of mergers in Switzerland was only 13 percent; it rose to 36 percent in 1999. Figure 9.2, which takes into account the number and not the value of mergers and acquisitions, undervalues the importance of this phenomenon (see *Handelszeitung*, 2000).

Fourthly, in addition to the increase in mergers and acquisitions, a lot of restructuring also took place in the large industrial companies and was

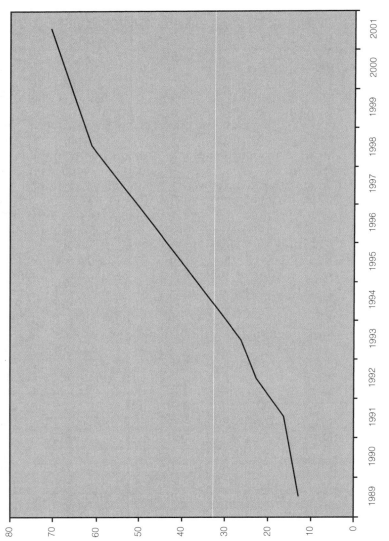

Figure 9.1 Proportion of Swiss quoted companies with a "single share" in their capital structure, 1989–2001 (%)
(*Source*: Kunz, 1998, 2002)

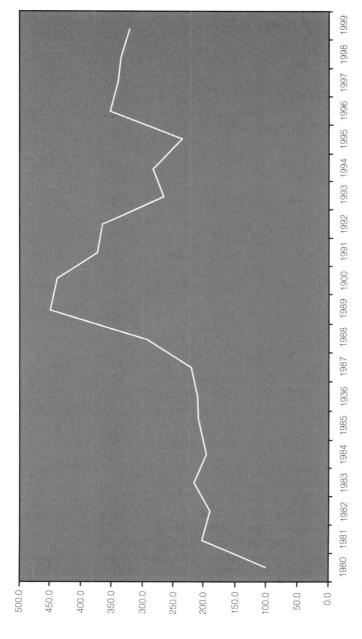

Figure 9.2 Mergers and acquisitions in Switzerland, 1977–99 (1977–80 = 100)
(*Source: Handelszeitung*, 2000)

generally motivated by the intention to concentrate these companies' activities on their core business and to abandon less profitable segments. This was the case of ABB, Sulzer, and Algroup, some of the largest Swiss industrial firms. In the chemical and pharmaceutical sector, too, the largest companies (Novartis and Roche) "outsourced" their chemical specialties with the creation of Cibas CS and Clariant. This restructuring was completely in line with the view of those advocating shareholder value.

Fifthly, one of the leitmotifs of the proponents of the shareholder value ideology is the professionalization and downsizing of boards. There has also been a tendency toward making the boards of large Swiss companies smaller and recruiting new board members through a more formal selection process than along the lines of group representation and personal relations, as was the case before. Nonetheless, this should not lead to an extensive loosening of the network of cross-holding:

> ... the leading banks will probably retain and, in the event of a continuing concentration in the financial sector, even extend their central position. . . . The average number of seats held by linkers will probably decline, but at the same time, the big linkers will increasingly get rid of the seats of medium-sized corporations and just keep a few lucrative mandates with large corporations. (Nollert, 1998: 55)

Lastly, several regulatory reforms concerning financial markets and corporate governance mechanisms were introduced during the last decade. These reforms cannot be assimilated to a process of "deregulation," but of "reregulation": new rules have been established in order to formalize and codify the new functioning of corporate governance. Two of these regulatory reforms were particularly important: (1) the reform of the Company Law (1992); (2) the adoption of a new Law on Stock Exchange and Securities Trading (1995).[10] All these reforms were aimed at more transparency in disclosure rules and presentation of accounts, but they did not represent a brutal change in the national regulatory framework and were the result of compromises between the decisive actors.

In short, some general and summary conclusions can be outlined from these recent changes. Firstly, the increasing power of national and foreign institutional investors and the reorientation of the large universal banks toward more lucrative activities, such as investment banking and private banking instead of traditional lending practices, mean that Swiss companies are much more exposed to the pressure of stock market evaluation and to the critical appreciation of institutional investors, focusing on the promotion of shareholder value. Secondly, the progressive changes in ownership concentration and in the behavior of central financial actors call into question the traditional extent of cross-shareholdings and interlocking directorates in the Swiss corporate governance system. The regulatory reforms, even if not of major importance, also favored this tendency and reinforced the role of institutional investors and opened the way for changing the practices of Swiss companies. Lastly, whereas regulatory changes do not seem to be extensive and do not confirm the hypothesis of a strong convergence toward Anglo-Saxon rules, the changing preferences, strategy, and power relations between central economic actors (shareholders, managers, and labor) indicate an evolution toward a more market-driven corporate governance system.

9.3.3 The "Swedish model" under pressure

Like Switzerland, Sweden, despite the high degree of internationalization of its economy, also resorted to some "selective-protectionist" measures concerning corporate governance mechanisms during the period of economic growth after World War II. Concentration of ownership was combined with foreign exchange controls, voting-rights distortion, and pyramiding. These characteristics have come under increasing pressure during the last 20 years.

In contrast to Switzerland, which never relied on foreign exchange controls and always had a liberal policy concerning financial markets, the liberalization of financial markets and the abolition of foreign exchange controls were a much more sensitive issue in Sweden during the second half of the 1980s. The liberalization of financial markets represented an important break with traditional Swedish macroeconomic policy, characterized by an active coordination of fiscal, monetary, and wage policies. After various attempts to restore economic growth and fight unemployment through coordinated macroeconomic management, and after several devaluations of the krona and wage moderation, the Swedish government finally decided to liberalize its capital markets and abandon foreign exchange controls during the second half of the 1980s. The main reasons for this choice were firstly a strategy to attract new foreign credits and the increasing difficulty in the context of technological innovation to maintain foreign exchange controls (see Jörnmark and Strandberg, 2001).

The decision to liberalize financial markets had a very important impact on the major characteristics of Swedish corporate governance, especially by increasing foreign ownership, and questioning specific regulations of ownership restrictions (see Reiter, 2003 and Henrekson and Jakobson, 2003a, b on which the following pages are largely based).

Firstly, these decisions clearly accelerated the transnationalization of the Swedish economy through a sharp increase of inward and outward FDI. Outward FDI, already representing 10.7 percent of GDP in 1985, reached more than 50 percent in 2000. These data illustrate the increasing internationalization of Swedish multinational companies through their expansion abroad. On the other hand, the liberalization of financial markets also favored a sharp increase of inward FDI, from 5.4 percent of GDP in 1990 to 36.1 percent in 2000 (see Table 9.5 above).

Secondly, the deregulation of financial markets at the end of the 1980s considerably increased the attractiveness of portfolio investments and the stock market (Table 9.7). The abolition of restrictions on foreign acquisitions of Swedish shares contributed to this evolution by allowing foreign ownership in Swedish companies. Since the beginning of the 1990s, foreign ownership in listed Swedish companies increased considerably, more than doubling between 1990 and 2000. Up to the mid-1980s, acquisition of Swedish shares by foreigners was limited by exchange controls and by legislation. With the suppression of exchange controls and legal restrictions on foreign purchasers, foreign ownership of shares increased steadily during the 1990s (for more details see Isaksson and Skog, 1994; Adolfsson et al., 1999).

The rapid growth of foreign ownership was also accompanied by the emergence of new domestic financial actors, such as insurance companies and portfolio managers, who have gained a much more important role in the market in comparison to other traditional ownership categories. These actors tend to replace more traditional investment companies as the major domestic investors and owners on the Swedish stock market (Henrekson and Jakobson, 2003b). The liberalization of financial markets and the emergence of new domestic institutional investors contribute to the redistribution of ownership and, in a second step, to the questioning of ownership restrictions. Reiter (2003: 119) stresses that "global investors have affected the traditional ownership groups, not only through exerting direct pressure, but also because their preferences have been adopted and driven by

Table 9.7   Distribution of stock market value according to ownership categories (%)

Year	Households	Foreign owners	Swedish institutions	Total
1993	26.0	19.0	55.0	100
1994	25.0	24.0	51.0	100
1995	17.0	32.0	51.0	100
1996	18.3	34.9	46.8	100
1997	17.8	36.4	45.8	100
1998	30.6[a]	34.9	34.5	100
1999	29.9[a]	38.2	31.9	100
2000	30.8[a]	42.7	26.5	100
2001	29.2[a]	42.8	28.0	100

Notes: Refers to the situation at the beginning of each year.
[a] As of 1998, mutual funds are included in household ownership; the share of mutual funds is estimated at approximately 10%.
Source: Henrekson and Jakobson (2003a), from Sundin and Sundqvist (1993–2001), SIS Ägarservice, Stockholm.

national shareholders, such as insurance companies and fund/portfolio managers."

We have seen that Swedish companies resorted to one-share-one-vote distortion and to pyramiding as protective devices. Concerning the first instrument, proposals have been made for a long time to change the law that allows the differentiation of voting rights between shares. Foreign investors have repeatedly criticized this protective regulation of the Swedish system and asked for the introduction of "one-share-one-vote" principles. Even though the Swedish government has not followed these regulatory proposals, several companies voluntarily decided to suppress some discriminating measures against new owners, in particular since the second half of the 1990s (Table 9.8). Thus, some large companies, such as Electrolux and SKF, recently abolished their dual-share structure (Reiter, 2003). These changes clearly resembled those introduced in Switzerland by some large companies. However, even if ownership restrictions and voting-rights distortions are declining, the largest Swedish companies still continue to use differential voting shares.

Concerning the second protectionist instrument, that is pyramiding, some important changes have also taken place. Firstly, traditional owners, such as Investor and Industrivärden, have been forced to concentrate their investments in a fewer number of companies (Reiter, 2003: 113). Secondly, the Wallenberg group, symbol of the pyramidal structure in Sweden, has also seen its strong ownership influence weakening. The dissatisfaction of shareholders with the low performance of Investor, the Wallenberg invest-ment company, is one sign of its loss of influence (*The Economist*, 9.6, 2001: 75). The abolition of the dual-share structure in Electrolux and SKF, which also diminishes Investor's voting rights (from 45 to 21 percent in the first case and from 33 to 29 percent in the second), is another (Agnblad et al., 2001: 256; Henrekson and Jakobson, 2003b: 36). This phenomenon should not, however, be exaggerated: "... the Wallenbergs still have a major influence over Swedish industry" (Adolfsson et al., 1999: 8).

Table 9.8 The percentage of listed companies on the Stockholm stock exchange with dual class shares, selected years, 1968–98

Year	Share	No. of firms
1968	32	146
1972	36	134
1977	44	130
1981	54	128
1986	74	217
1992	87	202
1998	63	304

Source: Henrekson and Jakobson (2003b: Table 9).

The evolution concerning the ownership structures and corporate governance mechanisms during the last decade in Sweden represented a substantial shift in power relations among the business community. The dominance of traditional Swedish owners has been increasingly called into question. The decline of traditional owners has been linked to the rising importance of foreign ownership and of new domestic institutional investors. Related to this shift in power relations, there has been a trend toward more Anglo-Saxon corporate governance practices, stressing the rights of minority shareholders and favoring continual public evaluation of companies on the stock market.

These rapid changes during the last decade have had some major impacts on the Swedish economy. Isaksson and Skog (1994: 297), for example, underline that the number of mergers and acquisitions has increased constantly during the last decade. More generally, the transnationalization of Swedish ownership and the progressive abolition of the protectionist elements of Swedish corporate governance might call into question some characteristics of the "Swedish model." Even though it was largely neglected in the literature on the Swedish model, the concentration of ownership among traditional domestic owners and the system of differentiated voting rights were particularly important in maintaining the cohesion of the Swedish economy (Reiter, 2003). With the rise of new financial actors, foreign and national, less focused on the long-term growth of their companies, some central institutions of the Swedish model such as collective wage bargaining might be called into question by the change in the composition of ownership structures and corporate governance mechanisms (Henrekson and Jakobsson, 2003a).

9.4   Conclusion: dynamics of change and institutional inertia in corporate governance practices

The evolution of Swedish and Swiss corporate governance during the 1990s should be seen in a broader context: is there, in Continental Europe, a process of convergence toward the Anglo-Saxon model or are these nations able to keep their main corporate governance features?

In general there are two different answers. Firstly, due to the liberalization of financial markets and their growing importance, some authors put forward the hypothesis that a converging trend is under way, in which the Continental European model is undergoing far-reaching transformations and is beginning to look like the Anglo-Saxon model (Hansmann and Kraakman, 2001). The other line of argument rejects the idea of a smooth and rapid convergence toward an optimal and unified Anglo-Saxon system of corporate governance and insists on the persistence of national governance systems. Bebchuk and Roe (1999) thus argue that path-dependencies and the self-interest of those who benefit from existing structures slow down or prevent convergence (see Coffee, 1999a; Cioffi and Cohen, 2000; O'Sullivan, 2000).

As underlined in our two case studies, the changes in the international environment have triggered profound transformations in the preferences of national actors, who have become increasingly transnational, and in the power relationships at the national level. Thus, the functioning of corporate governance is changing progressively, much less through the formal reform of the "rules of the game" than through the modification of the preferences and strategies of economic actors. Even if regulatory reforms remained path-dependent and their scope was limited, it would be a mistake to underestimate the modification in the behavior of central economic actors and the changing logic of corporate governance functioning. Thus it seems particularly appropriate, as suggested by Gilson (2000), to distinguish between different forms of convergence in order to underline the interaction between "path-dependency" and adaptation of national systems of corporate governance. Gilson distinguishes three kinds of convergence: functional, formal, and contractual convergence. The first characterizes a situation in which "existing governance institutions are flexible enough to respond to the demands of changed circumstances without altering the institutions' formal characteristics." The second appears when "an effective response requires legislative action to alter the basic structure of existing governance institutions." Lastly, contractual convergence constitutes the response which takes the form of a contract "... because governance institutions lack the flexibility to respond without formal change, and political barriers restrict the capacity for formal institutional change" (Gilson, 2000: 33–4; see also Coffee, 1999a, 2000). In a similar argument, Streeck (2001) underlines that the combination of international economic pressure and the persistence of national institutional characteristics leads to the "hybridization" of national systems of corporate governance.

Functional convergence toward Anglo-Saxon practices, which does not imply (formal) changes in corporate or security law, is the result of the changing strategies and relationships between the different actors involved in the company. The rising role of institutional investors and the changing attitude of traditional actors, such as banks and large blockholders, who give priority to the profitability of their assets rather than to long-term relationships, contribute to the weakening of the traditional characteristics of corporate governance systems in small European countries. The description of the Swiss case highlighted the simplification of the capital structure of the largest firms, the increase in mergers and acquisitions during the 1980s and 1990s, in particular acquisitions by foreign companies, and the adoption of international accounting standards by multinationals. A similar evolution is under way in Sweden.

This functional convergence, however, does not for the time being threaten the core characteristics of the corporate governance systems of the two countries. Ownership concentration and selective protectionism in particular are not collapsing; the former still remains largely in place and the latter is adapted by the national actors. Moreover, formal convergence (for example differential voting rights codified in corporate law) is not taking place. Regulatory changes are therefore much more limited: we cannot speak of a *formal convergence*. In Switzerland and Sweden, where voting-rights distortions predominate, changes seem less extensive than in other small European countries, such as Belgium or Austria, where foreign investors have gained considerable influence (for more details, see David and Mach, 2001). One of the main reasons is that, in Sweden and Switzerland, these defensive mechanisms are formalized in corporate law and national legislation reforms are largely determined by interest group politics. In Switzerland, 30 years of discussions, experts' reports, and consultation procedures were necessary to replace the old company law and the new one remains very tolerant toward *Vinkulierung*, the main selective protectionist mechanism. In Sweden, the recurrent proposals to change the law concerning differential shares have not yet been successful. These reforms aiming at diminishing the protection and giving more influence to (minority) shareholders were to a large degree opposed by the dominant interest groups, notably the controlling shareholders.

Finally, a third form of potential change is what Gilson called *convergence by contract*. To illustrate this form of convergence, Gilson (2000: 25) gives an interesting example: the convergence through security designs. A company with differentiated voting rights raises equity capital from American institutional investors. The family who controls the company does not want to cede its control to the public by unifying its shares. Therefore, investors will be reluctant to invest in a company where it is very difficult to monitor externally the performance of the management chosen by the controlling shareholder. A limited partnership will take place between the two parties: the institutional investor could be sold low voting stock which, at the end of specified period, would become super voting if the company's performance did not meet a specified standard. This example shows that, in a case of one-share-one-vote distortion, pressure related to globalization (here the necessity for the firm to raise capital from international investors) does not lead to a convergence toward Anglo-Saxon corporate governance mechanisms, but to an intermediate solution, a contractual approach which preserves the interests of both parties. Reiter (2003) gives some examples of Swedish companies that modified their capital structure progressively in response to new demands of foreign institutional investors. These examples illustrate the flexibility and the adjustment capacity of the corporate governance system of small countries.

Notes

1. We would like to thank Magnus Henrekson, Joakim Reiter, and Lars Swenson for helpful information on the Swedish case. We would also like to thank Frederick Kermisch for research assistance and Richard Kozul-Wright for supplying us with unpublished UNCTAD data. A preliminary version of this chapter was presented at the European Business History Annual Congress in Helsinki, 22–24 August 2002 and at the workshop of the Research Committee on Economic Sociology of the Swiss Society of Sociology, Fribourg 12 October 2002. This chapter is part of an ongoing research project on Swiss corporate governance funded by the Swiss National Science Foundation (Grant number: 1214-068112.02/1). Thomas David would like to thank the Fondation du 450[e] anniversaire of the University of Lausanne for its financial support.
2. For La Porta et al. (1998) the nature of legal systems is what explains ownership concentration. French, German, and Scandinavian law systems afford minority stockholders poor protection, whereas common law countries (Anglo-Saxon countries) have the strongest protection for outside investors. This argument has been criticized by Coffee (2000: 8) who argues that although "'law matters' legal developments tend to follow rather than precede economic change."
3. Big banks (Crédit Suisse and UBS) and state-owned cantonal banks are the main lenders to firms, with a combined market share of over 75 percent (Hertig, 1998: 813).
4. Whereas Schröter (1999: 204) considers that this form of "cooperative capital-ism" reached its peak development during the 1930s (because of its focus on cartelization), we think that these cooperative characteristics remained in place during the postwar period.
5. Some authors have already made a similar statement about the correlation between the existence of corporatist institutions and the high density of inter-locking directorships (Stokman et al., 1985; Windolf and Nollert, 2001). This argument is similar to the "varieties of capitalism" approach, which stresses the institutional complementarity between the four spheres of national production systems: the industrial relations system, the education and training system, the financial/corporate governance system, and the rules governing intercompany relationships (see Hall and Soskice, 2001).
6. But also at the international level concerning the large export-oriented com-panies.
7. Bebchuk et al. (2000) underline that the instrument of dual class shares is the most efficient means to separate ownership from control (see also Agnblad et al., 2001 on Sweden).
8. Even though it is very difficult to get precise data on the evolution of share own-ership structure during the last ten years, one indicator of the increasing role of institutional investors is the evolution of the proportion of shares (instead of other financial assets, such as loans or bonds) held by these new financial actors. The proportion of shares held by institutional investors increased steadily during the 1990s (see OECD, 2001).
9. In 1988, Nestlé was the first Swiss company to lift the prohibition against foreign buyers of its registered stock. One of the reasons put forward by the board to the press and the stockholders was the company's international image: Nestlé's takeover practices abroad during the 1980s had been somewhat controversial. Nestlé was expanding abroad through the acquisition of foreign

companies, while shielding itself from unwanted suitors. In 1988, for fear of reprisals in other countries, Nestlé took the decision to open itself to foreign investors (Loderer and Jacobs, 1995: 320–2). However, more important than the public image, the extension of the foreign activities of multinational companies in the 1980s also meant that Nestlé should increase its equity in order to finance its development, which implies raising more equity abroad and thus opening its capital structure.

10. In 2002, the Federation of Industry and Commerce adopted a code of best practice, which, although not compulsory, should improve the functioning of the companies.

10
European Integration and Corporate Governance in Central Europe: Trajectories of Institutional Change

Heather Grabbe

10.1 Introduction[1]

This chapter considers how the process of European integration is shaping various dimensions of corporate governance in Central Europe. The literature on corporate governance in Central and Eastern Europe (CEE) has so far made little connection with that on EU integration, and this chapter aims to open a research agenda on exploring how and where the accession process is influencing the development of corporate governance in the CEE region. In this chapter, corporate governance is construed very broadly, as both regulation of the activities of firms and also the relations between firms, the state, and trade unions. Systematic comparison of emerging corporate governance patterns in CEE has long been constrained by lack of consistent and comparable data across CEE countries, particularly at the micro level, and by the dynamic nature of institutional reform in post-communist transformation. Nevertheless, it is clear that a major external constraint on the development of corporate governance is the socio-economic order created by EU integration, which is now starting to govern the CEE economies as well.

The study of corporate governance in CEE has not made much use of work on Europeanization, but the theoretical insights of the Europeanization literature provide a useful background for an empirical study of the EU's effects in CEE. The growing literature on "Europeanization" explores numerous dimensions of the EU's impact on its member states. It has highlighted in particular processes of economic and institutional adaptation, as well as exploring specific mechanisms of Europeanization (in both public policy and political structures) and forms of "cognitive adaptation," whereby the EU is used to justify and legitimate policy choices. In extending this concept to encompass the EU's effects in Central Europe, I use a definition based on Radaelli (2000): Europeanization is the set of processes through which the EU changes the logic of political behavior at national level, by becoming part of domestic discourse, political structures, and public policies. Europeanization in the context of CEE corporate governance is seen as a process whereby the EU exports models of market regulation to CEE, and it affects the relations between firms, the state, and trade unions.

Section 10.2 reviews briefly the issues emerging in recent literature on CEE corporate governance. Section 10.3 sets out a prima facie case about how the EU accession process is starting to affect both corporate rule-making and the nexus of relations that structure economic activity. Section 10.4 outlines several directions for further research on the EU's impact at firm level. The focus of the chapter is on the Czech Republic, Hungary and Poland, but with reference to other CEE countries where relevant.

10.2   The rhetoric of choice and the power of paths

Since 1989, Central European policymakers have often claimed to be following Western models. A strong element in debates about economic reform, in particular, is the idea that comparing Western countries' experiences could help CEE to emulate "best practice" in areas like corporate governance. A common perception in CEE is that convergence with West European models is part of economic and social "modernization" and the "return to Europe." Early on in the process of post-communist transformation, it was politically expedient for CEE policymakers to claim to be emulating Western models: such models gave a sense of direction that helped to gain domestic support for reforms, and also to gain the financial support of international institutions and foreign governments that were keen to establish a neoliberal economic and democratic consensus in CEE.

Favored models in the 1990s tended to be neoliberal in character, a choice that reflects both the influence of Western advisors (particularly from US and international agencies) and also the desire of CEE policymakers to make a complete break from the discredited socialist models of the past. After all, it is easier in a time of revolution to advocate the opposite of past policies than to aim for a middle path. Famously, Vaclav Klaus claimed to be following in the footsteps of Hayek and the Chicago School in formulating Czech voucher privatization, explicitly rejecting West European social democratic models (Klaus, 1994). In Poland, "shock therapy" owed much to the neoliberal economic orthodoxy of the IMF and the Harvard Institute for International Development (see Sachs, 1994; Hare et al., 1999). Hungarian politicians, by contrast, tended to refer more to Austrian and German models of *Sozialpartnerschaft*, particularly under the Horn government of 1994–98 (Halpern and Wyplosz, 1998).

However, the typologies used in these debates have been vague: emulating particular models of capitalism has been more of a rhetorical device than a basis for substantive debate among policymakers. The major reform "plans" used to break political deadlock at key points – such as those of

Leszek Balcerowicz in Poland and Lajos Bokros in Hungary – have in practice combined a number of elements from the Anglo-American and Rhenish models. Particularly in the area of macroeconomic governance, Poland and Hungary used a mixture of measures in the first half of the 1990s, selecting à la carte rather than going for the set menu of a particular model. Neoliberal elements of fiscal austerity, withdrawing the role of the state, and promoting labor market flexibility were combined with the more Germanic/Latin characteristics of maintaining cooperation between social partners.[2] The Czech strategy under the Klaus government was presented as more radical, in moving toward a market-oriented rather than network-oriented system, but the aggressive rhetoric used by the government hid a lack of institutional development and the growth of informal networks of insider ownership.

In practice, Central European policymakers have innovated, adapting elements of different models to fit the complex situation facing them at different points in transition. Corporate structures borrow elements from different models and mix in novelties of their own, resulting in what has been called "mutant capitalism" (see Chavance and Magnin, 1997). For example, the Czech experience encompassed old German-style concentration of ownership, owing to the inadequacy of legal protection for minority shareholders, but later also US-style securities regulation as the government tried to lure back Western portfolio investors (Coffee, 1998). New experiments in corporate governance have also been tried, most notably the creation of investment privatization funds to collect ownership certificates from the population to buy packages of shares, such as in the Czech Republic and Slovenia. After all, the task of corporate governance in CEE is wide, including not only regulation of firms' activities but also reconstruction of markets; it is thus hardly surprising that different elements have been combined together in ways that are not directly comparable with particular Western models.

The outcomes of these attempts at mimesis for corporate governance are very mixed. Indeed, it is debatable whether emerging models of capitalism are even comparable with advanced economies at all, given the variance in responses to the challenges of post-communist transition (as argued by Grabher, 1994a; Bohle, 1996). Empirical work on corporate governance patterns in Central Europe points to a diversity of institutional solutions to the problems of transition across countries and across time, rather than an evident convergence with Western models. In particular, scholars stress that the forms of "network capitalism" that have emerged depend strongly on the political and economic environment (see Federowicz on Poland and Voszka on Hungary in this volume), rather than on attempts at institutional mimesis.

To sum up a very complex picture, the literature points to gaps at three levels in the period between the debate of the early 1990s and the situation at the end of the EU accession negotiations in 2002.

1. The first gap is between initial rhetoric and outcomes. The most ideologically motivated approaches to reform have often been the least successful, the most notorious being the Klaus government's approach to financial sector development. At the heart of the Czech problems was the voucher privatization program, which put the investment market in the hands of a small number of banks still largely controlled by the state; inefficient industry was propped up and restructuring avoided as a result of inadequate regulation of markets (see Stiglitz, 1997). The privatization process resulted in cross-ownership among banks, investment funds, and firms along the lines of the Rhineland model, but it was unregulated, with negative consequences for economic growth, company behavior, and capital market development (Neumann and Egan, 1999). The manifest market failure that ensued put the Czech economy into recession and forced the government to introduce regulatory and capital market reform along Anglo-Saxon lines from 1997 onwards. By contrast, the more gradualist approaches adopted in Hungary and Poland have resulted in more effective regulation, but also hybrid forms of production regime (see Stark and Bruszt, 1998; Zysman and Schwartz, 1998).

All three cases illustrate the difficulties of implementing new rules of corporate governance, especially in a period of such radical change in all parts of the economy:

> The governance institutions of the region are facing a very different task than those in more advanced economies. Corporate governance institutions in the advanced economies function in an environment in which most changes are marginal in nature ... , while Eastern European institutions, precisely because they function in an environment of transition, face a situation in which most reforms must be global. (Frydman et al., 1996: 5)

The nature of the resulting web of relationships between firms and banks is strongly correlated to the extent of bank privatization undertaken in each country (Frydman et al., 1996; OECD, 1997a). Hungary has been fastest in breaking firm–bank–state ties, having sold off some 90 percent of the financial sector, largely to foreign owners, by the end of 1997, while Poland has privatized more slowly but steadily. By contrast, the Czech Republic was very reluctant to sell its banks, with privatization starting in earnest only in 1999. The extent of firm–bank–state links in these countries is still opaque, but banks are less open to being used to channel soft credits and political favors once they have been sold off.

Attempts at imitating corporatism in interest group relations have also had mixed results. Discredited models of social partnership and of social welfare under communism produced wariness among the policymakers, employers, and trade unions alike in the Czech Republic and Slovakia to aim at *Sozialpartnerschaft*. By contrast, there was much greater willingness to set up formal structures of interest conciliation in Poland, Bulgaria, and Hungary (as detailed by Iankova, 1998). However, in the Hungarian case it has proved to be impossible to operationalize them. The center-right Orban government abolished the Interest Conciliation Council in April 1999, without much grief on the part of the trade unions which had found the system unworkable and their voices unheeded.[3] This is partly because of the shadow of the past: Kádárist individualism and communist-era compulsory membership had discredited the trade unions in Hungary, whereas in Poland the unions – the focus of protest under martial law – have retained a greater role. The difficulties in establishing a working relationship between social partners and with the state in CEE demonstrate problems in trying to foster democratic corporatism from the top down. At firm level, worker participation in decision-making remains extremely limited. In Slovenia, for example, middle management retains the dominant role in distinctive hierarchies left over from the Yugoslav self-management system during the socialist period, with worker representation almost irrelevant (Jaklic, 1997).

2. The second gap is between formal privatization programs and completed institutional reforms. A major theme emerging from studies across the CEE countries is the path-dependency of the outcomes of privatization (Grabher, 1994a; Hausner et al., 1995; Bohle, 1996; Chavance and Magnin, 1997; Comisso, 1998; Stark and Bruszt, 1998).[4] A consistent theme in the literature on privatization is that different methods used to move firms out of state control play only a secondary role in determining governance structures compared with the complex institutional legacies of partial reforms under socialism. As a result, institutional reforms remain much less complete than privatization programs, and microeconomic restructuring has been more limited than expected. Cross-country assessments of the extent of these reforms by the EBRD (published in its annual *Transition Reports)* indicate that whereas large and small-scale privatization have taken Central European countries steadily toward the EBRD's top mark of 4 (denoting a "well-functioning market economy"), enterprise restructuring and regulatory reforms have been more uneven and much slower.

Attempts at a comparative analysis between CEE transition and economic development in Western Europe and Asia – such as that made by Whitley (1999) – show the often contradictory effects of institutional transformation. Communism did not leave CEE with an institutional tabula rasa; rather, there is a patchwork of market institutions that have been subject to a complex process of demolition, reconstruction, and construction from scratch (see Crawford, 1995). The governance structures of transforming economies are complicated by the coexistence of newly initiated change mechanisms alongside underlying continuities from the socialist system. As Hayri and McDermott put it, "[communist economies] were less strict hierarchies or atomized agents than a complex of vertical and horizontal networks, in which firms, plants and banks largely remain embedded" (Hayri and McDermott, 1996: 3).

In Poland and Hungary, the institutional structures are partly a legacy of market socialist reforms from the early 1980s, which created hybrid organization forms and interorganization links between the formal and informal economies (Bohle, 1996), and these linkages have shaped highly individualistic paths of development in CEE after 1989. The combinations of inherited and new forms of relationship between firms have resulted in what Stark (1996) calls a "bricolage" of institutions.

3. The third gap is between reform of the institutional framework and changes in actual governance practices. In legal terms, Central European corporate governance structures are based on Continental rather than Anglo-Saxon legislation. Hungarian corporate governance structures are close to the German model of a two-tier system of supervisory boards and boards of directors, and many aspects of corporate law are similar, for example (see Török, 1998). However, even if the structures are similar to Germany, practices are still rather different. Despite their firm legal foundations, Hungarian corporate governance structures frequently have no real influence on a company's strategy, let alone everyday management (Török, 1998; Estrin et al., 1995). Moreover, shareholders are largely inactive, even in countries with effectively functioning securities markets: Hungary did not experience its first hostile takeover attempt until 1999, while in Poland shareholders had limited powers until 2001 and they tend to be too small to exercise effective control. Within firms, the macroinstitutional changes in governance structures have not been matched by changes at the level of work systems (Jaklic, 1997).

In the last couple of years, there has been more attention paid to the emergence of interenterprise links, particularly between the *Mittelstand* of Poland and Hungary. Informal networks between firms, and with banks and parts of the state, have compensated for the structural shortcomings of the formal organization of the economy at the start of transition, keeping the economy running during times of political paralysis. However, the danger is that these informal networks can also (paradoxically) exacerbate the structural shortcomings themselves by bypassing regulatory controls (Grabher, 1994a). The problems encountered in the Czech Republic and Slovakia are different, but both invite comparison with features of the Latin version of "network capitalism" in Southern Europe. Where the Czech experience diverges from the southern developmental model is that rent-winning groups were not organized into coherent state–society networks that could manipulate political institutions to protect their rents (Gould, 1999) and reregulation has been possible in the Czech republic. This is not so throughout the region: Gould contrasts the Czech experience with that of Slovakia under the government of Vladimir Mečiar, where economic reform and institutional weakness were very closely linked. "Nomenclature privatization" transferred assets to Mečiar's political allies, forming iron triangles between firms, banks, and the state that have proved to be difficult to dismantle. So successful were these networks at capturing regulatory institutions that Mečiar's successors had to start reprivatizing major enterprises after the election of September 1998.

The question now is whether such networks can indeed be transformed into benign forms of coordination within thriving market economies, or whether some of the CEE countries will end up with corrupt, rent-seeking networks that hinder efficiency and international competitiveness. Will Central European economies end up with healthy forms of democratic corporatism, or with crony capitalism? For several countries in the region, this remains an open question.

In sum, the fostering of particular corporate governance models borrowed from the West is constrained by three factors in CEE:

- The shadow of the past: the institutional legacies of socialism;
- The shadow of the present: the transformation strategies adopted since 1989;
- The shadow of the future: preparations for EU membership – the focus of the rest of this chapter – have had a significant impact both on market institutions and on sectoral policies.

What are the potential trajectories for CEE corporate governance now? The previous section has suggested that the constraints imposed by the countries' different pasts and presents have hindered the top-down fostering of particular models. Their future is now being shaped by EU integration, but will the EU encounter the same problems in trying to impose a one-size-fits-all set of regulatory policies? The next section discusses briefly why EU influence in CEE in greater than it is in the current member states and outlines the areas where the accession process is influencing corporate governance.

10.3   The growing force of Europeanization

So far, the literature on post-socialist transformation has located the epicenter of decisions about institutional design in domestic politics. This focus may have been appropriate for the first near-decade of transformation, when external influences have largely played a subordinate role to domestic actors and structures in designing institutions. However, we now need to pay more attention to outside influences, above all to the EU, which is starting to penetrate deeply in the sphere of economic governance. This decade will show far-reaching effects of "Europeanization" because the comprehensiveness of EU policy competences makes it a very significant force for legislative change in CEE, and the EU's influence on the reconstruction of markets in CEE is more significant than that of other international agencies. International financial institution (IFI) influence is now waning in Central Europe as countries are graduating out of the policy remits of the World Bank and IMF. But the influence of the EU is growing rather than diminishing, and developments in accession conditionality since 1997 have given it a far more pervasive force than any other external actor in CEE. In any case, the IFIs have more limited policy aims – such as macroeconomic stabilization (in the case of the IMF) or development goals (World Bank) – than does the EU. IFI policies generally restrain the redistributive functions of states, but they are less concerned with regulatory functions; by contrast, the EU started with the latter (particularly under the Single Market program) and increasingly covers the former as well (owing to the Maastricht convergence criteria for monetary union).

Moreover, the EU's impact on CEE is becoming both deeper and wider than the role it has played in shaping corporate governance in its own current member states. The agent of the EU in this analysis is primarily the Commission, because the focus here is on accession policy, which has been promulgated and managed by the Commission; although the Commission has throughout acted under the approval of member states, it has had considerable latitude for policy entrepreneurship in CEE (see Grabbe, 1999). However, it is important to note that the Commission is not the only agent of the EU in the region; in fact, the EU has multiple routes of influence into CEE, both at state and market levels, and from both EU institutions and member states.

10.3.1   The extent of EU influence

What kind of policy convergence should we expect with the EU in CEE? The experience of the EU's current member states would suggest the scope is not wide, but I argue it will be considerably greater for CEE than studies of previous Europeanization effects would lead us to expect. There has been only limited convergence within the EU itself toward a European "model of capitalism"; indeed, the continuing diversity of capitalisms across Western Europe has been well documented (see Berger and Dore, 1996; Crouch and Streeck, 1997; Rhodes and Apeldoorn, 1998; among others).

National models of capitalism have remained diverse partly because of the characteristics of EU policy-making, three of which are particularly important in resisting convergence. First, the EU's key governance function is regulation of social and political risk rather than resource redistribution (Hix, 1998) – which means it has more influence on market regulation than on macroeconomic policy. Secondly, the EU's policy framework for the Single Market remains a patchwork (Héritier, 1996), so it does not force member states to converge on a particular model of capitalism. Thirdly, policy actors in member states have been able to mitigate the impact of regulatory alignment on their domestic political economies, leading to uneven implementation and hence differentiated effects on national regimes (McGowan and Wallace, 1996). However, owing to the eastern accession process, these three characteristics do not apply in the same way to the CEE applicants, and so greater convergence is likely for Central Europe.

It is still too early to measure the detailed effects of European integration in CEE, but we can draw on the literature about the EU's effects on existing member states to obtain likely parameters of EU influence. There are three grounds for a hypothesis that the EU accession process is pushing the applicant countries toward greater convergence with particular policy models than has occurred within the existing EU.

1. The first factor is the speed of adjustment. The formal accession process sets out to adapt CEE institutions and policies to the EU much faster and more thoroughly than the adaptation of current EU-15 members. Whereas it took Greece well over a decade to adapt just to EU Single Market norms (Featherstone, 1998), prospective CEE members are expected to have oriented their institutions and policies to the EU prior to membership, from a much lower starting-point, and with very limited transitional periods. The EU has been able to push CEE policy reforms faster than they would otherwise have gone because of the priority accorded to accession by their governments and because of the institutional lacunae resulting from the communist era.

2. The second factor is the openness of CEE to EU influence. What was called "deregulation" under the Single Market program means radical reregulation in the CEE case, and sometimes imposing regulation where there was none (for example, for most of financial services). The process of throwing off communist-era legislative frameworks and creating new ones for a capitalist market economy made CEE more receptive to EU regulatory paradigms than its member states were, because EU models were being presented at the same time as CEE policymakers were seeking a model to implement. Moreover, mitigating the impact of EU policies is more difficult for applicant countries than it was for states that had already gained membership because of the asymmetric power relationship between applicants and the EU. EU institutions have much greater leverage over applicants than member states because member states are already inside.

The European "regulatory state" may still be embryonic, but it is the key starting-point for the development of national models of economic governance in CEE. In a broader sense, the EU is establishing or changing many of the "rules" of market-building and market intervention that are key to understanding how new markets develop in a society (as argued in Fligstein, 1996). EU competition policy, sectoral policies, and industrial standards are forming the core building blocks for the construction of market regulation. Wilks argues that European regulation affects the evolution or choice of a model of capitalism by shaping the creation of markets, given that "markets are social institutions governed by a set of rules, many of which are framed by the public authorities" (Wilks, 1996: 538–9). If we apply this argument to countries in transition, the EU has an extraordinary opportunity to shape the rules that constitute and define the development of new market economies.

3. The third factor is the breadth of the EU's agenda in CEE. The EU can also affect CEE in ways that lie beyond the limits of its economic governance role within the current member states as defined by the *acquis communautaire*.[5] To start with, applicants have no possibility of opt-outs from parts of the agenda, such as the Social Chapter or EMU opt-outs obtained by the UK. Hence the applicants are committed to converging with a maximalist version of the EU's policies. EU institutions (the Commission and the Council) have tended to define a "maximalist" version of the *acquis* for CEE (as discussed in Brusis, 1998).

More importantly, the EU's economic governance agenda in CEE has become wider than that for current member states through the membership conditions established for the eastern applicants. The conditions set at Copenhagen (quoted in Box 10.1) go beyond those for any previous applicant, stating that not only do prospective members have to take on the "obligations of membership" – which include the whole body of EU legislation known as the *acquis communautaire* – but they must also have a "functioning market economy" and "the capacity to cope with competitive pressure and market forces within the Union."

Through the Copenhagen conditions, the EU is having a twofold impact on CEE corporate governance: first, it is influencing market regulation and sectoral policies by presenting Single Market rules and norms that have to be adopted inflexibly, with very limited transitional periods. Secondly, the EU presents additional demands for changes in regulations and policies ad hoc to CEE. The general nature of the conditions thus allows the EU

Box 10.1   The Copenhagen Conditions

1. Membership requires that the candidate country has achieved stability of institutions guaranteeing democracy, the rule of law, human rights, and respect for and protection of minorities.
2. Membership requires the existence of a functioning market economy as well as the capacity to cope with competitive pressure and market forces within the Union.
3. Membership presupposes the candidate's ability to take on the obligations of membership including adherence to the aims of political, economic, and monetary union.
4. The Union's capacity to absorb new members, while maintaining the momentum of European integration, is also an important consideration in the general interest of both the Union and the candidate countries.

Source: European Council (1993).

(particularly the Commission, which manages accession policy) a wide margin for policy entrepreneurship in setting demands that change the macroinstitutional frameworks of these countries. Since 1993, the EU's demands on the applicants have become more specific as it has defined more clearly what would constitute meeting the Copenhagen conditions. The Commission's 1995 Single Market White Paper set out the market regulation part of the *acquis* for adoption, building on the Europe Agreements (that cover trade liberalization and competition policy, among other areas) signed from 1993 onwards. The Accession Partnerships issued from 1998 onwards are wider still, and aid and other benefits are conditional on meeting the priorities set out in them.[6]

Conditionality for accession now extends the reach of EU influence considerably more deeply into domestic policy-making in CEE than it has done in the member states, which have only had to implement policies resulting from "the obligations of membership" (the third condition) and have never been judged on the first two conditions. The democracy and market economy conditions have led the EU (in this case, mainly the Commission) to influence many policy areas that lie beyond the reach of Community competence for the member states. Whereas in the EU only certain policy domains have moved to the supranational level (see Stone Sweet and Sandholtz, 1997), in CEE there is a much wider policy remit for the Union's institutions. In the agenda presented to CEE, the distinctions between Community and national competences that are so carefully guarded within the EU are not acknowledged. Indeed, the Accession Partnerships cover several areas where member states have long been very resistant to extending Community competence for themselves. The political criteria take the EU into areas such as judicial reform and prison conditions; the economic criteria are interpreted to include areas such as reform of pension, taxation, and social security systems; and the measures for "administrative capacity to apply the acquis" bring EU conditions to civil service reform in CEE, for example. To indicate the breadth of the EU's agenda, Box 10.2 sets out the short-term economic priorities that were set in the first Accession Partnerships issued by the European Commission in 1998.

We might expect a large number of parallels with the impact that Europeanization has had on the poorer member states that joined in the 1980s (Greece, Portugal, and Spain), but also some contrasts. Particularly important are two potential parallels with the southern EU member states: the EU's penetration of state administration practices and the effects of aid dependence. However, contrasts immediately arise too: global forces have had more impact in CEE than for the Mediterranean countries, since it was not just the EU that forced liberalization in the 1990s. Penetration of state administrations is unlikely to be as deep because not all EU policies have yet been transferred, and they have had less time to penetrate; moreover, EU agencies in government were not so integrated or influential prior to

Box 10.2   Short-term economic reform priorities for 1998 (Accession
Partnerships)

Czech Republic	• implement policies to maintain internal and external balance
	• improve corporate governance by accelerating industrial and bank restructuring; implementing financial sector regulation; enforcing Securities and Exchange Commission supervision
Estonia	• sustain high growth rates, reduce inflation, increase level of national savings
	• accelerate land reform
	• start pension reform
Hungary	• advance structural reforms, particularly of healthcare
Poland	• adopt viable steel sector restructuring program by 30 June 1998 and start implementation
	• restructure coal sector
	• accelerate privatization/restructuring of state enterprises (including telecoms)
	• develop financial sector, including banking privatization
	• improve bankruptcy proceedings
Slovenia	• act on market-driven restructuring in the enterprise, finance, and banking sectors
	• prepare pension reform
Bulgaria	• privatize state enterprises and banks transparently
	• restructure industry, financial sector and agriculture
	• encourage increased foreign direct investment
Latvia	• accelerate market-based enterprise restructuring and complete privatization
	• strengthen banking sector
	• modernize agriculture and establish a land and property register
Lithuania	• accelerate large-scale privatization
	• restructure banking, energy and agri-food sectors
	• enforce financial discipline for enterprises
Romania	• privatize two banks
	• transform *régies autonomes* into commercial companies
	• implement foreign investment regime
	• restructure/privatize a number of large state-owned industrial and agricultural companies
	• implement agreements with international financial institutions
Slovakia	• tackle internal and external imbalances and sustain macroeconomic stability
	• progress on structural reforms
	• privatize and restructure enterprises, finance, banking, and energy-intensive heavy industries

Source: Author's summary drawn from the individual countries' Accession
Partnerships.

the start of negotiations as they are for member states. Finally, flows of aid to CEE have been much less than those to the main recipient member states as a proportion of GDP.

It is important to note that greater policy convergence is not necessarily the same thing as higher levels of compliance with the EU's *acquis*. CEE applicants are working from a much lower starting-point than applicants in terms of institutional development, human and financial resources, and economic capacity, so their capacity to adopt the *acquis* fully will be much less than that of a West European state. However, the EU's impact on their political economies is likely to be much greater precisely because of these underdeveloped conditions, which receive EU policies with less institutional resistance (in terms of existing policies) than do more developed member states.

10.3.2 Deconstructing the EU's agenda for corporate governance

The preceding section has suggested a powerful role for the EU in shaping policy and policy-making across a range of areas. But into what shape is the EU molding its applicants? It is difficult to say because the conditions for accession have emerged in stages and do not contain a complete blueprint for corporate governance, owing to the uneven development of supranational governance within the existing EU. For CEE, the EU is influencing both regulation and redistribution, classic concerns of the state, but these elements are developed to different degrees. Policies for CEE are much less detailed in areas that lie outside regulatory policy: the content consists of exhortations for "major efforts" to improve or strengthen policies and institutions, without the means being specified.[7]

Nevertheless, when put together, the EU's accession policy documents do contain implicit policy models for CEE. This is most evident on the economic side, where the thrust of the agenda is neoliberal, emphasizing privatization of the means of production, a reduction in state involvement in the economy (particularly industry), and further liberalization of the means of exchange. Competition policy has also been presented early on, with EU priority to state aids legislation from 1993, and later more attention to antitrust and merger control (Heinz, 1999).

Considering the variety of models of capitalism to be found among EU member states, the Accession Partnerships promote a remarkably uniform view of what a "market economy" should look like. The socioeconomic system they implicitly promote has a more "Atlantic" than "Rhenish" or "Latin" flavor. There is little attention to industrial policy, for example, or to consultation with social partners. The Accession Partnership priorities are largely anti-interventionist in terms of state involvement in managing the economy, and the Commission's regular reports have emphasized fiscal stringency (in order to prepare for eventually joining monetary union – CEC, 1998). Priority is given to the development of capital markets as a method of ensuring finance to industry and improving corporate governance (for example, in the priorities for the Czech Republic). The short-term priorities involved the setting of timetables for bank privatization in Romania, restructuring coal and steel in Poland, and preparing pensions reform in Estonia.

A major question is how consistent implementation of EU regulation will be. The countries' capacities to implement these priorities and their will to do so vary greatly across policy areas. At the same time, the EU's agenda is presented through several different fora, each with its own emphasis. The EU is deregulating in some areas (like labor codes) and reregulating in others (such as the financial sector). There are differences of emphasis from different parts of the Commission too: for example, under the Santer Commission, DGV (Employment, Industrial Relations, and Social Affairs) presented a more maximalist version of the social *acquis* to CEE than most member states had accepted (Brusis, 1998), while DGXV (Single Market and Financial Services) presented product regulation as coming before process regulation (Sedelmeier, 1998).

EU practices and norms were then brought directly into the policy-making process by member state officials working within CEE ministries through the "twinning programs" that started in 1999. Twinning marked a change from the Phare aid program, whose effect on policy-making was blunted by the use of consultants as advisors. Twinning means that bureaucrats accustomed to their own countries' methods of working and assumptions about policies and policy-making processes advise on implementation from within CEE governmental structures. Is their advice consistent with that of different parts of the Commission? Or do they bring in national views of how corporate governance should work? It makes a significant difference whether Greek, German, British, or Swedish civil servants are advising on implementation in particular policy areas.

10.4 Implications of Europeanization for CEE corporate governance

The preceding section has argued that the EU has an important role in setting the macroinstitutional framework that determines key rules of the game for corporate activity in CEE. But how much does it influence the structure of incentives and constraints facing individual firms? This section sets out some directions for future research on the impact that EU requirements are having on corporate governance in the region.

The case of CEE integration into the EU raises new challenges for several current literatures. It moves beyond the focus of comparative political economy on advanced capitalist societies to ask similar questions about those still emerging into capitalism, adding new cases for study. CEE countries are changing their policies not just because of international competition, but because of the foreign policy goal of EU membership. This case also adds further dimensions to research on how policies and institutions are transferred across national boundaries, because the EU–CEE integration process includes both voluntaristic and coercive transfer conditions. And it raises questions for the international political economy literature about the interaction of simultaneous processes of globalization and regionalization. Examination of this interaction leads us to further questions about the potential effects of EU accession on governance, state power, and transnational enterprises; for example, how might the EU be providing "transnational substitutes" (Strange, 1997: 183) for state power in CEE?

The role that the EU integration process has played in the process of transition is currently under-researched, and it is a critical part of understanding two sets of interactions: between political and economic change in the region, and between domestic and international pressures on policy and policy-making. The comprehensiveness of the EU accession process and the depth to which it has penetrated CEE policy-making make it more than just a dimension of globalization or an example of regional economic integration. The question being asked is how the EU has affected one of the central concerns of political economy, that is "the institutional underpinnings of government policy and social organization that are fundamental to the operation of economics" (Crouch and Streeck, 1997: ix).

Given the limited quantity of empirical work so far on the micro-economies of East–West integration, it is still unclear how far CEE firm behavior is becoming comparable to that of EU firms. However, there does seem to be a danger that overly rigid application of EU models may result in perverse outcomes owing to the very different circumstances prevailing in CEE, and this issue needs further investigation. The EU is clearly having an impact on the regulatory systems that institutionalize the internal firm and industry organization of market economies, what Gourevitch (1996) calls the "micro-institutions of capitalism." But, as he argues, these regulatory systems in turn have to be adapted to reflect changes resulting from international competitive pressures, and this adaptation does not appear to be happening in CEE at a satisfactory pace. The EU has focused during the accession process on rote adoption of legislation, with little attention to the impact of the resulting microinstitutional structures on efficiency. The concern that CEE should not engage in social or environmental "dumping" nor be allowed any leeway in applying Single Market rules has caused the EU to demand inflexible transposition of its frameworks, whatever the circumstances. Following Gourevitch's argument, this suggests that outcomes will be inefficient, as macroframeworks will fail to react to micro changes.

If path-dependence has so far caused outcomes to diverge from the stated plans of political leaders (as argued in Section 10.2), EU-imposed blueprints seem likely to encounter the same obstacles in implementation. The EU has generally ignored the social embeddedness of economic actors, seeking to use the same plans in all the countries. This fits the logic of the Single Market – minimum harmonization and mutual recognition are the bases of the level playing field, and they require a high degree of consistency in implementation to work. But does this approach fit the objective of real integration between CEE and EU production networks? How are firms changing the way that they organize and structure their interrelationships in response to EU-inspired regulatory reforms?

More empirical work is needed on how pressures for convergence with EU regulatory models at state level interact with the dynamics of market-level integration. This issue is important in seeing how appropriate the nascent European regulatory model is for the forms of capitalism emerging in CEE. There is a paradox that CEE applicants have been trying to converge with EU public policy models at a time when the future of many of these models appears open to question. Is the Single Market framework appropriate for regulating the emerging microinstitutional structures of CEE capitalism? Already there are questions concerning the appropriateness of the competition policy model implied by the EU's conditions for CEE, given the forms of corporate governance emerging in the region (see Wilks, 1997). Given the extent to which competition policy depends on being embedded in regulatory culture and adapted to national circumstances, it is questionable that the EU approach is optimal for developing effective regulation. One important axis of variation to explore empirically is which kinds of firms – for example, privatized versus *ab initio* new private companies – are closer to EU norms, and hence are more likely to foster the climate of regulatory compliance needed to make EU regimes work.

More detailed study of the dynamics of firm-level integration with EU production networks is needed as well. Are firms ready for the EU? The answer varies across the region; for example, a study undertaken by Carlin et al. (1999) found that at country level, progress in transition seems to be consistent with improvements in compliance with the major components of the *acquis*. Similarly, awareness of and compliance with EU directives at firm level was significantly greater in a country close to EU membership (Poland) than one far behind in the accession process (Romania).

EU firms may be playing a role here as well. The dominance of EU trade and investment in overall flows into the region raises the question of whether the activities of EU firms in the CEE region are exerting pressures for convergence with the various EU models of capitalism. A few authors have asked this question, but there is little empirical evidence yet. This issue is particularly pertinent for German influence, given its dominant role in both trade and investment. Is "Modell Deutschland" being exported along with goods, services, and capital, as some have indeed argued (e.g. Katzenstein, 1997)? Or is the opposite being attempted? A contrasting analysis is presented by Lankowski (1996), who argues that German firms are trying to escape the straitjacket of the German institutional framework by moving into CEE, rather than replicating it in the East.

Much of the literature comparing systems of corporate governance is aimed at assessing their advantages and disadvantages for sustainable competitiveness in international markets. In the context of this debate, what are the dangers of adapting to Europe as a response to global and domestic pressures? Grabher and Stark have argued that "limiting the search for effective institutions and organizational forms to the familiar Western quadrant of tried and proven arrangements locks in the post-socialist economies to exploiting known territory at the cost of forgetting (or never learning) the skills of exploring for new solutions" (Grabher and Stark, 1997: 1–2). From an evolutionary perspective, such institutional homogenization might foster adaptation in the short run, but the consequent loss of institutional diversity will impede adaptability in the long run (according to Grabher, 1994b). Certainly the EU restricts policy options in responding to international competition. Whether or not Europeanization is in tension with globalization depends partly on what you think is the best response to globalization, particularly whether convergence toward neoliberalism is inevitable and EU integration just speeds it up. But accession and transition are not synonymous, and we need to look more carefully at synergies and tensions between the tasks of integrating CEE into the EU, on the one hand, and into the world economy on the other.

10.4.1 Emerging into diverse models of capitalism from diverse models of socialism

Official EU policy toward CEE transition has largely conformed to the neoliberal consensus about what is good for transition, rather than reflecting the economic policy debates within the EU's current borders about the role of the state in promoting competitiveness and employment. In EU aid and trade policies toward CEE, the stress has been on liberalization, marketization, and privatization as the essential prerequisites for both transition and membership of the Union. The EU agenda for accession is mostly in line with that of the IFIs, which have themselves been criticized for being very neoliberal (see, for example, Gowan, 1992). Indeed, EU conditionality reinforces that of the IFIs: implementation of agreements with the development banks is part of Romania's 1998 Accession Partnership, for example, and the IMF's focus on macroeconomic stability is reinforced by EU conditions for maintaining internal and external balance in the economy.

The assumption in much of the language used in official EU publications on enlargement is that accession and transition are part of the same process and that preparations to join the EU are coterminous with overall development goals. There are reasons to be skeptical about this assumption: EU policies and regulatory models were created to fit economies and societies at a very different level of development, and they contain anomalies that are the outcome of a bargaining process between different interests and traditions (Héritier, 1996). They were not designed for countries in transition, and often require a complex institutional structure for implementation that is little developed in CEE. Moreover, the EU's emphasis on regulatory alignment has potential contradictions with the process of economic restructuring.

However, no explicit rationale is presented for this agenda. The conditions have been presented as if they are self-evident, with no acknowledgement of the policy debates going on in the EU and outside about the appropriate role of the state in the economy and the diversity of models of capitalism. It is possible to make convincing arguments as to why many of the EU conditions are necessary in CEE; for example, the need to reduce the power of social networks to promote competition, and the problems caused by lack of appropriate regulation of the financial sector in several countries. However, no such rationale has been presented, despite the fact that this is such a wide agenda from such an important external influence. It is characteristic of the asymmetric power relationship between the EU and the applicants that no justification is presented for these demands beyond the fact that they come in the name of joining the EU.

What happens if the EU applies inappropriate policies to CEE? The emphasis in EU accession policy on legal harmonization has meant much less attention to the incentive structures established at microeconomic level. The result has been a tendency for what sociologists call "functional dualism" to develop, whereby an exterior "ceremonial" structure is created that mitigates the impact on the actual activities of the organization (Jacoby, 1998). It is not clear how far this dualism yet extends, but it could be exacerbated by rapidly growing informal networks between firms. The EU's insistence on "the *acquis*, the whole *acquis* and nothing but the *acquis*" is certainly causing rapid harmonization of legislation and adaptation of macroinstitutional structures. However, it may also be encouraging a two-tier system whereby there is formal convergence in the system of rules, but also widespread market-level evasion of unimplemented regulations.

10.5   Conclusions

This chapter has argued that the regulatory side of corporate governance is becoming "Europeanized" in CEE to a significant degree through the accession process: not only are Single Market norms penetrating deeply into corporate rule-making in CEE, but EU influence extends well beyond the *acquis communautaire* that governs member states. However, it is not evident that Europeanization at state level is matched at firm level: transfer of the EU's rules and policies has not been matched by recognizably

"European" forms of firm–firm and firm–union relations, at least not yet. The post-1989 transformation of CEE corporate governance has led to hybrid organizational forms and a complex mixture of Anglo-American and Rhenish characteristics, rather than a clear choice between models of capitalism.

Harmonizing legislation with Single Market regulation and EU sectoral policies brings a certain logic that imposes some order on a fluid institutional framework in each country. However, the effects of the integration process on corporate governance in CEE are uncertain because both the capacity and the will to implement EU legislation vary greatly across policy areas and across countries. The institutional "bricolage" that has emerged in Central Europe makes it difficult to ensure uniform application of market rules across countries and sectors, and the ability of CEE regulators to enforce such inappropriate governance frameworks is equally doubtful.

The debate over which competing models of capitalism to choose has played a significant role in the political economy of post-communist transformation. However, attempts to mimic particular styles of capitalism have not resulted in convincing imitations. The corporate governance problems already emerging in Central Europe demonstrate the difficulty of trying to embed institutions in a dynamic social framework that contains many pre-1989 institutional obstacles. The EU is likely to stumble over these same obstacles in trying to impose its own policy agenda on economies in transition, which would exacerbate the "functional dualism" already emerging between formal rules and actual practice. Direct transfer has proved to be increasingly difficult, and the problems encountered in operationalizing transferred policy models, particularly the inadequacy of implementation and enforcement in many areas so far, demonstrate the inadequacy of the social settings necessary for economic institutions to work.

The rhetorical dance performed by the EU and CEE over accession conditionality has clouded the view of how far and in which areas regional patterns of state–market relations are converging and diverging. As Jean-Paul Fitoussi has asked, "Are we referring to conceptual or to concrete systems?" (Fitoussi, 1997: 149) when we discuss what system of capitalism the CEE economies are moving toward and what system of socialism they are emerging from. In an oft-repeated variant of the old communist joke, CEE policymakers are in a position of "They pretend to let us join, and we pretend to be ready." The EU tells the candidates to adopt a pure form of neoliberal capitalism if they want to join – ignoring the diversity across its current member states – while the applicants restate their commitment to rapid adoption of this model – ignoring the diversity of economic systems developing in their countries. Neither side has yet acknowledged the open question of whether the EU models that CEE countries are supposed to be adopting are appropriate to their economic systems in terms of effective market regulation, long-term competitiveness, and good governance.

Notes

1. The author would like to thank participants at workshops at the Wissenschaftszentrum, Berlin, and the European University Institute, Florence, for comments on earlier versions of this chapter, particularly Ruth Aguilera and Michał Federowicz.
2. To use Rhodes and Apeldoorn's typology of capitalist systems in Western Europe, developed from Albert (1991): see Rhodes and Apeldoorn (1998).
3. Author's interviews with employers' organizations and trade unions, Budapest, April 1999.
4. In the CEE literature, the term "path-dependency" is used loosely, and often does not meet the conditions used in the path-dependency literature in economics (such as David, 1985 on QWERTY). Rather, it is used most commonly to mean that "history matters" in the sense that pre-1989 structures and practices have left heavy institutional legacies. The term remains a subject of debate, and I am grateful to Bernard Chavance, Michal Federowicz, and Stewart Wood for discussion of this point.
5. *Acquis communautaire* is the term used to refer to all the real and potential rights and obligations of the EU system and its institutional framework; the accession *acquis* is the whole body of EU law and practice – see Grabbe (1999).
6. The evolution of the conditions for membership and the scope of their coverage are discussed in Grabbe (1999).
7. The Commission's emphasis is on having coherent policies and functioning institutions, rather than specific prescriptions for policy content. The policy detail is filled in by each country's "National Programme for Adoption of the Acquis" (published from June 1999 onwards), putting the onus on the applicants to decide how to meet the specified objectives. However, EU preferences in policy content emerged through which projects receive Phare funding and in the Commission's regular reports on each country's progress.

Bibliography

Ábrahám, Á. (1996) 'Corporate Governance in the Hungarian Manufacturing Industry', mimeo.

Adolfsson, P., U. Ask, U. Holmberg and S. Jönsson (1999) *Corporate Governance in Sweden: a Literature Review* (Göteborg University, European Project: Corporate Governance and Product Innovation, COPI).

Agnblad, J. E. Berglöf, P. Högfeldt and J. Svancar (2001) 'Ownership and Control in Sweden: Strong Owners, Weak Minorities and Social Control' in F. Barca and M. Becht (eds) *The Control of Corporate Europe* (Oxford: Oxford University Press), 228–58.

Aguilera, R. V. (1999) 'Elites, Corporations and the Wealth of Nations: How Do Historical Institutional Settings Shape Intercorporate Relations in Italian and Spanish Capitalism?' Harvard University, PhD dissertation.

Aguilera, R. and G. Jackson (2003) 'The Cross-National Diversity of Corporate Governance: Dimensions and Determinants', *Academy of Management Review*, 28 (3), 447–65.

Albert, M. (1991/1993) *Capitalism against Capitalism* (London: Whurr, 1993); or *Capitalisme contre capitalisme* (Paris: Le Seuil, 1991).

Alchian, A. (1977) *Economic Forces at Work* (Indianapolis: Liberty Press).

Amable, B. and B. Hancké (2001) 'Innovation and Industrial Renewal in France in Comparative Perspective', *Industry and Innovation*, 8(2), August, 113–35.

Amar, Michel and Bruno Crépon (1990) 'Les deux visages de la concentration industrielle: efficacité et rente de situation', *Économie et Statistique*, 229, 5–20.

Amatori, F. (1995) 'The Tormented Development of Large Industrial Enterprises between the Government and Families: Italy' in G. Airoldi, F. Amatori, and G. Invernizzi (eds) *Ownership and Governance: the Case of Italian Enterprises and Public Administration* (Milan: EGEA), 243–55.

Amatori, F. (1997) 'Italy: the Tormented Rise of Organizational Capabilities between Government and Families' in A. D. Chandler, F. Amatori, and T. Hikino, *Big Business and the Wealth of Nations* (Cambridge, New York: Cambridge University Press), 246–76.

Amatori, F. and F. Brioschi (1997) 'Le Grandi Imprese Private: Famiglie e Coalizioni' in F. Barca, *Storia del Capitalismo Italiano dal Dopoguerra a Oggi* (Rome: Donzelli Editore), 117–53.

Amsden, A. H., J. Kochanowicz and L. Tylor (1994) *The Market Meets Its Match* (Cambridge, London: Harvard University Press).

Anderson, M. and T. Hertig (1994) 'Institutional Investors in Switzerland' in T. Baums, R. M. Buxbaum and K. J. Hopt (eds) *Institutional Investors and Corporate Governance* (Berlin, New York: W. de Gruyter), 489–529.

Andreff, W. (1998) 'Privatisation and Corporate Governance in Transition Countries', mimeo.

Antal, L. (1985) *Gazdaságirányítási és pénügyi rendszerünk a reform útján* (Reforms of the Economic Mechanism and the Financial System) (Budapest: Közgazdasági és Jogi Könyvkiadó).

Antal-Mokos, Z. (1998) *Privatisation, Politics, and Economic Performance in Hungary* (Cambridge, UK, New York: Cambridge University Press).

Antalóczy, K. (1999) *Privatizáció a gyógyszeriparban* (Privatization in the Pharmaceutical Industry) (Budapest: Állami Privatizációs és Vagyonkezelő Rt.).

Aoki, M. (2000) *Information, Corporate Governance, and Industrial Diversity: Competitiveness in Japan, the USA, and the Transnational Economies* (Oxford: Oxford University Press).

Arruñada, B. (1990) *Control y Regulación de la Sociedad* (Madrid: Alianza Editorial).

Balassa, Á. (1996) 'A magyar bankrendszerkonszolidációja és jelenlegi helyzete' (The
Consolidation and the Current Situation of Hungarian Banking System),
Külgazdaság, Nos 4, 5, 4–21.

Balcerová, Z. (1998) 'Devìt let znovuzrození českého bankovnictví' (Nine Years of
Rebirth of the Czech Banking Sector), *Hospodářství*, 11–12.

Balcerowicz, L. (1995) *Socialism, Capitalism Transformation* (Budapest, London, New
York: CEU Press).

Banco de España (1999) *Annual Report.*

Baranovsky, O. (2003) 'The Banking System of Ukraine: the Present and the Future',
Zerkalo Nedeli, No. 14 (439) (Saturday, 12–18 April 2003) (http://www.mirror-
weekly. com/ie/show/439/38244).

Barca, F. (1996) *On Corporate Governance in Italy: Issue, Facts and Agenda*, Working
Paper of Fondazione Eni Enrico Mattei (Milan).

Barca, F., M. Bianco, L. Cannari, R. Cesari, C. Gola, G. Manitta, G. Salvo, and
L. F. Signorini (1994) *Assetti Proprietari e Mercato delle Imprese*. Vol. I. *Proprietà,
Modelli di Controllo e Riallocazione nelle Imprese Industriali Italiane* (Bologna: Il
Mulino).

Bauer, Michel (1988) 'The Politics of State-Directed Privatization: the Case of France,
1986–88', *West European Politics*, 11, 49–60.

Bauer, M. and B. Bertin-Mourot (1995) *L'Accès au Sommet, des Grandes Entreprises
Françaises, 1985–94* (Paris: CNRS Observatoire des Dirigeants and Boyden).

Baumol, W. (1959) *Business Behavior, Value and Growth* (New York: Macmillan).

Baums, T., R. M. Buxbaum, and K. J. Hopt (1994) *Institutional Investors and Corporate
Governance* (New York: Walter de Gruyter).

Bebchuk, L. A. , R. Kraakman, G. G. Triantis (2000) 'Stock Pyramids, Cross-
ownership and Dual Class Equity: the Mechanisms and Agency Costs of Separating
Control from Cash-flow Rights' in R. Morck (ed.) *Concentrated Corporate Ownership*
(Chicago: University of Chicago Press), 295–314.

Bebchuk, L. and M. Roe (1999) 'A Theory of Path Dependence in Corporate
Ownership and Governance', *Stanford Law Review*, 52, 127–70.

Becht, M. and F. Barca (2001) *The Control of Corporate Europe* (Oxford: Oxford
University Press).

Becht, M. and A. Röell (1999) 'Blockholdings in Europe: an International Comparison', *European Economic Review*, 43, 1049–56.

Belka, M, S. Estrin, M. E. Schaffer and I. J. Singh (1994) *Enterprise Adjustment in
Poland: Evidence from a Survey of 200 Private, Privatised and State-Owned Firms*
(London: Centre for Economic Performance, London School of Economics and
Political Science).

Béret, Pierre (1992) 'Salaires et marchés internes: quelques évolutions récentes en
France', *Economie Appliquée*, 45, 5–22.

Berger, Suzanne (1972) *Peasants against Politics* (Cambridge, UK and New York:
Cambridge University Press).

Berger, Suzanne (1995) 'Trade and Identity: the Coming Protectionism?' in G. Flyn
(ed.) *Remaking the Hexagon: the New France in the New Europe* (Boulder: Westview
Press), 195–210.

Berger, S. (1996) 'Introduction' in S. Berger and R. Dore (eds) *National Diversity and Global Capitalism* (Ithaca: Cornell University Press).

Berger, S. and R. Dore (eds) (1996) *National Diversity and Global Capitalism* (Ithaca: Cornell University Press).

Berger, Suzanne and Michael J. Piore (1980) *Dualism and Discontinuity in Industrial Societies* (Cambridge, Mass.: Cambridge University Press).

Berglöf, E. (1990) 'Capital Structure and Mechanisms of Control: a Comparison of Financial Systems' in M. Aoki, B. Gustafson, and O. Williamson (eds) *The Firm as a Nexus of Treaties* (London: Sage Publications), 237–62.

Berglöf, E. (1994) 'Ownership of Equity and Corporate Governance: the Case of Sweden' in T. Baums, R. M. Buxbaum, and K. J. Hopt (eds) *Institutional Investors and Corporate Governance* (Berlin, New York: W. de Gruyter), 311–23.

Berglöf, E. (1995) 'Corporate Governance in Transition Economies: the Theory and Its Policy Implications' in M. Aoki and H. K. Kim (eds) *Corporate Governance in Transitional Economies* (Washington, DC: The World Bank).

Berglöf, E. and E. Perotti (1994) 'The Governance Structure of the Japanese Financial Keiretsu', *Journal of Financial Economics*, 36, 259–84.

Berglöf, E. and H. Sjögren (1998) 'Combining Arm's-length and Control-oriented Finance Evidence from Main Bank Relationships in Sweden' in K. J. Hopt et al. (eds) *Comparative Corporate Governance. The State of the Art and Emerging Research* (Oxford: Clarendon Press; New York: Oxford University Press), 787–808.

Berle, A. A. and G. C. Means (1932) *The Modern Corporation and the Private Property* (New York: Harcourt, Brace, and World).

Best, M. H. (1990) *The New Competition: Institutions of Industrial Restructuring* (Cambridge, Mass.: Harvard University Press).

Bianchi, M., M. Bianco, and L. Enriques (1998) *Pyramidal Groups and the Separation between Ownership and Control in Italy* (Brussels: European Corporate Governance Network).

Bianco, M., C. Gola, and L. F. Signorini (1996) *Dealing with Separation between Ownership and Control: State, Family, Coalitions and Pyramidal Groups in Italian Corporate Governance*, Working Paper of Fondazione Eni Enrico Mattei (Milan).

Bianco, M. and S. Trento (1995) 'Capitalismi a Confronto: i Modelli di Controllo delle Imprese', *Stato e Mercato*, 43 (April), 65–93.

Birchler, U. (1995) 'Aktionärsstruktur und Unternehmenspolitik – Bedeutung für die Sicherheit des Bankensystems', *Quartalshefte der SNB*, 3, 265–77.

Birnbaum, Pierre (1994) *Les sommets de l'état. Essai sur l'élite du pouvoir en France* (Paris: Le Seuil).

Blair, M. (1995) *Ownership and Control: Rethinking Corporate Governance for the Twenty-first Century* (Washington, DC: The Brookings Institution).

Błaszczyk, B. (1997) 'Syndrom nie dokończonej prywatyzacji' (A Syndrome of Non-completed Privatization) in J. Mujzel (ed.) *Przedsiębiorstwa w procesie transformacji* (Warsaw: INE PAN).

Błaszczyk, B. and A. Kamiński (1999) 'Przebieg i charakter przekształceń własnościowych a rodzaje zachowań przedsiębiorstw' (Ownership Change and Enterprise Behavior) (Warsaw, manuscript, INE).

Block, T. H. (1998) '*Financial Market Liberalization and the Changing Character of Corporate Governance*', New School University, Center for Economic Policy Analysis, Working Paper Series III, No. 3.

Blommstein, H. (1998) 'Impact of Institutional Investors on Financial Markets' in OECD (ed.) *Institutional Investors in the New Financial Landscape* (Paris: OECD), 29–101.

Boda, D. and L. Neumann (1999) *MRP és MBO a hazai privatizációban* (Employee and Management Buy Out in Hungarian Privatization) (Budapest: Állami Privatizációs és Vagyonkezelő Rt.).

Boguszewski P., M. Federowicz, K. Kloc, W. Mizielinska, and T. Smuga (1993) *Banki a Przedsiębiorstwa* (Bank–Firm Relations: Empirical Study) (Warsaw–Gdansk: IBnGN).

Bohle, D. (1996) 'Governance im Spätsozialismus. Die Herausbildung hybrider Vernetzungen in Ungarn und Polen in den achtziger Jahren', *WZB Working Paper* (Berlin: Wissenschaftszentrum), 96–102.

Bohle, D. (2000) 'Internationalisation: an Issue Neglected in the Path-dependency Approach to Post-communist Transformation' in Dobry, M. (ed.) *Democratic and Capitalist Transitions in Eastern Europe: Lessons for the Social Sciences* (Kluwer Academic Publishers, Dordrecht, Boston, London).

Boltho, Andrea (1996) 'Has France Converged on Germany?' in S. Berger and R. Dore (eds) *National Diversity and Global Capitalism* (Ithaca, NY: Cornell University Press), 89–104.

Bonaccorsi di Patti, E. and G. Gobbi (2001) *The Effects of Bank Consolidation and Market Entry on Small Business Lending*, Discussion Paper No. 404, Servizio Study, Banca D'Italia.

Borodiuk, V. M. and O. V. Turchinov (1999) *Shadow Economic Policy. In Economic Growth and Equity*, World Bank Discussion Paper, No. 407.

Borodiuk, V. M, O. V. Turchinov, and T. Prykhod'ko (1996) 'Estimation of the Scales of a Shadow Economy and its Influence on the Dynamics of Macroeconomic Indices' (in Ukrainian and Russian), *Ekonomika Ukrainy*, Kiev, No. 11 (November), 4–16.

Bouin, O. (1996) 'Enterprise Restructuring at Different Stages of Ownership Transformation: the Czech Republic and Poland' in Blaszczyk B. and R. Woodward (eds) *Privatization in Post-Communist Countries* (Warsaw: Center for Social and Economic Research).

Bourdieu, Pierre (1989) *La Noblesse d'État. Grandes écoles et esprit de corps* (Paris: Éditions de Minuit).

Boyer, Robert (1997) 'French Statism at the Crossroads' in C. Crouch et al. (eds) *Political Economy of Modern Capitalism* (London: Francis Pinter), 71–101.

Boyer, R. and J.-P. Durand (1993) *L'après-fordisme* (Paris: Syros).

Bragantini, S. (1996) *Capitalismo all'Italiana. Come i Furbi Comandano con i Soldi degli Ingenui* (Milan: Baldini & Castoldi).

Brioschi, F., L. Buzzacchi, and M. G. Colombo (1990) *Gruppi di Imprese e Mercato Finanziario. La Struttura di Potere nell'Industria Italiana* (Rome: La Nuova Italia Scientifica).

Brunello, G., C. Graziano, and B. Parigi (1999) *Ownership or Performance: What Determines Board of Directors' Turnover in Italy?* (University of Padua).

Brusis, M. (1998) 'Residual or European Welfare Model? Central and Eastern Europe at the Crossroads' in M. Brusis (ed.) *Central and Eastern Europe on the Way into the European Union: Welfare State Reforms in the Czech Republic, Hungary, Poland and Slovakia* (Munich: Centrum für Angewandte Politikforschung), 1–19.

Buchtíková, A. (1996) 'Privatization in the Czech Republic' in Blaszczyk, B. and R. Woodward (eds) *Privatization in Post-Communist Countries* (Warsaw: Center for Social and Economic Research).

Cals, J. and A. Garrido (1999) 'Sistema y mercados financieros' in J. L. Garcia Delgado (ed.) *Lecciones de Economía Española* (Madrid: Ed. Civitas), Ch. 12.

Campbell, J. C. and O. K. Pedersen (1996) 'The Evolutionary Nature of Revolutionary Change in Postcommunist Europe' in J. C. Campbell and O. K. Pedersen (eds)

Legacies of Change: Transformation of Postcommunist European Economies (New York: Gruyter Inc.).

Cameron, David R. (1996) 'Exchange Rate Politics in France, 1981–1983: the Regime-Defining Choices of the Mitterrand Presidency', in A. Daley (ed.) *The Mitterrand Era. Policy Alternatives and Political Mobilization in France* (London: Macmillan – now Palgrave Macmillan), 56–82.

Čapek, A. and P. Mertlík (1996) *Organizational Change and Financial Restructuring in Czech Manufacturing Enterprises 1990–1995* (Prague: Czech National Bank, WP 55).

Capra, L., N. D'Amico, G. Ferri, and N. Pesaresi (1994) 'Assetti Proprietari e Mercato delle Imprese', Vol. III, *Gli Intermediari della Riallocazone Proprietaria in Italia* (Bologna: Il Mulino).

Carlin, W., S. Estrin and M. Schaffer (1999) *Measuring Progress in Transition and towards EU Accession: a Comparison of Manufacturing Firms in Poland, Romania and Spain*, CERT Discussion Paper, 99/02 (Edinburgh: CERT).

Carlin, W. and D. Soskice (1997) 'Shocks to the System: the German Political Economy under Stress', *National Institute Economic Review*, 159(1), 57–76.

Casper, S. (1999) *National Institutional Frameworks and High-Technology Innovation in Germany*, Discussion paper series, WZB.

Casper, Steven and Bob Hancké (1999) 'Global Quality Norms within National Production Regimes: ISO 9000 Norm Implementation in the French and German Car Industries', *Organization Studies*, 20(6), 961–85.

Castronovo, V. (1995) *Storia Economica d'Italia. Dall'Ottocento ai Giorni Nostri* (Turin: Piccola Biblioteca Einaudi).

Cauchon, Christophe (1997) 'La hiérarchie face aux réformes de la grande entreprise de service public en réseau et de son marché interne de travail: les cadres de la SNCF'. PhD thesis, University of Aix-Marseille.

CCP (Consejo Consultivo de Privatizaciones) (2001) *Evolución del Programa de Privatizaciones* (Madrid: Ministerio de Economia).

CEC (Commission of the European Communities) (1998) *Composite Paper: Reports on Progress towards Accession by Each of the Candidate Countries* (http://www.europa.eu.int/comm/dg1a/enlarge/report1198en/composite/index.html) (4 November).

Ceola, A., P. M. Reedtz, A. Geremia, and C. Scarenzio (1994) *La Prassi dei Fidi Multipli e l'Evoluzione del Raporto Banca-Impresa* (Milan).

Charap, J. and A. Zemplinerová (1993) *Restructuring in the Czech Economy* (London: EBRD, WP 2).

Charkham, J. P. (1994) *Keeping Good Company: a Study of Corporate Governance in Five Countries* (Oxford: Clarendon Press; New York: Oxford University Press).

Chavance, B. (1997) 'National Trajectories of Post-Socialist Transformation: Is There Convergence towards Western Capitalism?' paper presented at the Workshop 'Institution Building in the Transformation of Central and Eastern European Society', Budapest, December.

Chavance, B. and A. Labrousse (1998) 'Regulation Theory and Post-socialist Transformation', paper presented in 'Wirtschaftsordungspolitik: Der deutsche Ordoliberalismus und die französische *Ecole de la régulation* im Vergleich', WZB, Berlin, 8–9 May.

Chavance, B. and E. Magnin (1997) 'Emergence of Path-dependent Mixed Economies in Central Europe' in A. Amin and J. Hausner (eds) *Beyond Market and Hierarchy: Interactive Governance and Social Complexity* (Cheltenham: Edward Elgar), 196–232.

Chavance, B. and E. Magnin (1999) 'La contribution des économies post-socialistes à la diversité du capitalisme' in B. Chavance, E. Magin, R. Motamed-Nejad, and

J. Sapir (eds) *Capitalisme en perspective: évolution et transformation des systemes économiques* (Paris: La Decouverte).

Chavance, B. and E. Magnin (2000) 'National Trajectories of Post-socialist Transformation: Is there a Convergence towards Western Capitalism?' in Dobry, M. (ed.) *Democratic and Capitalist Transitions in Eastern Europe: Lessons for the Social Sciences* (Dordrecht–Boston–London: Kluwer Academic Publishers).

Ciocca, P. (1991) *Banca, Finanza, Mercato: Bilancio di un Decenio e Nuove Prospettive* (Turin: Einaudi).

Ciocca, P. (2000) *La nuova finanza in Italia: una difficile metamorfosi 1980–2000* (Turin: Bollati Boringhieri).

Cioffi J. and S. Cohen (2000) 'The State, Law and Corporate Governance: the Advantage of Forwardness' in G. Boyd and S. Cohen (eds) *Corporate Governance and Globalization: Long Range Planning Issues* (Cheltenham, UK; Northampton, Mass.: Edward Elgar), 307–49.

Coffee, J. C. (1996) 'Institutional Investors in Transitional Economies: Lessons from the Czech Experience' in R. Frydman, Ch. W. Gray, and A. Rapaczyński (eds) *Corporate Governance in Central Europe and Russia*. Vol. 1: *Banks, Funds, and Foreign Investors* (Budapest: CEU Press).

Coffee, J. C. (1998) 'Inventing a Corporate Monitor for Transitional Economies: the Uncertain Lessons from the Czech and Polish Experiences' in K. Hopt, H. Kanda, M. Roe, E. Wymeersch, and S. Prigge (eds) *Comparative Corporate Governance: the State of the Art and Emerging Research* (Oxford: Clarendon Press), 67–138.

Coffee, J. C. (1999a) 'The Future as History: the Prospects for Global Convergence in Corporate Governance and its Implications', *New Northwestern University Law Review*, 93, 641–707.

Coffee, J. C. (1999b) *Privatisation and Corporate Governance: the Lessons from Securities Market Failure*, Working Paper No. 158, The Center for Law and Economic Studies, Columbia Law School.

Coffee, J. C. (2000) *Convergence and its Critics: what are the Preconditions to the Separation of Ownership and Control?*, Columbia Law School Working Paper, No. 179.

Cohen, Elie (1989) *L'état brancardier. Politiques du déclin industriel 1974–1984* (Paris: Calmann-Lévy).

Cohen, Elie (1996) *La tentation hexagonale* (Paris: Fayard).

Cohen, S., J. Galbraith and J. Zysman (1985) 'The Control of Financial Policy in France' in S. Bornstein, D. Held and J. Krieger (eds) *The State in Capitalist Europe* (London: Allen & Unwin).

Collin, S. O. (1998) 'Why are these Islands of Conscious Power Found in the Ocean of Ownership? Institutional and Governance Hypotheses Explaining the Existence of Business Groups in Sweden', *Journal of Management Studies,* 35(6), 719–46.

Colombo, G. E. and G. B. Portale (1991) *Tratatto delle Societa per Azioni* (Turin: UTET).

Comisión Nacional del Mercado de Valores (CNMV) (2000) *Informe Anual sobre los Mercados de Valores* (Madrid: CNMV).

Comisso, E. (1998) 'Implicit Development Strategies in Central East Europe and Cross-National Production Networks' in J. Zysman and A. Schwartz (eds) *Enlarging Europe: the Industrial Foundations of a New Political Reality* (Berkeley: University of California Press), 380–423.

Commissariat Général du Plan (1996) 'Globalisation, Mondialisation, Concurrence: La planification française a-t-elle encore un avenir?' (Paris: Commissariat Général du Plan).

Conigliani, C. (1990) *La Concentrazione Bancaria in Italia* (Bologna: Il Mulino).

Consob (1998, 1999, 2000) (Commissione Nazionale Per le Societa' e la Borsa) *Annual Report* (Rome) (http://www.consob.it/eng_index.htm).

Consob (2001) 'Relazione per l'anno 2000' Dati e analisi sull'attivitŕ della CONSOB e sull'evoluzione del quadro di riferimento (Rome, 31 March) (http://www.consob.it/index.htm).

Costa, M. T. (1996) 'La Empresa: Características, Estrategias y Resultados' in J. L. García Delgado, R. Myro, and J. A. Martínez Serrano, *Lecciones de Economía Española* (Madrid: Civitas), 285–303.

Courtois, G. (1995) 'Education et Formation: Grandes Tendances' in *L'Etat de la France 95–6* (Paris: La Découverte, 1995), 85–90.

Crawford, B. (1995) 'Post-Communist Political Economy: a Framework for the Analysis of Reform' in B. Crawford (ed.) *Markets, States and Democracy: the Political Economy of Post-Communist Transformation* (Boulder: Westview Press), 3–42.

Crouch, C. and W. Streeck (eds) (1997) *Political Economy of Modern Capitalism: Mapping Convergence and Diversity* (London: Sage).

Crozier, Michel (1964) *Le phénomène bureaucratique* (Paris: Le Seuil).

Crozier, Michel (1970) *La société bloquée* (Paris: Le Seuil).

Cuervo-Cazzura, A. (1997) *Estructura de Propiedad y Comportamiento de la Empresa: Objetivos Alternativos de los Accionistas en España* (Salamanca: Universidad de Salamanca).

Dąbrowski J., M. Federowicz and A. Levitas (1991) 'Polish State Enterprise and Its Adjustment', *Politics and Society*, 19(4).

Dąbrowski J., M. Federowicz, and A. Levitas (1993a) 'State Enterprise in the Process of Transformation 1992–1993', *Economic Transformation Series*, No. 38 (Warsaw: IBnGN).

Dąbrowski J., M. Federowicz, T. Kamiński, and J. Szomburg (1993b) 'Privatisation of Polish State-Owned Enterprises', *Economic Transformation Series*, No. 33 (Warsaw–Gdansk: IBnGN).

Daily, C. M. and D. R. Dalton (1994) 'Bankruptcy and Corporate Governance: the Impact of Board Composition and Structure', *Academy of Management Journal*, 27(6), 1603–17.

Daley, Anthony (1996) *Steel, State, and Labor: Mobilization and Adjustment in France* (Pittsburgh: University of Pittsburgh Press).

D'Anieri, P., R. Kravchuk and T. Kuzio (1999) *Politics and Society in Ukraine* (Boulder: Westview Press).

David, P. (1985) 'Clio and the Economics of QWERTY', *American Economic Review*, 75, 332–7.

David, T. and A. Mach (2001) 'The Fortress of the Alps between National Interests and Transnational Capital: the Transformation of Swiss Corporate Governance in Comparative Perspective', paper presented at the Conference 'Small States in World Markets – Fifteen Years Later' (Göteborg, 27–29 September).

Deacon, B. (1997) *Global Social Policy: International Organizations and the Future of Welfare* (London: Sage).

De Bonis, R. and A. Ferrando (2000) *The Multiplemarket Contacts Theory: an Application to Italian Banks*, Discussion Paper No. 387, Servizio Study, Banca D' Italia.

De Cecco, M. and G. Ferri (1996) *Le Banche d'Affari in Italia* (Bologna: Il Mulino).

Demsetz, H. (1982) *Economic, Legal and Political Dimensions of Competition* (Amsterdam, New York: North-Holland).

Dermine, J. (1990) *European Banking in the 1990s* (Oxford, UK: Blackwell).

Diamond, D. W. (1996) 'Financial Intermediation as Delegated Monitoring: a Simple Example', *Federal Reserve Bank of Richmond Economic Quarterly*, 82(3), 51–66.

'Dimensions and Determinants' (2003) *Academy of Management Review*, July, forthcoming.

d'Iribarne, Alain (1989) *La compétitivité: Défi social, enjeu éducatif* (Paris: Presses du CNRS).

Dittus, P. (1994) *Corporate Governance in Central Europe: the Role of Banks* (Basle: Bank of International Settlements).

Dittus, P. and S. Prowse (1995) 'Corporate Control in Central Europe and Russia: Should Banks Own Shares?' (Washington: World Bank, mimeo).

Djankov, S. (1999) *Ownership Structure and Enterprise Restructuring in Six Newly Independent States*, World Bank Policy Research Working Paper, No. 2047.

Dobry, M. (ed.) (2000) *Democratic and Capitalist Transitions in Eastern Europe: Lessons for the Social Sciences* (Dordrecht–Boston–London: Kluwer Academic Publishers).

Dore, R. (2000) *Stock Market Capitalism: Welfare Capitalism. Japan and Germany versus the Anglo-Saxons* (Oxford, UK: Oxford University Press).

Dore, R., W. Lazonick and M. O'Sullivan (1999) 'Varieties of Capitalism in the Twentieth Century', *Oxford Review of Economic Policy*, 15(4).

Duchéneaut, Bertrand (1995) *Enquête sur les PME françaises. Identités, Contextes, Chiffres* (Paris: Maxima).

Duclos, L. and N. Mauchamp (1994) *Bilan-perspectives des relations sociales et professionnelles à EDF–GDF* (Paris: GIP Mutations Industrielles).

Duval, Guillaume (1996) 'Les habits neufs du taylorisme', *Alternatives Economiques*, No. 137, 30–9.

Duval, Guillaume (1998) *L'entreprise efficace à l'heure de Swatch et McDonald's. La seconde vie du taylorisme* (Paris: Syros).

Earle, J. and S. Estrin (1997) *After Voucher Privatization: the Structure of Corporate Governance in Russian Manufacturing Industry*, CEPR Discussion Paper Series, No. 1736, December.

EBRD (1996) 'The Report on Privatization in the Central and Eastern Europe', mimeo.

EBRD (1997) *Transition Report* (London).

Edwards, J. and K. Fisher (1994) *Banks, Finance, and Investment in Germany* (New York: Cambridge University Press).

Eguidazu, S. (1999) *Creación de Valor y Gobierno de la Empresa* (Barcelona: Ediciones Gestión 2000).

EIU (Economist Intelligence Unit) (2000) *Country Profile Italy* (London: The Economist).

El País (2001) *Anuario El País* (Madrid: El País).

Elster, J., C. Offe and U. K. Preuss (1998) *Institutional Design in Post-communist Societies: Rebuilding the Ship at Sea* (Cambridge: CUP).

Estrin, S. (ed.) (1994) *Privatization in Central and Eastern Europe* (London: Longman).

Estrin, S., J. C. Brada, A. Gelb and I. Singh (eds) (1995) *Restructuring and Privatization in Central Eastern Europe: Case Studies of Firms in Transition* (New York: M.E. Sharpe).

Estrin, Saul and Peter Holmes (1983) *French Planning in Theory and Practice* (London and Boston: Allen & Unwin).

Estrin, S., and A. Rosevear (1999) 'Enterprise Performance and Corporate Governance in Ukraine', *Journal of Comparative Economics*, 27(3), 442–58.

European Council (1993) *European Council in Copenhagen: Presidency Conclusions*, 21–22 June.

Evans, P. (1995) *Embedded Autonomy. States and Industrial Transformation* (Princeton, NJ: Princeton University Press).

Eyraud, F. and R. Tchobanian (1985) 'The Auroux Reforms and Company Level Industrial Relations in France', *British Journal of Industrial Relations*, 23(2), 241–59.

Fabregat, X. and J. Bermejo (1990) *Business Law Guide to Spain* (New York: CCH Editions Limited).

Fama, E. F. (1980) 'Agency Problems and Theory of the Firm', *Journal of Political Economy*, 88, 288–307.

Fama, E. F. and M. C. Jensen (1983) 'Separation of Ownership and Control', *Journal of Law and Economics*, 26, 301–25.

Featherstone, K. (1998) ' "Europeanization" and the Centre Periphery: the Case of Greece in the 1990s', *South European Society and Politics*, 3, 23–39.

Federowicz, M. (1994) *Poland's Economic Order: Persistence and Change* (Warsaw: Friedrich Ebert Foundation).

Federowicz, M. (2000) 'Anticipated Institutions: the Power of Path-finding Explanations' in M. Dobry (ed.) *Democratic and Capitalist Transitions in Eastern Europe: Lessons for the Social Sciences* (Dordrecht–Boston–London: Kluwer Academic Publishers).

Federowicz, M. and K. Jasiecki (1998) 'Herausbildung und Rolle von Wirtschaftseliten in Polen. Erste Ergebnisse empirischer Untersuchungen', in J. Kleer (ed.) *Transformation in den Neuen Bundesländern und Polen. Zwei Wege zur Marktwirtschaft* (Warsaw: Friedrich Ebert Stiftung), 19–36.

Federowicz, M., W. Kozek, and W. Morawski (1995) 'Poland' in J. Thirkell, R. Scase and S. Vickerstaff (eds) *Labour Relations and Political Change in Eastern Europe: Comparative Perspective* (London: UCL Press).

Federowicz, M. and A. Levitas (1995) 'Works Councils in Poland: under Communism and Neo-liberalism' in J. Rogers and W. Streeck (eds) *Works Councils: Consultation, Representation, and Cooperation in Industrial Relations* (Chicago, Ill.: University of Chicago Press).

Fernández Ordóñez, M. A. (2000) *La Competencia* (Madrid: Alianza).

FIBV (Fédération Internationale des Bourses de Valeurs) (2001) www.fibv.com

Filotto, U. (1995) 'The Institutional Bank Model: the Evolution of Legal Categories' in G. Airoldi, F. Amatori, and G. Invernizzi (eds) *Ownership and Governance: the Case of Italian Enterprises and Public Administration* (Milan: EGEA), 86–102.

Financial Research Ltd (2000) *A magyar gazdaság helyzete és kilátásai 1999–2000* (The Results and Perspectives of the Hungarian Economy 1999–2000) (Budapest).

Fitoussi, J. P. (1997) 'Following the Collapse of Communism, is there still a Middle Way?' in C. Crouch and W. Streeck (eds) *Political Economy of Modern Capitalism: Mapping Convergence and Diversity* (London: Sage), 148–60.

Fligstein, N. (1996) 'Markets as Politics: a Political–Cultural Approach to Market Institutions', *American Sociological Review*, 61 (August), 656–73.

Fligstein, N. and R. Freeland (1995) 'Theoretical and Comparative Perspectives on Corporate Organization', *Annual Review of Sociology*, 21, 21–43.

Fogel, D. S. (ed.) (1994) *Managing in Emerging Market Economies, Cases from the Czech and Slovak Republic* (Boulder: Westview Press, Inc.).

Franks, J. and C. Meyer (1990) 'Corporate Ownership and Corporate Control: a Study of France, Germany and the UK', *Economic Policy*, 1, 189–232.

Franks, J. and C. Meyer (1993) 'Corporate Control: a Synthesis of the International Evidence', *LBS IFA Working Papers*, 165–92.

Freyssenet, Michel (1998) 'Renault: from Diversified Mass Production to Innovative Flexible Production', in Michel Freyssenet, Andrew Mair, Koichi Shimizu, and Giuseppe Volpato (eds) *One Best Way? Trajectories and Industrial Models of the World's Automobile Producers* (Oxford: Oxford University Press), 365–94.

Friedman E., S. Johnson, D. Kaufmann, and P. Zoido-Lobatón (2000) 'Dodging the Grabbing Hand: the Determinants of Unofficial Activity in 69 Countries', *Journal of Public Economics*, June (http://www.worldbank.org/wbi/governance).

Frydman, R., Ch. W. Gray, and A. Rapaczyński (eds) (1996) *Corporate Governance in Central Europe and Russia: Banks, Funds and Foreign Investors*, Vol. I (Budapest, London and New York: Central European University Press).

Frydman, R., A. Rapaczyński and J. Earle (1994) *The Privatization Process in Central Europe* (Budapest: CEU Press).

Fukao, M. (1995) *Financial Integration, Corporate Governance, and the Performance of Multinational Companies* (Washington, DC: The Brookings Institution).

Galgano, F. (1997) *Diritto Commerciale* (Bologna: Zanichelli).

Galve G., C. and V. Salas Fumás (1992) 'Estructura de Propiedad en la Empresa Española', *Información Comercial Española*, 701, 79–90.

Galve Gorriz, C. and V. Salas Fumás (1993) 'Propiedad y Resultados de la Gran Empresa Española', *Investigacione Económicas*, 17(21), 207–38.

Gámir, C. L. (1999) *Las Privatizaciones en España* (Madrid: Ediciones Pirámide).

Ganne, Bernard (1992) 'Place et évolution des systèmes industriels locaux en France. Economie politique d'une transformation' in Georges Benko and Alain Lipietz (eds) *Les régions qui gagnent. Districts et réseaux: les nouveaux paradigmes de la géographie économique* (Paris: Presses Universitaires de France), 315–45.

Gardawski, J. (1998) 'Formy i struktura wlasności' (Form and Structures of Ownership) in M. Jarosz (ed.) *Prywatyzacja bezpośrednia* (Warsaw: ISP PAN).

Gatsios, K. Easter (1996) 'European Lessons on Economic Restructuring: a Synthesis of the Literature' in Scholtes, P. R. (ed.) *Industrial Economics for Countries in Transition* (Cheltenham, UK: UNIDO).

Genesca, E. and V. Salas (1995) 'Convergencia Microeconomica España–Europa (1982–1992)', *Papeles de Economía Española*, 63, 146–61.

Gerlach, M. (1987) 'Business Alliances and the Strategy of the Japanese Firms', *California Management Review*, Fall.

Gerlach, M. (1992) *Alliance Capitalism: the Social Organization of Japanese Business* (Berkeley, Calif.: University of California Press).

Gilson, R. J. (2000) *Globalizing Corporate Governance: Convergence of Form or Function*, Columbia Law School Working Paper No. 174.

Gilson, R. J. and M. J. Roe (1999) 'Lifetime Employment: Labor Peace and the Evolution of Japanese Corporate Governance', *Columbia Law Review*, 99, 508–83.

Glyn, Andrew (1997) 'Does Aggregate Profitability *Really* Matter?' *Cambridge Journal of Economics*, 21, 593–616.

Gorgeu, A. and R. Mathieu (1993) 'Dix ans de relations de sous-traitance dans l'industrie française', *Travail*, No. 28, 23–44.

Gorgeu, A. and R. Mathieu (1995) 'Stratégies d'approvisionnement des grandes firmes et livraisons juste à temps: quel impact spatial?' *L'Espace géographique*, 24(3), 245–59.

Gould, J. (1999) *Winners, Losers and the Institutional Effects of Privatization in the Czech and Slovak Republics*, RSC Working Paper No. 99/11 (San Domenico di Fiesole (FI): European University Institute).

Gourevitch, P. (1996) 'The Macropolitics of Microinstitutional Differences in the Analysis of Comparative Capitalism' in S. Berger and R. Dore (eds) *National Diversity and Global Capitalism* (Ithaca: Cornell University Press), 239–62.

Gowan, P. (1992) 'Old Medicine, New Bottles: Western Policy towards East-Central Europe', *World Policy Journal*, 1–33.

Goyer, Michel (1998) 'Governments, Markets, and Growth Revisited: Corporate Governance in France and Japan, 1965–98', paper presented to the American Political Science Association annual meeting, Boston, September.

Grabbe, H. (1999) *A Partnership for Accession? The Implications of EU Conditionality for the Central and East European Applicants*, RSC Working Paper No. 99/12 (San Domenico di Fiesole (FI): European University Institute).

Grabbe, H. and K. Hughes (1998) *Enlarging the EU Eastwards*, Chatham House Paper (London: Cassell/The Royal Institute of International Affairs).

Grabher, G. (1994a) 'The Elegance of Incoherence: Institutional Legacies, Privatization and Regional Development in East Germany and Hungary', *WZB Working Paper*, Berlin: Wissenschaftszentrum), 94–103.

Grabher, G. (1994b) *Lob der Verschwendung. Redundanz in der Regionalentwicklung* (Berlin: Edition Sigma).

Grabher, G. and D. Stark (eds) (1997) *Restructuring Networks in Post-Socialism: Legacies, Linkages, and Localities* (New York: Oxford University Press).

Granovetter, M. (1985) 'Economic Action and Social Structure: the Problem of Embeddedness', *American Journal of Sociology*, 91 (3), November, 481–510.

Gray, Ch. W. and K. Hendley (1995) 'Between Old and New: Developing Commercial Law in Hungary and Russia', paper presented for the J. M. Olin Lecture Series, Harvard University, May.

Greskovits, B. (1998) *The Political Economy of Protest and Patience: East Europe and Latin American Transformations Compared* (Budapest: CEU Press).

Greskovits, B. (2000) 'Rival Views of Postcommunist Market Societies: the Path Dependence of Transitology' in M. Dobry (ed.) *Democratic and Capitalist Transitions in Eastern Europe* (Dordrecht–Boston: Kluwer Academic Publishers).

Grossfeld, I. and G. Roland (1995) *Defensive and Strategic Restructuring in Central European Enterprises*, CEPR Discussion Paper Series No. 1135 (March).

Guatri, L. and S. Vicari (1994) *Sistemi d'impresa e capitalismi a confronto: creazione di valore in diversi contesti* (Milan: EGEA).

Guillemard, Anne-Marie (1991) 'France: Massive Exit through Unemployment Compensation', in Martin Kohli, Martin Rein, Anne-Marie Guillemard, and Herman van Gunsteren (eds), *Time for Retirement. Comparative Studies of Early Exit from the Labor Force* (Cambridge/New York: Cambridge University Press), 127–80.

Guillén, M. F. (2000) 'Organized Labor's Images of Multinational Enterprise: Divergent Foreign Investment Ideologies in Argentina, South Korea, and Spain', *Industrial and Labor Relations Review*, 53, 419–42.

Halimi, Serge (1992) *Sisyphe est fatigué. Les échecs de la gauche au pouvoir* (Paris: Robert Laffont).

Hall, P. A. (1985) 'Patterns of Economic Policy: an Organizational Approach' in S. Bornstein, D. Held and J. Krieger (eds) *The State in Capitalist Europe* (London: Allen & Unwin), 21–53.

Hall, Peter A. (1986) *Governing the Economy. The Politics of State Intervention in Britain and France* (Oxford: Oxford University Press).

Hall, P. (1995) 'The Political Economy of Europe in an Era of Interdependence', paper prepared for presentation to the Seminar on the State and Capitalism since 1800, Center for European Studies, Harvard University.

Hall, P. and D. Soskice (eds) (2001) *Varieties of Capitalism: the Institutional Foundations of Comparative Advantage* (Oxford, New York: Oxford University Press).

Halpern, L. and Ch. Wyplosz (eds) (1998) *Hungary: Towards a Market Economy* (Cambridge: Cambridge University Press).

Hancké, Bob (1998) 'Trust or Hierarchy? Changing Relationships between Large and Small Firms in France', *Small Business Economics*, 11, 237–52.

Hancké, B. (2002) *Large Firms and Institutional Change. Industrial Renewal and Economic Restructuring in France* (Oxford: Oxford University Press).

Hancké, B. and S. Casper (1996) *ISO 9000 in the French and German Car Industry. How Institutional Quality Standards Support a Variety of Capitalism*, discussion paper series, WZB.

Handelszeitung (2000) *Wer übernahm wen? Fusionen und Beteiligungen 2000* (Zurich).

Hannan, M. and J. Freeman (1989) *Organizational Ecology* (Cambridge, Mass.: Harvard University Press).

Hansmann, H. and R. Kraakman (2001) 'The End of History for Corporate Law', *Georgetown Law Journal*, 89, 439–68.

Harding, R. (1998) 'The Internationalisation of German R&D: an End to the Economic Miracle?', paper presented to Wissenschaftszentrum Berlin workshop, 23–24 October.

Hare, P., J. Batt, and S. Estrin (eds) (1999) *Reconstituting the Market: the Political Economy of Microeconomic Transformation* (Amsterdam: Harwood).

Hart, Jeffrey A. (1992) *Rival Capitalists. International Competitiveness in the United States, Japan, and Western Europe* (Ithaca, NY: Cornell University Press).

Hart, O. (1995) *Firms, Contracts and Financial Structure* (Oxford, UK: Oxford University Press).

Hart, O. and J. Moore (1990) 'Property Rights and the Nature of the Firm', *Journal of Political Economy*, 98, 1119–58.

Hausner, J., B. Jessop and K. Nielsen (1995) 'Institutional Change in Post-Socialism' in K. Nielsen, B. Jessop, and J. Hausner, *Strategic Choice and Path-Dependency in Post-Socialism: Institutional Dynamics in the Transformation Process* (Aldershot: Edward Elgar), 3–46.

Havel, J. (1994) *Changes in Governance Structure of Czech Enterprises 1989–1994* (Prague: Charles University, Reform Round Table Working Paper 20).

Hayri, A. and G. A. McDermott (1996) 'The Network Properties of Corporate Governance and Industrial Restructuring: a Post-Socialist Lesson' (Prague: CERGE-IE, mimeo).

Heinz, O. (1999) 'The Present Challenges of Competition Law and Policy in Central and Eastern Europe' in P. Hare, J. Batt, and S. Estrin (eds) *Reconstituting the Market: the Political Economy of Microeconomic Transformation* (Amsterdam: Harwood), 65–80.

Hellman, J. S. (1998) 'Winners Take All: the Politics of Partial Reform in Post-communist Transitions', *World Politics*, 50, January.

Henrekson, M. and U. Jakobsson (2003a) 'The Transformation of Ownership Policy and Structure in Sweden: Convergence towards the Anglo-Saxon Model?', *New Political Economy*, 8(1), 73–102.

Henrekson, M. and U. Jakobsson (2003b) *Two Attacks on the Swedish Corporate Model: from Wage-earner Funds to Corporatist Pension Funds*, Stockholm School of Economics Working Paper No. 521.

Héritier, A. (1996) 'The Accommodation of Diversity in European Policy-making and its Outcomes: Regulatory Policy as a Patchwork', *Journal of European Public Policy*, 3(2), 149–67.

Hertig, G. (1998) 'Lenders as a Force in Corporate Governance. Criteria and Practical Examples for Switzerland' in K. J. Hopt et al. (eds) *Comparative Corporate Governance. The State of the Art and Emerging Research* (Oxford: Clarendon Press; New York: Oxford University Press), 809–35.

Higley, J. and J. Pakulski (2000) 'Elite Power Games and Democratic Politics in Central and Eastern Europe' in M. Dobry (ed.) *Democratic and Capitalist Transitions in Eastern Europe: Lessons for the Social Sciences* (Dordrecht–Boston–London: Kluwer Academic Publishers).

Hildebrandt, Swen (1996) 'Berufsausbildung in Frankreich zwischen Staat, Region und Unternehmen: Neuere Entwicklungen in der Region Provence-Alpes-Côte d'Azur.' Berlin: Wissenschaftszentrum Berlin für Sozialforschung, *WZB discussion paper FS I*, 96–101.

Hix, S. (1998) 'The Study of the European Union II: the "New Governance" Agenda and its Rival', *Journal of European Public Policy*, 5(1), 38–65.

Hoang-Ngoc, Liêm (1998) *La facture sociale: Sommes-nous condamnés au libéralisme?* (Paris: Arléa).

Hoffmann, L. and A. Siedenberg (eds) (1997) *Aufbruch in die Marktwirtschaft. Reformen in der Ukraine von innen betrachtet* (Frankfurt/Main: Campus Verlag GmbH).

Hofstede, Geert (1980) *Culture's Consequences* (London: Sage).

Hoshi, T. (1998)'Understanding Japanese Corporate Governance' in M. J. Roe (ed.) *Corporate Governance Today* (Columbia, NY: Columbia Law School), 659–86.

Hoshi, T., A. Kashyap and D. Scharfstein (1991) 'Corporate Structure, Liquidity, and Investment: Evidence from Japanese Industrial Groups', *Quarterly Journal of Economics*, 106.

Howell, Chris (1992) *Regulating Labour. The State and Industrial Relations in France* (Princeton: Princeton University Press).

Iankova, E. A. (1998) 'The Transformative Corporatism of Eastern Europe', *East European Politics and Society*, 12(2), 222–64.

INSEE (1993) *Tableaux de l'économie française* (Paris: INSEE).

INSEE (1996) *Tableaux de l'économie française 1996–1997* (Paris: INSEE).

Institute for Economic Research and Policy Consulting (2003) *Quarterly Enterprise Survey*, No. 1(3), Kiev (February).

International Centre for Policy Studies (ICPS) (1999a) *Business Opinion Review (Industry and Agriculture)*, No. 4, Kiev (April).

International Centre for Policy Studies (ICPS) (1999b) *Business Opinion Review (Industry)*, No. 5, Kiev (July).

Isaksson, M. and R. Skog (1994) 'Corporate Governance in Swedish Listed Companies', in T. Baums, R. M. Buxbaum and K. J. Hopt (eds) *Institutional Investors and Corporate Governance* (Berlin, New York: W. de Gruyter), 287–310.

Jackson, G. (2001) 'The Origins of Non-liberal Corporate Governance in Germany and Japan', in W. Streeck and K. Yamamura (eds) *The Origins of Non-liberal Capitalism: Germany and Japan in Comparison* (Ithaca: Cornell University Press), 121–70.

Jacoby, W. (1998) 'Talking the Talk: the Cultural and Institutional Effects of Western Models', paper for the conference 'Post-communist Transformation and the Social Sciences: Cross-disciplinary Approaches', Berlin, 30–31 October.

Jaklic, M. (1997) 'Changing Governance Structures and Work Organization in Slovenia' in R. Whitley and P. H. Kristensen (eds) *Governance at Work: the Social Regulation of Economic Relations* (Oxford: Oxford University Press), 209–23.

Jakubowicz, S. (1989) *Niezależne samorządy pracownicze* (Independent Employee Self-management) (Warsaw: Instytut Socjologii, Uniwersytet Warszawski).

Jasiecki, K. (2001) *Elita biznesu w Polsce* (Business Elite in Poland) (Warsaw: IFIS Publishers).

Jensen, M. C. (1993) 'The Modern Industrial Revolution, Exit, and the Failure of Internal Control Systems', *The Journal of Finance*, 48, 831–80.

Jensen, M. and W. H. Meckling (1976) 'Theory of the Firm: Managerial Behavior, Agency Costs and Ownership Structures', *Journal of Financial Economics*, 3, 305–60.

Ježek, T. (1994) 'Ohlédnutí za privatizací' in *Dnešní fáze restrukturalizace vlastnických vztahů v české ekonomice* (Review of Privatization) (Prague: Česká ekonomická společnost).

Johnson, Ch. (1982) *MITI and the Japanese Miracle: the Growth of Industrial Policy, 1925–1975* (Stanford: Stanford University Press).

Jörnmark J. and U. Strandberg (2001) 'Large Companies in Small States – Internationalisation from Within', paper presented at the 'Conference Small States in World Markets – Fifteen Years Later', Göteborg, Sweden, 27–29 September.

Kadushin, Charles (1995) 'Friendship among the French Financial Elite', *American Sociological Review*, 60, 202–21.

Karsai, J. (1993) 'Fedőneve: reorganizáció' (Pseudonym: Reorganisation), *Közgazdasági Szemle*, No. 11.

Katzenstein, P. (1985) *Small States in World Markets. Industrial Policy in Europe* (Ithaca, NJ: Cornell University Press).

Katzenstein, P. (ed.) (1997) *Mitteleuropa: between Europe and Germany* (Providence, Oxford: Berghahn Books).

Kaufmann, D. (1994) 'The Plan and Administrative Regulation – the Way to Spontaneous Liberalization?', paper presented to the International Conference on 'The Societies in Transition: the Experience of Market Transformation for Ukraine', Kiev, May 19–21 (in Ukrainian).

Kaufmann, D. (1997) *The Missing Pillar of a Growth Strategy for Ukraine: Institutional and Policy Reforms for Private Sector Development* (Cambridge, Mass.: Harvard Institute for International Development).

Kaufmann, H. and B. Kunz (1991) *Shareholder Restrictions in Switzerland* (Zurich: Bank Julius Bär).

Keasy, K. T. and M. Wright (1997) *Corporate Governance: Economic and Financial Issues* (New York: Oxford University Press).

Kester, W. C. (1992) 'Governance, Contracting, and Investment Time Horizons: a Look at Germany and Japan', *The Continental Bank Journal of Applied Corporate Finance*, 8 (2), Summer, 83–98.

Kester, W. C. (1996) 'American and Japanese Corporate Governance: Converging to Best Practice?' in S. Berger and R. Dore (eds) *National Diversity and Global Capitalism* (Ithaca: Cornell University Press).

Kindleberger, Charles P. (1963) 'The Post-war Resurgence of the French Economy', in S. Hoffmann, C. P. Kindleberger, L. Wylie, J. R. Pitts, J.-B. Duroselle and F. Goguel (eds) *In Search of France* (Cambridge, Mass.: Harvard University Press).

Klaus, V. (1994) 'Systemic Change: the Delicate Mixture of Intentions and Spontaneity', address to the Mont Pélerin General Meeting, Cannes, 26 September.

Kläy, H. (1997) *Die Vinkulierung. Theorie und Praxis im neuen Aktienrecht* (Basle: Helbing & Lichtenhahn).

Klipper, M. Z. (1995) *The Governance of Privatized Firms: Problems of Power and Control* (Prague: CERGE-EI, WP 71).

Kloc, K. (1993) 'Charakterystyka systemu bankowego w Polsce i dynamika jego zmian' (Characteristics of the Banking System in Poland and its Dynamics of Change) in P. Boguszewski et al. *Banki a Przedsiębiorstwa* (Bank–Firm Relations: Empirical Study) (Warsaw–Gdansk: IBnGN).

Kocka, J. (1980) 'The Rise of the Modern Industry Enterprise in Germany' in A. D. Chandler and H. Daems, *Managerial Hierarchies: Comparative Perspectives on the Rise of Modern Industrial Enterprise* (Cambridge, Mass.: Harvard University Press), 77–117.

Kohli, Martin, Martin Rein, Anne-Marie Guillemard, and Herman van Gunsteren (1991) *Time for Early Retirement. Comparative Studies of Early Exit from the Labor Force* (Cambridge: Cambridge University Press).

Kormusheva, K. (2003) 'Change of Behavior in Transition: the Bulgarian Protests in January 1987', *Polish Sociological Review*, forthcoming.

Korpi, W. (1982) 'The Historical Compromise and its Dissolution' in B. Ryden and V. Bergström (eds) *Sweden: Choices for Economic and Social Policy in the 1980s* (London, Boston: Allen & Unwin).

Kouba, K. (1997) 'Privatization as a Process of Property Right Redistribution', *Prague Economic Papers*, 4 (Prague).

Kovách, I. and A. Csite (1999) 'A posztszocializmus vége. A magyarországi nagyvállalatok tulajdonosi szerkezete és hatékonysága 1997-ben' (The End of Post-Socialism. The Ownership Structure and the Effectiveness of Big Hungarian Firms), *Közgazdasági Szemle*, No. 2, 121–32.

Kovács, J. M. (ed.) (1994) *Transition to Capitalism? The Communist Legacy in Eastern Europe* (New Brunswick, NJ: Transaction Publishers).

Krajewska, A. (1999) 'Restrukturyzacja finansowa przedsiębiorstw, efekty ustawy o restrukturyzacji finansowej przedsiębiorstw i banków' (Financial Restructuring of Firms and Banks) (Warsaw: INE, mimeo).

Kuisel, Richard F. (1981) *Capitalism and the State in Modern France. Renovation and Economic Management in the Twentieth Century* (Cambridge: Cambridge University Press).

Kunz, R. M. (1998) *Shareholder Value durch Financial Engineering. Stimmrechte. Einheitsaktien und Aktiensplits* (Berne: Haupt).

Kunz, R. M. (2002) 'Simplification of Equity Capital Structure and Market Value', *Financial Markets and Portfolio Management*, 16(1), 30–52.

Kurzer, P. (1993) *Business and Banking. Political Change and Economic Integration in Western Europe* (Ithaca: Cornell University Press).

Kuzio, T., R. S. Kravchuk, and P. D'Anieri (eds) (1999) *State and Institution Building in Ukraine* (Basingstoke: Macmillan – now Palgrave Macmillan).

Labbé, D. (1992) 'Renault: les trois âges de la négociation', *Travail*, No. 26, 73–95.

Lane, Christel (1989) *Labour and Management in Europe. The Industrial Enterprise in Germany, Britain and France* (Aldershot: Edward Elgar).

Lane, D. (2001) *Russian Banks and the Soviet Legacy*, Working Paper No. 9, University of Cambridge.

Lankowski, C. (1996) *Whither Modell Deutschland?*, paper SMW-15.996 (Washington, DC: American Institute for Contemporary German Studies, Johns Hopkins University).

La Porta, R. F. L. de Silanes, and A. Shleifer (1999) 'Corporate Ownership around the World', *Journal of Finance*, 54 (2), 471–517.

La Porta, R. F. Lopez-de-Silanes, A. Shleifer, and R. W. Vishny (1998) 'Law and Finance', *Journal of Political Economy*, 106 (6), 1113–55.

Lazonick, W. and M. O'Sullivan (2000) 'Maximizing Shareholder Value: a New Ideology for Corporate Governance', *Economy and Society*, 29(1), 13–35.

Lehrer, M. (1996) *The German Model of Industrial Strategy in Turbulence: Corporate Governance and Managerial Hierarchies in Lufthansa*, Discussion Paper Series, WZB, Berlin.

Levy, Jonah (1999) *Toqueville's Revenge. Dilemmas of Institutional Reform in Post-dirigiste France* (Cambridge, Mass.: Harvard University Press).

Lewandowski, J. and J. Szomburg (1985) *Samorząd w dobie 'Solidarności'* (Self-Management in the 'Solidarność' Time) (London: Odnowa).

Lincoln, J. R., M. L. Gerlach, and Ch. L. Ahmadjian (1996) 'Keiretsu Networks and Corporate Performance in Japan', *American Sociological Review*, 61, 67–88.

Lincoln, J. R., M. L. Gerlach, and P. Takahashi (1992) 'Keiretsu Networks in the Japanese Economy: a Dyad Analysis of Intercorporate Ties', *American Sociological Review*, 57, 561–85.

Lindgren, H. (1987) *Banking Group Investments in Swedish Industry: on the Emergence of Banks and Associated Holding Companies Exercising Shareholder Influence on Swedish Industry in the First Half of the 20th Century*, Uppsala Papers in Economic History No. 15.

Lindgren, H. (1994) *Aktivt ägande. Investor under växlande konjonkturer* (Stockholm: Stockholm School of Economics).

Linhart, Danièle (1991) *Le torticolis de l'autruche. L'éternelle modernisation des entreprises françaises* (Paris: Le Seuil).

Lipietz, Alain (1998) *La société en sablier* (Paris: La Découverte).

Loderer, C. and A. Jacobs (1995) 'The Nestlé Crash', *Journal of Financial Economics*, 37, 315–39.

Loubet, Jean-Louis (1998) 'Peugeot Meets Ford, Sloan, and Toyota', in Michel Freyssenet, Andrew Mair, Koichi Shimizu, and Giuseppe Volpato (eds) *One Best Way? Trajectories and Industrial Models of the World's Automobile Producers* (Oxford: Oxford University Press), 339–64.

Lukauskas, A. J. (1994) 'The Political Economy of Financial Restriction: the Case of Spain', *Comparative Politics*, 27 (1), 67–89.

Lundström, R. (2001) 'Taxes and Corporate Structure in Sweden', in M. Larsson, M. Henrekson and H. Sjögren (eds) *Entrepreneurship in Business and Research* (Stockholm: EHF, Handelshögskolan & Probus Förlag), 73–112.

Lunina, I. (1999) 'Perspektyvni doslidzhennya' (Inviable Enterprises Produce Budget Imbalance), *Policy Studies*, No. 1, Kiev (January), 2–16.

McCarthy, F. D., Ch. Pant, K. Zheng, and G. Zanalda (1994) *External Shocks and Performance Responses during Systemic Transition: the Case of Ukraine*, The World Bank Policy Research Working Papers, No. 1361 (September).

Macchiati, A. (1996) *Privatizzazioni. Tra economia e politica* (Rome: Donzelli Editore).

McDermott, G. A. (2002) *Embedded Politics: Industrial Networks and Institutional Change in Post-Communism* (Ann Arbor: University of Michigan Press).

Macey, J. (1998) 'Italian Corporate Governance: One American's Perspective' in M. J. Roe (ed.) *Corporate Governance Today* (Columbia, NY: Columbia Law School), 687–703.

McGowan, F. and H. Wallace (1996) 'Towards a European Regulatory State', *Journal of European Public Policy*, 3(4), 560–76.

Maclean, M. (1995) 'Privatization in France 1993–94: New Departures or a Case of Plus ça Change?', *West European Politics*, 18 (2), 273–90.

Magnani, M. and S. Trento (2001) 'Corporate Governance and Industrial Relations in Italy', paper presented at the Exploratory Workshop on 'European Corporate Governance and Human Resource Management', Manchester, UK.

Major, I. (1995) 'A magántulajdon terjedése és a vállalatok gazdasági teljesítményei' (Expansion of Private Property and Economic Performance of Enterprises), *Közgazdasági Szemle*, No. 2.

Marris, R. (1964) *The Economic Theory of Managerial Capitalism* (Illinois, Ill.: Free Press of Glencoe).

Martin, R. (1998) 'Central and Eastern Europe and the International Economy: the Limits to Globalization', *Europe–Asia Studies*, 50(1), 7–26.

Martin Aceña, P. and F. Comín (1991) *INI-50 Años de Industrialización en España* (Madrid: Espasa Calpe).

Maurice, M., F. Sellier and J-J. Sylvestre (1986) *The Social Foundations of Industrial Power* (Cambridge, Mass.: MIT Press).

Maurice, M., F. Sellier and J-J. Sylvestre (1988) 'The Search for a Societal Effect in the Production of Company Hierarchy: a Comparison of France and Germany', in Paul Osterman (ed.) *Internal Labour Markets* (Cambridge, Mass.: MIT Press), 231–70.

Meier-Schatz, C. (1993) 'Legal Aspects and Institutional Realities of Corporate Governance in Switzerland', *Financial Markets and Portfolio Management,* 7(3), 309–21.

Mejstřík, M. (ed.) (1997) *The Privatization Process in East-Central Europe: Evolutionary Process of Czech Privatization* (Dordrecht: Kluwer Academic Publishers).

Mejstřík, M. (1999) 'Privatization, Foreign Investment and Corporate Governance' (Prague: mimeo).

Mejstřík, M. and A. Zemplinerová (1998) 'Final Report of EU-ACE Research Project P96-6171-R "Corporate Governance, Privatization and Industrial Policy"' (Prague: mimeo).

Melis, A. (1999) 'Corporate Governance. Le imprese non Finanziarie Quotate alla Borsa di Balori di Milano', *Auditing,* 36.

Melis, A. (2000) 'Corporate Governance in Italy', *Corporate Governance,* 8 (4), 347–55.

Menzel, U. (1988) *Auswege aus der Abhängigkeit. Die entwicklungspolitische Aktualität Europas* (Frankfurt am Main: Suhrkamp).

Mertlík, P. (1997) 'Restructuralization of Czech Manufacturing Industry in the Economic Transformation'(Prague: Czech National Bank, mimeo).

Mervart, J. (1998) *České banky v kontextu světového vývoje* (Czech Banks in the Context of World Development) (Prague: Nakladatelství Lidové noviny).

Midler, Christopher and Florence Charue (1993) 'A French-style Sociotechnical Learning Process: the Robotization of Automobile Body Shops', in Bruce Kogut (ed.) *Country Competitiveness. Technology and the Organizing of Work* (Oxford: Oxford University Press), 156–75.

Mihályi, P. (1997) *Corporate Governance during and after Privatization: the Lessons from Hungary* (Frankfurt: Institute for Transformation Studies).

Mihályi, P. (1998) *A magyar privatizáció krónikája* (The Chronicle of Hungarian Privatization) (Budapest: Közgazdasági és Jogi Könyvkiadó).

Mlčoch, L. (1992) *The Behavior of the Czechoslovak Enterprise Sphere* (Prague: Institute of Economics of the Czechoslovak Academy of Sciences).

Mlčoch, L. (1995a) 'Privatizace jako problém institucionálního evolucionismu' (Privatization as the Problem of Institutional Evolutionism), *Finance a úvìr,* 45 (Prague), 198–207.

Mlčoch, L. (1995b) 'The Restructuring of Property Rights through the Institutional Economist's Eyes', *Prague Economic Papers,* 4 (Prague), 148–58.

Möbus, Martine, and Eric Verdier (eds) (1997) *Les diplômes professionnels en Allemagne et en France. Conception et jeux d'acteurs* (Paris: l'Harmattan).

Móra, M. (1991) 'Az állami vállalatok (ál)privatizációja' (The Pseudo-privatization of State Firms), *Közgazdasági Szemle,* No. 6, 565–84.

Morikawa, H. (1992) *Zaibatsu: the Rise and Fall of Family Enterprise Groups in Japan* (Tokyo: University of Tokyo Press).

Morin, François (1995) 'Les mutations au cœur financier et son rôle dans les privatisations', in *L'Etat de la France 1995–96* (Paris: La Découverte), 427–30.

Morville, Pierre (1985) *Les nouvelles politiques sociales du patronat* (Paris: La Découverte).

Moss, D. (1997) '"Path Dependence": Career and Application', paper prepared for IFiS seminar, April, Institute of Philosophy and Sociology, Polish Academy of Sciences, Warsaw.

Muñoz, J. (1970) *El Poder de la Banca en España* (Vizcaya: Zero).

Neumann, S. and M. Egan (1999) 'Between German and Anglo-Saxon Capitalism: the Czech Financial Markets in Transition', *New Political Economy,* 4, 173–94.

Nicodano, G. (1998) 'Corporate Groups, Dual-Class Shares and the Value of Voting Rights', *Journal of Banking and Finance*, 22, 1117–37.

Nollert, M. (1998) 'Interlocking Directorates in Switzerland: a Network Analysis', *Revue suisse de sociologie*, 24(1), 31–58.

Nunnenkamp, P. (1998) *The German Model of Corporate Governance: Basic Features, Critical Issues, and Applicability to the Transition Economies* (Kiel: The Kiel Institute of World Economics).

OECD (various issues) *Institutional Investors Statistical Yearbook* (Paris).

OECD (1994–95) *OECD Economic Surveys, Italy*.

OECD (1995) 'Financial Markets and Corporate Governance', *Financial Trends*, 26, 13–35.

OECD (1996) *OECD Economic Survey: the Czech Republic 1996*.

OECD (1997a) *The New Banking Landscape in Central and Eastern Europe: Country Experiences and Policies for the Future*.

OECD (1997b) *Economic Synopses: Bulgaria 1997*.

OECD (1998) *Financial Market Trends*, No. 69.

OECD (2000) *Financial Market Trends*, No. 76.

OECD (2001) *OECD Economic Surveys, Spain*.

Olson, M. (1982) *The Rise and Decline of Nations: Economic Growth, Stagflation and Social Rigidities* (New Haven: Yale University Press).

Osiatyński, J., W. Pańków, and M. Federowicz (1985) *Self-Management in the Polish Economy in 1981–1985* (Biblioteca Walter Bigiavi, Facolta' Di Economia E Commercio, Universita Bologna).

O'Sullivan, M. A. (1996) *Innovation, Industrial Development, and Corporate Governance* (Cambridge, Mass.: Harvard University Press).

O'Sullivan, M. A. (2000) 'The Innovative Enterprise and Corporate Governance', *Cambridge Journal of Economics*, 24, 393–416.

Ozawa, T. (2000) 'Japanese Firms in Deepening Integration: Evolving Corporate Governance' in S. S. Cohen and G. Boyd (eds) *Corporate Governance and Globalization. Long Range Planning Issues* (Northampton, Mass.: Edward Elgar), 216–44.

Pańków, W. (1993) *Work Institutions in Transformation* (Warsaw: F. Ebert Foundation).

Pańków, W. and B. Gąciarz (1998) 'Skuteczne strategie w prywatyzacji bezpośredniej' (Effective Strategies in a Direct Privatization) in M. Jarosz (ed.) *Prywatyzacja bezpośrednia* (Direct Privatization) (Warsaw: ISP PAN).

Pannier, D. (ed.) (1996) *Corporate Governance of Public Enterprises in Transition Economies* (Washington: The World Bank).

Pérez, S. (1997) *Banking on Privilege: the Politics of Spanish Financial Reform* (Ithaca and London: Cornell University Press).

Philipenko, A. and B. Bandera (eds) (1996) *The Ukrainian Economy in Transition* (in Ukrainian) (Kiev: Akademia).

Pinto, B., M. Belka, and S. Krajewski (1993) *Transforming State Enterprises in Poland: Microeconomic Evidence on Adjustment*, The World Bank Working Paper No. 1101, Washington, DC.

Piore, M. J. and Ch. F. Sabel (1984) *The Second Industrial Divide. Possibilities for Prosperity* (New York: Basic Books).

Pistor, K. (2000) *Patterns of Legal Change: Shareholder and Creditor Rights in Transition Economies*, Working Paper Series (EBRD).

Pistor, K. and J. Turkewitz (1996) 'Coping with Hydra-State Ownership after Privatization: a Comparative Study of Hungary, Russia, and the Czech Republic' in R. Frydman, Ch. W. Gray and A. Rapacyński (eds) *Corporate Governance in Central Europe and Russia: Insiders and the State*, Vol. II (Budapest, London, and New York: Central European University Press).

Pitti, Z. (1999) 'A külföldi érdekeltségű vállalkozások működésének 1992–1998 közötti jellemzői, különös tekintettel a befektetői döntések motiváló tényezőire' (Characteristics of Companies with Foreign Owners between 1992 and 1998, with Special Regard to Motivations of the Investors' Decisions) (mimeo).

Plotnikov, A. (1995) *The Problems of the Development of Financial and Industrial Groups in Ukraine* (in Russian) (Kiev: Mira).

Pokrytan, A., P. S. Yeschenko, V. I. Golikov, and A. V. Maryenko (1999) 'The Character of Institutional Change in Ukraine' in V. M. Heyets (ed.) *The Transformation of Ukraine's Economic Model (Ideology, Contradictions, Prospects)* (in Ukrainian) (Kiev: Logos).

Porter, M. E. (1990) *The Competitive Advantage of Nations* (London: Macmillan Press – now Palgrave Macmillan).

Prowse, S. (1994) *Corporate Governance in International Perspective* (Basle: Bank of International Settlements).

Prowse, S. (1995) 'Corporate Governance in an International Perspective: a Survey of Corporate Control Mechanisms among Large Firms in the United States, the United Kingdom, Japan and Germany', *Financial Markets, Institutions and Instruments*, 4 (1), 1–63.

Pyke, F., G. Becattini, and W. Sengenberger (1990) *Industrial Districts and the Interfirm Co-operation in Italy* (Geneva: International Institute for Labor Studies).

Quélennec, Michel (1997) *L'industrie en France* (Paris: Nathan).

Radaelli, C. (2000) 'Whither Europeanization? Concept Stretching and Substantive Change', paper prepared for the international workshop 'Europeanization: Concept and Reality', Bradford University, 5–6 May.

Reiter, J. (2003) 'Financial Globalization, Corporate Ownership, and the End of Swedish Corporatism?', *New Political Economy*, 8(1), 103–25.

Rhodes, M. and B. van Apeldoorn (1998) 'Capitalism Unbound? The Transformation of European Corporate Governance', *Journal of European Public Policy*, 5(3), 406–27.

Rochard, M. B. (1987) *La sous-traîtance: entreprises et emplois. Le secteur de l'électronique professionnelle* (Paris: CEE–CEREQ–SESSI).

Roe, M. J. (1993) 'Some Differences in Corporate Structure in Germany, Japan, and the United States', *Yale Law Journal*, 102(8), 1927–2003.

Roe, M. J. (1994) *Strong Managers, Weak Owners. The Political Roots of American Corporate Finance* (Princeton, NJ: Princeton University Press).

Romanowska, M., M. Trocki, and B. Wawrzyniak (eds) (1998) *Grupy kapitałowe w Polsce* (Industrial Goups in Poland) (Warsaw: Defin).

Rusterholz, P. (1985) 'The Banks in the Centre: Integration in Decentralized Switzerland' in F. N. Stokman, R. Ziegler, and J. Scott (eds) *Networks of Corporate Power: a Comparative Analysis of Ten Countries* (Cambridge: Polity Press; Oxford, New York: Blackwell), 131–47.

Sachs, J. (1994) *Poland's Jump to the Market Economy* (Cambridge, Mass.: MIT Press).

Salais, Robert (1988) 'Les stratégies de modernisation de 1983 à 1986', *Économie et Statistique*, 213, 51–74.

Salais, Robert (1992) 'Modernisation des entreprises et Fonds National de l'Emploi. Une analyse en terme de mondes de production', *Travail et Emploi*, 51: 49–69.

Salas Fumás, V. (1991)'Relaciones Banca–Industria y Control del Capital' in A. Torrero (ed.) *Relaciones Banca–Industria. La Experiencia Española* (Madrid: Espasa-Calpe), 135–73.

Salmon, K. (1995) *The Modern Spanish Economy. Transformation and Integration into Europe* (London and New York: Pinter).

Sánchez-Calero, C. F. (1982) *Instituciones de Derecho Mercantil* (Madrid: Editoriales de Derecho Reunidas).

Sapir, J. (1997) 'Has the Transition in Russia and Ukraine been Completed? (The Establishment of Post-Soviet Neo-corporativizm)', *Political Thought*, No. 4, Kiev (September–December), 97–101.

Schluchter, W. (1981) *The Rise of Western Rationalism. Max Weber's Developmental History* (Berkeley: University of California Press).

Schmidt, Vivien A. (1996) *From State to Market? The Transformation of Business in France* (Cambridge: Cambridge University Press).

Schröter, H. G. (1993) *Aufstieg der Kleinen. Multinationale Unternehmen aus fünf kleinen Staaten vor 1914* (Berlin: Duncker & Humblot).

Schröter, H. G. (1999) 'Small European Nations: Cooperative Capitalism in the Twentieth Century' in A. D. Chandler, F. Amatori, and T. Hikino (eds) *Big Business and the Wealth of Nations* (Cambridge: Cambridge University Press), 176–204.

Scott, J. (1997) *Corporate Business and Capitalist Classes* (Oxford: Oxford University Press).

Sedelmeier, U. (1998) 'The European Union's Association Policy towards the Countries of Central and Eastern Europe: Collective EU Identity and Policy Paradigms in a Composite Policy', unpublished D.Phil. thesis, University of Sussex.

Senghaas, D. (1985) *The European Experience. A Historical Critique of Development Theory* (Leamington Spa, Warwickshire; Dover, NH: Berg Publishers).

SESSI (1997) *L'industrie française* (Paris: Ministère de l'Economie, des Finances et de l'Industrie. Service des Statistiques Industrielles).

Shleifer, A. and R. W. Vishny (1986) 'Large Shareholders and Corporate Control', *Journal of Political Economy*, 94, 461–88.

Shleifer, A. and R. W. Vishny (1997) 'A Survey of Corporate Governance', *Journal of Finance*, 52(2), 737–84.

Shonfield, Andrew (1965) *Modern Capitalism. The Changing Balance of Public and Private Power* (Oxford: Oxford University Press).

Sicsic, Pierre and Charles Wyplosz (1996) 'France, 1945–92', in N. Crafts and G. Tonioli (eds) *Economic Growth in Europe since 1945* (Cambridge: Cambridge University Press), 210–39.

Siedenberg, A. and L. Hoffmann (eds) (1998) *Ukraine at the Crossroads: Economic Reforms in International Perspective* (Berlin, New York: Physica. A Springer-Verlag Company).

Silitski, V. (1998) 'Evolution of the Banking System in Changing Political Circumstances', manuscript of Ph.D. dissertation, Budapest–Warsaw, CEU.

Silitski, V. (1999) 'Constraints and Coalitions: Politics of Economic Reform in Central and Eastern Europe after the Return of the Left', Ph.D. dissertation, Rutgers University.

Smelser, N. and R. Swedberg (1994) 'The Sociological Perspective on the Economy' in N. J. Smelser and R. Swedberg, *The Handbook of Economic Sociology* (New York: Russell Sage Foundation), 3–26.

Smith, W. Rand (1998) *The Left's Dirty Job. The Politics of Industrial Restructuring in France and Spain* (Pittsburgh/Toronto: University of Pittsburgh Press/ University of Toronto Press).

Soros International Economic Advisory Group Ukrainian Rapid Enterprise Survey (1996–98) (Kiev: SIEAG).

Soskice, D. (1994) *Germany and Japan: Industry-coordinated versus Group-coordinated Market Economy*, Conference on the Political Economy of the New Germany (Ithaca, NY: Cornell University).

Soskice, David (1997) 'German Technology Policy, Innovation and National In-stitutional Frameworks', *Industry and Innovation*, 4, 75–96.

Soukup, J. (1995) 'Commercial and Industrial Restructuring of Czech Enterprises' (Paris: Maison des Sciences de l'Homme, mimeo).

Stark, D. (1992) 'Path Dependence and Privatization Strategies in East Central Europe', *East European Politics and Science*, 6(1), Winter.

Stark, D. (1994) 'Recombinant Property in Eastern European Capitalism' (Budapest: Collegium and Ithaca, Cornell University, mimeo).

Stark, D. (1996) 'Recombinant Property in East European Capitalism', *American Journal of Sociology*, 101 (4 January), 993–1027.

Stark, D. and L. Bruszt (1998) *Postsocialist Pathways: Transforming Politics and Property in East Central Europe* (Cambridge: Cambridge University Press).

Stark, D. and Sz. Kemény (1997) 'Post-socialist Portfolios: Network Strategies in the Shadow of the State' (mimeo).

State Committee of Statistics of Ukraine (2003) *On the Social and Economic Situation in Ukraine* (January–March).

Steinherr, A. and Ch. Huveneers (1994) 'On the Performance of Differently Regulated Financial Institutions: Some Empirical Evidence', *Journal of Banking and Finance*, 18, 271–306.

Stiglitz, J. E. (1997) 'Comments on "Czech Republic: Capital Market Review Report"', Internal memorandum, Ministry of Finance, Czech Republic (9 May).

Stokman, F. N., R. Ziegler and J. Scott (eds) (1985) *Networks of Corporate Power: a Comparative Analysis of Ten Countries* (Cambridge: Polity Press; Oxford, New York: Blackwell).

Stone Sweet, A. and W. Sandholtz (1997) 'European Integration and Supranational Governance', *Journal of European Public Policy*, 4(3), 297–317.

Strange, S. (1997) 'The Future of Global Capitalism; or, Will Divergence Persist Forever?' in C. Crouch and W. Streeck (eds) *Political Economy of Modern Capitalism: Mapping Convergence and Diversity* (London: Sage), 182–91.

Stranghellini, L. (1995) 'Corporate Governance in Italy: Strong Owners, Faithful Managers. An Assessment and a Proposal for Reform', *Indiana International and Comparative Law Review*, 6, 91–185.

Streeck, W. (1996) 'Lean Production in the German Automobile Industry? A Test Case for Convergence Theory' in S. Berger and R. Dore (eds) *National Diversity and Global Capitalism* (Ithaca: Cornell University Press).

Streeck, W. (2001) 'La transformation de l'organisation de l'entreprise en Europe: Une vue d'ensemble' in R. W. Solow (ed.) *Institutions et croissance. Les chances d'un modèle économique européen* (Paris: Albin Michel), 175–230.

Suhonyako, O. (1999) 'Modern Problems of Development of Ukraine's Banking System' (in Ukrainian), *Ekonomichny tchasopis* (Economic Annals), No. 5 (May), 8–12.

Suleiman, Ezra (1979) *Les Elites en France* (Paris: Le Seuil).

Suleiman, Ezra (1995) *Les ressorts cachés de la réussite française* (Paris: Le Seuil).

Suleiman, Ezra and Henri Mendras (eds) (1995) *Le recrutement des élites en Europe* (Paris: La Découverte).

Swaan, W. (1996) 'Behavioral Constraints and the Creation of Markets in Post-Socialist Economies' in B. Dallago and L. Mittone (eds) *Economic Institutions, Markets, and Competition: Centralization and Decentralization in the Transformation of Economic Systems* (Cheltenham, UK and Brookfield, Vt: Edward Elgar).

Szelényi, I., G. Eyal, and E. Townsley (1996) 'Posztkommunista menedzserizmus: a gazdasági intézményrendszer és a társadalmi szerkezet változásai' (Post-communist

Managerism: Changes in Economic Institutions and Social Structure), *Politikatudományi Szemle*, Nos 2–3.

Taddéi, Dominique and Benjamin Coriat (1993) *Made in France. L'industrie française dans la compétition mondiale* (Paris: Librairie Générale Française).

Tamames, R. (1977) *La Oligarquía Financiera* (Barcelona: Planeta).

Tamames, R. (1993) *Introducción a la economía española* (Madrid: Alianza Editorial).

Tichý, L. (1997) *Dělba moci v privatizovaném podniku* (The Division of Power in a Privatized Enterprise) (Prague: Česká ekonomická společnost).

Todd, Emmanuel (1998) *L'illusion économique* (Paris: Gallimard).

Török, Á. (1995) *Corporate Governance in the Transition – the Case of Hungary. Do New Structures Help Create Efficient Ownership Control?* (Budapest: Hungarian Economy of Science, Institute of Economics).

Török, A. (1998) 'Corporate Governance in the Transition – the Case of Hungary: do New Structures Help Create Efficient Ownership Control?' in L. Halpern and Ch. Wyplosz, *Hungary: Towards a Market Economy* (Cambridge: Cambridge University Press), 159–91.

Torrero, A. (2001) *Internacionalización de las Bolsas y de las Finanzas. Funcionamiento del Patrón Oro y de la Moneda Unica Europea* (Madrid: Píramide).

Tortella, G. (1994) 'Patterns of Economic Retardation and Recovery in South-Western Europe in the Nineteenth and Twentieth Centuries', *Economic History Review*, 47(1), 1–21.

Tortella, G. and J. Palafox (1984) 'Banking and Industry in Spain, 1918–1936', *Journal of European Economic History*, 13(2), 81–111.

Tóth, I. J. (1998) 'Vállalkozások tulajdonosi kapcsolatai Magyarországon 1992–1996 között' (Ownership Relations of Companies in Hungary, 1992–1996), *Közgazdasági Szemle*, No. 6, 591–615.

Tuček, M. P. Machonin, L. Gatner, L. Konvička, and P. Šimoník (1998) 'Economic Elite – Czech National Report' (manuscript).

Tůma, Z. and M. Čihák (1995) *The Czech Republic: Growth after Stabilization*, Reform Round Table Working Paper 15 (Prague: Charles University).

Ukrainian–European Policy and Legal Advice Centre (UEPALAC) (1998–2002) *Ukrainian Economic Trends* (Kiev).

Ulrich, Karl (1995) 'The Role of Product Architecture in the Manufacturing Firm', *Research Policy*, 24, 419–40.

UNCTAD (2000) *World Investment Report 2000: Cross-Border Mergers and Acquisitions and Development* (Geneva: United Nations).

Uria, R. (1991) *Derecho Mercantil* (Madrid: Marcial Pons).

Useem, M. (1996) *Investor Capitalism: How Money Managers Are Changing the Face of Corporate America* (New York: Basic Books).

Várhegyi, É. (1998) *Bankprivatizáció* (Privatization of Banks) (Budapest: Állami Privatizációs és Vagyonkezelő Rt.).

Vedres, B. (2000) 'Koncentráció, polarizáltság és tulajdonosi hálózatok: a hazai nagyvállalatok tulajdonviszonyai a kilencvenes évek végén' (Concentration, Polarization and Ownership Networks: Ownership Structure of Big Hungarian Firms in the Late 1990s) (mimeo).

Velarde, J. (1969) *Sobre la Decadencia Económica de España* (Madrid: Editorial Tecnos).

Veltz, Pierre (1996) *Mondialisation, villes et territoires. L'économie d'archipel* (Paris: Presses Universitaires de France).

Verdier, Eric (1997) 'L'action publique en matière de formation professionnelle et les grandes entreprises: entre normes et décentralisation', paper presented at the workshop on 'Mutations industrielles et dynamiques territoriales'. Nantes, 28–29 March.

Vietor, R. H. K. (2001) 'Italy: From Welfare State to Market Capitalism', *Harvard Business School*, No. 9, 100–29.

Vitols, S. (1996) 'Corporate Governance versus Economic Governance: Banks and Industrial Restructuring in the US and Germany', Discussion Paper FSI 95–310, Wissenschaftszentrum Berlin für Sozialforschung, Berlin.

Vitols, S. (1999) 'Variety of Corporate Governance in Germany and the UK', WZB, manuscript.

Vitols, S., S. Casper, D. Soskice, and S. Woolcock (1997) 'Corporate Governance System in UK and Germany, Final Report', WZB, manuscript.

Voszka, É. (1997) *A dinoszauruszok esélyei* (Dinosaurs do not Want to Die) (Budapest: Pénzügykutató-Perfekt).

Voszka, É. (1998) *Spontán privatizáció* (Spontaneous Privatization) (Budapest: Állami Privatizációs és Vagyonkezelő Rt.).

Walter, I. (2000) 'Capital Markets and Control of Enterprises in the Global Economy' in G. Boyd and S. Cohen (eds) *Corporate Governance and Globalization: Long Range Planning Issues* (Cheltenham, UK; Northampton, Mass.: Edward Elgar), 95–127.

Weber, Henri (1990) *Le Parti des Patrons* (Paris: Le Seuil).

Wedel, J. (2003) '"State" and "Private": up against the Organizational Realities of Central and Eastern Europe and the Former Soviet Union', *Polish Sociological Review*, forthcoming.

Weiss, L. (1984) 'The Italian State and Small Business', *European Journal of Sociology*, 25(2), 214–41.

Whitley, R. (1999) *Divergent Capitalisms: the Social Structuring and Change of Business Systems* (Oxford, New York: Oxford University Press).

Wieviorka, M. and S. Trinh (1989) *Le Modèle EDF. Essai de sociologie des organisations* (Paris: la Découverte).

Wijnenbergen, S. van (1998) *Bank Restructuring and Enterprise Reform*, EBRD Working Paper No. 29 (London).

Wilks, S. (1996) 'Regulatory Compliance and Capitalist Diversity in Europe', *Journal of European Public Policy*, 3(4), 536–59.

Wilks, S. (1997) 'EU Competition Policy and the CEECs: the Institutions of a New Market Economy', paper prepared for a workshop on State Strategies and International Regimes in the New Europe, Thorkil Kristensen Institute.

Williamson, O. E. (1964) *The Economics of Discretionary Behavior: Managerial Objectives in a Theory of the Firm* (Englewood Cliffs, NJ: Prentice-Hall).

Williamson, O. E. (1985) *The Economic Institutions of Capitalism* (New York: Free Press).

Williamson, O. E. (1989) 'Transaction Cost Economics' in R. Schmalensee and R. Willig (eds) *Handbook of Industrial Organization* (Amsterdam, New York: North-Holland, New York: Sole distributors for the USA and Canada, Elsevier Science Pub. Co.).

Windólf, P. and J. Beyer (1996) 'Co-operative Capitalism: Corporate Networks in Germany and Britain', *British Journal of Sociology*, 47 (2), 205–31.

Windólf, P. and M. Nollert (2001) 'Institutionen, Interessen, Netzwerke: Unternehmensverflechtung im internationalen Vergleich', *Politische Vierteljahresschrift*, 42, 51–78.

Yarrow, G. and P. Jasinski (1996) *Privatization. Critical Perspectives on the World Economy* (London–New York: Routledge).

Yuschenko, V (1999) 'Improvement of Ukraine's Banking System is the Pledge of Consolidation of the Economy' (in Ukrainian), *Ekonomichny tchasopis* (Economic Annals), No. 5 (May), 3–7.

Zamagni, V. (1993) *Dalla periferia al centro: la seconda rinascita economica dell'Italia, 1861–1990* (Bologna: Il Mulino).

Zattoni, A. (1994) *'Le Aziende Italiane' Economia Aziendale, A. Cortesi* (Milan: EGEA).

Zeman, K. (2000) 'Competitiveness in Central and Eastern Europe', *Journal of Transforming Economies and Societies*, EMERGO, 7(1), Winter.

Zemplinerová, A., R. Laštovička, and A. Marcičin (1995) *Restructuring of Czech Manufacturing Enterprises: an Empirical Study*, WP 74 (Prague: CERGE-EI).

Ziegler, J. N. (1997) *Governing Ideas. Strategies for Innovations in France and Germany* (Ithaca, NY: Cornell University Press).

Zingales, L. (1994) 'The Value of the Voting Right: a Study of the Milan Stock Exchange Experience', *Review of Financial Studies*, 7, 125–48.

Zingales, L. (1998) *Corporate Governance* (London: Center for Economic Policy and Research).

Zon, H. van (2000) *The Political Economy of Independent Ukraine* (Basingstoke, London: Macmillan Press – now Palgrave Macmillan).

Zysman, John (1977) *Political Strategies for Industrial Order. State, Market and Industry in France* (Berkeley, Calif.: University of California Press).

Zysman, J. (1983) *Governments, Markets, and Growth: Financial Systems and the Politics of Industrial Change* (Ithaca, NY: Cornell University Press).

Zysman, J. and A. Schwartz (eds) (1998) *Enlarging Europe: the Industrial Foundations of a New Political Reality* (Berkeley: University of California Press).

Index

accountability   21, 68, 72, 137
acquisition *see* takeovers
administration   72, 77, 91, 93, 108,
    112, 133, 201, 212–13, 223, 257
adjustment   1, 3, 5, 7, 9, 18–19, 21, 64,
    73, 80–6, 96–7, 196–202, 204, 207,
    214–18, 224, 244, 255
    corporate   5, 196, 206, 216
    institutional   1, 3, 7, 9, 18–19
anomie   104–5, 118–19
anticipated institutions   7

Balcerowicz   154, 161, 164, 249
banking system   7, 9–10, 13, 49, 78–80,
    117–19, 146, 148, 159, 162–4, 168,
    208, 218
    Bulgarian   117–19
    French   208
    Italian   49
    Polish   162–4
    Ukrainian   78–80
bankruptcy   14, 83, 86, 96, 122, 129,
    131–2, 134, 142, 148, 171, 198,
    204
    law   14, 96, 129, 132, 148
bank(s)   8, 20, 25, 27–8, 31, 33, 42–3,
    48–66, 68, 73, 78, 80–1, 86, 93, 97,
    117–24, 126–7, 129–37, 139–42,
    146, 148, 152, 158–60, 162–5,
    167–8, 171, 174, 176–7, 179, 185,
    196, 199–201, 208–9, 217, 221–3,
    227–9, 232–4, 238, 243, 245, 250,
    253–4, 260, 263
    national (central) bank   78–80, 118,
        123, 162–3, 168
        National Bank of Ukraine (NBU)
        78–80
    investment bank(s)   25, 27, 49, 50,
        52, 81
    ownership   43, 57, 59, 63, 66, 68,
        133
    role of   42, 48–52, 54, 59–61, 66, 68,
        135, 140, 232–3
    see also financial institutions,
        institutional shareholders

boards   21, 24–5, 66, 77, 93, 98, 135,
    137, 163, 181, 187–9, 227, 238, 252
budget   72, 74, 79, 81–3, 95–7, 108,
    123, 125, 133, 176–7, 179–80, 202
Bulgaria (Bulgarian)   4, 14, 19, 21–2,
    100–20, 251
bureaucracy   13, 71, 73–4, 85, 90

capital
    accumulation   88, 93, 160
    allocation   83
    concentration   80
    dispersed   147
    equity   50, 131, 244
    financial   17, 65, 112, 117, 119, 152,
        155, 157–8, 162
    flight   83, 93
    foreign   25, 43, 58–9, 62–3, 65, 68, 78,
        131, 160–1, 163, 168, 180, 230
    formation   11, 17, 90, 145–6
    market(s)   7, 25, 27, 52–3, 59, 61–3,
        68, 83, 127–9, 131, 134, 139, 142,
        199–201, 203, 207, 209, 221–2,
        232–3, 239, 250, 259
    mobility   231
    outflow(s) of financial   86, 112, 162
    private   68, 145, 177, 179–80
    redistribution of (public)   73, 82, 90
    registered   83, 171, 179
    structure   43, 56, 228, 243–4
capitalism   2–4, 10–11, 15, 28, 31, 35,
    42, 51, 57, 74, 100, 103, 144, 166,
    170, 191, 199, 208, 217, 223, 225,
    249, 252–5, 259–65
    crony   253
    managerial   170, 191
    model(s) of, form(s) of   2, 15, 248–9,
        254–5, 259, 262–5
    network   249, 252
    political   35
    variety(varieties) of   1–2, 24
centrally planned economy   78, 95,
    137
civil service (civil servant(s))   187, 205,
    257, 260

clan(s)   71–4, 80–1, 97, 120
competence(ies)   73, 77, 125, 253, 257
competition   11, 13, 15, 27, 31, 60, 74,
   81, 83, 85–6, 88–9, 91, 96, 98, 140,
   149, 154–6, 158, 160–4, 166–7, 176,
   180, 184–5, 195, 199–201, 204, 208,
   218, 255, 257, 259, 261–262, 263,
   264
   international   11, 83, 160, 163, 263
   new forms of   199
competitive disinflation   204
competitiveness   16, 28–9, 64, 69,
   85–6, 180, 195, 200–1, 204, 214,
   226, 253, 263, 265
consensus   122, 150–1, 225, 248, 263
contract(s)   11, 14, 27, 82, 109, 111,
   130, 134, 142, 186–7, 205, 229,
   243–4
   law   11, 14
coordination   5, 27, 103–4, 110, 114,
   131, 139, 195–6, 200–1, 206–7, 217,
   239, 253
corporate
   actor(s)   100–3, 106–8, 116, 119
   adjustment   5, 196, 206, 216
   behavior   76, 100
   control   12–13, 44–8, 57, 59–60,
      65–7, 97, 128, 141, 148, 153, 156,
      158, 161–2, 164, 168, 220–1, 226
   finance, financing, financial   42, 48,
      50, 54–6, 62–3
   intercorporate holdings   174, 191–2
   model(s), form, system   8, 16, 25,
      27–8, 42, 45, 64, 68, 124, 141,
      164, 168, 182, 242
   ownership   42–4, 48, 58, 64
   performance   49–50, 56, 151
   strategy   147, 195
   structure   25, 27–8, 54, 68, 95,
      107–16, 159, 161, 168, 226, 249
   survival   204
   see also mergers
corporations   8, 11, 24–5, 27–9, 31,
   42–3, 46, 49, 56, 58–60, 62, 64–6,
   75–128, 135, 140–1, 144, 147, 152,
   161, 172, 174, 222–3, 231, 235, 238
corporatism, neo-corporativizm   81,
   250–1, 253
corruption   33, 86, 108, 153
cross-shareholding(s)   66, 200, 209,
   217, 220–1, 238

Czech Republic, Czech   14, 21–2,
   121–43, 152, 157–8, 165, 179,
   248–50, 252, 260

debt   33, 49, 52, 55–6, 60–3, 66, 68, 71,
   83, 118, 128, 131, 133, 162–3,
   177–80, 185, 191, 202, 204, 208,
   214, 234
decentralization   157, 176, 178, 199,
   215, 217
decision-making   7–10, 13, 76, 80–1,
   93, 96, 107–8, 113–14, 116, 132,
   137, 139, 144, 151, 160, 164–5, 178,
   181, 184, 187, 190, 207, 214, 251
deregulation   18, 28, 31, 52, 66, 122,
   176–7, 195, 199–201, 217, 235, 238,
   240, 255
design   20, 101,103, 110, 164–5, 216,
   224, 229, 253
directors   24, 28, 42, 58, 65, 72, 76–7,
   87–9, 93, 98, 112, 114–15, 135–7,
   147, 149, 153–5, 181–2, 184–9, 209,
   227, 252
   see also boards
distributive coalitions   105–14, 116–20
diversification   159
diversity   2–3, 11, 74, 103, 249, 254,
   263–5
dumping   261
Durkheimian   104

economic development   6, 9, 15–16,
   23, 33, 59–61, 85, 93, 98, 102, 105,
   111, 198–200, 251
economic structure   24, 58, 85, 97, 105
economy   1, 6–10, 12, 14–15, 23, 25, 27,
   33, 42, 47–8, 50, 52, 58–9, 62, 66, 71,
   73–5, 78, 80–1, 83–5, 87, 92, 95, 98,
   102–6, 111–12, 114, 120–1, 123–5,
   127, 130–1, 133–40, 142, 144–6,
   148–9, 151, 157–9, 164–6, 170,
   175–6, 180, 183, 195–200, 202–3,
   206, 216–17, 226–7, 232, 239, 242,
   250–2, 255–7, 259–61, 263–5
   command   71, 136
   global   15
   shadow   95
   SOE   72–3, 76–8, 82–3, 85, 88–91,
      109, 112, 114–15, 117–18,
      129–30, 138, 148–50, 152–8, 162,
      167

world   15, 263
see also capitalism, political economy
education   11, 16, 138, 200–1, 211–12, 215
efficiency   15–16, 20, 33, 52, 85–6, 91, 103, 112, 124, 130, 139, 142, 220, 233, 253, 261
elite   4, 9, 14, 16, 20, 101, 104–6, 108, 120, 124, 134, 158, 196–7, 200–1, 206–7, 217–18, 224–5, 231
employee   13, 24–5, 35, 43, 46, 55, 89, 114–15, 136–8, 141, 148, 150, 154, 156–7, 171–2, 174, 178, 181, 185, 187, 189–90, 192, 208
employment   27, 85, 122, 156, 180, 195, 199, 205, 212, 215–16, 239, 260, 263
Ente Nazionale Idrocarburi (ENI)   31
enterprises   25, 27, 31, 35, 43, 48, 56, 58, 72–9, 81–7, 89–92, 95–7, 107–18, 120–1, 124–5, 130–8, 140–2, 146–50, 153–8, 160, 163–5, 174–8, 181, 184, 187, 191, 231, 253, 261
  behavior of   96
  collective   76–7, 89–90
  private   92, 133
  privatized   89–90, 97, 109, 153
  state-owned (SOEs)   27, 31, 35, 48, 72–3, 76–8, 82, 85, 88–91, 93, 109, 112, 114–15, 117–18, 129, 138, 148–50, 152–8, 162, 167
entrepreneurs, entrepreneurship   33, 48, 52, 180, 254, 257
European Community   23, 64
European Union (EU)   3, 16, 18, 22, 24, 29, 31, 33, 58, 61–4, 66, 98, 106, 163, 195, 204, 234, 247–9, 253–7, 259–65
exchange rate   123, 139
executive power   147

financial crisis   101, 124
financial institutions (IFI)   13, 27–8, 48, 50, 55, 69, 81, 127, 144, 158, 160, 172, 254, 263
fiscal discipline   122
foreign
  direct investment (FDI)   4, 9, 14, 18, 20, 29, 31, 112, 142, 145–6, 153, 156, 161, 168, 180, 192, 232–3, 239–40

investment(s)   4, 29, 31, 63, 125, 142, 157, 161, 163, 171, 176, 191–2, 233
ownership   43, 59, 65, 67, 192, 231, 239–40, 242
France (French)   4–6, 9, 14–16, 19–22, 33, 56, 59, 64–5, 67, 192, 195–218, 235

Germany (German)   1, 4–5, 8–9, 12–15, 21, 25, 27–8, 55, 59, 65, 67, 106, 135, 148, 159, 165, 192, 195–7, 200, 204, 209, 211–13, 217, 222, 248–9, 252, 260, 262–3
globalization   16, 18, 28, 199, 233–4, 244, 261, 263
governance mechanisms   28, 220–1, 224, 226, 234, 238–9, 242, 244
governance structure   9, 11, 13–16, 18–19, 24, 93, 119, 144–7, 149, 151–2, 157, 163, 209, 222, 251–2
government   14, 19, 29, 31, 33, 35, 42, 48, 52, 58, 61, 63, 66–8, 71–4, 76, 78–85, 87, 89–91, 93–8, 103, 116, 118, 122–4, 126–7, 129–31, 133, 135, 139–41, 149, 153, 159, 163, 171–2, 174–80, 182–3, 187, 195, 199, 201–4, 206–8, 211–15, 218, 230–1, 233, 239, 241, 248–52, 255, 257, 260–1
government–financial–industrial groups (FIG, G-FIG)   79, 80, 81, 91, 97

harmonization (harmonize, harmonizing)   9, 16, 24, 29, 31, 42, 58, 64, 69, 234, 262, 264–5
Hungary (Hungarian)   4, 14, 21–2, 148, 150, 154, 170–92, 248–50
State Property Agency (SPA)   177–8

incentives   1, 8, 13, 29, 35, 63, 67, 80, 113, 117, 120, 131, 133, 153, 185, 190, 234, 260
industrialization   9, 23–5, 28–9, 31, 60
innovation   5, 12, 61, 75, 84, 99, 206–7, 213, 217, 239
insider ownership   249
see also management ownerships
institutional arrangements   4, 7–8, 10, 13, 16, 24, 93, 145–6, 167

institutional change   3–7, 10, 13–14,
   17–19, 21–2, 71, 91, 105, 121–2,
   124, 130, 144, 146, 152, 161, 164,
   166–8, 243, 247, 252
institutional legacies   24, 251, 253
institutional shareholders   25
institutions   2, 4–8, 13–14, 16–19,
   27–8, 48–50, 55, 64, 66, 69, 71–2,
   80–1, 94–7, 101–4, 106–7, 127, 137,
   144–6, 151, 158, 160, 169, 171–2,
   176, 178, 208, 213–15, 217, 220,
   224, 226, 242–3, 248, 250–7, 259,
   261, 263, 265
   financial   13, 27–8, 48, 50, 55, 69,
      81, 127, 144, 158, 160, 172, 263
   insurance   42–3, 56, 86, 120, 160, 176,
      186, 209, 221, 234–5, 240–1
   company(ies)   42–3, 56, 120, 160,
      209, 221, 234, 240–1
interest rates   79, 97, 178, 204, 214,
   233
interlocking directorships (directorates)
   25, 27, 220, 224–7, 238
International Monetary Fund (IMF)
   149, 248, 254, 263
internationalization   23, 28–9, 42, 53,
   61, 64, 105, 232–3, 239
investment   4, 10–11, 14, 25, 27, 29,
   31, 43, 49, 50, 52, 58, 62–3, 67–8,
   73–4, 78–9, 81, 83, 85–6, 90, 93–4,
   97, 108–13, 117, 120, 125–7, 134,
   139, 140–2, 145, 152, 157, 161, 163,
   167, 170–2, 176, 180–4, 189, 191–2,
   204, 208, 216, 223, 230–5, 238,
   240–1, 249–50, 262
   institutional   43
   privatization funds (IPFs)   62–3,
      126–9, 132, 134, 136–7, 140–1,
      180–1, 184, 208, 234, 249–50
investors   3, 25, 27–9, 31, 33, 35, 42–4,
   48, 52, 54, 56–9, 63, 68, 86, 89–91,
   93, 97, 105, 111, 118, 125–9, 131–2,
   134, 138, 140–2, 144–6, 152, 155–8,
   161, 167–8, 170–2, 174–5, 179–80,
   184, 186, 188–9, 191, 201, 207–9,
   221, 228, 230–5, 238–44, 249
   institutional   29, 35, 42–4, 56, 59,
      63, 68, 97, 180, 208–9, 221,
      233–5, 238–40, 242–4
Istituto per la Ricostruzione Industriale
   (IRI)   31, 33, 50

Italy (Italian)   4, 9, 21–3, 28–69, 195,
   197

Japan (Japanese)   1, 8, 12–13, 15, 20,
   27–8, 45, 55, 59, 62, 65, 68, 106,
   165, 196, 213
joint-stock company   75–6, 78, 89,
   135, 147
joint ventures   75–6, 138, 176

keiretsu   20, 27–28
Klaus, V.   123–4, 133, 248–50

labor   7, 12–13, 16, 25, 27, 29, 31,
   82–3, 94, 101, 115–16, 132, 138–9,
   146, 148, 154–6, 168, 195–200,
   202–3, 205–7, 210–11, 213–14, 217,
   220–1, 226–7, 231, 239, 249, 260
   costs   115
   productivity   31, 203
   union   115, 197–8, 202, 206–7,
      210–11, 213–14, 217, 231
   see also market
latecomers   23
Latin   21, 31, 249, 252, 259
   America   31
law   11, 14, 25, 27, 42, 47, 49–50,
   52–3, 58–9, 61, 64, 66–7, 72, 74–8,
   80, 82, 88–90, 94, 96, 98, 115, 119,
   127, 129–30, 132, 137, 147–51, 153,
   155, 158, 162–3, 166–7, 176–7, 179,
   220, 223–5, 227–9, 234, 238, 241,
   243–4, 251–2
   banking   14, 49–50, 66, 69, 78
   capital market   61
   on collective bargaining   115
   commercial   58
   common (tradition)   64
   company   42, 64, 75–7, 98, 174,
      176–7, 220, 224–5, 227–9, 234,
      238, 244
   contract   11, 14
   corporate   25, 27, 42, 58, 64, 96, 244,
      252
   on enterprise(s)   73–6
   new   53, 80, 238
   privatization   67, 88, 130, 148, 153,
      175, 179
   security   243
   stock market   52
leasing   179

legacy   16, 18, 57–9, 66, 71, 115, 127, 145, 252
legal
    framework (and regulatory)   42, 77, 127, 135, 145, 149–50, 175–6, 180
    infrastructure   35
legislation   16, 25, 28, 64, 72, 86, 94, 127, 129, 175, 181, 230, 240, 244, 252, 256, 259, 261, 264–5
liberalization   29, 33, 44, 50, 61, 66, 72–4, 85, 122–4, 139–40, 142, 156–7, 176–7, 221, 224, 232–4, 239–40, 242, 257, 259, 263
limited liability companies (LLC)   42, 58, 75–7, 147, 150, 156, 181
loans   55, 73, 78–81, 117, 131, 139, 178, 183, 208, 222, 233

management   9–10, 12–14, 20, 44, 48, 65, 72, 76–8, 84–6, 89–91, 93–5, 113, 115, 118–19, 129, 131, 134–8, 140–1, 147–9, 154, 156, 159, 172, 174, 176–8, 180–2, 184–92, 197–8, 201–2, 206–7, 209–14, 216, 218, 220–2, 226, 228, 239, 244, 251–2
management ownership   174, 190
managers   8–12, 20–1, 24, 50, 53, 66–7, 72, 77, 90, 93–4, 96, 105–7, 112–16, 121–2, 129, 131–2, 134, 136–9, 141, 144, 147, 151–2, 154–6, 160, 171, 177, 181, 183–90, 201, 213, 218, 220, 239, 240–1
market(s)
    capitalization   7, 14, 44, 46–8, 53, 56, 59–60, 62, 67, 233
    for corporate control   12, 66–7, 146, 148, 156, 164, 168, 220–1, 226
    economy(ies)   2, 71, 74–6, 78–80, 98, 102–4, 121, 170, 251, 253, 255–7, 259, 261
    financial   9, 14, 17, 29, 31, 33, 35, 44, 52, 57, 61, 63, 90, 161, 165, 186, 220–1, 224–5, 232–5, 238–40, 242
    institutions   80, 93–4, 96, 101, 176, 251, 253
    international   3, 16, 18, 111, 224–5, 263
    labor   7, 13, 16, 27, 132, 195–6, 199, 202, 211, 214, 226–7, 231, 249

product   3, 11–12, 15–18, 20, 25, 211–12, 226
reforms   57, 75, 250
regulation   16, 220, 248, 254–7, 265
securities   27, 55, 90, 252
share   47, 61, 183–4
Single Market   254–7, 260–2, 264–5
stock   12, 27–8, 42–5, 49, 52–6, 59–63, 67–8, 129–30, 198, 207, 233, 238, 240, 242
marketization   151, 155, 263
    see market reforms
mass media   168
mass production *see* production
merger(s)   12, 31, 35, 43, 50, 52, 61, 138, 163, 171, 176, 200, 207, 210, 235, 242–3, 259
ministry(ies)   28, 73, 78, 88, 94, 125–6, 137–9, 149, 154, 163, 211, 215, 260
    of Finance   126, 163
minority rights *see* shareholder(s)
modernization, modernize   64, 66, 74, 83–4, 88, 94, 196, 198, 200, 211, 214–15, 248
monitoring   11, 48–9, 56, 77, 117, 134, 137, 201, 208, 217
    bank   49
monopoly(ies)   72, 87, 95–6, 122, 125, 136, 183, 197, 208

network(s)   6, 17, 19, 24, 28, 42, 48, 59, 81, 106, 108, 110, 113–14, 120–1, 127, 134, 146–7, 150, 152, 155, 157–61, 165–7, 174–5, 191–2, 200–1, 205, 207, 214–16, 221, 224–7, 238, 249, 252–3, 262, 264
    corporate, intercorporate   48, 224, 226
    supplier   207, 214
networking   120, 159, 166–7

OECD   23–5, 29, 31, 35, 43, 45, 52, 54–6, 59, 62–3, 68, 117, 127, 195, 202, 204, 208, 216, 250
outside shareholders   221
owners   7–8, 10, 12, 14, 20, 35, 44, 48, 55, 58, 75–8, 90, 93, 97, 105–7, 109–11, 113–14, 116–18, 120, 124–5, 128–32, 134, 136–7, 140–1, 142, 144, 147, 151–2, 160, 165, 171–2, 174–5, 177–92, 208, 220, 222, 229, 235, 240–2, 250

owners – *continued*
  'real owner' 20, 91, 109, 141, 164–5
ownership 5, 10–14, 20, 25, 27, 31, 33,
  42–50, 56–60, 63–8, 72, 74–6,
  89–90, 107–8, 111, 114, 124–8,
  132–4, 136, 138–41, 147–8, 151–2,
  155–7, 160, 162, 168, 170–2, 174–7,
  179–80, 182–92, 197–9, 204, 207,
  209–10, 220–4, 226–7, 229–31,
  234–5, 238–42, 244, 249–50
  cross-ownership 5, 13–14, 47, 127,
    140, 155–7, 174, 209, 226, 250
  indirect 171
  interwoven 20, 160
  management of 72, 90, 136, 209,
    214
  rights 128, 134, 139, 177, 182, 188
  structure 14, 50, 90, 124, 128,
    140–1, 147, 152, 155, 157, 160,
    168, 170–2, 174–5, 179–80,
    183–4, 189–92, 207, 224, 231, 242
  and voting rights 44

path dependency, path-dependent
  5–7, 242–3, 251, 261
path-finding 6–7
pension funds 50, 68, 81, 160, 221, 234
performance 12, 15, 19–20, 49, 56, 71,
  76, 78, 81, 84, 89, 91, 97, 101,
  111–12, 114, 124, 139, 144, 151,
  162, 170, 176, 181, 185, 188–90,
  222, 241, 244
  enterprise 112
  see corporate performance
Poland (Polish) 21–2, 144–69, 248–52,
  260, 262
policy(cies) 5, 11, 14, 18, 25, 29, 33,
  43, 58, 82, 95–6, 109, 164, 175, 178,
  192, 196, 198–200, 203–6, 210, 212,
  214–17, 224–5, 231, 239, 248,
  253–7, 259–61, 263–5
political economy 1, 7, 9–10, 12, 14,
  17, 144, 195–7, 200, 202, 206,
  216–17, 232, 254, 259–61, 265
portfolio investment 29, 83, 90, 127,
  232–3, 240
post-communist 2, 3, 6, 13, 19–21,
  102–6, 110, 117, 120, 145, 155, 159,
  165, 247–9, 265
power 18, 25, 35, 42, 52, 65–6, 72, 77,
  81–2, 94, 96–7, 101, 105, 107–8,

  112, 115–16, 137–9, 141–2, 144,
  146–8, 154, 157, 159, 163, 171, 179,
  181–2, 198–200, 204, 215, 221, 226,
  231, 238–9, 242–3, 248, 252, 255,
  261, 264
discretionary 101
networks 81
price(s) 14, 72–3, 82, 85, 87–9, 106,
  110, 120, 122–5, 128, 130, 133, 139,
  142, 152, 158, 176, 178, 183, 186,
  195, 204, 206
  liberalization 73, 122–4, 139
  regulated 142
private sector 71, 88, 91–2, 97, 112,
  117, 121–2, 145–6, 150, 160–1, 171,
  197, 229
privatization 3, 11, 13–14, 19–21, 24,
  28–9, 31, 33, 35, 44, 46, 48, 52,
  66–7, 71, 74, 76, 78, 81, 84, 88–9,
  97, 100–2, 104–6, 109–10, 112–13,
  117–18, 120, 122–6, 128–30, 132–5,
  137–8, 140–2, 145, 148–58, 161,
  163–5, 167–8, 170–1, 175, 178–81,
  183, 191, 201, 207–10, 249, 251,
  253, 259–60, 263
  in Bulgaria 100–2, 104–7, 109–10,
    112–14, 117–18, 120
  in Czech Republic 122–35, 137–8,
    140, 142
  in France 198, 201, 207–10
  in Hungary 170–1, 175, 177–83, 191
  in Italy 31–5, 44–5, 48, 50–3, 66–7
  mass 129, 132, 167, 179
  massive (broad, extensive, large-scale)
    privatization 11, 29, 33, 46,
    122–5, 130, 165
  in Poland 145–58, 161, 164–5,
    167–8
  policies 175, 177, 179–80, 192
  process of 31, 33, 35, 46, 48, 52, 62,
    66, 91, 111, 130, 140, 142, 146–8,
    150, 154, 157, 159, 192, 198, 207,
    250
  in Romania 260
  in Spain 31–5, 62
  spontaneous 177
  of state-owned 53
  in Ukraine 71, 74, 76, 78, 81, 84,
    88–93, 97
  voucher 88–9, 125–6, 128–30, 132,
    136, 140, 248, 250

production   16, 75, 81, 84–9, 92, 94,
    110, 124, 136, 183, 191, 196, 201–6,
    208, 210, 212–14, 216, 221, 233,
    250, 259, 262
  mass   202, 206, 212
productivity   31, 139, 203, 206, 212
profits   86, 88–9, 94, 111, 120, 140,
    170, 184, 186, 202, 206
property   14, 20, 24, 72–5, 88–90, 98,
    107–12, 115–16, 119, 124–6,
    128–30, 144, 149–50, 154, 163, 165,
    168, 170, 174, 176–7, 190–2, 229
  recombinant   170, 174, 190–2
  rights 14, 24, 72, 107–8, 111–12, 116,
    119, 129, 144, 149, 176
  transformation   168
protection   25, 27, 42, 61, 72, 80, 98,
    122, 142, 166–7, 207, 229, 232, 244,
    249
protectionism   29, 69, 220–1, 224–7,
    230–1, 244
public administration   108
public services   183

quality
  quality (in the institutional context)
    17, 19, 90, 141–2, 152, 162, 167,
    204, 213
  quality (in the product context)   94,
    138–9, 183, 196–8, 206, 210,
    212–13

rationality   100, 107–8, 151
  economic   107
reform   3, 13, 16–18, 42, 47, 52–3, 57,
    65, 67, 71–2, 75, 78, 94–6, 101–6,
    111, 115, 121–4, 140, 142, 149,
    162–5, 169, 175, 195, 207–8,
    210–11, 213–15, 217, 238–9, 243–4,
    247–8, 250–3, 255, 257, 260, 262
region(s)   17, 31, 71, 95, 146, 148, 157,
    162, 215–17, 247, 250, 252–4, 260–2
regional   19, 103, 150, 182, 184,
    199–200, 202, 210, 215–17, 261,
    265
rent seeking   19, 80–1, 85, 124, 138,
    142, 218, 253
responsibility(ties)   72–3, 76, 89, 97,
    105, 134, 149, 178, 183, 186
restructuring   33, 73, 77, 80, 82, 84–5,
    91, 95–7, 105, 107, 112, 114, 116,

    120–1, 124–6, 129, 131–2, 134–5,
    138, 140–2, 148, 154, 156, 159–60,
    162–5, 167, 177, 180, 183, 190, 195,
    198–9, 202, 205–7, 210, 212–13,
    235, 238, 250–1, 260, 264
  in transition   249, 256, 262, 264–5
rights   25, 44, 46–7, 52–3, 72, 76,
    104–5, 119, 122, 127–8, 134, 137,
    139, 142, 149, 167, 176–8, 181–2,
    184, 188, 220, 225–6, 228–30, 235,
    239, 241–2, 244
  voting   44, 46–7, 220, 225–6,
    228–30, 235, 239, 241–2, 244
Romania   21, 260, 262–3
rule(s)   9–10, 12, 20, 43, 65, 72, 78–80,
    84–5, 88, 91, 93–6, 98, 104, 106–7,
    111, 120, 127, 139, 144, 168, 171,
    177, 179, 187, 204, 209, 226, 231,
    238–9, 243, 250, 255–6, 260–1,
    264–5
rule-making   248, 264
Russia, Russian   5, 21, 91, 112, 152,
    166, 213

segmentation   84, 145–6, 150–1, 153,
    161, 167
shareholders   9, 24–5, 27–8, 35, 42–3,
    45, 47–8, 51–3, 56, 58–60, 65, 77–9,
    89–90, 93, 98, 114, 119, 121–2,
    127–30, 135, 140–2, 147, 161, 170,
    172, 174–5, 180–1, 183, 185–91,
    207, 209, 220–2, 228–9, 233–5, 239,
    241–2, 244, 249, 252
  individual   25, 127
  minority (rights)   35, 42, 47, 53, 65,
    119, 127, 142, 161, 185, 190, 235,
    242, 249
  see also management ownership
shares   29, 35, 43, 45, 47, 53, 58, 61–2,
    65, 67, 75, 88–9, 126–8, 131–2, 134,
    140–1, 147–8, 150, 158, 162, 171–2,
    174–5, 177–80, 188, 191–2, 208–9,
    221–3, 226, 228–31, 233, 240–1,
    244, 249
Slovak Republic (Slovakia)   21, 117,
    122–3, 127, 250, 252
social structure   100, 175
society(ties)   12–13, 42, 71, 101–2,
    105–6, 151, 168, 196, 198, 252, 255,
    260, 263
SOE *see* enterprises

Soviet Union   6, 17, 21, 71–3, 81, 85, 148
Spain, Spanish   2, 4, 9, 21–2, 23–69
standard(s)   75, 78–80, 92, 94, 98, 102, 107, 114, 117, 147–8, 153, 159, 162–3, 165, 167, 171, 179, 183, 186, 197, 203, 215–16, 224, 231, 234–5, 243–4, 255
  accounting   234–5, 243
  international   224, 231
  ISO (9000, 9002)   138, 197
stakeholders   1, 7, 9, 12, 20, 56, 61, 121, 132, 136, 141, 221
state
  activity   19
  administration   72, 201, 257
  apparatus   199, 201, 217
  assets   73–4, 116, 130, 170–1, 176, 178
  bureaucracy   90 *see* bureaucracy
  capture   106
  control(ed)   48, 88–9, 144, 152, 158, 162, 197, 251
  coordination   5
  developmental   28
  dirigiste   5
  engagement   9
  enterprise   31, 117–18, 176–7, 184, 191
  holding(s)   31, 33, 177, 181–2, 187
  institution(s)   11, 19, 106, 137–8, 158, 171
  intervention, interventionism   27, 31, 33, 66, 118, 198, 225
  interventionist   42
  involvement   14, 140, 199, 204, 259
  member   2, 22, 44, 247, 253–7, 259–60, 264–5
  nation state   16
  nonstate   46–7, 89, 91, 191
  orchestrated by the state   27, 198
  owned enterprises (SOEs) *see* enterprise
  owned, state-owned   27, 31, 33, 35, 43–4, 46, 48, 53, 61, 64, 72–6, 88–9, 109, 118, 148–50, 152, 157, 163, 171, 174, 177, 181, 186–7, 189–90, 192, 198–9, 205
  ownership   43–4, 57, 64–5, 126, 132, 171, 174–7, 182–3, 186, 189
  parastate   171, 174, 180, 192

regulation   4
small European   220, 224–6, 232
state-led   204, 217
state-level   262, 264
state-protected   9
supra-state   29
treasury   89
welfare   68, 231
strategy(ies)   4–6, 8, 10, 12, 14, 19, 21, 27, 43, 54, 63, 81–4, 86, 88, 95–7, 103, 109–10, 116, 118, 121, 124, 128, 130, 133, 137–8, 141–2, 145, 147, 158–61, 163–5, 169, 181, 195–6, 200, 202, 207–8, 211–12, 215–16, 224–5, 229, 232, 234, 239, 243, 249, 252–3
subsidies   33, 81, 85, 90, 132–3, 140, 176–7, 183, 204–5, 225
Sweden (Swedish)   15, 22, 220–44, 260
Switzerland (Swiss)   15, 22, 220–44
systemic change   11, 122, 134, 138, 142, 153, 161, 164, 166

takeover(s), acquisition   27, 31, 35, 52, 55, 61, 66–7, 69, 83, 90, 110–11, 114, 117, 120, 131, 157–9, 161, 188, 192, 200, 204, 207, 209–10, 221, 224–6, 229–30, 235, 240, 242–3, 252
  see corporate control, mergers
tax   52, 79, 81–3, 86, 95, 97, 122, 142, 176, 209, 231
  burden   83
  income   176
  profit   176
technological innovation   239
transaction(s)   24, 72, 81–2, 84, 87, 90, 127, 131, 138, 157, 162, 178, 180, 183, 220, 222
  costs   24, 87, 131
transition   12, 23, 74, 82, 92, 96, 98, 198–9, 249–52, 256, 261–5
  see transformation
transformation   2, 4–6, 12–13, 16, 18–23, 28–9, 59, 71–4, 81, 94, 96–8, 100–7, 109, 112, 114–16, 119–25, 127, 133, 138, 140, 144, 145–6, 151–2, 155, 161, 164–5, 167–8, 175, 177, 191, 198, 232, 242–3, 247–8, 251, 253, 265
  systemic   74, 124

transparency   14, 19, 42, 44, 49, 52,
    61–2, 67–8, 77, 81, 91, 102, 114,
    137, 153, 160, 183, 221, 232, 238
  lack of   160
tripartite commission   115, 139
trust   11, 25, 48, 81, 86, 91, 259

Ukraine (Ukrainian)   2, 5–6, 17–18,
    21–2, 71–98
United Kingdom (UK, Britain, British)
    1, 14, 16, 43, 57, 59, 65–7, 195, 197,
    221–2, 233, 256
United States (US)   1, 14, 18, 25, 28,
    43, 45, 56–7, 59, 65–6, 164–5,
    221–2, 233–4, 243, 248–9
  corporate law   25

vertical integration   205

voucher privatization   88–9, 125–6,
    128–30, 132, 136, 140, 248, 250
  see investment privatization funds
    (IPFs)

wage(s)   83–4, 90, 122, 139, 176, 204,
    239, 242
worker(s)   10, 14, 74–5, 84, 89–90,
    93–4, 112, 114–16, 139, 144, 146,
    148–50, 153–6, 161, 167–8, 195,
    197, 199, 202–3, 205–6, 210–14,
    220–1, 251
  council(s)   146, 148–50, 153–4, 156,
    161, 167
  representation   114, 139, 146, 154–6,
    167, 251
works council(s)   115, 197
World Bank   254